Agriculture and Trade in the Pacific

Toward the Twenty-First Century

EDITED BY
William T. Coyle, Dermot Hayes,
and Hiroshi Yamauchi

Westview Press
BOULDER AND SAN FRANCISCO

Belhaven Press
LONDON

All rights reserved. No part of this publication may be reproduced or transmitted in any form or by any means, electronic or mechanical, including photocopy, recording, or any information storage and retrieval system, without permission in writing from Westview Press.

Copyright © 1992 by Westview Press, Inc., except for Chapter 13, which is copyright by the Australian government and Chapters 1, 7, 8, 10, and 11, which are works of the U.S. government.

Published in 1992 in the United States of America by Westview Press, Inc., 5500 Central Avenue, Boulder, Colorado 80301-2847

Published in 1992 in Great Britain by Belhaven Press (a division of Pinter Publishers Limited), 25 Floral Street, London WC2E 9DS

Library of Congress Cataloging-in-Publication Data
Agriculture and trade in the Pacific : toward the twenty-first century
  / edited by William T. Coyle, Dermot Hayes, and Hiroshi Yamauchi.
    p.   cm.
  Includes index.
  ISBN 0-8133-8277-7
  1. Produce trade—Pacific Area. 2. Agriculture—Economic aspects—
Pacific Area. I. Coyle, William T. II. Hayes, Dermot James.
III. Yamauchi, Hiroshi, 1932–
HD9018.P16A37   1992
338.1'099—dc20   91-48043
                                                                                                      CIP

British Library Cataloguing in Publication Data
A CIP catalogue record of this book is available from the British Library.
  ISBN 1-85293-254-6

Printed and bound in the United States of America

∞ The paper used in this publication meets the requirements
    of the American National Standard for Permanence of Paper
    for Printed Library Materials Z39.48-1984.

10   9   8   7   6   5   4   3   2   1

DEPARTMENT OF RURAL SOCIOLOGY
WASHINGTON STATE UNIVERSITY
PULLMAN, WASHINGTON 99164

Agriculture and Trade
in the Pacific

Contents

Preface   xi

**1 Pacific Rim Agriculture and Trade:
   Toward the Twenty-First Century**   1
   William T. Coyle

   Introduction, 1
   Agricultural Policy Reform in Japan, 6
   Regionalism in the Western Pacific, 8
   The Future Agricultural Comparative Advantage
     of China and ASEAN, 9
   Agricultural Policy Reform in the Region's
     Exporting Nations, 10
   References, 11

PART ONE
OVERVIEW

2 Pacific Basin Economic Prospects, 1990-1994   15
   Lawrence R. Klein

   Projections of Output, Consumption, and Inflation, 20

**3 Agricultural Development and Trade
   in the Pacific Rim Countries**   29
   Kym Anderson

   Introduction, 29
   Conceptualizing Agricultural Development
     in a Growing Economy, 30
   Empirical Support for the Theory, 32
   Future Economic Growth and Policy Reform Prospects, 46
   Conclusion, 58

4 Prospects for U.S. Agricultural Exports in the Pacific: The Role of Fast-growing Countries 67
John W. Mellor

Introduction, 67
Facts About Pacific Rim Countries, 69
The Conceptual Framework, 81
An Effective U.S. Policy to Encourage
  Agricultural Exports, 85
Notes, 88

PART TWO
COUNTRY PERSPECTIVES

5 Development of Agricultural Policy in Postwar Japan 91
Yutaka Yoshioka

Introduction, 91
Three Basic Agricultural Laws, 91
The Internationalization of Agriculture
  in Postwar Japan, 93
The World Food Crisis and the Emergence of
  Food Security Policies, 95
The New Phase of Internationalization in Agriculture, 96
References, 100

6 Japanese Agricultural Policy: Unfair and Unreasonable? 101
Fumio Egaitsu

Introduction, 101
Three Decades of Changes in Japanese
  Agricultural Protection, 103
Trends in the Price Gaps Between Domestic
  and World Markets, 107
Domestic Forces for and Against Protection, 112
Conclusion, 116
Notes, 117
References, 117

Notes, 60
References, 61

7 Japanese Agriculture in the 1990s: An American Perspective 119
Alan J. Webb and William T. Coyle

Introduction, 119
Structural Characteristics of Japanese Agriculture, 121
Emerging Conflicts Within Japanese Agriculture, 127
Declining Support for Agricultural Protection, 129
Policy Options, 130
Notes, 132
References, 132

8 Policies and Profitability in Livestock Feed Sectors of the ASEAN Countries 133
Allan Rae, Liborio Cabanilla, Tan Siew Hoey, Faisal Kasryno, and Suthad Setboonsarng

Introduction, 133
The Livestock Production and Trade Situation, 135
International Competitiveness of ASEAN Livestock Production, 136
Conclusions and Scope for Regional Cooperation, 146
References, 147

9 The Response of Thai Agriculture to the World Economy 149
Ammar Siamwalla, Suthad Setboonsarng, and Direk Patamasiriwat

Introduction, 149
The Rules of the Game, 150
The World Market and Thailand's Response: Some Preliminaries, 155
The World Market and Thailand's Response in Crop Production, 157
Thailand's Comparative Advantage in the Livestock Subsector, 161
Thailand's Comparative Advantage in the Fisheries Subsector, 164
Government Policies Towards the Agricultural Sector, 165
Conclusion, 173
References, 174

10 China Agricultural Trade Developments and Prospects: With Emphasis on Pacific Rim Countries   175
Francis C. Tuan and Shi Ru

Brief Historical Perspective, 175
Agricultural Trade Growth in the 1980s, 176
Agricultural Trade with Pacific Rim Countries, 179
Agricultural Trade Policies in the 1980s, 189
Impact of Recent Political Unrest on Agricultural Production and Trade, 190
Agricultural Trade Policies and Outlook for Trade with Pacific Rim Countries in the 1990s, 192
References, 196
Appendix: China's Trade Statistics, 197

11 Soviet Economic Reforms, Republic Sovereignty, and Pacific Rim Agriculture and Trade   199
Sergei B. Iliukhin and Kenneth Gray

Introduction, 199
The Difficult Course of Perestroika's Economic Reforms, 199
Centrifugal Economic Forces, 200
Progress in Rationalization of Farm and Retail Food Prices, 205
External Economic Relations, 205
The USSR in Pacific Rim Agricultural Trade, 207
Conclusion: The Future National Market and External Trade, 210
Notes, 211

12 Economic Reforms and New Zealand Agriculture   213
Ron A. Sandrey

The Setting, 213
The Reforms, 215
The Consequences, 217
The Future, 220
Conclusions and Lessons for Others, 226
References, 227

Contents

PART THREE
A SAMPLING OF APPLIED MODELING RESEARCH

13 EMABA: An Econometric Model of Pacific Rim Livestock Markets   233
David Harris and Ian Shaw

Introduction, 233
An Overview of EMABA, 234
An Application of EMABA: Liberalization of the
  North Asian Beef Trade, 251
Future Directions for EMABA, 257
References, 258

14 Exchange Rate Pass-Through Effects in Agriculture   261
Julian M. Alston, Colin A. Carter, and Marilyn D. Whitney

Introduction, 261
Previous Literature, 263
Comparative Statics of Exchange Rate
  Pass-Through, 268
Economic Models and Hypotheses, 281
Conclusion, 288
Notes, 289
References, 291

15 The Japanese Beef Policy:
Political Preference Function   295
Thomas Wahl, Dermot Hayes, and Andrew Schmitz

Introduction, 295
Optimal Government Behavior, 296
Estimating the Implied Weights of the
  Political Preference Function, 299
Summary and Conclusions, 302
Notes, 304
References, 305

PART FOUR
PROBLEMS AND ISSUES FOR FUTURE RESEARCH

16 **Problems and Issues for Future Research on Pacific Rim Agriculture and Trade** 309
Hiroshi Yamauchi

Concluding Statements of Panel Speakers, 310
From the Floor and Rejoinders, 324
Wrap-up, 326
Notes, 328

About the Book and Editors 329
List of Contributors 331
Index 335

Preface

The International Agricultural Trade Research Consortium (IATRC) is a group of economists from around the world who are interested in fostering research and providing a forum for the exchange of ideas relating to international trade of agricultural commodities. Each summer the IATRC sponsors a symposium on a topic relating to trade and trade policy from which proceedings are published. For a list of past symposia and related publications, contact Laura Bipes, IATRC Administrative Assistant, Department of Agricultural and Applied Economics, University of Minnesota, St. Paul, MN 55108, United States of America.

The editors acknowledge the help of Laura Bipes of the University of Minnesota and Lynn Haramoto of the East-West Center for making arrangements for the symposium in Honolulu. Also thanks to Charles Morrison of the East-West Center for providing the conference facility and the agricultural and resource economics department, University of Hawaii, and Agriculture Canada for financial support. The IATRC appreciates the assistance as well as the stimulating luncheon comments of Seiji Naya of the East-West Center. Thanks also are extended to Don McClatchey of Agriculture Canada, who organized and found financial support for the session on the Pacific Rim developing countries and Ed Rossmiller of Resources for the Future, who, along with Hiroshi Yamauchi, organized the agribusiness panel. Michael Lopez of ERS, and Walt Robertson and Jan Williams of the University of Hawaii College of Tropical Agriculture and Human Resources, provided editorial assistance. Nancy Ottum also provided editorial assistance and prepared the final camera-ready copy for this book.

William T. Coyle
Dermot Hayes
Hiroshi Yamauchi

1

Pacific Rim Agriculture and Trade: Toward the Twenty-First Century

William T. Coyle

Introduction

While institutional and political changes in Europe are grabbing the headlines, the steady growth of Pacific Rim economies and their increasing role in world trade are transforming the region and ensuring its economic leadership in the twenty-first century. Over recent decades, the Pacific has shown a vitality and dynamism surpassing that of other regions. Economic growth and trade are defining characteristics that bind together this region of disparate countries and that "have brought about a shift in the world's political and economic center of gravity" (Linder, 1986, p. 1) away from the Atlantic. Exemplifying the region's extraordinary role in trade, Hong Kong, a tiny city-state, exports more manufactured products than the Soviet Union and East Europe combined (Copper, 1990, p. 483).

Literally defined, the Pacific Rim includes the Pacific Ocean and all countries lying within and bordering on it. However, the term often explicitly excludes some Pacific coastal areas such as the USSR, Canada, the United States, and Latin America but almost always includes East Asia (including the PRC), Southeast Asia and Oceania. While the Americas are clearly Pacific nations, they also face toward the Atlantic. This book emphasizes the markets that make up the western side of the Pacific Rim: a group of countries with diverse resource endowments, cultural backgrounds, population densities, and levels of agricultural and economic development (Table 1.1).

The International Agricultural Trade Research Consortium (IATRC), consistent with its goal of encouraging economic research and discussion in areas critical to world agriculture and trade, sponsored a two-day

TABLE 1.1 Pacific Rim Countries: Selected Indicators, 1987 (Index, United States = 100)

	United States	Japan	S. Korea	Taiwan	Hong Kong	PRC	Philippines	Indonesia	Malaysia	Thailand	Singapore	Canada	Australia	New Zealand
Total population	100	50	17	8	2	439	25	74	7	22	1	10	7	1
GNP total	100	43	3	2	1	7	1	2	1	1	0	9	4	1
Pop./Sq Km of total area	100	1243	1631	2126	20643	431	786	363	190	397	16203	10	8	47
GNP per capita	100	85	16	20	44	2	3	2	10	5	43	81	60	44
GDP in agriculture	100	150	525	250	20	1690	1205	1300	1000	805	25	150	225	395
Cal. intake per cap per day	100	77	79	80	79	72	57	69	72	63	79	94	91	97
Fertilizer use per hectare	100	466	454	505	--	252	70	115	154	31	1971	52	31	783
Total ag product.	100	13	4	3	--	115	5	14	4	8	--	12	11	4
Food self-sufficiency	100	50	69	38	4	95	93	90	106	114	19	142	118	104
Ag. prod per ag worker	100	9	3	1	5	1	2	1	5	1	28	80	82	91
Total exports	100	91	19	21	19	16	2	7	7	5	11	39	10	3
Total ag exports	100	3	2	6	7	23	4	9	13	13	6	23	26	13
Total imports	100	36	10	8	11	10	2	3	3	3	8	22	7	2
Total ag imports	100	95	18	16	22	18	3	5	7	4	11	25	6	2

Sources: U.S. Dept. of Ag., Economic Research Service, World Agricultural Trends and Indicators, 1970-89, Statistical Bulletin No. 815.

symposium bearing the title of this book on August 1-2, 1990, at the East-West Center in Honolulu, Hawaii.

These proceedings include a global overview of the region, country-specific perspectives, and a sampling of applied research on agricultural trade patterns and issues relevant to Pacific Rim countries.

The global overview chapters (2, 3 and 4) establish the importance of the region to the world economy and to agricultural trade. The region's importance derives from its large economic size, its history of rapid growth, and its promise of future growth. The region has become an essential element in the global agricultural trade picture. The land-poor East Asian markets (Japan, South Korea, Taiwan, and Hong Kong) have shown the most significant growth in trade of any subregion in the Pacific, growing from 10 percent of world agricultural imports in 1970 to 14 percent in 1989 (Table 1.2). Japan, by itself, surpassed the EC-12 as an overseas market for U.S. farm exports in 1989. East Asia now accounts for one-third of all U.S. agricultural exports and is similarly important to other major exporters around the Pacific: Canada, Australia, New Zealand, the PRC, and the ASEAN.

The most important factors affecting the future of the region's agriculture and trade are the sustainability of high rates of economic growth and the response to this growth by agricultural policy in each of the region's countries. The Pacific Rim has grown rapidly in the recent past; most observers (including Anderson and Klein) believe that it likely will continue surpassing the growth of other regions and, thus, become even more economically important by 2000. The forecast of continued growth is predicated on the continued role of many growth-promoting characteristics in the economies making up the region. Some of these are decentralized markets, an export-orientation, high investment and savings rates, and political stability. Factors such as the

TABLE 1.2 Share of World Agricultural Trade

	1970		1980		1989	
	Imports	Exports	Imports	Exports	Imports	Exports
People's Republic of China	1.0	1.6	2.2	1.4	2.1	2.8
East Asia	10.0	1.6	10.5	1.5	14.1	2.4
S.E. Asia	2.8	4.9	2.7	5.9	2.9	6.0
Oceania	0.9	6.7	0.8	5.7	0.9	6.0
North America	13.7	19.3	10.2	22.1	10.8	18.2

Source: U.N. trade data.

Confucian work ethic and an emphasis on education are other important building blocks for economic development.

But there are uncertainties, both political and economic, about the future of the region that need to be acknowledged because they could derail our optimistic projections. We must remember that there have been 2 wars in the Pacific since World War II (Korea and Vietnam) and while the region is reasonably stable at the moment, circumstances can change quickly. Today the internal political situation is tenuous in a number of the countries. Since the student demonstrations in Tiananmen Square of June 1989, the future of economic reform in China is uncertain. Hong Kong's reversion to China in 1997 raises fundamental questions about its future. "Instability in the Philippines could contribute to turbulence in the region" despite collaboration, there are potential rivalries within ASEAN (Crowe and Romberg, 1991, p. 124). Despite Vietnam's withdrawal of military forces from Cambodia, its neighbors remain suspicious of its long-term ambitions in that part of the world . On the economic side, demographic changes in Japan are leading to lower savings and investment rates and structural shifts in that economy toward greater consumerism.

Economic growth affects agricultural markets in several ways. It raises demand for food and it leads to changes in the dietary pattern, away from food grains like rice, wheat, and barley and towards livestock products and other foods. This phenomenon has been observed in many markets over recent decades. Mellor points out (Chapter 4) that income changes have a big impact, particularly on the livestock sector and on the derived demand for feedgrains. Increased consumption of livestock products is particularly evident in East Asia, where income growth has been rapid for a long time and diets are going through a process of Westernization. With limited agricultural resources, East Asian economies must import feed grain and protein meal to support expansion of their livestock industries. More recently, production constraints have been overcome by increased meat imports.

At the same time that economic growth raises the demand for food and changes dietary patterns, it also leads to an almost inevitable decline in agriculture's share of an economy's output and employment (Chapter 3). As income rises, the demand for food rises more slowly than for many other goods and services. This causes resources to be bid away from agriculture and into other more remunerative activities. Thus, there is a strong tendency for agriculture's share of an economy's gross domestic product and employment to decline. This decline is especially fast in densely populated and rapidly growing markets like those in the Western Pacific.

At early stages of development, governments often choose to tax agriculture to spur development in other sectors. In later stages, governments commonly choose to subsidize agriculture to ease the adjustment pressures imposed on that sector by economic development. This pattern is pointed out by Anderson in Chapter 3. It has occurred in many Pacific Rim countries. While it does not apply to the very lightly assisted agricultures of Australia and New Zealand, it does apply to less-developed China and some of the ASEAN countries where governments tax agriculture and to the more developed countries of East Asia and North America, where governments subsidize agriculture. Anderson explains that there are "good politico-economic reasons for expecting such a trend in policy" which have to do with the distributional implications of policies, the costs of collective action that change as a population becomes more urbanized and food becomes less important as a wage good, and the general values and preferences of society that change during the development process.

Will the positive relationship between economic development and government assistance to agriculture that Anderson describes necessarily continue at ever higher stages of development? Maybe not. The ongoing GATT negotiations and the agricultural policy debates in the United States, the EC, and Japan underscore the growing reluctance of taxpayers to continue to finance support for agriculture. Ron Sandrey documents in Chapter 12 a sudden withdrawal of government support from agriculture in New Zealand starting in 1984. Webb and Coyle, in Chapter 7, address the inevitability of liberalization in the Japanese farm sector because of eroding political support. Even Anderson raises the possibility of a "third stage" in his conclusion by stating that protection may be reduced when an industry declines to such an extent that its political support is less than its political opposition. Other sectors of the economy that are increasingly dependent on an open trading system may oppose agricultural assistance because it makes them vulnerable to trade retaliation or because the agricultural subsidies make the whole economy less efficient in a time of increased economic integration across economies. Anderson also cites pressure to reduce subsidies from individual trade partners and from the world trading community as represented by the GATT.

The commitment of the region's countries to economic growth through trade ensures that, over the long haul, comparative advantage will determine specialization in agricultural production and the patterns of trade in the Pacific. While government intervention will remain an important factor both in the short run and the long run, it will not change the basic conditions in countries like Japan and South Korea, with their large populations, limited land area, and serious environmental constraints. They will continue to depend on imports of agricultural commodities for the foreseeable future. Government intervention will affect market growth and the composition of trade. The same holds for North America and Oceania, where government policy will likely not fundamentally alter their status as net exporters in agricultural commodity markets.

Generally, economic growth and the response of agricultural policy to this growth are the broad factors that will shape the agricultural economies and trade of the Pacific Rim region. Four more specific factors are also addressed either directly or indirectly in this book:

- Agricultural policy reform in Japan
- Regionalism
- The future agricultural comparative advantage of China and ASEAN
- Policy reform in the agricultural exporting nations

Agricultural Policy Reform in Japan

That three chapters in this book are devoted to Japanese agriculture and policy reflect not only the sheer size of the Japanese market but also the potential insights which studying this economic leader may give about policy evolution in similar but currently less developed East Asian markets.

Japan has the world's second largest economy; its per capita income recently surpassed that of the United States. Japan's great affluence combined with very limited agricultural land resources has made it the world's largest net importer of agricultural products (Japan's land area is about the size of California, while its population is about 4 times that of California).

Japan has pursued a protectionist agricultural policy for the past 30 years, particularly with respect to rice. Even with high levels of agricultural subsidies, Japan's agricultural self-sufficiency has declined from 80 percent in 1960 to 45 percent today, reflecting a strong comparative disadvantage in agriculture.

The future of the Japanese agricultural market will be influenced primarily by the effects of economic growth, but in some important instances, by the effects of policy changes.

Japan's 1988 agreement to open up its beef market, first by doubling import quotas over three years and then by using tariffs as the only means of import restraint, has and will have an important impact on Japanese consumption, production and imports of beef. Reform in Japan's rice policy could also have important implications for domestic production and regional rice trade, but more fundamentally it would set a different course for Japanese agriculture.

Do the 1988 beef agreement and other recent policy changes made by Japan represent a watershed in Japanese agricultural policy? Is policy change in Japan on the verge of accelerating?

According to Egaitsu in Chapter 6, agricultural policy change in Japan will be, as it has been in the past, slow. Those potentially most affected, farmers, are well organized, while consumers are indifferent. Consumers are not greatly concerned about high food prices because income growth has been rapid and the income share going to food consumption has progressively declined. Egaitsu links consumers' strong demand for a better quality of life with the importance of maintaining domestic farming and rural communities through government farm policy.

Webb and Coyle (Chapter 7), on the other hand, see an erosion of political support for agricultural protection, an increasing rural-urban conflict and an inevitability of reform. In their view, these developments should lead to more rapid policy reform. The declining role of farm income as a component of farm household income indicates to them that agricultural subsidies are no longer central to the viability or the stability of rural Japanese communities. Agricultural income as a percent of farm household income in Japan dwindled from about 50 percent in 1960 to 15-20 percent in 1990.

The second reason Japan is emphasized in this book is that Japan's experience may be a leading indicator, giving us insights about the way agricultural policy might evolve in other similar countries in the region, like South Korea and Taiwan. Yoshioka (Chapter 5) documents the evolution of postwar Japanese agricultural policy from an inward-looking period of democratic institution building (land reform and the development of the farm cooperatives), to a period of concern about food security (the soybean embargo of 1973), to a period of coping with trade frictions arising from the internationalization of Japan's agriculture and economy (the 1980s).

One would expect the evolution of agricultural policy in South Korea and Taiwan to be similar to Japan's because of strong similarities in their agricultures: rice-centered farming, a predominance of small-scale operations, and a rising importance of livestock production dependent on imported feedstuffs. There are differences in their agricultures, however, which will give a unique twist to their policy. Taiwan, for example, has been an important exporter of pork (this may change in the future because of environmental constraints) and is generally more export-oriented with respect to agricultural commodities than Japan or

South Korea. South Korean farmers are much more dependent on farm income than their counterparts in Taiwan and Japan.

Regionalism in the Western Pacific

If the world is becoming a global village, then regions are becoming its neighborhoods. The European Community, formed by the Treaty of Rome in 1957, is the best example of such an economic grouping. More recent ones include the U.S.-Canadian Free Trade Agreement and the Closer Economic Relations (CER) arrangement of Australia and New Zealand. The tendency for nations to coalesce in geographic groupings seems to be growing for both strategic and economic reasons. There is security in association and there are economic gains to be made from specialization and trade that come from access to a wider market. Some argue that the rise of trading blocs is a harbinger of the demise of an unwieldy and ineffective GATT.

The Western Pacific has also been flirting with the idea of a grouping known as the Asia-Pacific Economic Cooperation Council, although nothing concrete has materialized—perhaps because of the region's diversity and its great trade success without a tightly-knit association. More recently, Malaysia has proposed an East Asia Economic Grouping to provide a mechanism for the smaller Asian countries to speak with one economic voice.

The book addresses some of the economic and political forces that are pulling the Western Pacific economies closer together. The rapid economic growth in many of these countries has been important in stimulating intra-regional trade. Rising wages and higher costs in some parts of the region have caused capital to seek out better investment opportunities in other parts of the region. The Japanese textile industry is a good example: once an ascendant industry, it is now adjusting to competition from neighboring Asian economies. Japanese textile companies are now investing in countries where labor and other production costs are lower; many of these investments are being made in the region, particularly in Southeast Asia.

The region is also trading relatively less with the United States. Klein (Chapter 2) points out that the U.S. market is becoming less important to East Asia and other Western Pacific economies because of reduced import growth, better inflation control, and the revival of manufacturing growth in the United States. Reform in China (Chapter 10) has increased its exports, including agricultural products, to its Pacific Rim neighbors. And Australia and New Zealand are now much more closely tied to the Pacific than they were twenty years ago when they maintained special trading arrangements with the UK before it joined the EC.

Economic progress in the region may lead to political changes and broader economic ties with countries in the region that had been isolated. Economic reforms in China and the Soviet Union may have a demonstration effect, giving impetus to reforms in North Korea and Indochina. The former has potential as a large import market and the latter as a net exporter of agricultural commodities. Vietnam, for example, became a major exporter of rice when plantings and yields increased after production decisions were decentralized in 1989.

And opening up the Soviet Far East could lead to the exploitation of important complementarities between a resource-rich and sparsely populated area (only 8 million people) with vast forestry, fishery, and mineral resources and the resource-poor but capital-rich East Asian countries (Chapter 11). Such an opening would in the long term promote economic growth and trade through regional specialization and would affect indirectly the region's agriculture and trade.

The Future Agricultural Comparative Advantage of China and ASEAN

Oceania and North America will clearly be net exporters of agricultural commodities in the next decade and beyond, while East Asia will be a net importer. The future role of agriculture in China and in the Association of Southeast Asian Nations (ASEAN) is less certain. Will these areas be net importers or exporters of agricultural products in the next decade?

After the reforms of the late 1970s, China's agricultural production grew rapidly, leading to its emergence in the mid-1980s as a net exporter of agricultural products and a major competitor in world corn, soybean and cotton markets. But continued economic growth in China, as in many other economies, could lead to the relative decline of its agriculture. This is pointed out by Anderson, who sees China becoming a growing import market for coarse grains and wheat over the next decade.

The evidence concerning China's future role in agricultural trade is ambiguous. On the one hand, there are serious limits to China's capacity to expand production: yields are already relatively high and further expansion of the irrigated land area is limited. These supply-side factors coupled with urban food subsidies and the potential for strong income growth suggest that China will become a big net importer in the future. On the other hand, hard-currency constraints, a centrally controlled and planned trading system, and the limited capacity of the country's infrastructure to absorb imports mitigate against dramatic changes in the near term.

In the ASEAN, particularly Indonesia, Malaysia, and Thailand (other members are the Philippines, Singapore and Brunei), rapid economic growth will stimulate dietary changes similar to those observed in East Asia. Meat consumption, for example, is rising but is still about 10-20 years behind the level in Korea. The big difference between ASEAN and East Asia is on the supply side; ASEAN has more abundant land resources. Greater domestic resources and uncertainty about how they may be developed make it difficult to project production and net trade for this area. Rae et al. (Chapter 8) found that four of the ASEAN countries are "socially profitable producers" of broilers, eggs, and pork, but not dairy products. They also found that farmers except in Malaysia were economically efficient producers of corn and cassava, although land constraints are likely to limit future expansion. Siamwalla (Chapter 9) projects Thailand to be a net exporter of agricultural products at least until 1995 and probably until 2000. This will happen despite rapid shifts in comparative advantage towards manufacturing which have been ongoing since 1980. He also alludes to a potential land problem that would constrain expansion in the livestock industries; he predicts that sooner or later Thailand will be a net importer of corn.

Agricultural Policy Reform in the Region's Exporting Nations

The GATT negotiations have brought to public awareness the relationship between domestic agricultural policies and their external consequences. For net exporting countries, policies that cut the link between internal and external markets cause distortions that affect export performance. Such policies can be very costly and a drag on a country's economy. In a world of increased trade and specialization, it is in the interest of countries to enhance their overall economic performance. This can be done by reforming policies to make them consistent with the country's comparative advantage. New Zealand embarked on such a reform path in 1984.

Many countries have danced around the principle of free trade while New Zealand embraced it. Reforms were undertaken primarily in farm policy, macroeconomic policy, and in the public sector. Ron Sandrey (Chapter 12) documents the historical precursors to reform, the nature of the reforms, and their consequences for agriculture. While the removal of agricultural subsidies clearly makes sense for this pastoral nation that depends on agricultural commodities for 60 percent of its exports, New Zealand has done much less to reform its manufacturing sector or to increase the flexibility of its labor market.

What is of particular concern about the New Zealand experiment is that the outcome so far is equivocal. Was this a good thing to do? The indicators for New Zealand agriculture in 1990 compared with 1984 were mostly negative: income was down, asset values were down, and unemployment was up. Any liberalization process by its nature produces winners and losers. Agriculture in New Zealand for the time being is still "adjusting," and its prospects for the 1990s are uncertain. The unfinished business of liberalizing the labor and manufacturing markets is cited as being, in part, responsible for the slow adjustment of agriculture. Perhaps the most salient lesson for other countries is that agricultural reform is a painful process in which the costs are initially more obvious than the benefits and in which the costs are potentially more severe if the reforms are not part of a broad-based multi-sectoral program.

References

Copper, John F., "U.S. Perspectives on the Pacific Rim," in *Vital Speeches*, vol. LVI, No. 16, June 1, 1990.

Crowe, William J., Jr. and Alan D. Romberg, "Rethinking Security in the Pacific," in *Foreign Affairs*, vol. 70, No. 2, 1991.

Linder, Staffan Burenstam, *The Pacific Century: Economic and Political Consequences of Asian-Pacific Dynamism*, Stanford Univ. Press, 1986.

PART ONE

Overview

2

Pacific Basin Economic Prospects, 1990-1994

Lawrence R. Klein

The Asia-Pacific area of the world economy has attracted economic attention because of its high and impressive economic performance. Also, the apparent grouping of the countries of Europe and of North America into well-defined trading areas, with institutional structure, has prompted the Asia-Pacific countries to think about the prospects of their own integrated groupings. I want to consider the geographical makeup of these countries and to look at their present economic prospects.

First let me define some subgroups within the broader area. The ASEAN countries, the four "New Japans" (Hong Kong, Singapore, Taiwan, and Republic of Korea), and the developed countries of the Pacific (Australia, New Zealand, and Japan) distinguished themselves by establishing fast-growing modern economies that flourished in environments that seemed to be troublesome for many other countries.

The Asian-Pacific countries listed above came through oil shocks, in which only Indonesia was a major oil surplus economy; through debt crises; and world recession emerging stronger than other areas of the international economy. There was some inflation in Asia, but prices never got out of control for long; output growth was strong, even on a per capita basis; and export expansion was particularly impressive. True enough, there have been individual bad years for selected countries, but in viewing the region as a whole, it was possible to identify it in the 1970s and 1980s as the outstanding regional group on the world scene. Also there were some small countries in the region that never did participate in the general prosperity.

Progress still continues, but the coming decade that rounds out the century poses new challenges and probably some economic adjustments. The world's regional focus has shifted from the Asia-Pacific area to Europe. The challenge that is implicit in this shift comes from the institutional trading system that is associated with the enhancement of the Common Market into a *Single Market* after January 1, 1993. The final configuration is not clear because the relationship with the countries of EFTA and CMEA has not yet taken definite shape. Also some countries in Europe may change status by joining the Common Market. Possibilities are for Austria and Norway to join. Of course, East Germany is being absorbed by West Germany and brought into the market that way. In any event, a large, powerful, economic entity is being formed in Europe, and this new entity will be a formidable competitor for the Asia-Pacific countries. The fact that Switzerland, a European country that has often remained aloof from international organizations, is considering membership in the International Monetary Fund is indicative of the changing attitudes in Europe.

North America is changing too. In many Pacific Basin gatherings, Canada and the United States participate as though they are fully fledged Pacific nations. That is true enough, but they are also Atlantic and Caribbean nations. They are looking inward to some extent and are ready to welcome Mexico as well. It is, however, more than likely that the North American countries, even if tied together in a free trade zone, will continue to cooperate and coordinate policies with the Asia-Pacific countries.

A major question has arisen about the fitting of China into the Asia-Pacific grouping. At the beginning of the economic reform period in 1978, China was being implicitly reclassified from a "centrally planned economy" to an "Asian developing economy." World Bank tabulations across countries confirmed this classification.

Now the concept of "centrally planned economies" has changed drastically because of the upheavals in Europe. The Eastern European countries are moving away from central planning, and the Soviet Union may move too. Just when China seemed to be de-emphasizing central planning by freeing up or liberalizing agriculture and small enterprise, the political disturbances of last summer introduced a pause if not a reversal. For the moment, China should still be regarded as an Asian developing country, but trading relationships with some leading Pacific Basin economies appear to be developing more slowly than was expected, just prior to last June's student demonstrations. There may be some restoration of expanding trading relationships, but there is considerably less optimism for expansion in this area, particularly involving South Korea, Japan, Taiwan, and Hong Kong. In any event, Chinese economic expansion has slowed considerably. In the best years after the move towards liberalization in 1978, overall growth exceeded 10 percent annually. In the natural course of events, a slowing of growth to a more comfortable level between 5 and 10 percent per annum was fully expected but, in fact, the slowdown appears to have been more severe in 1989. Inflation, which caused much of the trouble in 1988-89, has been cut back to more manageable levels, but export growth, the trade balance, and financial reserves have all deteriorated.

The slowing of economic expansion in China is partly a domestic matter and partly related to the general slowing down among several Asian economies. Other Asian countries will be in the 5 to 10 percent range together with China, but few will be at the upper end of that range. While China is now reducing inflationary pressures, other Asian economies, from the most advanced cases such as Japan to the developing countries, are experiencing higher price rises. In some cases, wage rates are moving up smartly, and this is a source of pressure.

In the Japanese case, higher prices have been a consequence of yen depreciation and higher interest costs, which have been transmitted by world pressures, stemming to a large extent from Germany and the rest of Europe. Raw material prices have been favorable for buyers, and these tendencies have worked to prevent the price increases from breaking out into rapidly accelerating inflation rates.

An important characteristic of the Asia-Pacific region has been export-led growth. Economic strategy based on this concept goes back to the outstanding performance of Japan during the 1960s. The process continued in the 1970s and 1980s, spreading to Taiwan, South Korea, Hong Kong, Singapore, Thailand, Malaysia, and Indonesia. Now most of these economies are experiencing export resistance of one form or another. This will affect the ability of many developing countries in the area to pursue self-financing for needed imports and to manage international debt service burdens.

Why have exports been meeting resistance? First consider the lucrative American market. It has been the overt policy of the United States to curtail import dependence on the rest of the world, but especially on the Asia-Pacific area. The United States has negotiated for slower import growth and has become much more competitive through dollar depreciation, inflation control, and revival of manufacturing productivity growth. The large American market is still there, but it will become increasingly difficult to penetrate. There is a general tendency for the US trade account (net exports of goods and services) to move towards more favorable balance (from the US point of view). This has been a slow process that followed a policy of dollar depreciation, starting in February 1985. It is finally having some effect, abetted by pressures on Taiwan and South Korea to allow their currencies to appreciate. Recently, however, the US dollar has strengthened again and, with a time lag, this may retard the improvement in the American net export position.

There are several implications in these developments for the economies of the Asia-Pacific region. There must be more outward-looking policies towards Europe. The Common Market countries will resist exports from Asia, but the Eastern bloc countries that are now modernizing desperately need goods that Asian economies can produce in abundance. Financing needs to be developed and expanded in Eastern Europe and the Soviet Union, but there will be very large market opportunities there for the future. Also, Latin America will eventually recover, and there, too, a need for Asian manufactures will eventually provide some export outlets for the Pacific Basin countries.

Yet another geographical configuration can form an effective outlet for export expansion, namely, more trade within the Asia-Pacific region. At first, this trading pattern will develop in the normal course of events within the present institutional framework, but there should be increasing attention paid to the formation of an Asia-Pacific Common Market. Eventually, such an institutional scheme could include the economies of North America (the United States, Canada, and Mexico), which are Pacific as well as Atlantic countries. The European Common Market may grow into being such a formidable competitor that a trading coalition that includes both North America and the Asian Pacific Basin countries (plus Australia and New Zealand) will be needed to put up a strong cooperative front.

The origins of the Common Market in Europe were based on liberalizing of merchandise trade relationships. That should also be the first consideration for closer economic cooperation in the Asia-Pacific area, but there should also be close attention to capital flows and movements of financial capital, and people. At present, the Common Market is working intensively to liberalize both financial capital flows and movements of people. These developments are at the very heart of preparations for the Single Market after January 1, 1993. The establishment of liberalized capital markets with fewer and fewer barriers across countries is of extreme importance to the countries of the Pacific. Sophisticated and active financial markets already exist in Tokyo, Sydney, Hong Kong, and Singapore. Others will develop more intensively and extensively, too. But the established Pacific markets are already flourishing at the international level, and they do not have to wait on the completion of first steps with regard to merchandise traffic. The latest financial instruments, software, hardware, and exchange experience are already in operation. It is only a matter of breaking down the remaining international barriers and bringing more countries into this new sophisticated financial network. Their established financial markets are already big earners for the host countries. Their earnings can grow in an environment that allows free flow of capital.

Some remarks about "fringe" countries may be in order. They are intended to provide a more rounded view of the situation. The word "fringe" is not meant, in any sense, to be pejorative; it is simply a matter of where they lie in relation to the Pacific Basin economies. If we use the broader expression, Asia-Pacific, then we clearly ought to include India and Pakistan in the area's economic analysis. India is second, only to China, in population and Pakistan's 105 million people are hard to ignore.

A reason for commenting on their economic performance in discussions of the Pacific Basin results is that they are, in a sense, sleeping giants. They have both grown very well, not at the spectacular rates near 10 percent, as in the most dynamic of the Pacific Basin economies, but steadily near 5 percent, year after year, and there are some impressive gains to be noted. It is true, of course, that population growth has been rapid, at 2.0% (India) and 3.0% (Pakistan); these rates have diluted, in a sense, the output gains, but these two countries have made distinct progress.

They have experienced neither uncontrolled inflation nor extraordinary balance-of-payment problems. The main sources of economic instability have been either political or weather-related. Weather problems average out over the years, and at present, political instabilities are not unusual, certainly not as serious, it would appear, as in the Philippines or Hong Kong, where economic performance has been more eye-catching.

When many developing countries were taking on large amounts of debt, only to become burdened with intolerable servicing requirements, India and Pakistan managed to get along without resorting to unusual borrowing. India's self-reliance for capital financing has been overstated because deposits of Indians in the far-flung diaspora were not properly counted as financial liabilities in figuring international indebtedness. India actually has a debt of more than $70 billion, which is quite large, but there has not been a servicing crisis, as in so many other developing countries. India was very negative towards foreign equity capital, but that attitude has changed. Steady expansion looks promising, and if we extend the concept of the Pacific Basin, or revise it to become the Asia-Pacific area, then we should actively add two steady stalwarts to the group of economies being considered. Information is less substantial for Sri Lanka, Nepal, Afghanistan,

Samoa, Burma, Vietnam, North Korea, and other Asian countries, but they are mixed in performance and not so large as India and Pakistan. In general, they are not strong economies, but Vietnam may be one of the surprises for the near future.

Projections of Output, Consumption, and Inflation

Within the Asia-Pacific area and including the North American advanced industrial market (Canada/United States), the statistical estimates indicate a slowing of growth—sometimes cyclical as in 1990 or 1991 and sometimes along a medium-term trend—and a pickup in inflation. The growth slowdown is not disastrous, and some economies are projected to expand for several years running (Tables 2.2, 2.3, 2.6). The price pickup is not strongly inflationary. In most cases, prices are expected to be higher in the early 1990s with a slight falling off of the inflation rate towards mid-decade (Tables 2.5, 2.8). Pacific developing countries are expected to show improving trade balances (Table 2.1).

Some cross-country tabulations are extracted from the project LINK forecast of April 1990 and attached. First let us look at GDP estimates (Tables 2.2, 2.6). Canada and the United States should experience their slowest years during 1989-91 and then gradually approach the modest rate of 3% (or slightly less) expansion. Japan, too, appears to be slowing down and not recovering briskly. Growth in 1990 and 1991 may be a bit higher than estimated by LINK—as strong as 5%. Australia exhibits a pattern like that in North America, but New Zealand appears to be ready for modest expansion after coming off very poor years in 1988 and 1989. The unemployment figures for developed countries in the East (Japan, Australia, and New Zealand) are dominated by the low figures for Japan (Table 2.4).

In the Pacific Basin, all the growth rates of developing countries are below their historical best values. In most cases, they fall by about one or two percentage points between 1989 and 1994. China is expecting to regain some of last year's setback, possibly not as much as indicated in the LINK tables, but they end the period with a growth rate that is under their best years by one-half. The estimated slowdown for Hong Kong in 1990 appears to exaggerate the situation. Growth could be as high as 3 percent. Although these estimates show a slowing tendency in the Pacific Basin, it must be stressed that the results are not bad, and there is promise ahead for a very decent rate of expansion, better than 5% in most cases.

Consumer spending growth reported in Table 2.7 is not much different from production growth in most industrial countries being examined, but the six-year mean for consumer spending is below the six-year mean for

TABLE 2.1 World Exports, Imports and Trade Balances (f.o.b.)[a] (Billions of U.S. $)

	1989	% chg.	1990	% chg.	1991	% chg.	1992	% chg.	1993	% chg.	1994	% chg.
Developed Market Economies[b]												
Exports	2183.70	8.6	2425.13	11.1	2681.23	10.6	2962.11	10.5	3271.66	10.5	3605.95	10.2
Imports	2220.91	9.8	2466.81	11.1	2724.57	10.4	3006.22	10.3	3314.97	10.3	3656.23	10.3
Balance	-37.21		-41.68		-43.34		-44.11		-43.31		-50.29	
North America												
Exports	492.82	14.2	530.56	7.7	586.55	10.6	650.59	10.9	725.15	11.5	799.62	10.3
Imports	601.13	9.0	636.54	5.9	690.97	8.6	752.42	8.9	818.05	8.7	885.93	8.3
Balance	-108.30		-105.97		-104.42		-101.83		-92.90		-86.31	
Developed East												
Exports	321.08	7.0	337.91	5.2	364.80	8.0	395.91	8.5	426.59	7.7	460.28	7.9
Imports	247.78	21.0	269.85	8.9	297.60	10.3	328.36	10.3	361.29	10.0	401.52	11.1
Balance	73.30		68.06		67.20		67.56		65.30		58.76	
EEC												
Exports	1137.48	7.3	1296.95	14.0	1447.05	11.6	1603.37	10.8	1777.12	10.8	1973.12	11.0
Imports	1140.61	9.0	1301.52	14.1	1455.03	11.8	1616.50	11.1	1797.03	11.2	1996.29	11.1
Balance	-3.13		-4.57		-7.98		-13.13		-19.91		-23.17	
Rest of Industrialized												
Exports	232.33	6.1	259.70	11.8	282.83	8.9	312.23	10.4	342.80	9.8	372.92	8.8
Imports	231.39	5.6	258.91	11.9	280.97	8.5	308.94	10.0	338.60	9.6	372.49	10.0
Balance	0.93		0.80		1.86		3.29		4.20		.43	
Developing Countries[b]												
Exports	716.35	14.7	777.91	8.6	860.06	10.6	952.78	10.8	1056.63	10.9	1176.98	11.4
Imports	673.66	12.8	741.53	10.1	817.86	10.3	906.56	10.8	1006.56	11.0	1124.18	11.7
Balance	42.69		36.38		42.20		46.22		50.06		52.08	
Latin America, Caribbean												
Exports	114.97	7.2	122.77	6.8	131.87	7.4	143.01	8.4	155.16	8.5	168.70	8.7
Imports	91.89	6.3	97.50	6.1	105.43	8.1	114.97	9.0	126.31	9.9	141.18	11.8
Balance	23.8		25.27		26.44		28.04		28.85		27.52	

(*continues*)

TABLE 2.1 (continued)

	1989	% chg.	1990	% chg.	1991	% chg.	1992	% chg.	1993	% chg.	1994	% chg.
Africa												
Exports	61.44	15.4	64.60	5.2	69.55	7.7	75.28	8.2	81.20	7.9	88.37	8.8
Imports	69.56	7.8	74.14	6.6	79.97	7.9	86.82	8.6	94.03	8.3	101.97	8.4
Balance	-8.12		-9.54		-10.42		-11.54		-12.84		-13.60	
South, East Asia												
Exports	359.66	14.7	395.38	9.9	445.45	12.7	499.89	12.2	561.94	12.4	634.35	12.9
Imports	346.15	17.4	388.47	12.2	435.76	12.2	488.31	12.1	548.92	12.4	619.94	12.9
Balance	13.51		6.90		9.69		11.58		13.01		14.41	
China												
Exports	52.47	10.5	58.25	11.0	64.77	11.2	72.14	11.4	80.17	11.1	90.03	12.3
Imports	56.22	7.0	61.10	8.7	66.54	8.9	73.22	10.0	81.62	11.5	91.01	11.5
Balance	-3.75		-2.85		-1.77		-1.08		-1.45		-0.98	
West Asia												
Exports	72.26	28.6	77.08	6.7	83.00	7.7	90.87	9.5	99.97	10.0	109.88	9.9
Imports	33.80	6.7	37.43	10.07	40.29	7.6	45.21	12.2	48.53	7.4	52.74	8.7
Balance	-5.57		-6.76		-6.76		-8.21		-8.70		-8.95	
Eastern Europe, USSR												
Exports	220.86	-1.6	230.80	4.5	240.77	4.3	256.11	6.4	274.63	2.2	295.91	7.7
Imports	221.45	5.5	237.92	7.4	258.41	8.6	276.85	7.1	298.94	8.0	321.01	7.4
Balance	-0.59		-7.12		-17.64		-20.73		-24.31		-25.10	
World Exports	3120.91	9.1	3433.84	10.0	3782.05	10.1	4170.99	10.3	4602.89	10.4	5078.79	10.3
World Export Price	3.88	1.2	4.06	4.6	4.25	4.8	4.45	4.6	4.64	4.2	4.85	4.6
World Exports, Real	804.81	7.8	846.35	5.2	889.35	5.1	937.68	5.4	992.79	5.9	1047.12	5.5

Source: [a]Project LINK—United Nations/DIESA

[b]Definition of aggregates:

Aggregate	Definition
North America	Canada, U.S.A.
Developed East	Japan, Australia, New Zealand
EEC	Belgium/Luxemburg, Denmark, France, Germany (F.R.), Greece, Ireland, Italy, Netherlands, Portugal, Spain, U.K.
Rest of Industrialized	Austria, Iceland, Finland, Norway, Sweden, Switzerland, South Africa, Israel
Latin America and Caribbean	Argentina, Bolivia, Brazil, Chile, Colombia, Ecuador, Mexico, Paraguay, Peru, Uruguay, Venezuela, Caribbean
Africa	Algeria, Egypt, Ethiopia, Gabon, Ghana, Kenya, Libya, Morocco, Nigeria, Sudan, Tunisia, Other African countries, Africa least developed countries
South and East Asia	Hong Kong, Indonesia, Korea, Malaysia, Philippines, Singapore, Taiwan, Thailand, India, Pakistan, South East least developed, other South East Asian countries
West Asia	Iran, Iraq, Kuwait, Saudi Arabia, West Asia Oil Importers
Mediterranean	Other developed countries, Turkey, Yugoslavia
CPE	Bulgaria, Czechoslovakia, Germany (G.D.R.), Hungary, Poland, Romania, U.S.S.R.

Note: Regions are defined in the respective country tables.

TABLE 2.2 World Gross National Product (1970 U.S. $) (Percent change)

	1989[b]	1990[b]	1991[b]	1992[b]	1993[b]	1994[b]	Mean
Developed Market Economies[a]	3.4	2.7	3.1	3.0	3.0	2.9	3.0
North America	2.9	1.9	2.7	2.7	3.0	2.8	2.7
Developed East	4.9	4.3	4.1	4.1	4.2	4.4	4.3
EEC	3.7	3.4	3.5	3.0	2.7	2.5	3.1
Rest of Industrialized	1.8	1.4	0.9	2.2	1.8	2.0	1.7
Developing Countries	3.4	3.1	5.0	5.1	5.3	5.4	4.5
Lat. Am., Caribbean	0.8	-0.9	4.2	3.7	4.2	4.5	2.7
Africa	2.6	2.8	2.2	2.6	3.0	3.3	2.7
South, East Asia	6.4	5.8	6.2	6.1	6.0	6.1	6.1
China	3.9	5.1	6.1	6.5	6.5	6.4	5.7
West Asia	6.9	4.5	3.5	4.6	4.3	4.2	4.7
Mediterranean	1.1	0.0	4.0	5.6	4.9	4.8	3.4
CPE	-1.1	-1.2	0.2	1.7	2.2	2.7	0.7
World Total	2.7	2.2	3.0	3.2	3.3	3.3	3.0

[a]See Table 2.1, Definition of aggregates
[b]Growth Rates
Source: Project LINK United Nations/DIESA.

TABLE 2.3 Per Capita World Gross National Product (1970 U.S. $) (Percent change)

	1989[b]	1990[b]	1991[b]	1992[b]	1993[b]	1994[b]	Mean
Developed Market Economies[a]	2.9	2.3	2.7	2.6	2.5	2.4	2.6
North America	2.0	1.0	1.9	1.9	2.1	2.0	1.8
Developed East	4.3	3.8	3.5	3.5	3.6	3.8	3.8
EEC	3.7	3.4	3.4	3.0	2.6	2.5	3.1
Rest of Industrialized	1.2	2.4	2.2	3.3	2.6	2.5	2.4
Developing Countries	1.7	1.4	3.3	3.4	3.5	3.7	2.8
Lat. Am., Caribbean	-1.0	-2.6	2.2	1.7	2.2	2.5	0.8
Africa	-0.3	0.0	-0.5	-0.1	0.3	0.5	0.0
South, East Asia	4.6	4.1	4.6	4.4	4.4	4.5	4.4
China	2.7	3.9	4.9	5.3	5.3	5.2	4.5
West Asia	3.9	1.2	0.3	1.4	1.1	1.0	1.5
Mediterranean	-0.1	-1.1	2.9	4.5	3.8	3.7	2.2
CPE	-1.8	-1.9	-0.4	1.1	1.5	2.1	0.1
World Total	2.0	1.6	2.4	2.5	2.6	2.6	2.3

[a]See Table 2.1, Definition of aggregates
[b]Growth Rates
Source: Project LINK United Nations/DIESA.

TABLE 2.4 OECD Unemployment Rate (Percent change)

	1989	1990	1991	1992	1993	1994	Mean
OECD[a]	6.2	6.4	6.3	6.2	5.9	5.8	6.1
North America	5.4	5.8	5.7	5.5	5.0	4.9	5.4
Developed East	2.8	2.9	3.1	3.2	3.5	3.8	3.2
EEC	10.0	9.8	9.5	9.3	9.3	9.0	9.5
Rest of OECD	5.7	6.4	7.0	7.4	7.2	6.8	6.8

Note: Excl. Greece, Iceland, and Switzerland.
[a]See Table 2.1, Definition of aggregates
Source: Project LINK United Nations/DIESA.

TABLE 2.5 OECD Private Consumption Deflator (Percent change)

	1989	1990	1991	1992	1993	1994	Mean
OECD[a]	3.4	3.8	4.2	4.1	3.4	3.3	3.7
North America	4.4	4.2	4.5	4.9	4.6	5.0	4.6
Developed East	3.1	2.6	2.9	2.9	2.8	2.6	2.8
EEC	3.2	3.8	4.2	4.0	3.3	3.1	3.6
Rest of OECD	4.7	5.3	5.1	3.8	3.6	3.5	4.3

Notes: Inflation rate in local currency weighted with GNP in current U.S. $
[a]See Table 2.1, Definition of aggregates
Source: Project LINK United Nations/DIESA.

TABLE 2.6 Gross Domestic Product, in Local Currency (Percent change)

	1989	1990	1991	1992	1993	1994	Mean
Industrialized Countries[a]							
Canada	2.56	1.33	2.86	3.03	3.40	3.39	2.76
Japan	5.15	4.58	4.37	4.32	4.38	4.48	4.56
U.S.	2.99	1.95	2.71	2.70	2.96	2.74	2.67
Australia	3.70	2.30	2.40	2.59	3.08	3.79	2.98
New Zealand	0.90	1.60	2.80	1.30	2.50	2.90	2.01
Developing Countries & Regions[a]							
Indonesia	5.90	6.10	5.70	5.80	5.80	5.90	5.87
Thailand	10.95	9.29	8.68	7.67	7.36	7.89	8.63
China	3.89	5.08	6.12	6.51	6.50	6.41	5.75

[a]See Table 2.1, Definition of aggregates
Source: Project LINK United Nations/DIESA.

production except for Australia, where the consumption figure is slightly higher. The slowing down of consumption growth occurs most frequently during 1990-92. In Malaysia, the estimate is for sharply higher consumption than production growth. For industries that look to the consumer market for support, that situation does not appear to be bad, but the tendency to expand sharply is not apparent in most cases.

Finally, let us turn to inflation in Table 2.8—as measured by the index deflator of consumer expenditures. In Australia and New Zealand, the trend is downward. There is a slight pickup in the inflation figures for Japan, the United States, and Canada, but the results do not look seriously bad. It is a case of low, persistent inflation.

Among Pacific Basin countries studied, the Philippines are projected to experience the most inflation, averaging about 10 percent. Inflation in Taiwan, Hong Kong, and South Korea is likely to be higher than estimated in all cases, probably near 10 percent. In most other countries, inflation is fairly steady and comes down a bit after peaking early in the decade. Inflation restraint has been a characteristic feature of Pacific Basin economic performance, during the region's best years and during some very trying times in the world economy. It seems sensible, then, for countries in the region to do everything possible to keep inflation under strict control.

India and Pakistan are expected to grow at rates near their long-run averages. The LINK estimates are, in each case, just above 5% for GDP growth. The key assumptions behind these two estimates are that agricultural conditions remain normal for the next few years—for such things as crop moisture, harvest conditions, health of crops—and that present political configurations remain firmly in place. There are expected to be the usual amounts of inflationary pressure and balance-of-payment difficulties but natural or manmade disasters—as at Bhopal—do not appear.

This is not an economic environment of demand pressure. It appears to be a healthy situation for expansion without an uncontrollable acceleration of price rises. However, where inflation rates have strayed above the regional average, steps should be taken to restore price stability.

In some countries, particularly the Philippines, debt burdens remain heavy obstacles to good growth and overall performance. There will have to be further concessions or swaps in order to allow the expected growth path projected here. The new developments in economic priorities are clearly revealed by the fact that the Philippines and other heavily indebted developing countries have experienced net capital outflows in recent years, while the large creditor countries are now gearing up for significant capital inflows into Eastern Europe, even

TABLE 2.7 Real Private Consumption in Local Currency (Percent change)

	1989	1990	1991	1992	1993	1994	Mean
Industrialized Countries[a]							
Canada	3.71	1.20	0.30	1.30	1.53	2.40	1.73
Japan	3.34	4.32	4.25	3.90	3.80	3.80	3.90
U.S.	2.76	2.44	2.41	2.28	2.53	2.49	2.48
Australia	4.90	2.50	1.80	2.98	3.41	3.46	3.17
New Zealand	0.60	0.10	1.30	1.20	3.70	3.20	1.67
Developing Countries and Regions[a]							
Indonesia	12.50	9.70	6.50	6.80	8.31	7.41	8.52
Thailand	8.56	8.65	8.52	8.09	7.73	7.68	8.20

[a]See Table 2.1, Definition of aggregates
Source: Project LINK United Nations/DIESA.

TABLE 2.8 Consumption Deflator in Local Currency (Percent change)

	1989	1990	1991	1992	1993	1994	Mean
Industrialized Countries[a]							
Canada	4.15	4.52	5.79	5.06	4.98	4.90	4.90
Japan	2.71	2.07	2.38	2.53	2.54	2.38	2.44
U.S.	4.40	4.11	4.34	4.88	4.58	5.03	4.56
Australia	6.32	7.68	7.98	6.63	5.83	4.57	6.50
New Zealand	7.50	6.10	2.90	1.70	0.70	1.00	3.28
Developing Countries & Regions[a]							
Indonesia	6.40	6.80	9.30	8.80	9.20	9.30	8.20
Thailand	6.92	5.47	4.70	4.16	3.23	3.18	4.60

[a]See Table 2.1, Definition of aggregates
Source: Project LINK United Nations/DIESA.

into large debtor countries such as Poland and Hungary. There are also inflows into parts of Southern Europe.

For a number of years, starting in the mid-1970s, I have been very optimistic about economic expansion in the Asia-Pacific area. Japan's continuing into more economic maturity following the extreme expansion of the 1960s, Australia's diversification into minerals and manufactures, the abilities of Australia and New Zealand to reorient their interests to the Pacific area after the establishment of the Common Market in Europe, the ability of the area to cope with the two oil shocks of the 1970s, the development of the "New Japans" into lines of activity that previously led to expansion in Japan, the establishment of leading financial market centers in the area, the latest wave of expansions in

Asian countries, and the adoption of economic reforms by China in 1978 all contributed to heightened expectations for an already promising economic area. Though there have been some setbacks, particularly in recent years, and the most extreme of the good indicators have been trimmed or adjusted slightly, I remain as firmly convinced as ever that this is one of the most promising economic areas of the world economy. The work force, the environment and the attitudes of the population all point toward continuing economic achievement. Therefore, while I clearly recognize the new challenges from Europe and North America, I remain convinced that the Asia-Pacific area has outstanding economic promise for the next few years and probably well beyond the end of this century.

3

Agricultural Development and Trade in the Pacific Rim Countries

Kym Anderson

Introduction

What will be the impact of economic growth in Pacific Rim countries and elsewhere on the agricultural trade of those economies? This is of course a question of great importance to agricultural exporters in countries such as Australia, Canada, New Zealand, Thailand and the United States. But it is also of great interest to people in densely populated, newly industrializing nations who fear their agricultural sector and food security will decline as farmers become less competitive in the wake of industrialization. An all-too-common response to that fear is a call for protection from food import competition. When the call is heeded the protection inevitably is deemed insufficient, and so the escalation of agricultural protection begins. This in turn raises domestic food prices and reduces trade growth, thereby frustrating both domestic consumers and non-food exporters, not to mention overseas producers of farm products.

To understand likely developments in agricultural production and trade therefore requires looking at the determinants not only of agricultural comparative advantage but also of policy distortions to incentives affecting producers and consumers in each economy as it grows.

The first section of the paper briefly reviews standard trade and development theory as it applies to the agricultural sector of a growing economy. It shows that while it is virtually inevitable that agriculture's share of production and employment will decline with economic growth, the same is not necessarily true of agriculture's share of exports or of food self-sufficiency—even in an economy which remains undistorted. The latter is therefore even less likely in an economy whose

29

growth is accompanied by policy changes which increasingly favour the farm sector, as Western Europe clearly demonstrates.

The second section examines the extent to which empirical evidence from Pacific Rim countries supports the standard theory. It turns out their experiences conform very closely with that theory, particularly when account is taken of the changes to distortionary policies affecting farmers' incentives.

We often observe policies which discriminate against agriculture in poor countries and in favour of farmers in rich countries. Reasons for this gradual change, which tends to increasingly favour agriculture as an economy develops, are briefly canvassed in section three. This understanding of the political economy of policy trends, together with the empirically supported theory of changing comparative advantages, gives us confidence to say something in the final section about future prospects both for traditional agricultural-exporting countries as well as for newly industrializing countries and those contemplating major policy reforms.

Conceptualizing Agricultural Development in a Growing Economy

Why Agriculture's Relative Importance Declines

Why does the agricultural sector tend to decline in relative importance over time? When domestic savings accumulate or foreign capital flows in from abroad in the form of grants or loans, the economy's production possibilities expand and incomes rise. More is thus spent on the available goods, but not in the same proportions as before. In particular, the demand for essentials such as food rises relatively slowly (Engel's Law). In a closed economy—including the world as a whole—this Engel effect means that economic growth will be accompanied by a decline in the price of food relative to non-food products, ceteris paribus.[1] Any small open economy faced with such a price decline in world markets will tend to move resources out of agriculture into sectors producing other tradables. As well, as incomes grow in this economy the demand for nontradables tends to grow more than proportionately and thereby cause resources to be attracted to their production.[2] Thus both the relative price and the relative quantity of farm products tend to decline as incomes grow at home and abroad, and hence so too does agriculture's shares of gross domestic product and employment.

The only situation in which this would not happen in a small open economy is if output growth is sufficiently biased in favour of agriculture to offset the relative price decline for farm products. That requires either total factor productivity growth to be faster in agriculture than in other sectors, and/or the endowment of factors used relatively intensively in farming (most notably agricultural land) to increase relatively rapidly.[3] This is likely to be especially difficult to achieve in densely populated economies.

Must Agricultural Self-Sufficiency Also Decline?

What determines whether a country is a net agricultural exporter or importer at a point in time? And how will that position change with economic growth at home and abroad?

A modification by Anne Krueger (1977) of the standard theory of comparative advantage suggests that when a poor economy opens up to international trade, its exports initially will be specialized in primary products, because its stocks of non-farm capital relative to farm capital (principally land) are comparatively low.[4] The proportion of those primary exports that is agricultural will be larger, the greater this country's endowment of agricultural land relative to minerals compared with that ratio globally. If the country's domestic incomes and non-farm capital to labour ratio grow more rapidly than the rest of the world's (for example, because of a high domestic savings ratio or large borrowings from abroad),[5] its export specialization will gradually switch away from primary products (in raw or lightly processed form) to manufactures, in the absence of distortionary policies. This switch will begin at an earlier stage of economic development, and the manufactured goods initially exported will be more labour intensive, the more resource-poor or densely populated the country (population density serving as a crude inverse proxy for the stock of agricultural land and minerals per worker). Since many textile and clothing production activities tend to be intensive in the use of unskilled labour, this theory suggests they will be among the items initially exported by a newly industrializing, densely populated country, and that as the demand for textile raw materials by that country's expanding textile industry grows, so the country's net exports of natural fibre will diminish, or net imports of natural fibre will increase, ceteris paribus.

These smooth changes in comparative advantage can of course be disrupted by sudden shocks to the economy, such as a major institutional or relative price change. The introduction in rural China of large communes in 1958, and of the household responsibility system and huge producer price hikes in the late 1970s, are cases in point. Other examples are a sustained change in the international terms of trade for a country, such as happened with the petroleum price increases of 1973 and 1979-80 and their decrease in the mid-1980s before jumping again in late 1990, and a discovery of new mineral deposits (Corden 1984).

Empirical Support for the Theory

Global Cross-Sectional Evidence

This theory has strong empirical support from both cross-sectional and time series evidence.[6] The negative relationship between agriculture's shares of gross domestic product (GDP), employment (EMP) and exports (EXP) on the one hand, and income per capita (YPC) on the other, are very significant statistically. These shares are also negatively associated with population density per unit of agricultural land (PDA) although significantly so only for the export share equation. This is clear from the following OLS regression equations, from Anderson (1987), which are based on World Bank data for 1981 for 70 countries with populations in excess of one million (t-values in parentheses):

(1) GDP = 87 − 9.2lnYPC $\bar{R}^2$ = 0.80
              (6.7)

(2) EMP = 179 − 18.5lnYPC $\bar{R}^2$ = 0.80
              (6.6)

(3) EXP = 152 − 9.5lnYPC − 8.5lnPDA, $\bar{R}^2$ = 0.45
              (5.1)   (4.7)

The theory also suggests that the share of labour-intensive manufactures such as textile and clothing in total manufactured exports (TEX) would by very high at first as income per capita (YPC) increases from a low base and then would fall, and would tend to be higher the greater the population density of the country (PD, a crude index of the endowment of natural resources per capita suggested by Keesing and Sherk [1977], Bowen [1983] and Leamer [1984]). Evidence supporting this can be obtained by estimating an OLS regression equation from cross-sectional data. For example, using the data available for the year 1986 from the World Bank (1988) for 63 countries with populations exceeding one million, the following equation is estimated:

TEX = 25.6 + 7.77lnYPC − .523(lnYPC)2 + .163PD, $\bar{R}^2$ = 0.52
           (5.6)   (5.7)   (6.3)

These equations are clearly consistent with the theory of development and changing comparative advantage summarized above.

Time-Series Evidence from Pacific Rim Countries

Time-series evidence also is strongly supportive of the above theory of structural change and comparative advantage in growing economies. What is clear from columns 2 and 5 of Table 3.1 is that Northeast Asia's market economies and Singapore are extremely poorly endowed with agricultural land per worker and have enjoyed extremely rapid income growth during the past 25 years; that the other economies of East Asia have grown moderately rapidly and are moderately densely populated (China more so than is indicated because three quarters of its agricultural land is low-quality pastoral land); and that Australasia and North America are extremely well endowed with farm land per worker and their economic growth has been relatively sluggish.

This categorization does not imply that there is a causative link between income growth and population density (although there may be indirectly, in the sense that economies extremely poorly endowed in natural resources have to trade more and their openness enhances economic growth—compare columns 2, 5 and 7 of Table 3.1). Rather, it is to examine the extent to which the theory in section 1 is supported by the changing production and trade pattern of these three groups of economies.[7]

Specifically, the theory leads us to expect the relative importance of agriculture in Japan and its densely populated and rapidly growing neighbours to be declining rapidly, and for these countries to be losing comparative advantage in farm products while gaining it in (initially labour-intensive) manufactures. For the other market economies of East Asia one would expect similar though less rapid changes, and for Australasia and North America one would expect a slower decline in agricultural competitiveness with a lingering comparative advantage in farm products despite their advanced income status (apart from Mexico).

This is indeed what has occurred. Table 3.2 shows the extremely rapid decline in the relative importance of agriculture in Northeast Asia—including China even before the reforms began in 1978 but especially since then. In Indonesia and Thailand, too, agriculture's share of GDP has halved during the past two decades. The international competitiveness of East Asian agriculture also has declined rapidly, as shown in Table 3.3. The importance of agriculture in these economies' exports was more than twice the world average at the time they began to industrialize, but its relative importance has fallen precipitously. In Japan and the four NIEs (the newly industrialized economies of Hong Kong, Singapore, South Korea and Taiwan), farm products now constitute only a small fraction of their exports relative to agriculture's share

TABLE 3.1 Population, National Product, and Trade Orientation of Pacific Rim Economies

	Population, 1987		GNP, 1987	GNP Per Capita		Ratio of Exports to GDP (%)		Share (%) of World Agricultural Trade, 1987	
	Total (millions)	Per Unit of Agricultural Land[a]	(US$ billion)	US$ 1987	Real Growth Rate (%p.a.) 1965-1986	1960	1986	Exports	Imports
Northeast Asian MEs									
Japan	122	21.8	1,926	15,770	4.3	11	12	0.7	1.2
Hong Kong	6	>100	45	8,260	6.2	82	112	0.1	.7
Korea, Rep.	43	17.9	113	2,690	6.7	3	41	0.8	.8
Taiwan	20	20.0	108	5,400	6.9	11	61	1.1	.5
Southeast Asian MEs									
Indonesia	172	5.0	77	500	4.6	3	21	0.4	.7
Malaysia	16	3.4	29	1,800	4.3	4	57	0.5	.9
Philippines	58	5.9	34	590	1.9	1	25	0.2	.5
Singapore	3	>100	20	7,940	7.6	163	N/A	0.9	0.8
Thailand	53	2.4	45	840	4.0	17	27	1.7	0.4
East Asian CPEs									
China	1,086	2.8	600[b]	580[b]	5.1	4	11	2.4	.3
Kampuchia	8	0.7	N/A	N/A	N/A	N/A	N/A	0.0	.0
Korea, DPR	21	8.3	N/A	N/A	N/A	N/A	N/A	0.1	.0
Laos	4	2.1	N/A	N/A	N/A	N/A	N/A	0.0	.0
Vietnam	63	8.7	N/A	N/A	N/A	N/A	N/A	0.1	.1

Australasia									
Australia	16	0.03	176	10,900	1.7	15	29	3.1	0.6
New Zealand	3	0.2	27	8,230	1.5	22	16	1.6	0.2
North America									
Canada	26	0.3	390	15,080	2.6	18	27	6.0	2.1
United States	246	0.4	4,486	18,430	1.6	5	7	12.6	10.9
Mexico	83	0.8	149	1,820	2.6	10	16	0.8	0.6

[a] Agricultural land area per capita (arable land plus permanent crops and pastures) in the country shown relative to that in the rest of the world.
[b] Based on Perkins' (1988) estimate that China's per capita income in 1985 was US$ 500.

Source: World Bank (1988 a, b); FAO, Production Yearbook, and Trade Yearbook, Rome, 1988; Council on Economic Planning and Development, Taiwan Statistical Data Book, Taipei, 1988; International Economic Data Bank, World Trade Tapes, ANU, Canberra, 1990.

TABLE 3.2 Declining Importance of Agriculture in Northeast Asia, 1880 to 1987

	Share of Agriculture (%)		
	Employment	Domestic Product	Exports
Japan			
1880	74	38	63
1900	60	29	30
1920	51	22	23
1939	42	15	18
1960	33	13	11
1970	9	6	5
1980	1	4	2
1987	8	3	1
Korea, Rep			
1956	N/A	46	89
1960	66	40	56
1970	50	26	17
1980	34	15	10
1987	20	12	5
Taiwan			
1953	56	38	92
1960	50	33	68
1970	37	18	21
1980	20	9	9
1987	15	6	6
China[a]			
1949	N/A	68	N/A
1952	84	58	N/A
1957	81	47	55
1962	82	48	N/A
1967	82	47	51
1972	80	38	47
1978	71	33	34
1984	64	40	23
1987	60	34	18

[a]Some of the Chinese data refer to the average of several years centered on the year shown.

N/A = Not available

Source: See Anderson, 1990, Tables 2.1, 3.4, 3.6 and 3.7.

TABLE 3.3 Indexes of 'Revealed' Comparative Advantage[a] in Agriculture and in Textiles and Clothing in East Asia, 1899 to 1987

	Agriculture	Textiles and Clothing
Japan		
1899	>1.0	1.5
1913	0.7	2.6
1929	0.7	2.9
1937	0.5	4.1
1954-56	0.4	5.5
1964-66	0.3	2.7
1971-73	0.2	1.7
1976-78	0.2	1.0
1982-84	0.1	0.7
1985-87	0.1	0.5
Hong Kong		
1954-56	N/A	5.4
1964-66	N/A	7.0
1971-73	N/A	7.6
1976-78	N/A	9.2
1982-84	N/A	7.2
1985-87	N/A	6.7
Korea, Rep.		
1954-56	2.7	N/A
1964-66	1.6	4.3
1971-73	0.7	6.3
1976-78	0.6	6.6
1982-84	0.5	4.8
1985-87	0.4	3.9
Taiwan		
1954-56	2.6	N/A
1964-66	2.1	2.2
1971-73	0.8	4.8
1976-78	0.7	5.0
1982-84	0.6	4.1
1985-87	0.5	2.9
China		
1955-59	N/A	2.1
1965-69	2.1	3.3
1975-77	2.2	3.9
1978-80	1.9	4.6
1981-83	1.6	5.0
1984-87	1.4	5.1

(*continues*)

TABLE 3.3 (continued)

	Agriculture	Textiles and Clothing
ASEAN[b]		
1965-69	2.6	0.3
1970-74	2.5	0.5
1975-79	2.3	0.6
1980-84	1.9	0.7
1985-87	1.9	1.1

[a]Share of an economy's exports due to these commodities relative to those commodities' share in total world exports, following Balassa (1965). Agriculture is defined as SITC sections 0, 1, 2 (excluding 27, 28) and 4; textiles and clothing include SITC divisions 65 and 84.
[b]Association of Southeast Asian Nations (Brunei, Indonesia, Malaysia, Philippines, Singapore and Thailand).
N/A = Not available
Source: See Anderson, 1990, Tables 3.3 and 3.8.

of world exports. And even for the other ASEAN countries and China that ratio (the so-called revealed comparative advantage index) is fast approaching unity. Conversely, manufacturing exports have become increasingly more important for these economies, beginning with labour-intensive products such as textiles and clothing before moving to more skill- and technology-intensive products (see column two, Table 3.3).

For countries well endowed with agricultural land such as the United States and Australia, agriculture's share of exports is well above the OECD average and has declined much less rapidly than in East Asia, as expected. But, as Table 3.4 shows, agriculture's shares of employment and national product have nonetheless declined quite rapidly and to the very low levels of other OECD countries. This supports the theory which suggests that retaining a degree of international competitiveness is insufficient for preventing a decline in the importance of agriculture in the domestic economy. That is, even the most advantaged agricultural sectors are not immune from the need for structural adjustment of resources out of farming. Those adjustments are accentuated in the face of a minerals export boom, such as Australia faced from the late 1960s to early 1980s. (See especially column 3 of Table 3.4. Farmers in Canada, Indonesia, Malaysia and Mexico also were adversely affected by currency appreciation following the growth in their energy export earnings in the 1970s and early 1980s and will be again if the petroleum price rise in late 1990 is sustained.)

TABLE 3.4 Declining Importance of Agriculture in the United States and Australia, 1830 to 1989

	Share of Agriculture (%)		
	Employment	Domestic Product	Exports[a]
United States			
1830	71	N/A	85 (22)
1850	55	N/A	83 (21)
1870	53	35	81 (25)
1890	43	24	79 (42)
1910	31	16	55 (20)
1930	22	11	36 (14)
1950	12	6	33 (14)
1970	4	4	22 (11)
1987	3	2	N/A
Australia			
1910	24	24	76
1930	24	21	87
1950	13	24	89
1960	10	13	78
1970	8	7	53
1980	6	7	45
1989	5	5	37
OECD Average			
1960	22	7	23
1987	8	3	12

[a] The U.S. export data refer to all primary products, with food only shown in parentheses.
Sources: U.S. Department of Commerce (1976); OECD (1989); Freebairn (1987); Keating (1973); ABARE (1990).
N/A = Not available

The extent of the adjustments made by other Pacific Rim economies since 1965 are summarized in Table 3.5, along with indexes of their international competitiveness in agriculture and textiles and their land productivity. Southeast Asia has adjusted away from agriculture less rapidly and from a higher base than Northeast Asia's market economies, as expected given its lower economic growth rates and population density, but the adjustment has nonetheless been substantial. Notice from the final three columns of Table 3.5 that the loss in competitiveness is not necessarily correlated with crop yields per hectare. Indeed Northeast Asia has relatively high yields, reflecting the fact that government incentives encourage the heavy use of yield-enhancing inputs such as fertilizer and pesticides.

TABLE 3.5 Importance, Competitiveness, and Land Productivity of Agriculture in Pacific Rim Economies, 1965 to 1988 (percent)

	Share of Agriculture in:						Index of "Revealed" Comparative Advantage in:[a]				Grain Yield per ha, 1986-88[b]		
	Employment		Domestic		Exports		Agriculture		Textiles and Clothing		Rice	Wheat	Coarse Grain
	1965	1980	1965	1988	1965	1988	1965	1988	1965	1988			
Northeast Asia													
China	81	74	44	32	48	17	1.8	1.2	3.4	3.8	1.6	1.3	1.4
Japan	26	11	9	3	7	1	0.2	0.1	2.7	0.3	1.9	1.5	1.2
Korea, Rep.	55	34	38	11	25	5	0.9	0.4	4.3	3.2	1.9	1.4	1.1
Taiwan	47	20	27	6	54	6	2.1	0.4	2.3	2.4	1.1	1.5	-
Southeast Asia													
Indonesia	71	57	56	24	53	22	2.0	1.5	0.0	1.2	1.2	-	0.8
Malaysia	59	42	28	21	59	37	2.2	2.6	0.0	0.8	0.8	-	-
Philippines	58	52	26	23	84	26	3.1	1.9	0.1	1.1	0.8	-	0.5
Thailand	82	71	32	17	84	45	3.2	3.2	0.1	2.6	0.6	-	0.9
North America/Australasia													
Australia	10	7	9	4	73	38	2.7	2.7	0.1	0.1	2.1	0.6	0.6
Canada	10	5	6	4	35	20	1.3	1.4	0.1	0.1	-	0.8	1.3
Mexico	50	37	14	9	62	7	2.3	0.5	0.4	0.3	1.1	1.8	0.9
New Zealand	13	11	N/A	10	94	68	3.5	4.9	0.0	0.3	-	1.8	2.0
United States	5	4	3	2	27	17	1.0	1.2	0.4	0.3	1.9	1.0	2.3

[a]Share of an economy's exports due to these commodities relative to those commodities' share in total world exports.
[b]Yield in the country shown as a ratio of the global average.
Source: World Bank (1988a, 1990); International Economic Data Bank, World Trade Tapes, ANU, Canberra, 1990.
N/A = Not available.

As incomes rise in developing countries, the demand for livestock products and fruit and vegetables tends to rise by at least the same proportion while the demand for staples rises much more slowly. Fruit and vegetable production and intensive livestock production (pork, chicken, eggs) require relatively little land per dollar of output. Fresh fruit and vegetables, in addition, often enjoy natural protection from foreign competition because of their perishable nature, as does fluid milk.[8] Thus countries facing a declining comparative advantage in agriculture in general may nonetheless be able to profitably switch some farm resources into these activities. While this would reduce the need to import these items, it is likely that a large-scale expansion in intensive livestock production would necessitate increased dependence on imported feedgrains. In Northeast Asia, for example, exactly these types of changes have occurred. The shares of livestock products and fruit and vegetables in the gross value of their agricultural production have increased substantially at the expense of cereals over the past 30 years (Table 3.6). And self-sufficiency of intensive livestock products has been maintained at close to 100 percent while that of feedstuffs, especially corn and soybeans, has fallen dramatically (as it has for wheat and for beef to a lesser extent—Table 3.7). Similar trends have also occurred in other countries. Mexico in particular has expanded its production of fruit and vegetables to satisfy not only domestic demand growth but also growing United States import demand. In this case production is occurring close to the land border and the lower labour costs in Mexico provide it with a comparative advantage over the United States in producing these relatively labour-intensive foods. Notice from the bottom of Table 3.7, though, that despite the decline in agriculture's relative importance in the economies of Southeast Asia, ASEAN's food self-sufficiency has been maintained thanks to rapid farm output growth in Indonesia and Thailand.

The Role of Policy Interventions

Trends in the inter-sectoral pattern of production and trade depend not only on changes in comparative advantage but also on trends in the distortions to incentives due to government policies. There is ample evidence to suggest that advanced industrial economies tend to subsidize agricultural relative to other sectors while developing countries tend to effectively tax farm relative to non-farm producers (Schultz 1978; Anderson 1989). This suggests that the incentive structure which is distorted against agriculture in low-income countries may gradually be altered by governments to increasingly favour farmers as economic growth occurs. This has happened steadily in Western Europe and has

TABLE 3.6 Composition of Farm Household Income in Japan, Korea, and Taiwan, 1955 to 1987 (percent)

	Share of Gross Value of Farm Output[a] from:				Share[b]
	Grain	Livestock Products	Fruit and Vegetables	Other	
Japan					
1955-59	58	12	17	13	N/A
1960-64	50	18	20	12	68
1965-69	46	20	21	13	67
1970-74	37	25	26	12	63
1975-79	38	26	26	10	60
1980-84	31	28	26	15	53
1985-86	32	26	26	16	53
Korea, Rep.					
1955-59	N/A	N/A	N/A	N/A	N/A
1960-64	78	7	6	9	N/A
1965-69	60	13	13	14	N/A
1970-74	57	14	15	14	81
1975-79	53	16	22	11	78
1980-84	40	25	24	11	74
1985-87	42	25	26	7	67
Taiwan					
1955-59	56	20	7	17	66
1960-64	55	22	9	14	64
1965-69	46	26	13	15	63
1970-74	39	33	18	10	56
1975-79	34	36	20	10	54
1980-84	25	38	27	10	50
1985-87	21	40	28	11	49

[a]Valued at current domestic prices.
[b]Share of value added in the gross value of farm output.
Source: Anderson (1990, Table 3.11).
N/A = Not available.

occurred even faster in Japan and extremely rapidly in Korea and Taiwan (Anderson, Hayami and others 1986).

There are good politico-economic reasons for expecting such a trend in policy. They have to do with the income distributional effects of distortionary policies in rich as compared with poor countries, as well as changes in the costs of collective action by different groups and in the preferences of society. On preferences, it is not difficult to understand why a poor agrarian society may wish to encourage the infant industrial sector to "modernize," while in a rich industrial society people would be sympathetic to the small farm sector as it struggles to survive.

TABLE 3.7 Agricultural Self-Sufficiency and Agricultural Protection in Northeast Asia, 1961 to 1986

	Self-Sufficiency Index (production as a percentage of apparent consumption)								Average Nominal
	Wheat	Coarse Grain	Soybean	Rice	Beef and Sheepmeat	Pork and Poultry	Dairy Products	Sugar	Weighted Average[a]	Rate of Protection[b]
Japan										
1961-64	30	36	20	97	66	99	92	24	78	68
1965-69	20	19	8	109	51	97	90	27	77	87
1970-74	6	5	4	94	51	95	90	20	67	110
1975-79	5	3	4	110	45	92	87	20	67	147
1980-84	11	2	4	92	51	91	86	31	64	151
1985-86	14	2		107	52	90	88	34	67	N/A
Korea, Rep										
1961-64	20	87	89	100	100	100	26	0	92	3
1965-69	18	98	94	94	99	100	54	0	86	18
1970-74	7	68	81	91	89	102	85	0	77	75
1975-79	3	40	66	96	69	100	97	0	75	146
1980-84	3	22	58	93	69	100	96	0	69	195
1985-86	0	13	50	98	96	100	99	0	69	239
Taiwan										
1961-64	9	25	29	103	100	100	38	253	120	2
1965-69	5	16	20	105	100	100	33	254	115	2
1970-74	0	6	9	100	70	103	28	252	97	17
1975-79	0	4	5	111	16	103	23	187	85	36
1980-84	0	4	4	119	5	103	22	147	77	57
1985-86	0	7	1	104	5	107	29	125	77	N/A

(*continues*)

TABLE 3.7 (continued)

	Self-Sufficiency Index (production as a percentage of apparent consumption)									Average Nominal
	Wheat	Coarse Grain	Soybean	Rice	Beef and Sheepmeat	Pork and Poultry	Dairy Products	Sugar	Weighted Average[a]	Rate of Protection[b]
China										
1961-64	80	97	103	104	100	101	100	48	98	N/A
1965-69	86	101	104	103	101	102	100	78	100	N/A
1970-74	93	104	101	105	101	102	100	79	102	N/A
1975-79	96	103	99	104	101	101	99	72	101	N/A
1980-84	86	100	101	101	103	101	99	76	98	N/A
1985-86	87	96	108	100	104	101	98	80	96	N/A
ASEAN										
1961-64	0	118	94	102	96	100	13	171	104	N/A
1965-69	0	133	91	105	95	100	12	151	105	N/A
1970-74	0	133	89	101	95	100	14	164	104	N/A
1975-79	0	127	70	103	90	101	14	169	105	N/A
1980-84	0	126	47	109	93	102	18	153	109	N/A
1985-86	0	132	57	110	88	103	28	143	109	N/A

[a] Weights based on value of domestic production at border prices.
[b] The percentage by which the domestic producer price for grain and meat exceeds the international price at the country's border. The final period shown for Japan and Taiwan is 1980-82, and that for Korea is 1985.

Source: Anderson (1990, Table 3.4).
N/A = Not available.

Citizens may even judge that farm subsidies are a necessary price to pay to ensure political stability. But the distributional effects of policy choices and the relative costs of collective action by lobby groups in the two different types of economies are no doubt the main driving forces behind the observed pattern of distortions, for the following reasons.

If one were to assume that capital (including land) is sector specific and labour is the only mobile resource, then the distributional effects of altering the relative price of farm products depends importantly on its impacts on wage costs and on the share of the community's expenditure on food. In a poor economy where most people work in agriculture, raising the relative price of agricultural products has a large impact on the demand for labour, thereby raising wage rates substantially. This erodes much of the gain to landholders, and yet will be insufficient to offset the increase in the cost of living for labourers. Even more importantly, it reduces very substantially the income of industrial capitalists. These effects, plus the fact that farmers have much greater free-rider and other costs of getting together to lobby collectively than do urban groups, ensure there is a relatively weak demand for agricultural assistance policies relative to demands for industrial-sector assistance in poor agrarian economies.

In rich industrial economies, on the other hand, agriculture is a small employer and so raising the relative price of farm products has little impact on the demand for labour and hence wages. And since people spend much less of their income on farm products in these as compared with poor economies, the product price change affects the cost of living by less. Hence other groups, including industrial capitalists, have little incentive to oppose agricultural support policies in advanced economies.

When typical values for these and other parameters are included in a computable general equilibrium model of a poor agrarian economy and a rich industrial one, the income distributional effects of policy intervention contrast markedly. A simulation exercise by Anderson (1989) suggests a 10 percent increase in the price of farm products would raise farmers' real incomes by only 4 percent in the 'typical' poor country but would reduce the real incomes of industrial capitalists by 43 percent, while the same policy shock in the 'typical' rich country raises farmers' real incomes by 23 percent while lowering those of industrial capitalists by only 3 percent. And the real incomes of non-farm workers would be lowered by four times as much (2.5 percent) in the poor country as in the rich one, hence they too would be more inclined to join industrialists in opposing an increase in the relative price of food in the poor country, possibly by rioting.

While this is far from the full story, it goes some way towards explaining why we observe farm subsidies in rich countries but disincentives for agriculture in poor countries. It suggests that the tendency observed in Western Europe and Northeast Asia for policies to gradually change from discouraging to excessively encouraging agriculture in the course of economic development may occur in subsequent generations of newly industrializing economies too. Moreover, there tends to be a strong negative correlation also between agricultural protection and agricultural comparative advantage.[9] This suggests densely populated countries are likely to switch from being more to being less than fully self-sufficient in farm products at a slower rate than we might expect from the theory of comparative advantage alone.

Future Economic Growth and Policy Reform Prospects

Overall, the agricultural production and trade trends in Pacific Rim countries strongly support standard trade and development theory. Certainly there are many price and trade policies in place which distort trade in farm products, but in this region they tend to have merely weakened the degree of specialization and slowed the rate of decline of agriculture and the associated change in trade patterns. This allows one to use that theory with some confidence in speculating about likely future developments. In general, if relative economic growth rates continue as in the recent past, many of the trends in agricultural production and trade noted above will continue into the next century, around which there will no doubt be fluctuations due to weather and short-term policy changes. But to be more precise requires first assessing the longer-run growth prospects of economies within (and beyond) the region.[10]

Prospective Economic Growth Rates

Future economic growth rates will depend in large part on the attitudes and policy choices made in the various countries of the world. Japan and East Asia's NIEs have several characteristics which are conducive to continued rapid output and hence income growth. One is the high value placed on formal education and on-the-job training, which ensures that the work force is not only relatively highly skilled but also adaptable. Another is the capacity for social cohesion, which is manifest in the widespread acceptance of the ideology of economic growth and the preparedness of people to accept the inconvenient disruptions to life that necessarily accompany rapid growth. Thirdly, their postwar land reforms ensured an unusually equitable distribution of that important source of wealth. That fact, together with the necessary dependence on the productive use of labour in export-oriented manufacturing for output growth (in the absence of an abundance of natural resources), has ensured a remarkably equitable growth in incomes in these densely populated economies as real wages have risen. This growth has been facilitated not only by the exceptionally high propensity to save and invest but also by a willingness to import ideas, technology and other forms of capital from abroad, by a preparedness to let market forces generally dictate the allocation of productive resources, and by a political environment which supports investors with long-term horizons. It is true that the politics of these countries may be somewhat less stable in the 1990s than in recent decades, particularly as their labour markets tighten and their large current account surpluses decrease, but these changes are likely to have only a minor rather than a major dampening effect on their economic growth rates (Garnaut 1989).

China has several of these characteristics, and during the decade from late 1978 it had most of them. Not surprisingly, that decade was one of very rapid economic growth. The growth rate was exceptionally high in part because the takeoff was from a low starting point in terms of real wages and levels of technology, marketing and other management skills. Thus by liberalizing domestic markets, opening up to trade and allowing new ideas, technical know-how, financial capital and the like to be imported, the payoff was enormous. It would continue to be so for years to come should the government return to the economic reform agenda that in the late 1980s was put aside, especially in urban areas where reforms still have a long way to go. Moreover, a return to the agenda of gradually adopting market forces in China also would have positive spin-offs to growth in Hong Kong and to a lesser extent Taiwan, where investors are understandably nervous about the uncertainty in China's attitudes towards those territories as 1997 approaches.

For the rapid growth of these East Asian economies to continue in the long term, a continuing program of policy liberalization is required, according to Krueger (1990). It also helps to have favourable terms of trade. The low prices of primary products in international markets during most of the 1980s, particularly for energy, benefited resource-poor economies substantially.[11] At the same time, surplus savings have benefited from high interest rates abroad. Low primary product prices may well continue in the absence of major policy changes (discussed below), but earnings from the export of financial capital are less certain. On the one hand, the aging of Japan's population and the lower savings rates of its young workers are likely to reduce the supply of Japanese funds in international markets, at a time when the reconstruction of East European economies will increase the demand for such funds. On the other hand, as Klein (1990) points out, the ending of the cold war—which is making Eastern Europe's reform and reconstruction programs possible—will reduce the world's demand for funds for military investments. Only time will tell what the net effect of these forces—and of the Gulf crises of late 1990, should it be prolonged—will be on world interest rates and thereby on the growth rates of East Asian (and other) economies.

The end of the cold war and the growth performance of China in the early 1980s may encourage Asia's other centrally planned economies to open up. Already Vietnam is moving in that direction, a political settlement of the Cambodian issue seems closer, and even North Korea might eventually open up following the recent historic meeting between Presidents Gorbachev and Noh. Given the enormous scope for profitably importing foreign technology and capital, the potential is there for these socialist economies too to double their output in a decade, just as China did when it opened up in 1978, or at least to achieve the moderately fast growth rates of the ASEAN economies.

North America and Australasia may grow a little faster in the 1990s than in the 1980s because of the formation of their respective free-trade areas, but substantial changes from the relatively low growth rates of the past would require major reforms to their economic policies. It is expected that New Zealand's experiment with such reforms in the latter 1980s will bear fruit from the early 1990s if the reform process is allowed to continue. Australia is following New Zealand's example only to a minor extent: rapid growth there will not occur without substantial reductions in manufacturing protection, privatization of state enterprises and major reductions in the regulation of markets for labour and various services. In North America too, growth is dampened to some extent by the continued use of trade interventions aimed to appease powerful vested interest groups in agriculture, manufacturing and services.

Likely Trends in Agricultural Production and Trade

Given these expectations about future economic growth rates, theory and past experience allow us to anticipate the broad trends in future production and trade in farm products. Japan and the four newly industrialized economies of East Asia are likely to become ever-larger importers of wheat, corn and soybeans as well as tropical agricultural products. However, wheat imports will grow less rapidly than in the past, as income and population growth rates slow down and per capita consumption approaches its satiation point. Furthermore, growth in corn and soybean imports will depend crucially on whether the high levels of protection currently afforded meat (especially beef) and dairy products are raised further or lowered in the years ahead. In the latter event (discussed in the next section), imports of livestock products would substitute for imports of feedstuffs, and per capita consumption of meat and milk could rise substantially given their current relatively low levels (Table 3.8). Rice imports are unlikely to rise, unless a substantial liberalization of the rice market were to result from the Uruguay Round.

Japan's share of world imports of cotton and wool has been falling during the past decade, but it has been more than offset by the increase in the shares of the Northeast Asian NIEs and (until the late 1980s) to China. As a region, Northeast Asia now accounts for more than one-third of the world's natural-fibre imports. This trend can be expected to continue through the 1990s. If China were to open up its markets more, an increasing share of those imports would be used for producing textile and clothing exports from China rather than from the NIEs (Anderson 1991).

The ASEAN economies are likely to continue to lose comparative advantage in agriculture, but from a high base. To date, their self-sufficiency in temperate food products other than wheat, soybeans, and dairy products has remained high (Table 3.7). This is partly because per capita consumption of livestock products is still very low in ASEAN relative to other countries (Table 3.8). Should those consumption levels rise as ASEAN incomes grow, there is very considerable scope for growth in their imports of either livestock feedstuffs and/or livestock end products as the comparative advantage of the large agricultural suppliers (Indonesia and Thailand) continues to move rapidly towards light manufactures such as textiles and clothing (Tables 3.3 and 3.5).

China's agricultural production growth has slowed considerably in recent years, following the initial boost to yields that resulted from the increase in producer prices, the freeing of rural markets and, especially, the introduction of the household responsibility system in rural areas. Given that China's crop yields are already quite high by world standards (see Table 3.5), farm productivity growth in the 1990s is likely to be slower than in the late 1970s and early 1980s unless producer prices are again increased substantially. Indeed, if urban reforms were to improve incentives in non-farm activities and to allow rural-to-urban migration, there may well be a "de-agriculturalization" in China of the sort predicted by the booming sector theory and experienced in Korea and Taiwan in the 1960s and 1970s.

The equations in the first part of section 2 above predict quite accurately agriculture's shares of employment and GDP for China in 1986. They might therefore be used to project those shares for the year 2000. A conservative scenario could be GDP and population growing at 6 and 1.7 percent, respectively, while an optimistic scenario could involve

TABLE 3.8 Per Capita Consumption of Grain and Livestock Products, Pacific Rim Economies, 1961 to 1986 (kg per capita per year)

	Grains		Soybean	Meat		
	Direct	Indirect[a]	Products	Products	Dairy	Eggs
Japan						
1961-64	181	38	48	8	29	11
1985-86	156	117	93	36	69	18
N.E. Asian NIEs						
1961-64	245	7	19	10	1	4
1985-86	246	175	119	39	28	13
China						
1961-64	139	11	20	5	3	2
1985-86	243	44	21	19	5	6
ASEAN						
1961-64	138	4	3	6	3	2
1985-86	169	18	10	9	4	4
Australia						
1961-64	207	151	1	113	528	14
1985-86	145	206	19	116	322	15
Canada						
1961-64	228	526	49	78	423	16
1985-86	244	682	95	92	299	13
Mexico						
1961-64	183	13	2	25	64	4
1985-86	163	69	48	36	104	11
New Zealand						
1961-64	134	96	1	115	1236	18
1985-86	158	171	17	133	1245	16
United States						
1961-64	146	512	130	92	298	20
1985-86	234	571	240	110	277	17

[a]The estimates of indirect grain consumption via livestock assume that no rice is used in feedmixes.

Source: International Economic Data Bank, Agricultural Trade Tapes, ANU, Canberra, 1990.

growth rates of 9 percent for GDP and 1.3 percent for population. In the conservative scenario the employment share would fall from 61 to 50 percent between 1986 and the year 2000, while in the optimistic growth scenario it would fall to 43 percent, according to those equations. The GDP share would likewise fall, from 31 percent in 1986 to 25 percent in the conservative case and to 20 percent in the optimistic case. Tyers and Anderson (1991, Ch. 7) use their model of world food markets to see what these growth rates would mean for China's production and trade of particular commodities. Assuming that real prices of farm products are held constant through the 1990s in China, that the agricultural policies of other countries are not altered, and that the income elasticities of demand and price-independent productivity growth rates are as shown at the top of Table 3.9, they project China's food consumption, self-sufficiency and trade levels as shown in the lower parts of that table.

Even though the model used provides no more than a consistency framework for projecting trends given specific assumptions, it nonetheless provides results which can illustrate several points. First, in the conservative scenario China's self-sufficiency in these foods would continue to decline, even for livestock products, despite the large increase in import dependence on feedgrains (and soybeans, not shown in these results). Second, in the optimistic scenario in which both agricultural and nonagricultural production are assumed to grow 50 percent faster, food self-sufficiency nonetheless still drops to 90 percent because the faster production growth happens to be roughly matched by faster consumption growth (particularly of feedgrains by the livestock industries), given the higher rate of growth of real incomes in that scenario. And third, while China's grain imports would become much larger in the optimistic scenario (up to one-third instead of one-fifth of world trade in coarse grain in 2000, for example), the effect of this greater import volume on the international price of grain is relatively minor (no more than 5 percent—see bottom of Table 3.9). This is attributable to the flexibility of the world's agricultural producers in substituting out of one product and into another as market conditions change.

The continuing growth in import demand for agricultural products by East Asia, and in their export supply of manufactured goods, ensures that the land-abundant countries of North America and Australasia will continue to enjoy a comparative advantage in producing food, feed and fibre for those (and other) markets. However, the composition of that import growth will depend importantly on the extent to which livestock production is protected from import competition in East Asia.

Prospective Policy Changes

The above discussion is premised on a continuation of current policy trends (apart from the discussion of a possible return by China to its reform agenda). There are, however, several prospective policy changes in the next decade or so which could affect those projected patterns of

TABLE 3.9 Food Consumption, Self-Sufficiency and Trade of China, 1965 to 2000

	Wheat	Coarse Grain	Rice	Ruminant Meat	Non-Ruminant Meat	Dairy Products	Sugar	Weighted Average
Parameter Assumptions								
Income elasticity of direct demand	0.5	0.1	0.1	1.1	1.0	1.2	1.0	
Price-independent productivity growth rate (% p.a.)								
Conservative	3.5	2.5	2.0	5.0	5.0	5.0	5.0	
Optimistic	5.2	3.7	1.0	7.5	7.5	7.5	7.5	
Per capita Consumption (kg p.a.)								
Actual 1965-69	41	64	84	0.4	8	3	3	
Actual 1985-86	97	84	117	1.0	18	5	7	
Projected 2000								
Conservative	132	130	119	2.1	31	9	11	
Optimistic	159	184	123	3.1	41	13	16	
Self-Sufficiency (%)								
Actual 1970-74	93	104	105	98	101	100	79	102
Actual 1985-86	87	96	100	99	104	98	80	96
Projected 2000								
Conservative	75	73	101	82	97	92	91	90
Optimistic	78	62	102	78	89	87	87	90
Imports Net of Exports (mmt)								
Actual 1970-74	5	1	-2	0.0	-0.2	0.0	0.6	
Actual 1985-86	8	-4	-1	0.0	-0.2	0.1	1.5	
Projected 2000								
Conservative	45	48	-1	0.1	2.6	1.0	1.3	
Optimistic	46	94	-2	0.4	2.0	2.3	2.9	
% Difference Between Conservative and Optimistic Scenarios in the Year 2000								
International price	4	-1	0	2	-1	2	6	
World trade volume	-1	14	1	1	2	-0	3	

Source: Tyers and Anderson (1991, Tables 8.5, 8.6, 8.7, 8.9).

production and trade. Five possible developments come to mind: the Uruguay Round and associated GATT activities; the tendency towards more nationalism and regionalism; developments within Europe in particular; possible reforms in Indo-China and North Korea; and the greening of world politics. (Also of importance is the 1990 U.S. farm bill, but I leave that to more qualified analysts. The recently announced liberalizations of Japanese and Korean imports of beef and other farm products are important too, but their likely effects are fairly obvious.)

The Uruguay Round and Associated GATT Activities. A critical aspect of the Uruguay Round involves the negotiation of reductions in agricultural and other protectionism, particularly in OECD countries. The direct stakes are quite high: according to one recent study, a 50 percent phased reduction in OECD agricultural protection during the 1990s would yield a net benefit to OECD countries of U.S. $36 billion per year (in 1985 dollars) by the year 2000 (Anderson and Tyers 1990b). But the indirect stakes are far higher, because the U.S. negotiators in particular insist that the prospects for liberalizing non-farm trade in this Round depend heavily on a liberalizing outcome for agriculture. If the Round does conclude at the end of 1990 with a significant liberalization of both farm and non-farm trade, and if in addition the Multi-fibre Arrangement (which expires mid-1991) is replaced with a more liberal agreement on textile and clothing trade that is brought into the mainstream of the GATT, we can expect to see more specialization in production and trade and faster economic growth rates globally. This would accelerate East Asia's industrial development, ceteris paribus, and increase that region's capacity to import more food, feed and fibre from producers in North America, Australasia and elsewhere. It is to be hoped that the locking in of negotiations on non-farm trade liberalization with those for agriculture in the Uruguay Round will be sufficient incentive for the governments of agricultural-protectionist countries to lower their farm support despite the strong domestic political opposition from farmers discussed in section 3 above.

Nationalist and Regionalist Tendencies. The slow economic growth of the 1980s has encouraged an increase in nationalism, notably in the United States. There has also been an increased emphasis on regionalism, largely in response to the increasing economic integration associated with the Europe 1992 program in Western Europe. It has manifested itself in the Australia-New Zealand free trade agreement as well as in the United States' bilateral trade agreements with Canada, Israel, the Caribbean and prospectively Mexico and other Latin American countries. And it is also manifesting itself in inter-regional negotiations, most notably among North American and Western Pacific countries (the latest acronym for which is APEC—Asian-Pacific Economic Cooperation).

While such bilateral and regional arrangements run the risk of diverting rather than expanding trade (Krugman 1989), some of them at least are likely to expand trade. Indeed the APEC initiative is specifically aimed at encouraging trade and investment on a non-discriminatory MFN basis and supporting multilateralism through the GATT system (Drysdale and Garnaut 1989).

Moreover, the nationalist and regionalist tendencies are being offset—and perhaps will be more than offset in the 1990s—by a strong tendency towards internationalism. This is resulting from two sources. One is the growth of intra-firm international trade of multinational corporations. For example, even apparel firms in the United States are becoming ambivalent about U.S. import barriers which may inhibit the growth of their offshore export-oriented operations. The other is the blossoming of specialized service industries, such as international banking and insurance, whose growth is tied to the expansion in international trade. Both of these groups of producers are becoming ever-stronger advocates for the strengthening of GATT rules and disciplines. This tendency increases the prospects for liberalizing world trade and hence for greater specialization in production and exports, including farm products. Traditional agricultural-exporting countries would obviously gain if the relative price of farm products rose as a consequence of such liberalization. But, in addition, recent research suggests that so too would many developing countries that are net food importers, particularly if agricultural innovation is price-responsive (Anderson and Tyers 1990a).

Developments Within Europe. What are the likely implications of developments in Europe for Pacific Rim agriculture? The Europe 1992 program of eliminating barriers between the twelve member states of the European Community, the unification of the two Germanys, the granting of EC associate member status to nearby non-EC countries, and the dramatic reforms in Eastern Europe are developments that are becoming increasingly intertwined.[12] A probable effect of the Europe 1992 program will be increased specialization of production within the EC and faster economic growth there. It remains to be seen whether all internal barriers to agricultural trade (for example, those due to the use of MCAs) will be eliminated and whether national governments will resist the temptation to replace them with national farm support programs to maintain current protection levels. In the event that internal barriers are removed and governments limit themselves to adjustment assistance to farmers, then production would expand in the lowest-cost areas of the Community at the expense of high-cost areas. Whether this in combination with the rest of the Europe 1992 program would expand or contract the net agricultural export surplus of the EC—and hence its impact on Pacific and other economies—is an empirical question requiring detailed multi-country CGE modelling of the Community.

The unification of the two Germanys raises many complex issues and questions. Given that east Germany has twice as much agricultural land per capita as its neighbour, that its grain yields per hectare are only five-sixths of those in west Germany, and that it is poorer and so has a much larger share of its work force in agriculture, an increase in the relative price of farm products in the east to the levels prevalent in the west may well stimulate a considerable expansion in farm output. This would have the initial effect of expanding Europe's excess supply of food and so driving down international food prices. Over the longer term, however, east Germany's income growth would lead to an expansion in domestic food consumption, and the inflow of industrial capital would strengthen its comparative advantage in manufacturing relative to agriculture in the way described in section 1 above.

Reforms in the rest of Eastern Europe might be expected to be similar, in effect, though much less rapid than those in east Germany. The sequencing of market reform will of course have an important bearing on the medium-term outcome: if agricultural markets are reformed first, as was done in China, then net export surpluses of farm products might expand initially. But since these economies have barely half as much agricultural land per worker as the rest of the world and their real per capita incomes and wages are perhaps no more than a quarter of those in Western Europe, their comparative advantage would soon switch to relatively labour-intensive standard manufactures. Therefore, provided their domestic agricultural prices do not rise above international levels and their non-agricultural markets are also liberalized, they are likely to be competing with East Asian suppliers for markets for manufactured goods in Western Europe and North America. And this would be even more likely should they get preferential access to EC markets (as may associate members of the EC such as Turkey). This may dampen prospects for export expansion from East Asia's newly industrializing economies, particularly if the EC member states of Southern Europe demand increased external barriers to non-European imports of labour-intensive manufactures as a quid pro quo for tolerating preferential access of East European goods to EC markets (Hamilton 1991). Any such dampening would in turn slow East Asia's growth in import demand for farm products and so reduce the export prospects of farmers in North America and Australasia. Moreover, a proliferation of preferential trading arrangements in Europe may also weaken the GATT system of world trade in general. This too would be detrimental to the interests of Pacific Rim countries.

Reforms in Indo-China and North Korea. If China's growth experience of the 1980s and the ending of the cold war between the superpowers had the effect of stimulating economic reforms in and the opening up of Indo-China and North Korea, how would agricultural trade be affected? Indo-China undoubtedly would be initially a net agricultural exporter. Indeed we have already started to see an increase in rice exports from Vietnam recently. If Vietnam were opened up further to world markets and, as a consequence, grew rapidly (given that it has barely one-quarter as much agricultural land per capita as neighbouring Thailand [see Table 3.1]), it may not be too many years before this country of 63 million people would begin to transform its comparative advantage toward unskilled labour-intensive manufactures.

North Korea, like South Korea, has a productive work force and relatively little agricultural land. If opened up it would be likely to follow a pattern of trade and development similar to South Korea but a few years behind it. That is, it would become increasingly dependent on agricultural imports as it exploited its comparative advantage in (initially light) manufactures. Its market for agricultural imports would be no more than half the size of South Korea's, however, given the population difference.

The Greening of World Politics. The dramatic increase in recent years in the concern for the environment, both locally and globally, is going to have important impacts on Pacific and world production and trade in a number of ways. One immediate effect is the increase in concern for chemical residues in what we eat. In Western Europe this is manifesting itself in calls for banning imports of U.S. beef that has been produced with growth hormones. The fear is that this legitimate concern of consumers will be used to excess by agricultural protectionist interests, leading to a proliferation of such trade restrictions. As more information becomes available on the extent of the harmful effects of such chemicals, and on their presence in domestic as well as foreign food, one might expect to see consumers demand and be prepared to pay more for low-chemical foods. This would strengthen the agricultural comparative advantage of countries which use few chemicals (Australia, New Zealand, Thailand) at the expense of countries whose farming is relatively chemical-intensive (Japan and Western Europe). With incomplete information there may also be a bias by consumers of imported food in favour of produce from advanced as distinct from developing countries.

A second direct consequence of greater environmental awareness is the likelihood that, especially in densely populated countries, people will oppose the use of chemicals in farming and the intensive production of livestock because of the pollution it causes to local air and water. As it becomes more generally recognized that high product prices stimulate these polluting activities, then sympathy of non-farmers toward agricultural protection in Western Europe and Japan will weaken. This too will enhance the farm export prospects of both lightly populated countries, such as Australia and New Zealand, and developing countries more prepared to tolerate such pollution.

In addition, some other consequences of the greening of world politics may indirectly affect agricultural development and trade. In countries which introduce taxes on industrial pollution, the production of non-industrial goods, including farm products, may well expand. Pollution-intensive industries will thus tend to be relocated to developing countries, assuming the pollution-abatement costs imposed are positively correlated with countries' per capita incomes. Ceteris paribus, this effect will reduce the tendency for agricultural comparative advantage to move from advanced to developing countries in the course of global economic growth.

Trade is also going to be affected by the increasing awareness of the fact that pollution extends beyond national boundaries and has significant regional and global consequences. The relocation of heavy industrial activity from West to East Europe and from Japan and Korea to the north coast of China certainly has not eliminated the polluting effects of those industries from the viewpoint of the more advanced economies, because pollution is carried back by the rivers and prevailing winds. And the emission of greenhouse gases and the damage to the ozone layer have truly global consequences, such as rising temperatures and sea levels and altered rainfall patterns. Clearly the latter will affect agricultural production and trade directly.[13] But it may also affect farm trade indirectly insofar as it leads to attempts to set new international rules relating to environmental damage. There will be strong free-rider incentives for firms not to abide by such rules, so economic sanctions will be required to enforce compliance by offending nations. Given the emotionally charged nature of debates on the environment, it would not be surprising if first-best policy instruments were not used for coping with this problem. Most likely the sanctions would take the form of restrictions on trade and investment flows, which could seriously weaken the world trading system under the GATT and have adverse consequences for global resource allocation and economic growth. People involved in the setting and policing of rules aimed at maintaining a liberal world trade regime may need to be thinking sooner rather than later about how to respond to this likely change in international relations (Whalley 1990).

Conclusion

The standard theory of trade and development outlined in Section 1 is certainly helpful in understanding what has happened and what is likely to happen to agriculture in Pacific Rim economies, given details or assumptions about the openness and the growth rates of those economies. What that theory does not provide, however, is an understanding of what determines whether and when an insular country will choose to open its economy (as did Japan in 1868, South Korea and Taiwan in the early 1960s, China in 1978, and parts of Eastern Europe from the late 1980s). Nor does it explain the differing growth rates across countries, other than to point to the strong statistical correlation between openness and economic growth as evidence to support the gains from trade argument.

A better understanding of the dynamics of economic development is still clearly needed. Thankfully a resurgence of research on the topic has begun, in three distinct but closely related areas. The "new" trade theories emphasizing economies of scale and imperfect competition have shown theoretically and empirically that the gains from trade liberalization may be very much larger than our constant returns to scale/perfect competition models suggest. That is, they provide results that are closer to what trade economists instinctively believe to be the very substantial benefits of openness. (See, for example, Helpman and Krugman [1985] and the survey by Richardson [1989].)

Secondly, the "new" growth theories are seeking to understand the mechanisms by which economic growth and development are generated. They are addressing such questions as why do we not observe more capital flowing from capital-abundant to capital-poor countries, and what determines the rates of product innovation and international technology transfer. (See, for example, Grossman and Helpman [1990a, b], Lucas [1978, 1980] and Romer [1990].)

And thirdly, the "new" economics of politics is improving our understanding of why governments adopt the policies they do, and hence of what is required to change policies, and the rules that govern policy making, to encourage economic growth. (See, for example, Baldwin [1989], Brock, Magee and Young [1989], Hillman [1989] and Jones and Krueger [1989] on endogenous trade policies and Brennan and Buchanan [1985] on the designing of rules for government, as well as Olson [1982] on politico-economic reasons for the slowing of growth in OECD countries.)

A particularly important political economy question to address with the help of this literature is: Under what conditions will protection to declining industries such as agriculture cease growing or reverse? We have seen a few dramatic instances of the complete withdrawal of government support to industry, such as for Swedish steel production and shipbuilding in the 1970s and for its textile and clothing industries from 1992, as well as for the U.S. footwear industry. Cassing and Hillman (1986) suggest that aggregate political support from a protected declining industry may dwindle as the industry contracts until a point is reached where that support is less than the political opposition to that protection from other groups who are hurt by it. At that point protection could be fully withdrawn.

Another reason protection may be reduced is because of a shock to the political markets for protection policies. A recent example is the trade friction arising from Northeast Asia's current account surpluses and the U.S. twin deficits, which led to U.S. pressure being superimposed on the domestic political markets for beef and other agricultural import protection in Northeast Asia. The liberalizations of trade in those products, which is scheduled to occur in the 1990s, would almost certainly not have occurred without the addition of U.S. pressure. A second example is the growing realization that pollution from the use of agricultural chemicals is correlated with agricultural price levels, leading to environmentalists adding a new voice to opposition to agricultural protection for that reason too.

Finally, there is the prospect of reductions in protection though the setting of new trade rules, for example under the GATT. The extent and cost of agricultural protection escalated in the 1980s, galvanizing GATT contracting parties to place agriculture high on the agenda of the Uruguay Round of trade policy negotiations. Part of the motivation came from a realization of two facts. One was that the presence of new GATT rules limiting agricultural protection would make it easier for governments to deny farm lobbies further support—and even to wind back existing support. The other fact was that if all countries liberalized simultaneously, international food prices would rise and so the extent of price declines needed to reduce protection to a particular level would be less. Indeed even if protection levels were as much as halved over the 1990s, agricultural production levels would still expand somewhat in virtually all OECD countries, according to recent simulation results (Anderson and Tyers 1990b).

If the Uruguay Round is successful in getting countries to agree to limit their agricultural support programs, improved monitoring and dispute settlement mechanisms will need to be established. Such mechanisms would have the additional advantage of increasing the transparency of policies, thereby making it less costly for domestic groups harmed by distortionary policies to oppose them in the future (Spriggs 1990). Whether countries are prepared to give up their sovereignty over agricultural policies to that extent, however, is something that only time will tell.

Notes

Helpful comments from Bill Coyle, John Dyck, and other IATRC Symposium participants on the first draft of this paper are gratefully acknowledged. Since completing this paper, the author has joined the economic research staff of the GATT Secretariat in Geneva. The views expressed are the author's own and are not intended to reflect the view of the GATT Secretariat or GATT contracting parties.

1. The weight of empirical evidence supports the view that agricultural prices have declined relative to industrial product prices during the past century or so, although the difficulty of accounting for changing qualities of manufactured goods needs to be kept in mind (Spraos 1980; Sapsford 1985; Grilli and Yang 1988). This suggests that the outward shift in the supply curve for non-food products has not been sufficiently faster than that for food products as to offset the relatively slow growth in demand for the latter.

2. Available evidence suggests that the income elasticity of demand for services (which make up the vast majority of nontradables) is well above unity in developing countries and tends toward unity as incomes grow (Lluch, Powell and Williams 1977; Kravis, Heston and Summers 1983; Summers 1985; Theil and Clements 1987). So if productivity growth is no more rapid for nontradables than for tradables (indeed it is probably slower—see Clark 1957), but demand for nontradables expands more rapidly while demand for tradables expands less rapidly than aggregate output, then both the price and the quantity of nontradables relative to tradables will increase. Strong across-country evidence that the price of nontradables relative to tradables increases with real incomes is provided in Kravis and Lipsey (1988).

3.The agricultural growth bias in this economy has to be strong enough not only to offset the decline in the international price of food relative to prices of other tradables but also to offset the pull of resources into the production of nontradables (Anderson 1987).

4. See also Balassa (1979), Deardorff (1984), Eaton (1987), Leamer (1987), and Balassa and Bauwens (1988).

5. On why we observe so little capital flowing from capital-abundant to capital-scarce economies even when there are no government-imposed barriers to such flows, see Lucas (1990). The present analysis also begs the question of what determines rates of savings, investment and technology trade, issues which are currently being grappled with by the "new" growth theorists. (See, for example, Grossman and Helpman (1990a, b) and the references cited therein).

6. Since many empirical studies are available with such evidence, only a small sample of evidence is presented here. For more detailed evidence see, for example, Kuznets (1971) and Chenery, Robinson and Syrquin (1986).

7. For space reasons smaller economies are not discussed here, but the largest of those omitted—Papua New Guinea—is analyzed in Jarrett and Anderson (1989). Until very recently Central and South American countries have not been closely involved in Pacific Rim discussions and so are also omitted here, although they are examined in Anderson (1983).

8. Canned, dried and frozen fruit and vegetables and powdered and UHT vacuum-packed fluid milk are of course substitutes for the fresh produce and can be traded internationally. The c.i.f. price of imports of such substitutes would thus determine the ceiling on domestic prices of the fresh products in the absence of import restrictions.

9. Anderson and Tyers (1986) estimate the following regression equation for 30 countries/country groups spanning the world (t-values in parentheses):

$$NPC = 0.22 + 0.11\,YPC - 0.51\,CA \qquad \bar{R}^2 = 0.83$$
$$(8.7) \quad (5.6) \qquad (-10.7)$$

where NPC is the log of the weighted average nominal agricultural protection coefficient in 1980-82, YPC is the log of the ratio of an economy's per capita income to the global average per capita income in 1982, and CA is the log of the food self-sufficiency ratio at global free trade prices as estimated by the authors' model of world food markets. The main exceptions to the rule that rich countries subsidize agriculture are the agricultural-exporting countries of Australia and New Zealand, while important exceptions to the opposite rule for developing countries are the food-importing economies of Korea and Taiwan. All four economies have extreme values for CA and so are not inconsistent with the above political economy theory.

10. In what follows it is assumed that the current macroeconomic problems of East Asia's surpluses and the U.S. twin deficits are solved through appropriate adjustments to monetary, fiscal, and exchange rate policies.

11. The combined effects of East Asia's fuel-conservation measures, its adjustment away from energy-intensive activities, and the decline in international energy prices in the 1980s can be seen from data on the share of petroleum in the value of East Asia's imports. In 1980-82 that share was 36 percent in Japan, 25 percent in Korea and 21 percent in Taiwan, but by 1988 those shares were only 10, 7 and 5 percent, respectively. The earlier adjustments to high prices put these economies in a much sounder position to cope with subsequent petroleum price hikes such as in late 1990.

12. In the interests of brevity, the great uncertainty associated with developments in the USSR is not discussed here.

13. One preliminary attempt to quantify these effects is reported in the paper by Kane, Reilly and Bucklin (1989).

References

ABARE. 1990. *Agriculture and Resources Quarterly*. Vol. 2(1). Canberra: Australian Bureau of Agricultural and Resource Economics.

Anderson, K. 1983. "Economic Growth, Comparative Advantage and Agricultural Trade of Pacific Rim Countries." *Review of Marketing and Agricultural Economics* 51(3): 231-48. Also published as Ch. 2 in *Food, Agriculture and Development in the Pacific Basin*. Ed. by G. E. Schuh and J. L. McCoy. Boulder: Westview Press.

Anderson, K. 1987. "On Why Agriculture Declines with Economic Growth." *Agricultural Economics* 1(3): 195-207.

Anderson, K. 1989. "Rent-seeking and Price-distorting Policies in Rich and Poor Countries." Seminar Paper No. 428, Institute for International Economic Studies, University of Stockholm.

Anderson, K. 1990. *Changing Comparative Advantages in China: Effects on Food, Feed and Fibre Markets*. Paris: Organization for Economic Cooperation and Development.

Anderson, K. (ed.). 1991 (forthcoming). *New Silk Roads: East Asia and World Textiles Markets*. Cambridge: Cambridge University Press.

Anderson, K., Y. Hayami, et al. 1986. *The Political Economy of Agricultural Protection: East Asia in International Perspective*. Boston, London and Sydney: Allen and Unwin.

Anderson, K. and R. Tyers. 1986. "Agricultural Policies of Industrial Countries and Their Effects on Traditional Food Exporters," *Economic Record* 62(179): 385-99.

Anderson, K. and R. Tyers. 1990a. "Welfare Gains to Developing Countries from Food Trade Liberalization Following the Uruguay Round." Mimeo, University of Adelaide.

Anderson, K. and R. Tyers. 1990b. "Effects of Tariffication of Food Trade Barriers Following the Uruguay Round." Seminar Paper 90-02, Centre for International Economic Studies, University of Adelaide.

Balassa, B. 1965. "Trade Liberalization and 'Revealed' Comparative Advantage." *Manchester School of Economic and Social Studies* 33(2): 99-124.

Balassa, B. 1979. "The Changing Pattern of Comparative Advantage in Manufactured Goods." *Review of Economics and Statistics* 61(2): 259-66.

Balassa, B. and L. Bauwens. 1988. *Changing Trade Patterns in Manufactured Goods: An Econometric Investigation*. Amsterdam: North-Holland.

Baldwin, R. E. 1989. "The Political Economy of Trade Policy." *Journal of Economic Perspectives* 3(4): 119-35.

Bowen, H. P. 1983. "Changes in the International Distribution of Resources and Their Impact on U.S. Comparative Advantage." *Review of Economics and Statistics* 65(3): 402-14.

Brennan, G. and J. M. Buchanan. 1985. *The Reason of Rules*. Cambridge: Cambridge University Press.

Cassing, J. H. and A. L. Hillman. June 1985. "Shifting Comparative Advantage and Senescent Industry Collapse." *American Economic Review* 76(3): 516-23.

Chenery, H., S. Robinson and M. Syrquin. 1986. *Industrialization and Growth: A Comparative Study*. New York: Oxford University Press for the World Bank.

Clark, C. 1957. *The Conditions of Economic Progress*. London: Macmillan (3rd Ed.).

Corden, W. M. 1984. "Booming Sector and Dutch Disease Economics: Survey and Consolidation." *Oxford Economic Papers* 36: 359-80.

Deardorff, A. V. 1984. "An Exposition and Exploration of Krueger's Trade Model." *Canadian Journal of Economics* 17(4): 731-46.

Drysdale, P. and R. Garnaut. 1989. "A Pacific Free Trade Area?" in *Free Trade Areas and U.S. Trade Policy*. Edited by J. Schott. Washington, D.C.: Institute for International Economics.

Eaton, J. 1987. "A Dynamic Specific-Factors Model of International Trade," *Review of Economic Studies* 54(2): 325-38.

Freebairn, J. 1987. "The Natural Resource Industries." Ch. 6 in *The Australian Economy in the Long Run*. Ed. by R. Maddock and I. McLean. Cambridge: Cambridge University Press.

Garnaut, R. 1989. *Australia and the Northeast Asian Ascendancy*. Canberra: Australian Government Publishing Service.

Grilli, E. R. and M. C. Yang. 1988. "Primary Commodity Prices, Manufactured Goods Prices, and the Terms of Trade of Developing Countries: What the Long Run Shows." *World Bank Economic Review* 2(1): 1-48.

Grossman, G. M. and E. Helpman. 1990a. "Trade, Innovation and Growth." *American Economic Review* 80(2): 86-91.

Grossman, G. M. and E. Helpman. 1990b (forthcoming). "Comparative Advantage and Long-run Growth." *American Economic Review* 80.

Hamilton, C. 1990. "The New Silk Road to Europe: New Directions for Old Trade." Seminar Paper 89-07, Centre for International Economic Studies, University of Adelaide, Australia.

Helpman, E. and P. R. Krugman. 1985. *Market Structure and Foreign Trade*. Cambridge: MIT Press.

Hillman, A. L. (1989). *The Political Economy of Protection*. New York: Harwood Academic Publishers.

Jarrett, F. G. and K. Anderson. 1989. *Growth, Structural Change and Economic Policy in Papua New Guinea: Implications for Agriculture*. Canberra: National Centre for Development Studies.

Johnson, H. G. 1968. *Comparative Cast and Commercial Policy Theory for a Developing World Economy*. Stockholm: Almqvist and Wiksell.

Johnson, D.G. 1973. *World Agriculture in Disarray*. London: Fontana.

Jones, R. and A. Krueger, (eds.) 1989. *The Political Economy of International Trade*. Oxford: Basil Blackwell.

Kane, S., J. Reilly and R. Bucklin. 1989. "Implications of the Greenhouse Effect for World Agricultural Commodity Markets." A USDA paper presented at the Western Economic Association Conference, Lake Tahoe.

Keating, M. 1973. *The Australian Workforce, 1910-11 to 1960-61*. Canberra: ANU Press.

Keesing, D. B. and D. R. Sherk. 1971. "Population Density in Patterns of Trade and Development." *American Economic Review* 61(5): 956-61.

Klein, L. R. 1990. "The Economics of Turning Swords into Plowshares." *Challenge* 18-26.

Kravis, I. B., W. Heston and R. Summers. 1983. "The Share of Services in Economic Growth." *Global Econometrics*. Ed. by F. G. Adams and B. G. Hickman. Cambridge: The MIT Press.

Kravis, I. B. and R. E. Lipsey. 1988. "National Price Levels and the Prices of Tradables and Nontradables." *American Economic Review* 78(2): 474-78.

Krueger, A. 1977. *Growth, Distortions and Patterns of Trade Among Many Countries*. Princeton, N.J.: International Finance Section.

Krueger, A. O. 1990. "Asian Trade and Growth Lessons." *American Economic Review* 80(2): 108-112.

Krugman, P. 1989. "Is Bilateralism Bad?" NBER Working Paper No. 2972, Cambridge, Mass.

Kuznets, S. S. 1971. *Economic Growth of Nations: Total Output and Production Structure*. Cambridge: Harvard University Press.

Leamer, E. E. 1984. *Sources of International Comparative Advantage: Theory and Evidence*. Cambridge: MIT Press.

Leamer, E. E. 1987. "Paths of Development in the Three-Factor, n-Good General Equilibrium Model." *Journal of Political Economy* 95(5):961-99.

Lluch, C., A. A. Powell and R. A. Williams. 1977. *Patterns in Household Demand and Savings*. New York: Oxford University Press.

Lucas, R. E. 1988. "On the Mechanics of Economic Development." *Journal of Monetary Economics* 22(1): 3-42.

Lucas, R. E. 1990. "Why Doesn't Capital Flow from Rich to Poor Countries?" *American Economic Review* 80(2): 92-96.

Magee, S. P., W. A. Brock and L. Young. 1989. *Black Hole Tariffs and Endogenous Policy Theory: Political Economy in General Equilibrium*. Cambridge: Cambridge University Press.

OECD. 1989. *Historical Statistics 1960-1987*. Paris: Organization for Economic Cooperation and Development.

Olson, M. 1982. *The Rise and Decline of Nations: Economic Growth, Stagflation and Social Rigidities*. New Haven: Yale University Press.

Perkins, D. H. 1988. "Reforming China's Economic System." *Journal of Economic Literature* 26(2): 601-45.

Richardson, J. D. 1989. "Empirical Research on Trade Liberalization with Imperfect Competition." *OECD Economic Studies* 12: 7-51, Spring.

Romer, P. M. 1990. "Endogenous Technological Change." *Journal of Political Economy* 98.

Sapsford, D. 1985. "The Statistical Debate on the Net Barter Terms of Trade Between Primary Commodities and Manufactures: A Comment and Some Additional Evidence." *Economic Journal* 95(379): 781-88.

Schultz, T. W., ed. 1978. *Distortions of Agricultural Incentives*. Bloomington: Indiana University Press.

Spraos, J. 1980. "The Statistical Debate on the Net Barter Terms of Trade Between Primary Commodities and Manufactures." *Economic Journal* 90(357): 107-28.

Spriggs, J. D. 1990. "Transparency vs. Protectionism." Seminar Paper 90-03, Centre for International Economic Studies, University of Adelaide.

Theil, H. and K. W. Clements. 1987. *Applied Demand Analysis: Results from System-Wide Approaches.* Cambridge, Mass.: Ballinger.

Tyers, R. and K. Anderson. 1991. *Disarray in World Food Markets.* Cambridge: Cambridge University Press.

U.S. Department of Commerce. 1976. *Historical Statistics of the United States.* Bicentennial edition. Washington, D.C.: U.S. Department of Commerce.

Whalley, J. 1990. "Environmental Protection and International Trade." Paper presented to a conference, The Economics of Environmental Policy. Canberra.

World Bank. 1988a. *World Development Report 1988.* New York: Oxford. University Press.

World Bank. 1988b. *The World Bank Atlas 1988.* Washington, D.C.: The World Bank.

4

Prospects for U.S. Agricultural Exports in the Pacific: The Role of Fast-growing Countries

John W. Mellor

Introduction

The post-World War II period has been extraordinarily dynamic for food trade. We have every reason to expect that dynamism to continue. Major exporters such as the United States must increasingly turn to the developing countries for markets. In that context, they have a major interest in helping to accelerate the growth of those countries.

Western Europe has been transformed from a large importer of basic food staples and other agricultural commodities to a substantial net exporter; Eastern Europe and the Soviet Union have changed from modest net exporters to very large net importers; Japan has become the world's largest net importer of agricultural commodities; and a number of developing countries, primarily in the Pacific Basin, are emerging as large net importers. The most important factor determining these changes has been growth in effective demand, which is related to the level and rate of growth of per capita GNP. These changes most heavily affect the livestock sector and the derived demand for feedgrains for livestock.

Notably, the growth rates of agricultural production in Western and Eastern Europe have been similar over the last few decades. Yet agricultural imports have grown rapidly in Eastern Europe, while agricultural imports have declined and net exports have grown rapidly in Western Europe. The difference in performance lies in income level and rates of economic growth. In Western Europe, growth in demand for food has virtually halted as incomes have become high enough to satiate demand, whereas agricultural technology has added inexorably to output. In Eastern Europe, per capita income growth has been significant, though rising from a much lower income base. Consequently, marginal propensities to consume food have been much higher particularly for livestock commodities. Similar factors have come into play in Asia: first in Japan, then in the four fast-growth East Asian areas (Taiwan, Korea, Singapore, and Hong Kong), and increasingly in other developing countries. The end result is that Western Europe, formerly the biggest market for agricultural exports from the United States, has become a competitor; Eastern Europe has become an extremely large market but probably has little scope for further growth; Japan, too, has become a large market and probably has some additional scope for growth; and the fast growth developing countries of the Pacific Basin offer major opportunities for future growth.

The purpose of this paper is to examine the agricultural export market potentials of the fast growth developing countries of the Pacific Rim. The first section will begin with Japan—a country that has recently passed through a stage of extraordinarily rapid economic growth then moves on to the Gang of Four (Hong Kong, Singapore, Republic of Korea, and Taiwan)—which is now experiencing a long period of rapid growth. Next we will consider the Gang of Two (Malaysia and Thailand), which has appeared on the fast-growth scene somewhat more recently; Indonesia, which has yet to experience rapid growth in the demand for food; and the Philippines, which should have but has not. Finally, we will comment briefly on China and India, in order to gain perspective on large countries. That section will be followed by a discussion of the conceptual basis for understanding the interrelationships between accelerated agricultural growth, accelerated nonagricultural growth, growth in employment and effective demand for food, and the impact of all of those on trade relationships.

The paper closes with a discussion of the U.S. foreign economic and political policies needed to realize the tremendous agricultural export potentials that exist. The United States has considerable capacity to influence these processes. However, it may not even recognize that it has this capacity and tends to follow policies that are inconsistent with developing it. Although this paper deals with the prospects for U.S. agricultural exports, the United States will hardly be mentioned until the last section because our basic concern is with total market possibilities. We know that the United States has a strong underlying comparative advantage in agricultural exports and thus, as long as we see substantial market potential, it is then for the United States to develop its national policies in such a way that it becomes a strong competitor. Therefore, the final section deals with policies that encourage growth, that enable the United States to be a reliable supplier, and that foster open trade regimes so as to create larger markets in the fast growth developing countries.

Facts About Pacific Rim Countries

Background

These observations will focus on data for nine countries on the Pacific Rim. China is excluded from the basic analysis because of its immense size and complexity and the unusually large role that political factors have played, causing fluctuations in policy and economic performance, and thus making it difficult to look ahead for China. However, some data are presented separately for India and China.

Data for the nine countries chosen for analysis, which together comprise a population of about half a billion people, are divided into five sets (see Table 4.1). The first set comprises Japan, which, because of its large population and high per capita GNP, is important in its own right and a portent of things to come for the present group of middle-income, fast-growth countries. Until the mid-1970s, Japan had a high growth rate, similar to that of the Gang of Four; since the mid-1970s, its growth rate has slowed, although it is still somewhat on the fast side for a mature economy.

The second category is the Gang of Four. Hong Kong, Singapore, the Republic of Korea, and Taiwan are a heterogeneous group, including two city-states, one moderately large country and one medium-sized country. Their total population is 70 million, more than half the size of Japan. They all have very rapid rates of growth, with per capita GNP ranging from one-fifth to more than half that of Japan. Their growth rates show no signs of slowing.

The third category of countries includes Thailand and Malaysia, with a combined population equal to that of the Gang of Four, and comparable growth rates which show no signs of significant slowdown and may even be accelerating. But these two countries, as distinguished from the Gang of Four, have commenced rapid growth more recently, starting from a lower GNP base, and thus have average per capita GNPs less than one-third of those of the Gang of Four.

The fourth category is Indonesia. At times, Indonesia's growth rate has been more rapid than those of Thailand and Malaysia, but it has now slowed down because of the impact of oil revenue on past growth. It should remain relatively slow until a larger base of human and institutional capital can be built. Thus, we have a country with a

TABLE 4.1 Basic Economic Indicators of Selected Pacific Countries and China and India, Various Years

Country	Population mid-1987	GDP Avg. 1985-87	GNP per Capita Avg. 1985-87	Average Annual Change in Real GNP	
				1965-73	1973-86
	Millions	US$ billions	US$	Percent	
1. Japan	122.1	1,886.65	13,300	9.4	4.1
2. Hong Kong	5.6	33.17	7,070	N/A	N/A
Singapore	2.6	18.27	7,440	12.8	7.8
Rep. of Korea	42.1	101.90	2,403	6.1	7.2
Taiwan	19.7[a]	76.58	3,950[b]	11.0[c]	7.6[c]
Sub-total	70.0	229.91	3,398		
3. Thailand	53.6	42.73	820	7.7	6.0
Malaysia	16.5	35.70	1,880	6.9	6.3
Sub-total	70.1	78.43	1,068		
4. Indonesia	171.4	77.13	490	8.0	6.1
5. Philippines	58.4	32.57	577	5.5	3.1
6. Sum: groups 1-5	492.0	2,304.71	4,215		
7. India	797.5	200.10	287	4.1	4.5
China	1,068.5	276.93	300	7.8	7.6

Notes: Subtotals for population and GDP for each group were obtained simply by summing the relevant statistics in each group. The GNP per capita for each subtotal was obtained by first deriving the total GNP for each of the three years by multiplying GNP per capita in each year with population for each country and then summing each country's GNP. The total regional GNP is then divided by each subgroup's total population.

[a]The population figure for Taiwan is based on end of the year household registration data.
[b]The figure for Taiwan is GDP per capita.
[c]The figure for Taiwan is real GDP.

Sources: 1. Except Taiwan, population, GDP, and HNP per capita are from *World Development Report*. 1989. Washington, D.C.: The World Bank, 1989.

2. Except Taiwan, average annual changes in real GNP are from *World Resources 1988-89*. 1988. A report by the World Resources Institute and the International Institute for Environment and Development in collaboration with the United Nations Environment Programme. New York: Basic Books.

3. The data for Taiwan are from Statistical Yearbook of the Republic of China. 1988. Director-General of Budget, Accounting and Statistics, Executive Yuan, Republic of China, and from Taiwan Statistical Data Book, 1989. Council for Economic Planning and Development, Republic of China.

population 50 percent larger than Japan, with a very low per capita GNP and modest growth rates, but with great potential for acceleration of those growth rates over the longer run.

The fifth category is the Philippines, a country that in the mid-1950s clearly had as much potential for rapid growth as Taiwan and a somewhat higher per capita GNP. Even during its fastest period of growth, however, it has grown relatively slowly and has recently slowed considerably more. It is a country of substantial size—nearly 60 million people—somewhat larger than Thailand. Its economic potential is great but so far it has shown an inability to realize that potential.

We will return to India and China later. Suffice it to say that between the two of them they have nearly 2 billion people—four times the size of the nine countries examined here. Their GNPs are very low and their growth rates are modest, exaggerated in the case of China by the nature of its national income accounting system. Nevertheless, both countries have tremendous potential to affect overall international aggregates.

Trade in Major Cereals

Detailed information on imports, exports, and net imports of major cereal commodities for the nine Pacific Rim countries analyzed is provided in Table 4.2. Shown are the three-year averages for 1970-72 and for 1985-87, and for 1988. Several observations stand out.

First, trade in major cereals for the nine countries is dominated by corn, and within corn, Japan's imports dominate the totals. Between the two three-year periods Japan's corn imports increased more than 2.5 times. In the 1970-72 period, Japan accounted for about 75 percent of the corn imports of the nine countries. But, since some of the other countries increased their imports of corn even more rapidly, Japan's share had declined to only about 60 percent of total corn imports by the 1985-87 period. Thus, even recently, Japan's market has grown rapidly, but other countries have grown even more rapidly.

Second, both the Republic of Korea and Japan have increased their imports of corn tremendously—Korea by almost 13 times and Japan by 2.7 times between the two periods averaged, and by 1988 they had increased again—Korea by 30 percent and Japan by 9 percent between 1988 and the average of 1985-87. Malaysia has also experienced a sixfold increase in corn imports, but of course from a small base.

The grain trade increase is dominated by corn because it is a feedgrain import and represents the massive expansion of livestock production in

TABLE 4.2 Volume of Imports, Exports, and Net Imports of Major Cereal Commodities of Selected Pacific Rim Countries, Including China and India (Three-year averages of 1970-72, 1985-87, and 1988)

Crop/Country	Imports			Exports			Net Imports		
	1970-72	1985-87	1988	1970-72	1985-87	1988	1970-72	1985-87	1988
Corn									
1. Japan	5,692.0	15,127.0	16,555.0	0.2	0.0	0.0	5,691.8	15,127.0	16,555.0
2. Hong Kong	156.0	223.0	46.0	0.8	5.0	0.3	155.2	218.0	45.7
Singapore	195.0	399.0	426.0	88.0	103.0	216.0	107.0	296.0	210.0
Republic of Korea	301.0	3,881.0	5,051.0	0.0	0.0	0.0	301.0	3,881.0	5,051.0
Taiwan	825.0	3,265.0	N/A	0.0	1.0	N/A	825.0	3,264.0	N/A
Subtotal	1,477.0	7,768.0	5,523.0[a]	88.8	109.0	216.3[a]	1,388.2	7,659.0	5,306.7[a]
3. Thailand	3.0	1.0	0.5	1,645.0	2,787.0	1,209.0	-1,642.0	-2,786.0	-1,208.5
Malaysia	220.0	1,229.0	1,331.0	1.5	1.4	3.5*	218.5	1,227.6	1,327.5
Subtotal	223.0	1,230.0	1,331.5	1,646.5	2,788.4	1,212.5	-1,423.5	-1,558.4	119.0
4. Indonesia	0.0	110.0	64.0	195.0	4.0	38.0	-195.0	106.0	26.0
5. Philippines	72.0	112.0	25.0	0.0	0.0	0.1	62.0	112.0	24.9
Sum: Groups 1-5	7,464.0	24,347.0	23,498.5[a]	1,930.5	2,901.4	1,466.9[a]	5,533.5	21,445.6	22,031.6[a]
6. India	4.0	10.0	300.0*	1.0	5.0	0.0	3.0	5.0	300.0
China	207.0	740.0	N/A	66.0	5,298.0	N/A	141.0	-4,558.0	N/A
Wheat									
1. Japan	4,902.0	5,535.0	5,724.0	0.0	0.0	0.0	4,902.0	5,535.0	5,724.0
2. Hong Kong	124.0	119.0	113.0	6.0	4.0	0.0	118.0	115.0	113.0
Singapore	211.0	145.0	288.0	18.0	9.0	23.0	193.0	136.0	265.0
Republic of Korea	1,551.0	3,519.0	4,116.0	0.0	0.90	0.0	1,551.0	3,519.0	4,116.0
Taiwan	618.0	791.0	N/A	0.0	0.0	N/A	618.0	791.0	N/A
Subtotal	2,504.0	4,574.0	4,517.0[a]	24.0	13.0	23.0[a]	2,480.0	4,561.0	4,494.0[a]

3. Thailand	66.0	143.0	226.0	0.0	0.0	66.0	143.0	226.0
Malaysia	326.0	601.0	758.0	1.0	15.0	325.0	586.0	757.0
Subtotal	392.0	744.0	984.0	1.0	15.0	391.0	729.0	983.0
4. Indonesia	223.0	1,539.0	1,588.0	0.0	0.0	223.0	1,539.0	1,588.0
5. Philippines	598.0	765.0	1,074.0	0.0	0.0	598.0	765.0	1,075.0
Sum: Groups 1-5	8,619.0	13,157.0	13,888.0[a]	25.0	28.0	8,594.0	13,129.0	13,864.0[a]
6. India	1,950.0	0.0	2,000.0*	87.0	237.0	1,863.0	-237.0	2,000.0
China	4,219.0	8,232.0	N/A	0.0	2.0	4,219.0	8,230.0	N/A

Rice

1. Japan	43.0	19.0	16.0	564.0	0.0	-521.0	19.0	16.0
2. Hong Kong	291.0	373.0	364.0	42.0	12.0	349.0	360.0	352.0
Singapore	325.0	214.0	213.0	55.0	3.0	270.0	205.0	210.0
Republic of Korea	842.0	1.0	1.0	0.0	0.8	842.0	1.0	0.2
Taiwan	1.0	4.0	N/A	20.0	N/A	-19.0	-127.0	N/A
Subtotal	1,559.0	592.0	578.0[a]	117.0	15.8[a]	1,442.0	439.0	562.2[a]
3. Thailand	0.0	0.0	0.0	1,589.0	5,267.0	-1,589.0	-4,343.0	-5,267.0
Malaysia	268.0	272.0	288.0	5.3	5.0	262.7	270.7	283.0
Subtotal	268.0	272.0	288.0	1,594.3	5,272.0	-1,326.3	-4,072.3	-4,984.0
4. Indonesia	732.0	39.0	33.0	0.0	0.0	732.0	-103.0	33.0
5. Philippines	275.0	180.0	119.0	2.0	0.0	273.0	143.0	119.0
Sum: Groups 1-5	2,877.0	1,102.0	1,034.0[a]	2,277.3	5,287.8[a]	599.7	-3,574.3	-4,253.8[a]
6. India	472.0	39.0	684.0	19.0	200.0*	453.0	228.0	484.0
China	2.0	362.0	N/A	1,557.0	N/A	-1,555.0	631.0	N/A

Note: Net imports derived by subtracting exports from imports. Hence, a country with negative net imports exported more of a particular commodity than it imported.

N/A = not available.

Source: FAO 1988 *Agriculture Trade Standard Yearbook* Tape. Rome, RAO.

[a] Does not include Taiwan.

*Unofficial figure.

countries in which incomes are rising very rapidly from a modest base. This will be discussed further later in the paper.

Thailand, in the period shown, nearly doubled its corn exports. The peak was hit in the mid-1980s. Corn exports have declined since then in response to some small reduction in production and very major increases in domestic livestock feeding.

The second notable grain is wheat. As incomes rise, wheat consumption also rises. Japan, even by the early 1970s, had reached so high a level of income that further increases in wheat imports were relatively small. But the Gang of Four nearly doubled their wheat imports in that period; the Republic of Korea had especially large increases. Substantial increases in wheat imports also occurred in Thailand and Malaysia, but from a very small base. It is notable that even though Indonesia's income was low, it had a substantial increase in wheat imports. There was even a modest increase in the Philippines.[1]

Thus, wheat imports into this set of countries increased from 8.6 million tons to over 13 million tons in the period studied. This is not an insignificant increase. None of the countries provided significant exports, so net imports were about the same as gross imports.

The third implication from Table 4.2 is that rice imports into these countries are relatively insignificant and do not change much over time. The tendency is actually for some decline in imports, most notably in Indonesia, which reflects a high, but probably unsustainable, rate of growth in rice production as the result of the introduction of IR36 rice varieties, resistant to brown plant hoppers.

Thailand, of course, continues to increase its rice production rapidly, nearly tripling its exports in the period shown. We will comment on that in the conceptual section.

Thus, to summarize, except for Thailand's rice exports, the rice trade is not particularly dynamic. There is considerable dynamism in the wheat trade, with rapidly increasing imports associated with rising incomes, but that income effect peaks out by the time a country reaches the level of income of Japan. In contrast, corn imports grow much more rapidly and do not peak at as early a stage of development. Thus, Japan has continued to show a rapid increase in corn imports.

Meat Trade

There has been tremendous expansion in net meat imports into Japan, an almost threefold increase between the two periods analyzed (see Table 4.3). As for other Pacific countries, while their domestic consumption of meat increases, the changes in their imports depend on

TABLE 4.3 Volume of Imports, Exports, and Net Imports of Meat and Meat Preparations of Selected Pacific Rim Countries Plus China and India, Three-year Averages 1970-72 and 1985-87 (thousand metric ton)

	Meat and Meat Preparations					
	Imports		Exports		Net Imports	
Country	1970-72	1985-87	1970-72	1985-87	1970-72	1985-87
1. Japan	302.0	831.0	11.0	4.0	291.0	827.0
2. Hong Kong	86.0	235.0	1.2	22.0	84.8	213.0
Singapore	24.0	87.0	5.0	16.0	19.0	71.0
Rep. of Korea	3.0	17.0	3.0	12.0	0.0	5.0
Taiwan	0.5	42.0	6.0	102.0	-5.5	-60.0
Sub-total	113.5	381.0	15.2	152.0	98.3	229.0
3. Thailand	0.1	0.4	0.0	67.0	0.1	-66.6
Malaysia	10.0	52.0	0.1	3.0	9.9	49.0
Sub-total	10.1	52.4	0.1	70.0	10.0	-17.6
4. Indonesia	1.0	2.0	0.7	3.0	0.3	-1.0
5. Philippines	6.0	4.0	0.1	0.2	5.9	3.8
6. Sum: groups 1-5	432.6	1,270.4	27.1	229.2	405.5	1,041.2
7. India	0.0	0.1	2.5	38.0	-2.5	-37.9
China	0.0	12.0	203.0	302.0	-203.0	-290.0

Notes: Net imports are derived by subtracting exports from imports. Hence, a country with negative imports exported more than it imported.

Source: FAO 1988 *Agriculture Trade Standard Yearbook* tape. Rome: FAO.

their capability for domestic production. The city-states of Hong Kong and Singapore increased their imports, and Taiwan and Thailand increased their exports significantly. In the conceptual exposition, it will be noted that developing countries have a comparative advantage in many types of livestock production and can be expected to gradually become net exporters. The high transaction costs in livestock marketing may well restrain those potentials.

Fruit and Vegetable Trade

As in the case of meat, Japan is a large importer of fruits and vegetables, and imports have been growing rapidly (see Table 4.4). Again, wheat imports, which have more or less stabilized, may be contrasted with the meat and horticultural commodities imports, where rising incomes continue to provide scope for increasing

TABLE 4.4 Volume of Imports, Exports, and Net Imports of Fruits and Vegetables of Selected Pacific Rim Countries Plus China and India, Three-year Averages 1970-72 and 1985-87 (thousand metric ton)

	Fruits and Vegetables					
	Imports		Exports		Net Imports	
Country	1970-72	1985-87	1970-72	1985-87	1970-72	1985-87
1. Japan	1591.0	2734.0	133.0	74.0	1458.0	2660.0
2. Hong Kong	677.0	1211.0	96.0	352.0	581.0	859.0
Singapore	470.0	816.0	184.0	270.0	286.0	546.0
Rep. of Korea	7.0	261.0	16.0	74.0	-9.0	187.0
Taiwan	45.0	315.0	828.0	720.0	-783.0	-405.0
Sub-total	1199.0	2603.0	1124.0	1416.0	75.0	1187.0
3. Thailand	8.0	12.0	1409.0	7286.0	-1401.0	-7274.0
Malaysia	188.0	465.0	259.0	350.0	-71.0	115.0
Sub-total	196.0	477.0	1668.0	7636.0	-1472.0	-7159.0
4. Indonesia	17.0	77.0	416.0	682.0	-399.0	-695.0
5. Philippines	15.0	31.0	482.0	1343.0	-467.0	-1312.0
6. Sum: groups 1-5	3018.0	5922.0	3823.0	11151.0	-805.0	-5229.0
7. India	271.0	461.0	213.0	372.0	58.0	89.0
China	72.0	113.0	697.0	2292.0	-625.0	2179.0

Notes: Net imports are derived by subtracting exports from imports. Hence, a country with negative imports exported more than it imported.

Source: FAO 1988 *Agriculture Trade Standard Yearbook* tape. Rome: FAO.

consumption and where gradual trade liberalization has opened markets substantially. The two city-states have also increased their fruit and vegetable imports substantially, and the two together represent a market almost half of Japan.

As one would expect for labor-intensive commodities like horticultural products, which require a high state of technology, the fast-growing entities of Taiwan and Thailand are rapidly increasing their exports.

Vegetable Oils Trade

There has been great expansion in net vegetable oil imports by countries with higher per capita GNPs (see Table 4.5). Japan increased its net imports by 7.8 times between the two time periods and the Gang of Four by 6.0 times. Among the four, the Republic of Korea experienced a 57-fold increase from a low base. Apart from countries with high GNP,

TABLE 4.5 Volume of Imports, Exports, and Net Imports of Fixed Vegetable Oils and Fats of Selected Pacific Rim Countries Plus China and India, Three-year Averages 1970-72 and 1985-87 (thousand metric ton)

	Fixed Vegetable Oils and Fats					
	Imports		Exports		Net Imports	
Country	1970-72	1985-87	1970-72	1985-87	1970-72	1985-87
1. Japan	71.6	300.7	35.7	19.7	35.9	281.0
2. Hong Kong	50.6	110.5	5.1	27.2	45.5	83.4
Singapore	228.5	1004.9	232.6	930.8	-4.1	74.1
Rep. of Korea	2.7	141.3	0.3	1.4	2.5	139.9
Taiwan	9.5	23.0	0.1	2.8	9.4	20.2
Sub-total	291.4	1279.7	238.2	962.2	53.2	317.5
3. Thailand	0.6	24.3	1.7	20.7	-1.2	3.5
Malaysia	14.5	47.3	615.7	4036.8	-601.2	-3989.5
Sub-total	15.1	71.6	617.4	4057.5	-602.4	-3985.9
4. Indonesia	0.7	46.0	216.1	661.9	-215.5	-615.9
5. Philippines	9.7	21.5	399.3	833.3	-389.7	-811.8
6. Sum: groups 1-5	388.4	1719.5	1506.8	6534.5	-1118.4	-4815.1
7. India	76.6	1342.7	32.67	86.6	44.0	1256.1
China	47.3	250.0	63.5	166.9	-16.1	83.2

Notes: Net imports are derived by subtracting exports from imports. Hence, a country with negative imports exported more than it imported.

Source: FAO 1988 Agriculture Trade Standard Yearbook tape. Rome: FAO.

both India and China raised their net imports. India's increase was tremendous, increasing 28-fold during the 15 years. Thailand increased its imports by 40 times, consequently changing from a net exporter to a net importer.

The three palm-oil producing countries (Malaysia, Indonesia, and the Philippines) are net vegetable oil exporters. Palm oil production is restricted to countries with a tropical environment. One expects that as their agriculture grows, their net exports will also rise. During the 15 years, Malaysia's net vegetable oil exports increased by 6.6 times, Indonesia's by 2.9 times, and the Philippines' by 2.1 times.

Cotton Lint Trade

Although Japan is dominant in cotton lint imports among the nine Pacific Rim countries, its share dropped from 60 percent in the early

1970s to 33 percent in the mid-1980s (see Table 4.6). While Japanese net cotton imports slightly decreased, most Pacific Rim countries increased their net imports rapidly. The Republic of Korea, Taiwan, and Malaysia increased their net imports by more than 3.0 times, Thailand by 4.4 times, and Indonesia by 7.7 times.

Cotton consumption is related to the level of per capita income. The Japanese income level has already reached the saturation point for cotton consumption; therefore its imports did not increase. The income levels of other Pacific Rim countries are rising from lower bases. As their incomes increase, their cotton consumption, and consequently imports, will also increase until consumption reaches its peak.

Another factor related to cotton imports is the textile trade. Because the textile industry is labor-intensive, textile factories follow lower labor costs shifting first from Japan to the Gang of Four, and then to Thailand and Malaysia. Appropriate climates and lower land costs provide both China and India with an advantage in producing cotton. Their overall agricultural growth also promotes cotton production and imports. Both countries changed from being net cotton importers to net cotton exporters during the 15 years.

Overall Trade in Agricultural Products

The overall agricultural trade relationships follow from the preceding analysis of component parts. In total, Japan dominates net imports, having almost doubled the value of its imports in the 15-year period analyzed (see Table 4.7).

At a much lower level are the Gang of Four, which also are major net importers of agricultural commodities. They have increased their net imports by 2.6 times in the 15-year period analyzed. Whereas their population is about 60 percent as large as Japan's, the value of their net imports is only about 40 percent as high. Thus there is clear scope for continued substantial growth in those countries as net importers of agricultural commodities. They are clearly going the way of Japan.

Thailand and Malaysia both have excellent agricultural resources and have followed policies that have exploited them well; thus it is not surprising that they have become increasingly large net exporters of agricultural commodities. Their net exports have increased almost threefold in the 15-year period. It is clear that where countries have a large, underexploited land base and have their policies and projects for agricultural development well in place, they have the potential to increase agricultural production and agricultural exports. However, in both Thailand and Malaysia, domestic demands will certainly grow

TABLE 4.6 Volume of Imports, Exports, and Net Imports of Cotton Lint of Selected Pacific Rim Countries Plus China and India, Three-year Averages 1970-72 and 1985-87 (thousand metric ton)

	Cotton Lint					
	Imports		Exports		Net Imports	
Country	1970-72	1985-87	1970-72	1985-87	1970-72	1985-87
1. Japan	775.2	737.4	0.1	0.0	775.1	737.4
2. Hong Kong	152.9	269.5	1.5	71.0	151.4	198.4
Singapore	14.2	11.4	5.5	7.7	8.6	3.7
Rep. of Korea	112.2	388.4	0.0	0.0	112.2	388.4
Taiwan	130.4	397.4	0.0	0.0	130.4	397.4
Sub-total	409.6	1066.7	7.0	78.7	402.6	988.0
3. Thailand	43.6	191.8	0.3	1.6	43.2	190.3
Malaysia	8.1	28.7	0.4	0.1	7.7	28.6
Sub-total	51.7	220.5	0.7	1.7	51.0	218.8
4. Indonesia	22.2	170.5	0.0	0.0	22.2	170.5
5. Philippines	31.8	36.8	0.0	0.0	31.8	36.8
6. Sum: groups 1-5	1290.5	2232.0	7.8	80.4	1282.7	2151.6
7. India	132.6	2.1	21.9	524.6	110.7	-522.4
China	140.7	2.0	35.3	123.3	105.4	-121.3

Notes: Net imports are derived by subtracting exports from imports. Hence, a country with negative imports exported more than it imported.

Source: *FAO 1988 Agriculture Trade Standard Yearbook* tape. Rome: FAO.

beyond their capacity to increase production, particularly as their incomes rise to the level that allows substantial livestock production. Even Thailand can be expected to become a net importer of feedgrains, as it gradually absorbs its current corn exports into domestic feed consumption. In addition, Thailand has not positioned itself to raise its agricultural factor productivity as it runs out of land frontier, which has principally accounted for its production increases in past years. And in both countries, rapidly rising factor productivity in manufacturing will cause a relative shift of resources out of agriculture.

Indonesia has increased its net exports, while the Philippines' net exports have slightly decreased. However, these countries are not nearly as land-rich, relative to their populations, as Thailand and Malaysia. One might expect, as their growth rates accelerate, that they will begin to look a bit more like the Gang of Four.

TABLE 4.7 Volume of Imports, Exports, and Net Imports of Total Agricultural Products of Selected Pacific Rim Countries Plus China and India, Three-year Averages 1970-72 and 1984-86 (1980 US$ millions)

	Total Agricultural Products					
	Imports		Exports		Net Imports	
Country	1970-72	1984-86	1970-72	1984-86	1970-72	1984-86
1. Japan	10.0	17.8	0.7	0.8	9.3	17.0
2. Hong Kong	1.6	3.6	0.3	1.5	1.4	2.1
Singapore	0.9	2.5	0.6	1.9	0.3	0.6
Rep. of Korea	1.1	3.3	0.2	0.6	0.9	2.7
Taiwan	0.8	2.8	0.7	1.3	0.1	1.5
Sub-total	4.5	12.1	1.8	5.2	2.7	6.9
3. Thailand	0.2	0.6	1.2	3.5	-0.1	-2.9
Malaysia	0.7	1.5	1.5	3.9	-0.9	-2.4
Sub-total	0.9	2.0	2.8	7.4	-1.9	-5.3
4. Indonesia	0.6	1.0	1.0	2.5	-0.5	-1.5
5. Philippines	0.4	0.6	1.1	1.3	-0.8	-0.7
6. Sum: groups 1-5	16.3	33.6	7.5	17.2	8.8	16.4
7. India	1.2	1.6	1.5	2.3	-0.3	-0.7
China	1.2	2.5	2.2	5.5	-0.1	-2.9

Notes: Net imports are derived by subtracting exports from imports. Hence, a country with negative imports exported more than it imported.

Source: FAO 1988 Agriculture Trade Standard Yearbook tape. Rome: FAO.

Analysis of the United States' Share of Agricultural Trade with the Pacific Rim Countries

The countries analyzed here (excluding Taiwan) take more than 25 percent of U.S. cereals exports, a significant share that doubled during the 15-year period (see Table 4.8). U.S. exports of agricultural commodities to Taiwan also increased. As would be expected from the overall import data, Japan, the Republic of Korea, and Taiwan are the most important destinations for U.S. agricultural exports.

Concerning future growth potential, first, the opportunity for growth in this market is substantial. Second, the United States has participated in the past growth, having doubled the proportion of its own cereal exports to these countries. Third, the key commodities in the nine Pacific countries' imports were cotton and fruits and vegetables in the early 1970s and fruits and vegetables and meat in the mid-1980s. Among cereals, feedgrains are most important. Fourth, where agricultural imports are growing so rapidly, one would expect that some of the

TABLE 4.8 Volume of Imports of Total Cereals from the United States Averaged over Five-Year Periods, 1963-67, 1973-77, and 1983-87. The U.S. Cereal Exports to the Pacific Countries as Percentage of the U.S. Total Cereal Exports (Thousand tons of cereal equivalent)

Country	Total Cereal		
	1963-67	1973-77	1983-87
1. Japan	4942.0	12024.8	17307.0
2. Hong Kong	40.2	80.2	109.6
Singapore	3.2	54.6	92.2
Rep. of Korea	776.2	2732.6	4708.2
Taiwan	N/A	N/A	N/A
Sub-total	819.6	2867.4	4910.0
3. Thailand	5.2	55.8	98.0
Malaysia	7.4	20.6	102.0
Subtotal	12.6	76.4	200.0
4. Indonesia	85.8	597.8	767.0
5. Philippines	316.2	491.6	951.2
6. Sum: groups 1-5	6176.2	16058.0	24135.2
7. Item 6 as percent total U.S. cereal exports	14.7%	21.1%	28.8%
8. India	5767.8	3016.8	1023.6
China	0.0	1598.6	2758.0

Note: The data are for July-June.
N/A = Not available.
Source: USDA 1988. USDA PSD tape issued in 1988. Washington, DC: USDA.

commodity groups being imported would not be normal areas of U.S. comparative advantage but there may be small niches within those groups that should be examined for their potential. We will return to that point later. Now we proceed to the conceptual framework for viewing the dynamics of agricultural trade in developing countries as the basis for a proactive policy by major exporters, such as the United States.

The Conceptual Framework

The principal growth market for major agricultural exporters, particularly grain exporters, is in the developing countries. The Pacific Rim countries are the harbinger of the future in this regard. Many of them are already growing rapidly and becoming increasingly large importers, particularly of cereals. Indonesia and the Philippines are best described as incipient major markets.

What determines how these countries will grow? What positive role can international policy and the policies of major agricultural exporters play in these processes? The course of development and its impact on agricultural trade are subject to policy, both national and international. In this section, the underlying developmental relationships will be briefly explored. In the following section, the implications for policies will be drawn.

Figure 4.1 shows that, for Asian countries, there is a strong relationship between the rates of growth of the agricultural and nonagricultural sectors. If we remove four outliers (Burma, the Philippines, Singapore, and the Republic of Korea), we obtain an R-square of 0.91 and a β-coefficient of roughly 1.4, which means that for every 1.0 percent increment in the rate of growth of the agricultural sector, there is an increment of 1.4 percent in the rate of growth of the nonagricultural sector.

This is, of course, not a necessary relationship, which is why the four outliers are removed. Each is a country in which agriculture has, for one reason or another, not played a key, causal role in accelerating growth of the nonagricultural sector. The reasons why this is so for these four cases are themselves instructive. We remove Singapore because, for all practical purposes, it does not have an agricultural sector. We remove Burma because, although it has an extremely favorable physical environment for agriculture, it has had abysmal policies for encouraging either agricultural or nonagricultural growth, so that the sum result has been good growth in agriculture because of the good physical environment, despite the poor policies, while the nonagricultural sector has been left out. Similarly, we remove the Philippines because, although "the green revolution" succeeded because of good technological policy, skewed industrial policies co-opted the bulk of the capital and related resources into inefficient large-scale, capital-intensive industries, largely located in metropolitan Manila, resulting in a slow rate of overall nonagricultural growth. We remove South Korea because it followed favorable industrial policies, but in its early stages of development it largely neglected the agricultural sector. Finally, few of these countries followed vigorous policies for increasing the size of the multipliers between agricultural and nonagricultural growth. If they had, the size of their β-coefficient could have been much higher.

Why do we find this relationship between agricultural and nonagricultural growth important? What is the theory of causality? The

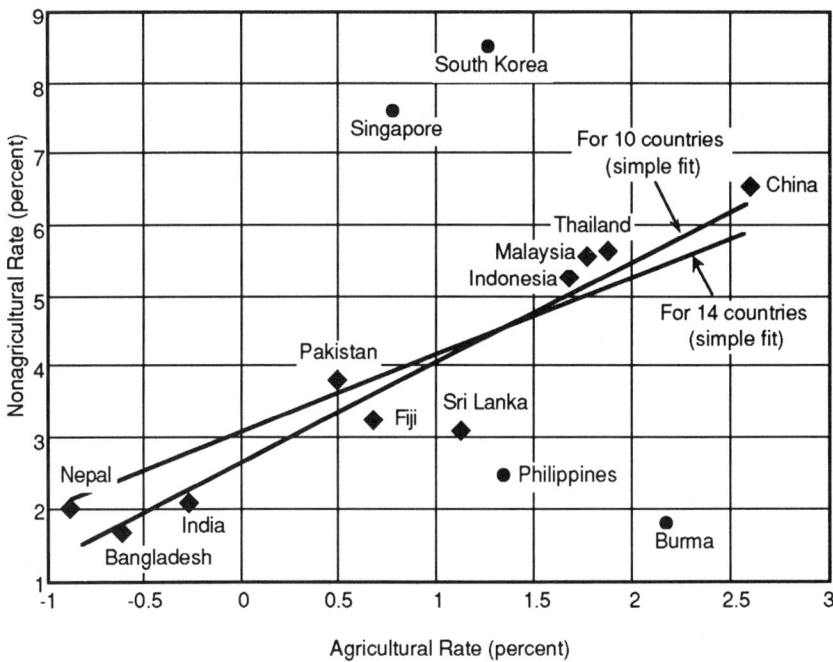

FIGURE 4.1 Growth Rates of Per Capita Agriculture and Nonagriculture GDP (various Asian countries and years, 1960-86)

Descriptive variables for simple fit of 10 countries (excluding Burma, Philippines, Republic of Korea, and Singapore): R-Square, 0.91; value of coefficient of agricultural growth rate, 1.43; T-stat. of agricultural growth rate, 9.33; and standard error of agricultural growth rate, 0.15.

Descriptive variables for simple fit of 14 countries: R-square, 0.23; value of coefficient of agricultural growth rate, 1.07; T-stat. of agricultural growth rate, 1.92; and standard error of agricultural growth rate, 0.56.

Source: The World Bank data.

Note: Constant 1980 Price GDT at market prices in local currency.

principal reason is that developing countries are, virtually without exception, countries in which a high proportion of the economy's productive resources, especially people, are engaged in the agricultural sector. Not only is it difficult to move the whole when only a small part is being accelerated, but there are powerful linkage effects between agricultural and nonagricultural growth. Growth in real incomes in agriculture, consistent with Engel's Law, results in expenditure patterns that vigorously stimulate the nonagricultural sector. This is particularly true of the service sector and the small-scale industrial sector, both of which are employment intensive. One effect is a reverse flow of expenditures from people newly employed in industry to the agricultural sector, creating a market not only for basic food staples, but also for livestock and horticultural commodities. These commodities have characteristics more like the nonagricultural sector, such as relatively high income elasticities of demand, a high degree of labor intensity, and low land intensity in production. Thus, accelerated growth in the nonagricultural sector significantly stimulates agriculture, which in turn further stimulates both.

It is extremely difficult to have growth rates in the agricultural sector in excess of 2.5 to 3 percent if the sector consists largely of basic food staples. However, as soon as there is effective demand for high income-elasticity, labor-intensive commodities, the agricultural sector will grow much more rapidly. For example, in a country like Thailand, the demand for livestock commodities is probably growing by close to 10 percent a year. This allows tremendous intensification in agriculture, as long as feed supplies are not limiting, and a great acceleration in the agricultural growth rate. The same, in a somewhat more modest way, can be said of the horticultural sector.

As demand for agricultural commodities accelerates, it becomes increasingly difficult to match those rates of growth with that of agricultural supply. This is particularly true of basic food staples, which are heavy land-users—the land base rapidly runs out. The result is an eventual shift to imports of the heavy land-using commodities. To put this another way, the comparative advantage shifts toward exports of labor, whether they be from agriculture or nonagriculture, and away from agricultural commodities which are extensive users of land, such as cereals, and especially feedgrains. This process moves very rapidly when the base of livestock consumption becomes large, and it is further accelerated when the land base for the basic food staples is contracted, even though modestly, by increased demand from the livestock sector and from the horticultural sector. It is then that we get explosive growth in net imports. We have seen this occur in Japan, Taiwan, and the Republic of Korea, and we are now seeing it in Thailand, although somewhat muted because it was initially a major exporter.

Without going into the details of these relationships, what can we conclude from this simple exercise? First, agricultural exporters need not fear accelerated growth in the agricultural sectors of developing countries. It is natural, more or less inevitable, and indeed should be encouraged. Second, induced accelerated growth in the nonagricultural sectors is not inevitable (consider the Philippines) and requires favorable macro policy. That leads us to specific recommendations for U.S. policy since the United States is the largest agricultural exporter, the largest provider of foreign aid to developing countries, and the single most important influence on international policy.

An Effective U.S. Policy to Encourage Agricultural Exports

Market development for agricultural exports to developing countries is complex because it depends on accelerated growth in per capita incomes. Thus, the core of policy must be development-oriented. An effective U.S. policy needs three key components: (1) to encourage overall growth, (2) to be a reliable supplier, and (3) to encourage open-trade regimes.

To encourage overall growth, the United States must first, and most importantly, encourage technological change that accelerates factor productivity increases in the agricultural sector. That is the base of agricultural growth, which is in turn the base of overall growth. This means the United States should play to its own comparative advantage in building institutions for technological change in agriculture by assisting and developing agricultural research systems, extension systems, and higher educational systems for training the people who will run the numerous complex institutions needed for rapid technological change in agriculture.

Second, there are two areas where massive investment is needed: rural infrastructure, including roads, and education. Numerous studies at IFPRI and elsewhere have demonstrated the critical role of roads in integrated agricultural development. There is no need to lecture to trade economists on this issue. What one is after is to reduce transaction costs for rural people so that they can gain the advantages of specialization and underlying comparative advantage. Further, technological change is becoming increasingly complex, and thus it is important that rural people be increasingly well educated. Road building, construction of other infrastructure, and provision of adequate and appropriate schooling require massive financial inputs that are difficult to raise for many poor countries. Capital assistance can be helpful in such instances.

Finally, there is a tremendously important role for food aid in this development context. It is an important means of market development, which arises from encouragement of the overall economic development process. Since the basic needs for infrastructure and schooling have a large labor component, and therefore a large food component, food aid can be used to break that bottleneck. Obviously, financial aid can be just as effective, but, as food, aid is politically cheaper; therefore, one should go in that direction, since food is in any case being underutilized initially.

Note that food aid is justified in terms of its development impact. It is often argued that food aid changes tastes in the direction of the commodity composition of the food aid: the relative increase in wheat consumption is often cited. However, it is far more likely that such changes in tastes are the product of rising incomes and the impact of modernization on the value of women's time. Thus, food aid should be allocated so as to most efficiently raise incomes. That will be the most effective form of market development. A shortsighted view of market development will be ineffective over the longer run.

Being a reliable supplier should be the second component of U.S. policy. If a country opts for heavy emphasis on agricultural development and rapid growth in employment and food consumption, it needs to reduce vulnerability in this extremely risky area. After all, if a country relies on agriculture for production, and food for consumption, it is moving into the area most vulnerable to weather fluctuation. What can the United States do in this respect? It can help the countries develop a stocking capacity to assure them of adequate supplies until imports can be brought in. It can provide technical assistance and capital assistance in building the storage facilities. It should complement that stocking policy with a stocking policy of its own. As the largest agricultural exporter in the world, the United States has a special interest in being a reliable supplier and therefore should see that holding stocks has a rate of return that is greater than indicated by the direct financial returns.

Being a reliable supplier, as any large corporation knows, is a sine qua non of building markets. In the same context, the United States must manage its production capacity in order to be a reliable supplier. When it sees its domestic and global stocks declining, it must bring acreage back into production in order to maintain stocks at a reasonable level so that it can continue to be a reliable supplier.

Finally, we must recognize that for developing countries, one of the biggest risks is not the supply of food as such, but the financing for it.

Developing countries are apt to find themselves in a poor bargaining position in purchasing existing supplies of food simply because of the lack of short-term financing. Given the tremendous financial pressures, it is perhaps too much to expect them to build monetary reserves for this purpose. Under such circumstances, the United States should be pressuring the International Monetary Fund to rehabilitate the now moribund Cereal Facility, which provided precisely that kind of financing. Such a facility should be a free-standing unit, with the single objective of seeing to it that developing countries have the finances to import food whenever their import bill is rising rapidly, whether it is because of domestic crop failures, rapidly rising international prices, or a combination of the two. The facility should not be hitched to other foreign exchange concerns. What we are after is reliability of food supplies, not only because they are important from the humanitarian point of view, but also because of their market development implications.

Finally, developing countries do, in general, require open trading regimes if they are to grow rapidly. This is particularly true if they are to import substantial quantities of livestock feed. If the United States is to fulfill its comparative advantage in exporting basic food staples and other agricultural commodities to developing countries, these countries must be able to develop rapidly, which requires earning foreign exchange for importing capital-intensive intermediate products and other goods and services and, more specifically, for purchasing the cereals that the United States wants to sell.

An open-trade regime must, of course, extend to agriculture. If Thailand has a comparative advantage in rice exports, we must encourage them with open trading regimes and perhaps in other ways, expecting to recoup on other agricultural commodities as their economy grows. As Thailand's livestock consumption grows and their livestock exports grow, their corn exports will decline rapidly, eventually turning into corn imports. We also would gain a large oilseeds market in that context. We will recoup on the rice market in West Africa, where we can expect the demand to grow far more rapidly than Thailand can fulfill.

As part of the pressure towards liberal trade regimes, we need to lobby in the GATT for openness with respect to horticultural commodities, including international rules for health and sanitation relations. For a country like the United States, with a powerful comparative advantage in agricultural exports, it is only common sense to work for open-trading regimes in which we will lose some markets to a very few developing countries but gain far more.

Notes

1. Increased wheat imports are driven in particular by the labor-saving potential of purchased baked bread. A paper, "The Effect of the Value of Time on Food Consumption Patterns in Developing Countries: Evidence from Sri Lanka," by Senauer, Sahn, and Alderman, tests the hypothesis that the bread consumption of an urban Sri Lankan household will increase as the opportunity cost of time of a primary woman in the household increases, with the data from a 1981/82 labor force and socioeconomic survey conducted by the Sri Lankan Department of Census and Statistics. The finding strongly supported the hypothesis. The paper concludes that the increased value of human time must be considered one of the factors underlying the shift from time-intensive traditional foods to time-saving foods, especially commercially baked bread, which is occurring quite widely in developing countries.

PART TWO

Country Perspectives

5

Development of Agricultural Policy in Postwar Japan

Yutaka Yoshioka

Introduction

The development of agricultural policy in postwar Japan can be divided into four phases. The first, in the 1940s and 1950s, was the establishment of democratic agricultural systems as a pillar of the Japanese democratization taking place at that time. The second, in the 1950s and 1960s, was the internationalization of agriculture, which went hand in hand with the rapid economic growth of the period. The third was the shift to a policy of food security prompted by the world food crisis from the early 1970s to the early 1980s. The fourth was the return, amid various political hindrances, to internationalization in the late 1980s.

Three Basic Agricultural Laws

Just as the current agricultural policy systems in the United States are based on the Agricultural Adjustment Act enforced during the Great Depression of the 1930s, the main structure of current Japanese agricultural systems was set up during the U.S. occupation of the late 1940s. Three laws enacted during this period were particularly important: the Farmland Law, the Agricultural Cooperative Law, and the Staple Food Control Law.

Like in the United States, where the Agricultural Adjustment Act was put together to tackle the depressed conditions of rural America, the three Japanese laws were also the product of their time—a time when Japan was faced with serious food shortages under a collapsed national economy and desperately needed to democratize its economy and society.

The Farmland Law

The Farmland Law aimed to provide a basis for Japanese democratization and agricultural development by redistributing farmland and setting up independent owner-farmers. To protect these newly established owner-farmers from commercial buyouts by nonfarm interests, and also to control unfair profits by farmers selling farmland originally bought at legally controlled minimum prices, the transfer of ownership was strictly regulated so that only farm producers were eligible to purchase farmland—nonfarm use of land was strictly controlled.

The Agricultural Cooperative Law

Newly established owner-farmers were encouraged to organize cooperatives in their villages to protect their interests against economically powerful former landowners, money lenders, and the merchants who had previously dominated the rural economies. Almost all of the farmers in a community participated in the cooperative, which was run according to traditional community rules. Most rural residents at that time were farmers. Therefore, the name of the agricultural cooperative became an alternative name for the community, village, or town. Furthermore, under the Agricultural Cooperative Law, a farmer in a cooperative could exercise formerly nonexistent equal voting rights.

Cooperatives organized prefectural federations, which in turn set up various national federations. Thus, a huge national network of agricultural cooperatives was established capable of providing various important economic services to member farmers and their communities. By means of their cooperative activities, farmers were able to protect themselves economically throughout the many years when rice was the major agricultural product for most of them.

The Staple Food Control Law

The Staple Food Control Law was enacted in the midst of food shortages during the Second World War. The government needed to secure a stable supply of rice and other staple foods, including wheat, barley, and later, yams, from the domestic agricultural sector, and distribute them to consumers under a rationing system. Immediately after the war, the supply-and-demand situation in staple grains worsened, so the law, as the most powerful policy tool available to combat the tight food situation, was used constantly. The government forced producers to sell all their rice and other staple foods, and sometimes even yams, to the Food Agency, holding back only that used for their own consumption. This produce was sold to the agency at relatively low prices compared with the much higher black market prices. So in this period, the law clearly aimed at protecting consumers, and for this reason, it was viewed by farming interests as one of the worst pieces of legislation as far as they were concerned.

Recap

We must bear in mind that these three basic laws were closely interrelated with the overall concept of rice and the paddy field. Moreover, the laws were put together and enforced in an extremely unusual domestic situation, and at a time when Japan was more isolated internationally than it had been at any time since the Meiji era. The laws were influenced by the particular situation and needs of postwar Japan.

The Internationalization of Agriculture in Postwar Japan

Entry into the GATT

Japan entered the General Agreement on Tariffs and Trade (GATT) in 1955, seven years after the organization was established. Most Japanese policymakers at that time, particularly in the agricultural sector, did not fully understand the character and importance of the GATT, but there was a firm consensus among government leaders that internationalization was the only way that Japan was going to rebuild its economy and raise living standards.

Self-Sufficiency in Rice

Achieving self-sufficiency in rice in the late 1950s relieved the manufacturing sector from the serious shortage of convertible foreign currencies such as U.S. dollars or British sterling. At the same time, rural economies—supported by increased farm income—provided a market for the manufacturing sector.

Import Liberalization in Agriculture

The 1960s and early 1970s saw a rapid growth of the national economy, boosted by ever-increasing industrial exports. This resulted in occasional trade surpluses. Trade friction with agricultural exporting countries, and in particular with the United States, began to emerge. Import restrictions on many agricultural products were quickly abolished, while tariffs on many others were lowered through bilateral and multilateral negotiations or as a result of Japan's unilateral initiatives. Farm imports increased rapidly to meet increasing domestic food consumption.

In the 1960s and 1970s, the Japanese diet started to become Westernized, marked by a rise in the consumption of livestock products—e.g., meat and dairy products—as well as green vegetables and fruits, and reduced consumption of fish and traditional grains like rice and barley. As a result, the gap between the national production capacity of rice and demand for the grain began to widen, and rice surpluses became a new policy problem. Switching paddy fields to the production of farm products for which demand was expected to grow became an urgent policy target. The government started to use the Staple Food Control Law to protect producers and adjust the use of their paddy fields, while deregulating the marketing and distribution of rice and wheat.

At the same time, a swift flow of young workers from rural areas to factories and urban areas started to cause labor shortages in farming areas. Domestic production of wheat and soybeans, which until then had been bolstered by surplus labor, began to shrink rapidly. Mechanization became a priority, so the government and agricultural organizations encouraged farmers to start using modern farm machinery and technologies. The nationwide mechanization of rice production—previously thought of as the most difficult area in which to mechanize—was achieved through the introduction of small tractors, replanters, and combines. So, the problem of sudden labor shortage in farming was solved without reducing agricultural output.

A further socioeconomic problem was the widening income gap between farm and nonfarm households caused by the rapid increase in industrial productivity. To tackle this grave national problem, improvements to raise productivity and support of farm incomes to bring them up to the level of nonfarm incomes became urgent policy goals.

As we are all well aware, structural changes in agriculture have been needed globally for many years. It is perfectly understandable that the government chose to pay for the income support policy by providing higher support prices. During the period of fast-paced economic growth, consumers seldom complained about the prices of food. The Ministry of Finance liked the price support system, which put the financial burden onto consumers, but disliked direct income support through deficiency payments, which can become a heavy burden on future national budgets. During this period, support prices for agricultural products, and for rice in particular, were raised considerably to narrow the income gap.

At the same time, for many small producers, the promotion of part-time employment was an important policy as far as achieving income equality was concerned. By means of special taxation policies and other measures, industries were encouraged to build plants in rural areas. Thus, the number of part-time farmers increased at a rapid pace, so their household incomes gradually grew while the importance of their farm incomes steadily decreased.

Throughout this period, agricultural markets except for rice were opened considerably. There was widespread consensus, even among leading conservative politicians, that in agriculture, too, free trade was a natural and desirable course for Japan to pursue. I still remember a promising congressman of the ruling party saying: "Full liberalization of the agricultural market, without giving farmers an inkling that it is taking place, is a most desirable course for Japan." If that attitude had prevailed, agricultural policy problems today would be quite different.

The World Food Crisis and the Emergence of Food Security Policies

The world food crisis, symbolized for the Japanese by the American soybean embargo in the early 1970s, prompted a decisive change in the direction of the internationalization of agriculture in Japan. Overnight, consumer groups switched their slogans from "cheaper food" and support of further agricultural liberalization to "higher self-sufficiency" and "safer food." These aims were to depend on the domestic market for their success.

Despite the fact that the supply of soybeans from the United States in the critical year of 1973 was almost equal to or a little more than the previous year's, public attention centered on the nation's low self-sufficiency of basic grains like wheat, feed grains, and soybeans, since the country was already self-sufficient in or had a surplus of rice. Quite naturally, this serious national concern was swiftly echoed by the agricultural sector, thus creating a firm alliance of agricultural and consumer groups. In this way, food security became a national slogan. All political parties cooperated to create various related agricultural and food policies.

Nevertheless, the end result of the government's study of possible policy measures to achieve food security was not a particularly extreme result, but, rather, a moderate and well-balanced one. Ensuring economic and financial feasibility, while at the same time avoiding serious adverse international reaction, meant that a responsible government was unable to find a single drastic solution.

The food security policy announced by the government consisted of four major themes: the maximum increase in domestic agricultural production compatible with economic and financial feasibility; the securing of guarantees from major agricultural exporting countries such as the

United States; the creation of reserves for basic grains such as rice, wheat, soybeans, and some feed grains; and the diversion of overseas supply sources, accompanied by agricultural development cooperation for developing countries such as Brazil and Indonesia.

During the 1960s and the early 1970s, Japan steadily reduced its import barriers on agricultural products. For example, the number of agricultural import quota items was reduced to 22 in 1974, from a peak of over 100. However, since the announcement of the food security policy, the Japanese government has until recently strongly opposed any further opening of the agricultural market. In addition, the government has adopted new policy measures to encourage higher price supports and the introduction of new subsidies as well as trying to increase domestic production of grains such as wheat, soybeans, and some other nongrain products for which the self-sufficiency rate was clearly low. The rice production diversion program was one such measure.

Because of the tight supply-and-demand situation for grains and other agricultural products, as well as the American ban on exports to the Soviet Union under the Carter administration, the food security policy did not come under heavy international fire during the late 1970s and the early 1980s. Because of the need to protect domestic agriculture, Japan did not lower its food security colors even after the surpluses became a major concern in world agricultural trade.

Thanks to the rapid increase in household income, higher food prices were no longer a heavy burden on the family purse. Consumer activists were busy demanding that the government guarantee the quality and safety of food to protect consumer interests, and so the government managed to avoid nonfarm criticism of the heavy farm protection.

I would like to draw your attention to just one point here: throughout this period, the Japanese government was able to make some contribution to the stability of the international grain market by refraining from the aggressive subsidization of exports or the dumping of rice in the form of aid. Such measures would have allowed the government to enforce a less rigorous rice production control program.

The New Phase of Internationalization in Agriculture

The fourth phase in the development of postwar Japanese agricultural policy is familiar to all trade specialists in the field. In world agriculture, surpluses and the serious trade competition that resulted among agricultural exporting countries have existed since the early 1980s. For Japan, agricultural trade friction with the United States, fanned by huge trade surpluses on the Japanese side, became the number one bilateral problem needing to be solved. In nonfarm sectors, social and economic structural reform was emerging not only as a domestic issue but also as an international one, particularly with the United States and other developed countries.

Faced with this urgent need to reform domestic systems, the Nakasone administration started to build national consensus for reform by establishing the Maekawa Committee, an informal advisory body to the prime minister. Among the members was a high-ranking former government official of the Ministry of Agriculture, Forestry, and Fisheries.

The Maekawa Report emphasized, among other points, the importance of the internationalization of Japanese economic and agricultural systems. In agriculture, such policy reforms as the promotion of structural improvements to create higher productivity, the review of current pricing policies to encourage greater market orientation and internationalization, and a steady increase in foreign access for all agricultural products except basic ones were recommended.

With the Liberal Democratic Party's landslide victory in the 1986 general election, gained with the support of urban voters, the government clearly signaled its intention to shift from its traditional pro-farm policy to a more balanced, urban-based agricultural policy.

Following the principles laid down in the Maekawa Report, the Agricultural Policy Research Council submitted recommendations to the prime minister in 1986 that set out more detailed guidelines for agricultural policy reforms. These recommendations included the following five major policy targets:

- Establishment of high-productivity paddy farming
- Enlargement of the scale of farming operations and the securing of efficient farmers
- Introduction of competitive agricultural production and marketing
- Adoption of a pricing policy reflecting the production costs of the larger core farmer and the market situation, as well as reform of the Staple Food Control system to make it more market-oriented
- Increase of import access under, for example, a system of tariffs that reflect international market prices, allowing import quotas only in special cases

Under the guidelines set forth in the report, later endorsed by the Cabinet, the Ministry of Agriculture, Forestry, and Fisheries started to work toward policy changes. The government purchase prices for rice from producers were lowered for two consecutive years—1987 and 1988—and negotiations on 12 categories of agricultural products and on beef and citrus were concluded between Japan and the United States as well as with other exporting countries. So when it came to agricultural negotiations in the present Uruguay Round of the GATT, the Japanese government was expected to contribute positively.

However, the landslide defeat of the ruling Liberal Democratic Party in the 1989 Upper House election abruptly changed the domestic situation. The LDP lost its Upper House majority, while the opposition parties, such as the Japan Socialist Party, the Japan Communist Party, the Democratic Socialist Party, and Komeito were able to approve or veto bills concerning the national budget, among other matters. These parties lean more toward protectionism than the LDP, and so increased internationalization and market orientation in agricultural policy were stalled politically.

Many political observers gave three factors as reasons the LDP lost the election: introduction of a consumption tax, political scandals, and agricultural market liberalization. The government and the LDP quickly shifted their agricultural policy reform to one of maintaining the traditional status quo on protectionism.

Thus, the government purchase prices for rice were fixed at the preceding year's levels in 1989 and were reduced only 1.5 percent in 1990, even though many policymakers thought it was important to reduce the prices further. After such careful preparation, the LDP managed to win a majority of seats in the 1990 Lower House election. Moreover, the minority opposition parties—who held the majority in the Upper House—were pressed by the public to become more realistic and responsible over important national issues.

The swift political and economic changes in the Soviet Union and Eastern Europe, together with the ending of the Cold War between the United States and the Soviet Union, have caused public fears over national security to lessen somewhat, and have made a lot of people think again about the meaning and importance of international interdependence and a free global economic system.

In my judgement, it is important for the government and the LDP to breathe new life into the Agricultural Policy Research Council's guidelines. They were, after all, once endorsed by the Cabinet. How can this be done? This is always a political problem in any country's agricultural sector. That is why I feel that the rice issue will be such an important yardstick by which to judge Japanese agricultural policy reform in the near future.

Professor Egaitsu has discussed the socioeconomic factors underlying Japanese agricultural protection over the past three decades. I would like to approach the issue of rice from a broader political institutional perspective.

Development of Agricultural Policy in Postwar Japan   99

As I mentioned, rice has been the core agricultural product supporting the entire agricultural system since the postwar period. Even now, the basic situation is not that different. For example, the Food Agency still employs about 12,000 officials whose main job is to examine the quality of rice marketed by producers. To deal with the domestic handling, distribution, transportation, and quality checks of rice and wheat, the agency maintains 47 prefectural offices and many branch offices. The agency's labor union is known as one of the most activist of all governmental labor unions, and it is strongly influenced by the Japan Socialist Party.

The nationwide system of agricultural cooperatives is decisively propped up by the business activities connected with rice marketing, purchasing, saving, credits, and so on. Rice is marketed almost exclusively by rural cooperatives, their prefectural federations, and the national economic federations. Money from these sales flows back through the system so that payments to individual producers are automatically kept in savings accounts in their agricultural cooperatives. All farming and living costs for member farmers are automatically deducted from these deposits. Traditionally, rural cooperatives have served as sole bankers and retailing institutions for their communities.

According to 1987 statistics, there were 4,300 general agricultural cooperatives organizing 5.5 million farmers and 2.4 million associate members. These organizations employed about 300,000 officials, forming a powerful national labor union. These agricultural cooperatives accounted for 40 percent of the market for farm machinery, over 90 percent of that for fertilizers, over 60 percent of the market for agrochemicals, and over 40 percent of that for feed. Their total savings in the *Norinchukin* Bank, or the Central Agricultural Cooperative Bank, easily exceeded those of many of the larger Japanese city banks, while sales and purchases by the National Economic Federation of Agricultural Cooperatives were equal to those of the top-ranked Japanese trading companies. In rice-producing areas, agricultural cooperatives account for almost 100 percent of all rice marketed.

In Japan, there is also a national agricultural insurance system managed and subsidized by the government. All rice producers cultivating paddies of a certain acreage are obliged to participate in the scheme. By prior agreement, premiums are automatically deducted from their savings accounts with the agricultural cooperatives.

These are only a few examples of the way in which rice is integral to the Japanese agricultural system. When agricultural interests emphasize the importance of rice in Japanese society, they are also talking about such institutionalized aspects of the commodity. Therefore, whenever the Japanese government decides to reform its rice policy, it also has to tackle the difficult issues of how to change or overhaul the entire agricultural administrative system in the face of potentially tough resistance from people who are quite eager to maintain the status quo.

Nevertheless, Japan desperately needs some kind of reform in agricultural policy, and particularly in rice policy, because without substantial reform in this area, we cannot even think about meaningful policy reforms for other commodities. In light of all this, I believe that the Uruguay Round will be an extremely appropriate forum to start a new phase in, or return to, the already existing guidelines for Japanese agricultural policy.

References

Economic Council. 1986. Report of the Advisory Group on Economic Structural Adjustment for International Harmony (known as irst Maekawa report; later formalized in "Policy recommendations of the Economic Council" see next entry). Tokyo.

———. 1987. "Policy Recommendations of the Economic Council—Actions for Economic Restructuring" (second Maekawa report). Tokyo.

Foreign Press Center. 1988. *The Debate on Food Security in Japan.* Tokyo.

Japan Agricultural Policy Council. 1988. *The Basic Direction of Agricultural Administration Toward the 21st Century.* Prime Minister's Office, Tokyo.

Ministry of Agriculture, Forestry, and Fisheries. 1991. *Changes in Japan's Food Consumption.* Tokyo.

———. 1990. *Structural Changes in Japan's Agriculture.* Tokyo.

———. 1989. *Japan's Agricultural Trade.* Tokyo.

Miyahara, Yukinori. 1981. *Postwar Agricultural Policy and Agricultural Laws* (in Japanese). Norin Tohkei Kyohkai, Tokyo.

Toda, Hakuai. 1986. *Agricultural Policy in Modern Japan* (in Japanese). Norin Tohkei Kyohkai, Tokyo.

Yoshioka, Yutaka. 1988. *Food and Agriculture in Japan* (rev.). About Japan Series 18. Foreign Press Center, Tokyo.

6

Japanese Agricultural Policy: Unfair and Unreasonable?

Fumio Egaitsu

Introduction

Recently, Japanese agricultural policy has often been referred to as being both unfair and unreasonable. The import ban of rice is being blamed as an unfair barrier against foreign producers, and high food prices are being criticized as an unreasonable infringement of domestic consumers' rights. Certainly the policy is protective and interventionist.[1]

The objective of this chapter is to offer some material for the discussion of whether it is actually unfair and unreasonable, as it seems to be. The emphasis is placed on the second part of the question, namely whether it is actually unreasonable or not. This can be answered basically with evidence from the domestic scene. The answer to the first part, whether it is unfair or not, depends upon the rule of trade, which by its very nature should be an international matter. We should note, however, that the international rule itself is formulated on the domestic considerations of participating countries.

To begin with the conclusion, the answer to be found here is that Japanese agricultural policy from the domestic viewpoint is not as unreasonable as it may appear in the eyes of foreigners. This foregone conclusion should surely be disappointing to those who know how unreasonable Japanese food prices are by international standards. But it is my intention in the following pages to explore the reasons, if any, why Japan has maintained its seemingly unreasonable agricultural policy.

This question of unreasonableness can be approached in more than one way. A convenient partial equilibrium approach is to ask whether it is reasonable to reduce Japanese food prices, ceteris paribus, by opening its markets further to foreign suppliers. The answer, of course, should definitely be in the affirmative, which is why Japanese agricultural policy is deemed to be unreasonable. In this partial equilibrium context, there is no doubt about the unreasonableness of that policy as long as Japanese consumers could have enjoyed cheaper food prices and there were no countervailing losses to other parts of society to be concerned about. All that is left to debate is crammed into the clause ceteris paribus, a condition that is widely and safely assumed for classroom purposes but is by no means safe for actual policy analyses in the real world.

A general equilibrium approach is to ask how Japanese socioeconomic living conditions as a whole would have been had its agricultural policy been less protective over the past 10 or 20 years. The significance of this broader approach lies in the assumption that the interactions among different sectors of society cannot be overlooked in evaluating the long-term performances of policies of any kind. Some understandable reasons may be found for the apparent unreasonableness of protectionist measures if their contribution to other aspects of Japanese living are taken into consideration.

Table 6.1 compares eight socio-economic indicators of Japan against those of four other highly industrialized countries: United States, United Kingdom, West Germany, and France. For 1985, two basic economic indicators, per capita national income (in U.S. dollars) and Engel's coefficient (share of expenditures for foods in total household consumption expenditures) ranked Japan slightly below the United States but just among the three European countries.

For its relatively high level of income, Japanese per capita meat consumption is surprisingly low at less than a quarter of that of the United States. This may be, and to some extent is, related to the high price of beef due to the protective agricultural policy. In 1984, the nominal rate of protection, which reflected the gap between domestic and international prices of farm products, showed that Japan was the most protective among the five countries.

In spite of this high rate of protection, Japanese food self-sufficiency ratio is still the lowest, just slightly above 50 percent in terms of original energy. This shows how poorly endowed Japan is with respect to agricultural resources, especially farmland. In fact, Japan has only 0.045 hectares of farmland per person, less than one-tenth that of France and one-fiftieth that of the United States.

Japan stands out with respect to such indicators as crime rate, divorce rate, and income distribution. These figures confirm that Japan still has a very stable society when compared with the other highly industrialized countries. If Japan's social stability has any relationship with the protection that has maintained its rural farming communities, the

TABLE 6.1 Socioeconomic Indicators for Five Countries, 1985

	Japan	U.S.	UK	GFR	France
Per capita income ($)	8,851	13,349	6,023	7,904	7,031
Income distribution[a]	4.3	7.5	5.7	5.0	7.7
Engel's coefficient (%)	23	15	20	25	21
Per capita meat consumption (kgs)	28	117	74	100	109
Crime rate[b]	4.4	271.2	74.8	60.5	101.5
Divorce rate[c]	1.4	4.8	3.2	2.1	2.0
Nominal rate of agricultural protection[d]	102	6	15	49	25
Food self-sufficiency ratio[e] (%)	52	127	77	93	128

[a] Ratio of the share of the highest quintile income class in total personal income to the share of the lowest quintile class.
[b] Number of cases per 100,000 persons.
[c] Number of cases per 1,000 persons.
[d] Nominal rate of protection in 1984.
[e] In terms of original energy.

Sources: The Japanese Prime Minister's Office, *Statistical Yearbook of Japan* (1987), Japan MAFF, *Statistical Yearbook* (1987), Bank of Japan, *Economic Statistics Annual* (1987).

high food prices can, to some extent, be justified as the cost or sacrifice willingly paid by the Japanese people for such noneconomic benefits.

Three Decades of Changes in Japanese Agricultural Protection

Several quantitative indicators have been advanced to measure the degree of agricultural protection, such as nominal rate of protection (NRP), real rate of protection (RRP), producers' subsidy equivalent (PSE), and consumers' subsidy equivalent (CSE). With all these indicators, Japan is ranked among the most protective of OECD countries.[2] It is not my concern here to discuss whether Japanese agricultural policy is highly protective or not, nor is it to provide a more precise measurement of the degree of agricultural protection. There is not much left to be questioned about the protectiveness of Japanese agricultural policy as far as these numerical indicators are concerned.[3]

It is important, however, to understand how Japanese agricultural protection has changed over the past three decades. In Table 6.2, the major farm products are classed into four groups according to the mode of

TABLE 6.2 Changes in Japanese Agricultural Protection, 1960-1992

	PP	PU	UP	UU
1960	Rice, wheat & barley, potatoes for starch	fresh potatoes, meats (beef, pork, poultry), milk, eggs, fruits & fruit juice, sugar, vegetables, soybeans, feedgrains	—	—
1970	Rice, wheat & barley, potatoes for starch, manufacturing milk*	beef, pork, fruits & fruit juices	soybeans,* sugar*	poultry,* liquid milk,* eggs,* fresh potatoes,* vegetables,* feedgrains*
1980	Rice, wheat & barley, potatoes for starch, manufacturing milk	beef, oranges,* fruit juices*	soybeans, sugar	pork,*a poultry, liquid milk, eggs, feedgrains, fruits other than oranges,* fresh potatoes, vegetables
1990	— no change, all categories —			
1992	Rice, wheat & barley, potatoes for starch, manufacturing milk	—	soybeans, sugar, beef*b	pork, poultry liquid milk, eggs, feedgrains, fruit & fruit juices,* fresh potatoes, vegetables

* Changes from previous period.

a Although variable levies are applied to pork, the actual rates have not varied and instead have been fixed at a level that has not supported pork prices significantly above market levels.

b Tariffs fixed at sufficiently low levels that do not significantly distort domestic prices are ignored. In the case of beef, however, tariff rates will remain significantly high for the next three years (70% in 1991, 60% in 1992, and 50% in 1993) so that beef will remain substantially protected at the border. This scheme was designed as a temporary adjustment measure in the tariffication process.

Definitions: PP = Protected both at the border and within the country.
PU = Protected at the border but unprotected within the country.
UP = Unprotected at the border but protected within the country.
UU = Unprotected both at the border and within the country.

Source: Japan MAFF, *Statistical Yearbook* (1987).

government intervention in their respective markets. The first group, denoted PP, includes products that are protected both at the border and within the country. The second group, PU, includes products protected at the border but not domestically. The third group, UP, is unprotected at the border but protected within the country. The last group, UU, is not protected at all—at the border or within the country.

There is a wide range of protective measures in agricultural policy—strong and weak, direct and indirect, etc. But here, protection refers only to the strong and direct government interventions that support producer prices definitely above market equilibrium levels. Price stabilization measures are not included. At the border, protection means only import quotas and variable levies. Tariffs are not included for the following reasons: In principle, the specific distorting effects of tariffs on the operating production and marketing levels are indirect in terms of their actual extent, timing, and place. Also, although tariffs are widely used, the rates are relatively low except in the case of beef, which is subject to gradual decline. The inclusion of tariffs would blur the focus on the strong and direct forms of agricultural protection.[4] Within the country, protection means deficiency payment schemes and direct government purchases at politically determined guaranteed prices.

In 1960, all the major farm products were protected at the border, as shown at the top of Table 6.2. Domestic protection covered only three types of products: rice, wheat and barley, and potatoes (including sweet potatoes) for starch. Rice and wheat were under the strict regulation of the Food Control Act dating back to 1942 during the war and were exclusively purchased and distributed by the Food Control Agency. They have been under the regulation and protection of the same act up until now. Potatoes for starch have been protected by deficiency payments since 1953.

In the 1960s rice was (and to a lesser extent still is) by far the most important of all farm products to producers and consumers. It was grown by substantially all the farmers at that time, accounting for almost 50 percent of the total agricultural produce, and it provided consumers with nearly 50 percent of their total energy intake. The wheat and barley category was the second most important, especially as a winter crop. Potatoes were also important as an energy crop, and government intervention originated from wartime food shortages. But, deficiency payments were introduced when food supply became relatively abundant and the potato producers faced a sharp decline in prices. From their standpoint, potatoes were important local products in the upland crop areas where rice farming was difficult because of water shortage.

Over the next 10 years, to 1970, Japan opened its food markets to a very substantial extent. Only seven major products were left under import quotas. A deficiency payment scheme for soybeans and a guarantee price scheme for sugar were introduced to protect domestic producers who lost border protection measures for their crops. However, no such compensatory scheme was introduced for the other six products, even though they were also deprived of border protection. Border protection measures were maintained for manufacturing milk, beef, pork, and fruit because these sectors were considered to be infant industries. Although these products were relatively unimportant at that time in terms of total production and consumption, domestic demands were expected to sharply increase and induce rapid developments on the supply side.[5]

The markets for soybeans and sugar were liberalized, since they were not expected to be competitive against foreign supplies even in the future. Counterbalancing domestic measures were introduced for them, because soybeans were widely grown by farmers all over Japan, and sugar beets in Hokkaido and sugarcane in Okinawa were important local products. The import of feedgrains was liberalized without any compensatory measures, since there was no significant domestic production at that time, and there was little doubt as to the lack of future potential of these highly land-intensive crops.

The markets for poultry, liquid milk, eggs, fresh potatoes, and vegetables were also opened to imports without introducing any domestic protection measures. These products were already considered to be competitive or under some innate natural protection against overseas supplies. The introduction of a deficiency payment scheme for manufacturing milk in 1965 was a remarkable change in domestic policy. It was introduced not as a compensation for the loss of border protection but for the promotion of the dairy industry, which was in the throes of a takeoff. Although it started as a temporary measure for protecting what was seen as an infant industry at that time, the Japanese dairy industry is still under the same protective scheme today, 25 years later.

Over the following 10 years, Japanese food markets were opened for two more major product categories: pork and fresh fruits (except oranges). This time no new domestic countermeasures were introduced as far as strong support measures are concerned.

No substantial change was made during the next decade, to 1990. The classification table remained unaltered. However, import quotas are scheduled to be removed for three major products by 1992— beef, oranges, and fruit juices. After that, the only products that will remain under quotas will be rice, wheat and barley, manufacturing milk, and potatoes for starch. All these are also under domestic protection. A deficiency payments scheme is designed for the beef industry (feeder calf program) to compensate for the damages from losing border protection, but no such program is expected for the domestic fruit growers. Then no item will be left in the PU group, and the 1992 pattern will be as shown at the bottom of Table 6.2.

It is difficult to say anything more about the prospects of liberalization at this time, because that would depend upon the outcome of the Uruguay Round. But it is most probable that further liberalization will be accompanied by some sort of compensatory domestic protective scheme, especially deficiency payments. All four major products left with border protection—rice, wheat and barley, manufacturing milk, and potatoes for starch—are already heavily protected domestically. Rice and wheat are still under the Food Control Act and are purchased directly by the government at support prices several times higher than the world market price. Manufacturing milk and potatoes for starch are under deficiency payment schemes. Also, rice and milk have been suffering from overproduction and fettered by production quotas for more than 10 years. So it seems very unlikely that the Japanese government will open the markets for the remaining products under border and domestic protection (PP) without introducing some further form of domestic support measures.

Tables 6.3 and 6.4 show the trends in the shares of the above four groups in total supply (production and imports) at fixed 1960 values and at current values, respectively. Agricultural protection was significantly reduced in the decade between 1960 and 1970, and to some extent in the next decade to 1980. However, it remained almost unchanged after 1980. At current values, slightly more than half of agricultural supply will be traded without some form of intervention in 1992, after the liberalization of beef, oranges, and fruit juices. At 1960 values, however, about 70 percent will still be under protection in one way or another. The difference between these two results reflects the decline in the share of protected products, especially rice, in the total food supply.

Trends in the Price Gaps Between Domestic and World Markets

As is well known, Japanese food prices are now among the highest in the world. This section focuses on the past trends of price gaps between Japan and United States for the four major food items that have invariably remained under protection both at the border and within the country. U.S. prices are taken as the comparative basis because they are considered to represent the world market prices.

Table 6.5 shows the ratios of Japanese producer prices (in U.S. dollar terms) to American producer prices for wheat, rice, beef, and milk. The trends in the ratios are more significant than the absolute levels, because prices are not adjusted for quality differences. First, it is remarkable that no significant price gap existed between the two countries in 1955 when Japan was just starting on its long and continuous period of

TABLE 6.3 Shares of Major Farm Products Grouped by Mode of Protection in Total Agricultural Supply at 1960 Fixed Values

	PP	PU	UP	UU
1960	62.2	37.8	0.0	0.0
1970	63.6	11.2	4.2	20.8
1980	63.6	4.1	4.2	27.9
1990	63.6	4.1	5.4	27.9
1992	63.6	0.0	6.2	30.2

Note: See Table 6.2 for definitions.

Source: Japan MAFF, *Statistical Yearbook* (various years).

TABLE 6.4 Shares of Major Farm Products Grouped by Mode of Protection in Total Agricultural Supply at Current Prices

	PP	PU	UP	UU
1960	62.2	37.8	0.0	0.0
1970	46.1	10.7	5.4	37.8
1980	41.1	6.7	5.4	46.8
1990	40.1	8.3	4.1	47.5
1992	40.1	0.0	9.7	50.2

Note: See Table 6.2 for definitions.

Source: Japan MAFF, *Statistical Yearbook* (various years).

TABLE 6.5 Japan/U.S. Price Ratios (U.S. = 1.00)

	Wheat	Rice	Beef	Milk
1955	1.30	1.37	0.94	0.83
1960	1.51	1.50	0.85	0.76
1965	1.98	2.17	1.41	1.04
1970	2.16	2.62	1.86	1.03
1975	2.55	3.52	2.92	1.58
1980	6.06	3.99	3.80	1.70
1985	5.68	4.61	4.08	1.75
1988	8.22	6.88	6.13	2.59
1989	7.38	6.40	5.54	2.13

Notes: Quality differences are not taken into consideration.
Prices for wheat and rice are support prices in both countries.
Price of beef is for *Wagyu* steers and U.S. choice.
Price of milk is average price received by producers in Japan and all milk wholesale price in the United States.

Sources: Japan MAFF, *Statistical Yearbook* (various years), USDA, *Agricultural Statistics* (various years).

rapid economic growth. Even Wagyu beef, which now costs several times more than U.S. choice beef, could be purchased at a lower price than that of American steers. The price ratios rose uniformly during the 35 years since then, with the only exception being between 1988 and 1989. In part, this may reflect the detrimental effects of government intervention that curbs competitive incentives towards productivity increase on the side of Japan. However, it is also natural to assume some intrinsic factors behind this long-term trend.

Table 6.6 shows the decomposition of the changes in the price ratios for rice into three factors, namely, changes in Japanese price in terms of yen, changes in the U.S. price in terms of dollars, and changes in the yen-dollar exchange rate. For the first decade, 1960-1970, the relative rise in price was dominated by the rise in Japanese price, which was only slightly affected by the rise in U.S. price. The exchange rate did not play any role, because it was fixed at 360 yen to a dollar. Over the next five years, 1970-1975, the rise in Japanese price was still the most important factor. Although the rise in U.S. price accounted for a more significant portion, the ratio increased by an average of 6 percent per year, boosted by the appreciation of the yen.

Over the next five years to 1980, the rapid increase in the U.S. price was almost fully canceled by the appreciation of the yen, and the ratio rose by as much as the rise in the Japanese price. During 1980 to 1985, the ratio rose by 2.9 percent a year, of which nearly half was attributed to the rise in Japanese price and the other half to the fall in

TABLE 6.6 Factors in the Rise of Japanese Rice Price Relative to U.S. Price

	Price Ratio	P_{JP}	P_{US}	E/R
1960-65	7.8	9.5	1.6	0.0
1965-70	3.9	4.8	1.0	0.0
1970-75	6.0	13.5	10.5	3.2
1975-80	2.6	2.9	8.3	7.9
1980-85	2.9	1.1	-1.4	0.3
1985-88	14.3	-3.6	-2.1	13.7

Notes: All variables represent the average annual rate of change (%).
Price Ratio = P_{JP}/P_{US}.
P_{JP} = Japanese rice price (government purchase price).
P_{US} = U.S. rice price (target price).
E/R = Exchange rate (yen/$).

Sources: The Japanese Prime Minister's Office, *Statistical Yearbook of Japan* (various years), Japan MAFF, *Statistical Yearbook* (various years), Bank of Japan, *Economic Statistics Annual* (various years).

U.S. price. The most significant rise in the ratio occurred in the three years to 1988, which was almost exclusively accounted for by the steep appreciation of the yen.

In sum, the Japanese rice price rose against the U.S. price due to the rise in its own level during the period between 1955 and 1975, but after that, most of the rise was due to the appreciation of the yen. While the U.S. rice price rose by 27 percent from 1975 through 1989, the Japanese price in its own currency rose by only 8 percent. The Japanese price in terms of U.S. dollars, however, rose by 30 percent during the same period.

With reference to the factors that account for changes in the Japanese rice price in terms of yen, Table 6.7 provides a decomposition for the domestic price similar to that for price ratios in Table 6.6. Here, the changes in price are attributed to changes in wage rates, labor productivity, and relative share of labor costs in the total cost of production. All through the period between 1960 and 1988, labor productivity in the Japanese rice industry kept rising at the fairly high rates of 4 to 5 percent per year. Up until 1981, however, all the gains in labor productivity were undermined by the far more rapid rise in wage rates. Even when the productivity of labor was rising at an annual average rate of 9.3 percent in the five years to 1975, it could not bring about a decline in price because of the even higher rise in wage rate, 17.9 percent per year. The rise in wage rate can be attributed to various factors, but no doubt the most important was the galloping expansion of the manufacturing industries. Since 1980, labor productivity increased faster than wages, which rose only moderately with the approaching maturity of the Japanese economy.

Table 6.8 presents data on the future potential for increase in labor productivity and consequential fall in product price in the Japanese rice industry. In Japan, rice is produced on two types of farms. Type A farm is operated by a family with at least one adult male member who is fully engaged in farming. Type B farm is operated by a family that has no adult male full-time worker and lives mainly on incomes from off-farm sources. The average size of Type A farms is 3.45 hectares, fairly large by Japanese standards, while that of Type B farms is less than 1 hectare. Labor productivity differs greatly between these two types of farms, 100 to 41.

The major portion of total rice output is produced on the small and inefficient Type B farms. If this structure was reversed to make Type A farms produce most of the domestic rice, the average labor productivity would increase substantially. Such a structural change would certainly reduce the average cost of production, and consequently lower the price of rice. The welfare of Type B farmers would not suffer much from losing

TABLE 6.7 Factors in the Changes of the Japanese Rice Price in Yen

	Producers' Average Price	Wage Rate	Labor Productivity	Labor Share of Total Cost
1960-65	9.7	16.7	4.0	2.3
1965-70	5.1	11.9	5.6	0.9
1970-75	13.1	17.9	9.3	-5.2
1975-80	2.9	13.1	3.3	6.4
1980-85	1.0	3.8	4.7	-1.9
1985-88	-2.2	2.5	3.9	0.9

Note: All variables are shown in terms of average annual rate of change (%).
Source: Japan MAFF, *Costs of Production Survey (Rice)* (various years).

TABLE 6.8 Two Types of Farmers in Japan, 1988

	Type A	Type B
Share of Total Production (%)	24.4	75.6
Average Size of Farm (hectare)	3.45	0.86
Labor Productivity Gap	100	41
Household Income Gap	100	118
Share of Agricultural Income in Total Farm Income (%)	65.9	6.5

Notes: Total production and labor productivity with reference to rice. Size of farm covers all farmland.
Source: Japan MAFF, *Farm Household Economy Survey (1988)*.

their rice production. At present, their per capita household income exceeds that of Type A farmers by nearly 20 percent. If the Type B farmers were to lose all their farming activities, the income loss would amount to only 6.5 percent of their total income. Considering these factors, it can be safely said that the present structure of rice farming in Japan is highly irrational and needs to be reformed without any serious external consequences.

The policy basis for the existing inefficient structure of the rice industry is the Food Control Scheme, dating back from wartime. The repeal, or at least the announcement of repeal after a lapse of time for adjustment, of this out-of-date scheme should be the first goal of structural reform. However, the necessary structural change is by no means easy to accomplish. Apart from social and political impediments, it requires the transfer of a huge number of tiny farmland plots currently possessed by millions of part-time farmers into the hands of a relatively small number of full-time farmers. In any case, it is possible, at least technically, to reduce the Japanese price of rice substantially through structural improvements.[6]

Thus, it is expected that in the coming years the domestic price of rice in yen will fall at a moderate rate. Whether it will fall against the world price depends almost entirely upon the future movement of exchange rate. If the yen continues to appreciate at the rapid rate it did in 1985 to 1988, it would be beyond the scope of possible productivity growth to reduce the Japanese price of rice in terms of U.S. dollars. In any case, it will take a long time to restore the competitiveness of Japanese rice farming in the world market.

Domestic Forces for and Against Protection

There is a fairly large amount of room for the reduction of the domestic prices of rice and other major farm products of Japan that are currently under government protection without reducing the level of production. This can be achieved through gradual but steady cuts of support prices over several years. The Food Control Scheme with its strong and unnecessary interventionist measures should be repealed after a certain transition period. In this way, the nominal rate of agricultural protection (NRP) in Japan, in terms of price gaps, can be reduced considerably.

There are limits, however, to such prospects. It is highly unlikely that the price gaps can be reduced to zero in the foreseeable future without seriously damaging domestic production. This means that the price gaps consist of two parts, one that can be safely removed without damaging production and another that cannot. The protectionist measures responsible for the part that can be safely removed are certainly unreasonable. Such measures can hardly be justified from any point of view, and there is no doubt that Japanese food prices are unreasonably high as long as this part of the gap continues.

The second part of the price gap is, on the other hand, necessary for the maintenance of domestic farming and rural communities. It cannot be justified from a purely market economic standpoint, but it may still be justified on some other, nonmarket, considerations. With respect to this part of the price gap, Japan faces an alternative choice of whether to reduce the level of protection at the cost of losing a part of its domestic farming or to maintain it at the cost of high food prices. This is a kind of trade-off problem, so it is natural that some domestic forces support the reduction of agricultural protection while others are against it. This section examines such forces and underlying factors.[7] Apparently, there are two major forces that can benefit from the reduction of agricultural protection: the domestic consumers seeking cheaper foods and the foreign producers seeking larger export markets. The problem of the foreign producers is not fully discussed here, except to note that they may find their allies among Japanese industrial exporters who are afraid of the world markets for industrial products becoming more restrictive.

There are two domestic forces against the further reduction in agricultural protection. One is, of course, the producers. The other is the people who find their reasons in two factors: food security and the extra-market values of farming and rural communities. The extra-market values here relate mainly to environmental quality considerations and to social stability.[8]

Consumers in Japan quite naturally prefer cheaper foods, just as their counterparts do in other countries. But, as opinion polls show, they are rather hesitant about the further opening of Japanese food markets to foreign producers.[9] So, the question to be addressed here is why Japanese consumers do not bother much about food prices that appear to be unreasonable by American or European standards. The question can, in part, be answered by the data presented in Table 6.9. What the data show is that Japanese consumers have had a remarkable improvement in their living conditions over the past 30 years. Their per capita income is now higher than that of their American counterparts. This is more than a satisfactory result, considering that it was less than 20 percent of the American level in 1960.

Per capita meat consumption is still very low by Western standards, as shown in Table 6.1. The rate of increase, however, has been quite satisfactory. The average Japanese consumer, who used to buy only 5.2 kg of meat a year in 1960, can now afford to buy about 30 kg, five times as much.

Engel's coefficient has declined from 41.6 percent in 1960 to 25.5 percent in 1988, close to the European level, even with food prices as high as they have been in Japan. Housing conditions, represented by the number of dwelling rooms per house, have also improved steadily.

What this all means is that Japanese consumers are quite satisfied with their present living conditions. They live in the best economic conditions that they have ever experienced. They are not fussy about food prices, because they can afford to buy more foods, better in quality and richer in variety, than ever in the past without paying much attention to the impacts on their purses. It is by no means an urgent matter for the average Japanese to cut his or her food expenditures by buying cheaper items from abroad. It is quite natural for Japanese consumers to evaluate their present living conditions relative to a standard based upon their past experiences.

TABLE 6.9 Changes in Japanese Living Conditions

	Per Capita Income (U.S. = 100)	Engel's Coefficient (percent)	Per Capita Meat Consumption (kgs)	Number of Dwelling Rooms per House
1960	16.4	41.6	5.2	3.60
1970	40.4	34.1	13.4	3.84
1980	77.6	29.0	22.5	4.52
1985	66.3	27.0	25.1	4.73
1988	115.4	25.5	28.2	4.80

Sources: The Japanese Prime Minister's Office, *Statistical Yearbook of Japan* (various years), Japan MAFF, *Statistical Yearbook* (various years), Bank of Japan, E*conomic Statistics Annual* (various years).

Thus, at the moment, they pay more attention to the noneconomic aspects of agriculture and agricultural protection than the price of foods. They recognize two positive roles of agricultural protection: food security and the maintenance of rural communities. Much has been said about food security, so only one point needs to be repeated for emphasis. This concerns the geo-political conditions of Japan, which are quite different from those of the Western countries. Japan is a small island nation confronting two communist superpowers, China and the Soviet Union, far away from most of its democratic allies. Thus, it is no wonder that the Japanese are much more sensitive about the issues of food security than the Western nations. For the majority of Japanese, food security will not lose its significance until these two superpowers become its reliable allies both politically and economically.

Turning to the issue of maintaining rural communities, Japan still has a very stable society for its high degree of industrialization. This was, in part, shown by the low crime and divorce rates for the nation as a whole (Table 6.1). Whether this social stability is related to the preservation of farming and rural communities is a difficult question to settle. Indeed, there is insufficient evidence, and it is almost impossible to argue for or against such a relationship with the evidence at hand.

Nevertheless, differential rural-urban social indicators may shed some light on the issue. Table 6.10 shows that crime rates and divorce rates are both significantly lower in the rural areas of Japan than in the largest two cities. This is no more than very fragmental evidence, but it still suggests that rural communities contribute to social stability. Generally speaking, the rural communities represent stable and conservative aspects of a society while cities represent dynamic and progressive sides. The low mobility or the sluggish attitudes toward changes in culture and way of life is a rural characteristic. By contrast, cities

TABLE 6.10 Two Social Indicators for Tokyo, Osaka, and the Rest of Japan

	Crime Rate (per 100,000 persons)		Divorce Rate (per 1,000 persons)	
	1970	1985	1970	1985
Tokyo	17.9	19.3	12.4	15.1
Osaka	13.0	18.5	12.2	16.5
Rest of Japan	10.0	12.1	10.3	13.3

Source: The Japanese Prime Minister's Office, *Statistical Yearbook of Japan* (various years).

are characterized by high mobility and innovations. Whether to prefer traditions or to prefer innovations is, to some extent, a matter of value judgment which by nature should belong to individuals. But still it should be a kind of golden rule for any society to find a good balance between the two extremes.

Considering the very rapid and more than satisfactory improvement in the economic conditions of Japan, it is quite reasonable that Japanese consumers are much more sensitive to the possible deterioration to their society than to a little more amelioration in their economy. They are rather reluctant towards the further opening of their food markets, for they feel uneasy about the uncertain impacts on their rural communities.

Agricultural producers in Japan prefer protection, just as farmers do everywhere in the world. Two points are worth noting here. First, in Japan almost all farmers are organized into a single body of agricultural cooperatives, which have a national federation for political activities. Their political demands are most strongly represented. Second, the agricultural cooperatives and their federations at the national and prefectural levels have long been benefiting from the present schemes of agricultural protection, especially from the Food Control Act dating from 1942.

It is only natural that the political parties in Japan are all reluctant to reduce or eliminate agricultural protection when consumers are rather indifferent about food prices whereas producers are highly organized politically to resist price reductions. Thus, in Japan all the major political parties are in support of agricultural protection. Especially, the Japan Socialist Party, which is the largest opposition to the ruling Liberal Democratic Party, is the most protective and interventionist in its agricultural policy.[10]

Conclusion

For the foreseeable future, it will be difficult for operators in the major agricultural sectors in Japan to restore their competitive advantage against foreign suppliers. During the period 1960 to 1975, the rapid rise in industrial wage rates eroded their competitiveness. This was aggravated over the next 15 years by the rapid appreciation in exchange rates. Now, it seems that the time to recover some of that lost competitiveness has come, but it will take a long and arduous effort to narrow the existing gaps between domestic and world prices. Moreover, a lot will depend upon the future course of currency exchange rate changes.

Even after several rounds of liberalization, most of the farm products that are still protected at the border are also heavily protected within the domestic markets. Indeed, there is considerable room for the reduction of the price support levels through the removal of domestic measures of protection. The existing price gaps between domestic and world markets can be narrowed to a considerable extent without damaging domestic production and rural communities. But a part of the gap will inevitably remain, even after structural improvements take place on the largest possible scale. So a significant level of protection in one form or another will be necessary for the survival of the farm and the rural communities in Japan.

Consumers, at least for the present, do not regard high food prices as a serious problem. Rather, they are more concerned with the issues of food security and the probable negative effects of losing rural communities on environments and social stability in the long run. This attitude of Japanese consumers to the farm problem is rooted in the fact that they are quite satisfied with the performance of their economy over the past three decades. They now seek to improve the quality of life with something more than just income valued in market terms.

The asymmetry in attitudes toward reducing food prices between rather skeptical consumers and very vulnerable producers makes all the major political parties in Japan conservative regarding agricultural policies. Among them, the Japan Socialist Party—the largest opposition party—is the most protective.

Japanese agricultural policy is a joint product of these socio-political factors.[11] Certainly, it is distorted by the political lobbying of producer and other interest groups, but it should not be regarded as an irrational or unreasonable policy that has no sound basis in the behavior of Japanese consumers. Were it not for such reasons, agricultural protection could not have survived for such a long time.

To conclude: from the domestic point of view, the most important factor in reforming agricultural policy in Japan is the consumers' strong demand for a better quality of life. While better quality of life means many things, security and stability are among the most important elements. To maintain domestic farming and rural communities is reasonable as far as it contributes to food security and social stability. Japanese consumers are ready to pay the necessary cost for them.

In Japan, domestic farming needs protection, which inevitably collides with the general rule of free trade. This is a collision between domestic and international interests, and the solution can be found in nothing but a reasonable compromise between the two.

Notes

1. See Gale Johnson (ed., 1987) and Yujiro Hayami (1988). See also ABARE (1988), which is the most comprehensive book available in English on the present state of Japanese agricultural policy.
2. See OECD (1987) and Hayami and Homma (1986).
3. With regard to the policy implications of these indicators, I have earlier questioned and cautioned against the forming or reforming of agricultural policy on the basis of any single numerical element, whatever it may be (Egaitsu, 1987).
4. This focus on strong and direct forms of government interventions draws attention to the kinds of non-tariff barriers that support prices at significantly higher levels than what could otherwise be considered as market equilibrium.
5. According to government projections published in 1962, domestic demands for beef and pork were expected to triple, and for fruit double over the following ten years.
6. Projections by the Ministry of Agriculture, Forestry, and Fisheries of Japan expect the costs of production to be reduced by 30 to 50 percent for rice, by 40 to 60 percent for wheat, and by 40 to 50 percent for soybeans through the structural improvement measures.
7. See Kenzo Hemmi (1982).
8. See Fumio Egaitsu (1987).
9. See the *Opinions on Foods and Agriculture* (in Japanese). The Prime Minister's Office, 1989.
10. Recently, the Japan Socialist Party proposed to double the self-sufficiency ratio of foods in terms of grains in its New Farm Policy.
11. An interesting quantitative analysis on the dynamics of agricultural policy adjustments for the Korean rice case is found in Kwon and Yamauchi (1989).

References

Australian Bureau of Agricultural and Resource Economics (ABARE). 1988. *Japanese Agricultural Policies.*
Bank of Japan. Various years. *Economic Statistics Annual.*

Egaitsu, Fumio. 1987. "A Plan for Removing Production Quotas." *Japan Echo*, Vol. XIV, No. 1.
Hayami, Yujiro, and Masayoshi Homma. 1986. "Structure of Agricultural Protection in Industrial Countries." *Journal of International Economics*, 20.
Hayami, Yujiro. 1988. *Japanese Agriculture Under Siege*. London: Macmillan.
Hemmi, Kenzo. 1982. "Agriculture and Politics in Japan." Emery Castle and Kenzo Hemmi (eds). *U.S.-Japanese Agricultural Trade Relations*. Resources for the Future/Johns Hopkins University Press.
Japan Ministry of Agriculture, Forestry & Fisheries (MAFF). 1988. *Farm Household Economy Survey*.
Japan Ministry of Agriculture, Forestry & Fisheries (MAFF). Various years. *Statistical Yearbook*.
Japan Ministry of Agriculture, Forestry & Fisheries (MAFF). Various years. *Cost of Production Survey (Rice)*.
Johnson, Gale (ed). 1987. *Agricultural Reform Effects in the United States and Japan*. New York University Press.
Kwon, Yong Dae, and Hiroshi Yamauchi. 1989. "Agricultural Policy Adjustments in East Asia: The Korean Rice Economy." International Agricultural Trade Research Consortium (IATRC) Working Paper No. 89-9.
Organization for Economic Cooperation and Development. 1987. *National Policies and Agricultural Trade*.
The Japanese Prime Minister's Office. 1989. *Opinions on Foods and Agriculture* (in Japanese).
The Japanese Prime Minister's Office. 1989. *Statistical Yearbook of Japan*, various years.
USDA, *Agriculture Statistics*, various years.

7

Japanese Agriculture in the 1990s: An American Perspective

Alan J. Webb and William T. Coyle[1]

Introduction

Japan faces a restructuring of its agricultural sector in the next decade. To some extent, the changes that take place will be the result of policy changes that have already been initiated, such as the liberalization of beef and citrus imports. But to a much larger extent, this restructuring will be the culmination of powerful demographic and economic forces that have been under way in all the major developed countries over the past three decades. Although these changes are inevitable, the shape of the agricultural sector will depend on the future Japanese policy response.

Current Japanese agricultural policies arise out of a concern for adequate food supplies. Japan has stimulated domestic production of food staples by providing high support to producers. This has meant high food prices for consumers. As national income has increased over the past three decades, producer prices have been raised in an attempt to maintain income parity between the rural and urban sectors.

The evolution of Japanese policy thus fits well into the paradigm of Anderson and others who argue that the level of support for agriculture is directly related to a country's level of development. Two well-known scholars of Japanese agricultural policy—Yujiro Hayami and Fumio Egaitsu—recognize this policy evolution in their historical discussion of Japanese policy formation. Hayami (1988) identifies three periods:

1. A period of overcoming the food problem from the beginning of the Meiji Restoration to the end of the First World War
2. A period of rural poverty from WWI to the early 1950s

3. The period of the agricultural adjustment problem from roughly 1960 to the present

Egaitsu (1982) takes a shorter historical perspective but concludes, like Hayami, that the primary objective of current Japanese agricultural policy is to facilitate structural adjustment.

The underlying implications are clear in the writings of both authors. The primary concern of Japanese agricultural policy has shifted from one of merely improving the income of the rural sector to one of trying to improve its competitiveness. For Japan, agricultural sector competitiveness should not be viewed in the context of the international market but in the context of the domestic demands for labor, capital, and land and water resources. Despite high price supports and trade barriers, labor resources have continued to flow out of the agricultural sector over the past three decades. Policy and institutional barriers in Japan have prevented the consolidation of land resources, and this has inhibited the adjustments in scale that have allowed the farming operations in other developed countries to compete for labor and management resources with the industrial and service sectors.

We argue in this paper that Japan has now entered a fourth era in its agricultural policy evolution in which it will finally have to come to grips with the structural adjustment problem. High price supports have stifled the effect of reforms designed to improve the efficiency of the sector and have done little to improve farm income or abate the flow of young people to urban job opportunities. This is an era in which government price supports will be reduced, forcing Japanese agriculture to become more competitive with other sectors of the economy. In the process, agriculture will become more open to the world market. New policy instruments may emerge that will directly target the social and environmental problems associated with a rapidly changing society. The policy issue for Japan is whether to use the opportunity offered by the GATT Uruguay Round negotiations to liberalize trade—and in the process provide adjustment mechanisms for a smooth transition to a more viable agricultural sector—or to ignore these changes and wait until circumstances force a larger, more rapid adjustment. We base our arguments on two sets of observations.

First, current policies will lead to growing conflict within the Japanese agricultural sector itself. As a result, producers themselves will become disillusioned with the policy. Second, there are already signs of eroding political support for agricultural protection. The younger generation has very weak ties to agriculture, and even those with links to the sector through part-time farming have a larger interest in national tax policies and the state of the economy than they do in farm price supports. Anderson has alluded to this in his paper and we will extend his arguments and apply them to Japan.

Before we develop the reasoning behind each of these two observations, we will briefly review the current structure of Japanese agriculture and provide our interpretation on how it has evolved. Egaitsu has already covered some of this ground, but we wish to reemphasize some of the points that bear on our subsequent remarks. The final section will discuss some broad policy alternatives for Japan and their implications for the future evolution of the Japanese agricultural sector and how this will ultimately affect Pacific Rim agricultural trade.

Structural Characteristics of Japanese Agriculture

The current structure of agriculture in Japan is the direct result of rapid economic growth in an agricultural policy environment shaped by two major policy sets—a land policy set and an income support policy set. Rapid economic growth has been the hallmark of postwar Japan. Between 1965 and 1988, Japan's gross domestic product (GDP) increased 30-fold, compared with a 7-fold increase for the United States and a 10-fold increase for the Federal Republic of Germany (*World Bank*, p. 183). This remarkable period of sustained economic growth has wrought massive changes in the Japanese economy. The agricultural sector, despite attempts to shield it from these changes, has been greatly affected by this transformation of the Japanese economy. Agriculture has declined from 9 percent to 3 percent of Japan's GDP over the past 25 years, and the percentage of the labor force in agriculture has fallen from 26 percent to 11 percent in the same period.

The Policy Set

The decline in agriculture's role in the overall economy is no different from the changes that have occurred in the United States and other developed countries since the end of World War II. The unique elements in the Japanese experience are the speed at which change has occurred and the way two key policy sets—the Agricultural Land Law of 1952 and the Agricultural Basic Law of 1961—have shaped adjustments within the agricultural sector.

Agricultural Land Law of 1952. The Agricultural Land Law "imposed a limit on landholding to 3 hectares (12 hectares in Hokkaido) in order to prevent the revival of landlordism" (Hayami, 1985). The major significance of the law—apart from its effect on the distribution of wealth—was to create a major institutional barrier to the consolidation of landholdings. This prevented an increase in farm size. Over the past three decades, the average size of farms cultivated by farm households in Japan has remained virtually unchanged, compared with a 50 percent increase in average farm size in the United States and a 33 percent increase in the European Community over the same period (Figure 7.1).

Increasing the size of the farm enterprise is one of the ways farmers can maintain incomes comparable with opportunities in an expanding nonfarm sector. The Agricultural Land Law foreclosed this as an option. Although the institutional impediment to ownership of farms larger than 3 hectares was removed when the Land Law was amended in 1962, economic forces prevented consolidation. Rapidly increasing land prices driven by demand for nonagricultural uses reduced the agricultural returns to farmland from 7 percent in 1960 to 2 percent by 1975 and 0.6 percent by 1980 (Hayami, 1988). The purchase of land for agricultural uses was not economically viable.

Land leasing was not an option for expanding the size of farm enterprises, because the 1962 amendment of the Land Law did not relax the regulations on tenancy contracts (Hayami, 1988). Revisions to the Land Law in 1970, 1975, and 1980 have eased the restrictions on tenancy contracts but land leasing is still very limited in Japan. The history of strong legal rights for tenants since World War II has made potential landlords reluctant to lease their land for fear of losing control of it.

The Agricultural Basic Law of 1961. The Agricultural Basic Law was enacted to reduce the disparity in living standards between agriculture and the rest of the economy. A primary objective of the law was to increase farm income by improving productivity. The output of commodities whose demand was expected to expand was to be encouraged. Farm size was to be increased, and the marketing and processing of agricultural products and inputs was to be improved.

Despite the attempt to achieve higher farm income through improved productivity, the thrust of Japanese policy from 1961 to the early 1980s has been to encourage the production of all commodities with price supports and import restrictions. One estimate found that 80 percent of Japan's agricultural output was covered by pricing policies in 1982 (Konosu, 1982). Rice has been the focus of political lobbying and has received the most support based on estimates of total government transfers (Webb et al., 1990), even though, as will be discussed below, the demand for rice has been in steady decline for almost 30 years.

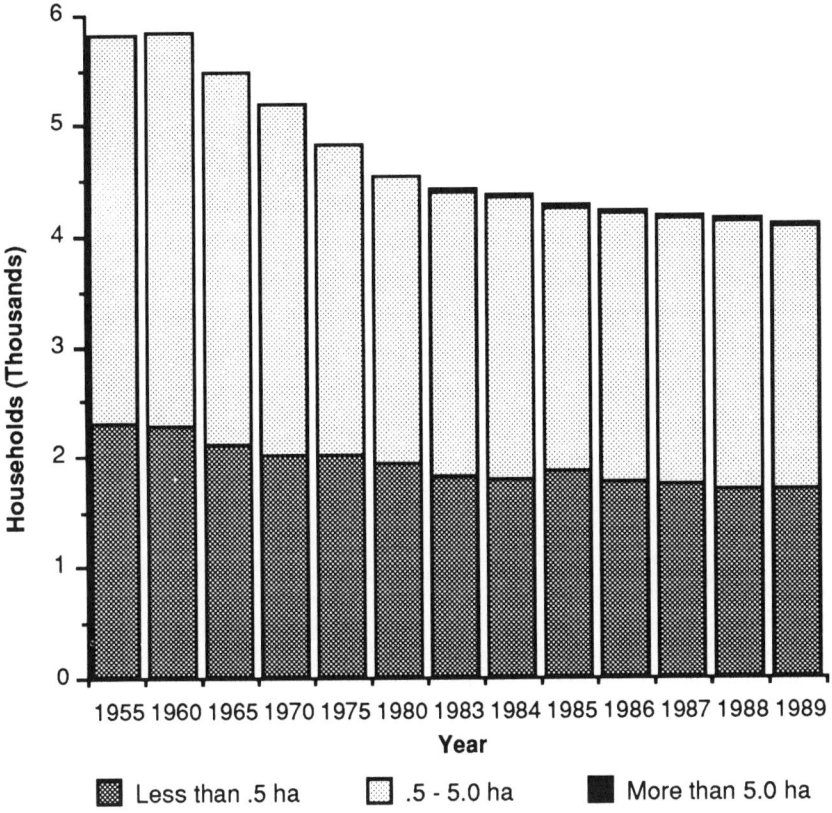

FIGURE 7.1 Distribution of Households by Farm Size

Structural Characteristics

With the increase of farm size ruled out by institutional and economic barriers, adjustment of the agricultural sector to the rapid expansion of the national economy had to occur elsewhere. The proximity of good employment opportunities in major agricultural areas, combined with the government policy to increase productivity, made part-time farming an attractive option for many farm households. Figure 7.2 shows the division of farm household income between farm and off-farm sources. Despite high support prices, income from farming has declined slightly over time, while income from nonfarm sources has risen sharply.

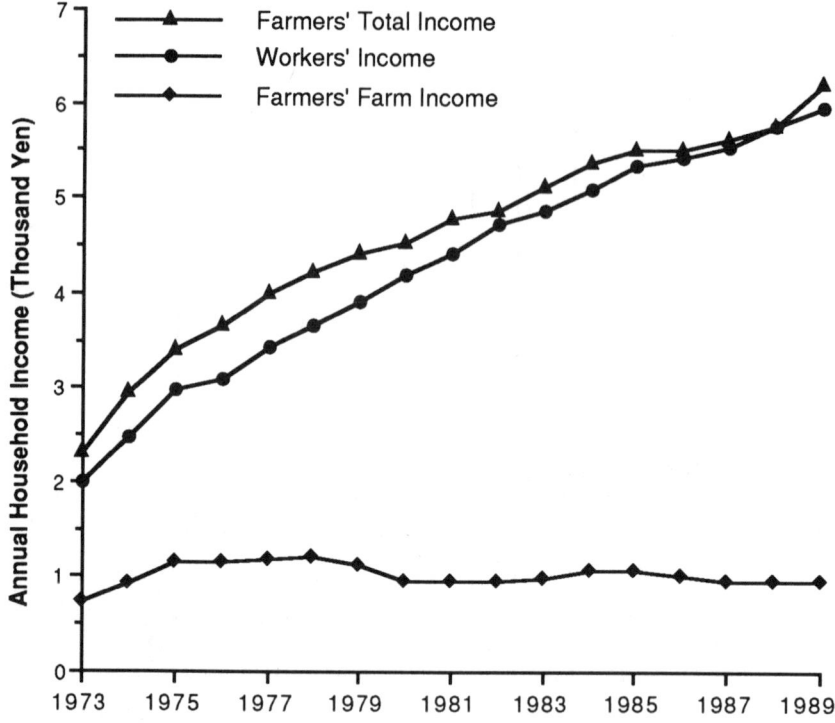

FIGURE 7.2 Farm Household Income from Farm and Off-farm Sources Compared with Workers' Household Income

The change in the sources of farm household income has been accompanied by a change in the composition of the farm work force. Better opportunities in the industrial and service sectors have drawn off a large numbers of workers—particularly those between 16 and 60 years of age (Figure 7.3). The number of both male and female workers over 60 has remained virtually unchanged since 1960. Hence, in 1989 elderly workers account for 42 percent of the farm work force primarily engaged in farming as compared with only 14 percent in 1960.

Rice is the single most important crop in Japan as a source of farm income (Figure 7.4). It has many advantages for an aging part-time farm work force. The small plots require sporadic care, and high price supports make it a worthwhile part-time activity. But a changing consumption pattern has reduced the importance of rice in the Japanese diet. Consequently, rice receipts as a percentage of total farm receipts

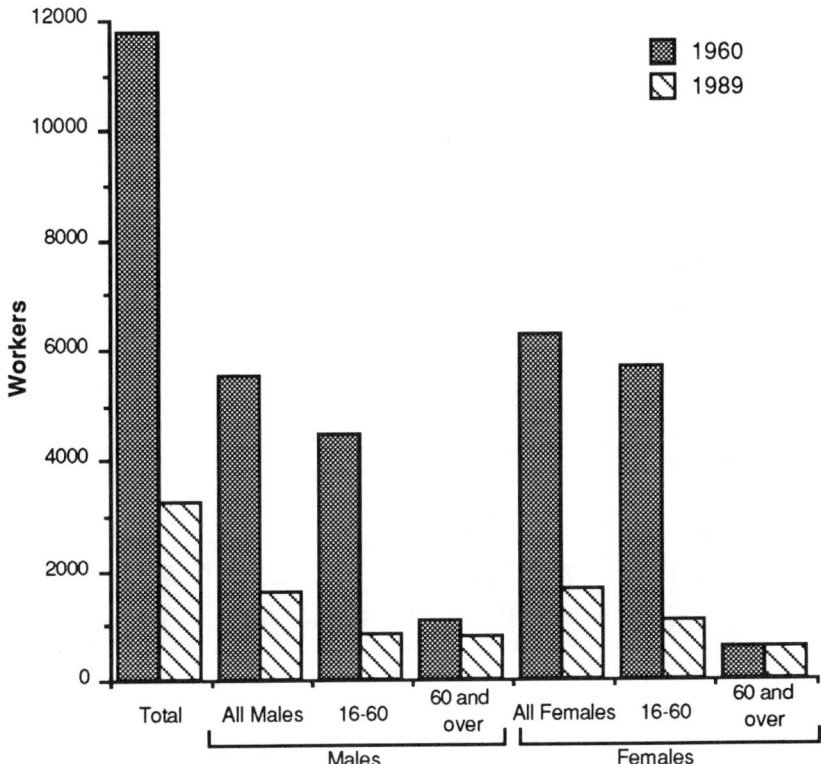

FIGURE 7.3 Demographic Changes in Japan's Agricultural Work Force (Principal persons engaged in farming by age and sex)

have declined in the last 20 years as returns from the production of vegetables, milk and livestock products have increased.

Rice holds a unique position in Japanese culture and policy. It is the basic food staple and a symbol of food security and national well-being. Egaitsu has articulated the Japanese view that rural farm communities based on rice production are essential to the long-term stability and prosperity of Japan. As a result of sentiments such as these and the disproportionate influence of the farm vote from rural election districts, rice has become the major focus of the government's agricultural support policies. In 1987, rice accounted for nearly 60 percent of the estimated transfers to producers of 10 major commodities (Figure 7.5). Other parts

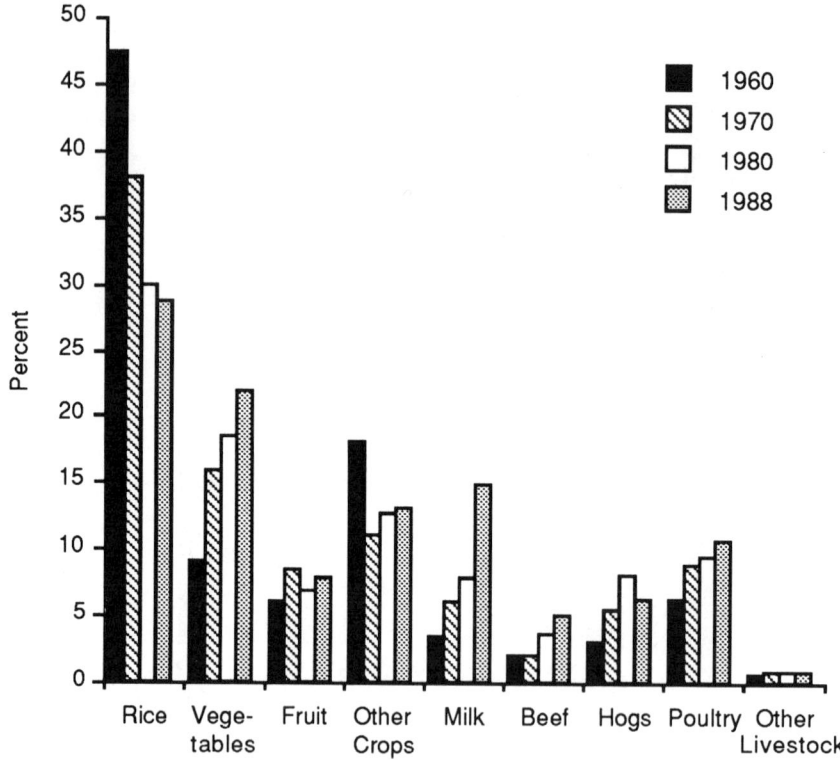

FIGURE 7.4 Distribution of Gross Returns for Major Agricultural Products in Japan

of the farm sector may receive comparable or higher levels of support, but no other commodity is as important as rice to Japanese agriculture.

In summary, the key agricultural policy problem in Japan, as it is in many industrial countries, is how to maintain income parity between the farm and the industrial/services sectors. Japanese agricultural policy for most of the past 30 years has attempted to maintain this parity through the increase in support prices and the adoption of measures that encourage the consolidation of farm enterprises. But because there has been virtually no increase in the size of farm operations on either an ownership or a rental basis (Figure 7.1), the increase in support prices has only slowed the decline in household income from farming (Figure 7.2). Instead, it has been the massive shift to part-time farming that has allowed many people to stay on the farm while earning the largest share of their income from off-farm sources. Reform

Japanese Agriculture in the 1990s: An American Perspective 127

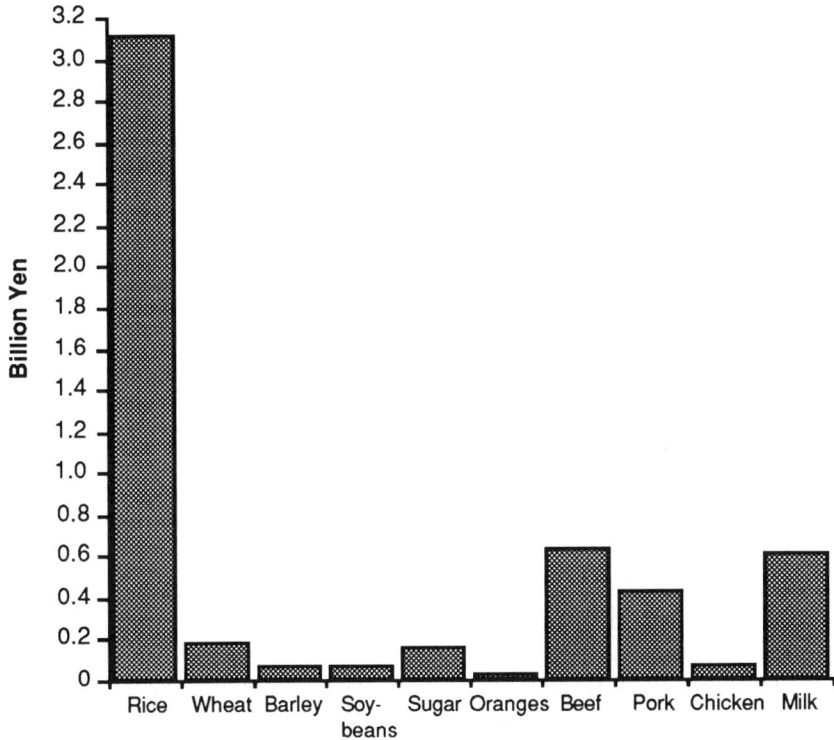

FIGURE 7.5 Policy Transfers to Producers in Japan for Major Agricultural Commodities (Source: Webb et al.)

of Japan's agricultural support policies, therefore, is likely to have a very limited effect on the incomes of the majority of Japanese farmers.

Emerging Conflicts Within Japanese Agriculture

Trends and events in the past five years make it clear that the level of Japanese support for agriculture will not be sustained. Reforms in one component of the sector generate an impetus for reforms in other areas. At the very least, we can expect major changes for beef, dairy, and citrus production as a result of the 1987 Beef and Citrus Agreement, which will give imports access to the Japanese market. Domestic beef production, particularly the lower-quality beef cuts coming from culled dairy cows, will face stiff competition from imports. High-quality Wagyu beef may hold a niche in the Japanese market that will allow it to command a substantial premium over imported beef. Although expanding consumer demand for beef and a complicated distribution system will blunt the price-depressing effects of cheaper imports, import access will put pressure on the beef and, to a lesser extent, on the dairy industries to cut costs and improve efficiency. These industries will, in turn, put pressure on the feed-compounding industry to increase the availability of cheaper feed rations.

Import access for beef also closes off a significant opportunity for small-scale, part-time farming. Over 300 thousand of Japan's 4 million farm households in 1989 (including both full and part-time households) were engaged in dairy or beef production (Management and Coordination Agency, 1990). For all of Japan except Hokkaido, the average number of milk cows per dairy household was 24 and the average number of beef cattle per beef production household was 10. Import access will accelerate the consolidation of beef and dairy production and will likely force many of the smaller part-time operations out of business or into the production of other farm products.

Conflicts are emerging in the production of rice as well. The long-term decline in the consumption of rice has serious implications for agricultural policy. Japan has been self-sufficient in rice since the mid-1960s. But declining rice consumption and increasing yields have resulted in a capacity to produce large surpluses. Japan has dealt with rice surpluses from time to time over the past 25 years by subsidizing exports, accumulating stocks, and diverting rice land to alternative uses. Subsidized rice exports in the form of food aid in the late 1970s and early 1980s, however, led to strong protests from the United States, and Japan has discontinued the policy. Thus, the only long-term solutions open to Japanese policy-makers are to divert or remove from production more paddy land or to reduce the incentive to plant rice by reducing price supports.

Land diversion has not worked well in Japan in the past, and the necessity to divert or idle ever-increasing surplus production capacity is a source of growing tension between farmers and those responsible for setting farm policy. But there is also tension within the farm community itself. High-quality rice commands premium prices in Japan, well above the support price. The allocation of the area to be diverted across prefecture therefore entails higher opportunity costs for the high-quality producing regions than for the lower-quality producing regions. Acreage control, however, "is imposed by government on all producers more or less at a uniform percentage of their paddy fields" (Hayami, 1988).

Diversion of rice area into other crops, over time, increases the production of these alternatives. Having higher production levels lowers prices or, in the presence of government price supports, displaces imports and creates trade tensions. In 1985, for example, area diverted from rice increased the area devoted to wheat and barley by 27 percent and the area devoted to pulses by 36 percent (ABARE, 1988).

Declining Support for Agricultural Protection

Over the past three decades, the literature on the political economy of protection has tried to identify the forces that explain why some industries have been successful in obtaining protection and others have not.[2] Anderson's work comparing rates of protection for food and agriculture across countries has made a major contribution to this literature. He observes that low-income countries tend to have small, politically active urban populations and large dispersed rural farm populations. For most low-income countries, it is politically expedient to employ policies that keep food prices low and impose the costs on farmers. As incomes rise, migration changes the rural-urban balance of population and political influence. Rural farm groups become smaller, better organized, and relatively more powerful, and urban consumers become more numerous and less concerned about food prices. Support shifts away from consumers to producers of agricultural commodities.

The evolution of policy does not end here. Cassing and Hillman (1986) argue that as an industry declines in economic importance, the balance of forces supporting and opposing protection changes in favor of those opposing it. Although their analysis has focused on the U.S. shoe industry, there are parallels to Japanese agriculture. Japan has reached the point where the forces opposing protection are strengthening and taking different forms (e.g., environmental concerns) and those favoring a continuation or an increase in protection for rice are waning. The predominance of part-time farming means that the removal of support would have only a marginal effect on the majority of households. Also, with 85 percent of farm household income coming from nonfarm sources, many farm households are likely to be less inclined to vote purely on the basis of changes in farm policies. Issues related to industrial growth, export expansion, environmental quality, and taxes may be far more important in determining voting behavior among the nation's 3 million part-time farmers than changes in rice support prices.

Policy Options

Egaitsu poses the question in his paper of whether Japanese agricultural policies are fair or reasonable. The answer, he argues, is that "Japanese agricultural policy from the domestic viewpoint is not as unreasonable as it may appear in the eyes of foreigners." We, in the United States and in other countries, cannot presume to judge what is fair or reasonable for Japan. We can certainly make our positions known and argue for policy reforms that are more favorable to our interests, but the choice of policy instruments and objectives is the prerogative of the Japanese public. The salient issue facing the Japanese electorate is to decide what objectives they wish to pursue relative to agriculture and rural communities and what policies should be used to achieve these objectives.

Egaitsu has implied that Japan's stable society is rooted in the value structure of its rural heritage. The preceding discussion, however, has shown that the stability of rural communities is no longer tied to Japanese farm policies. The price support policies initiated under the Basic Law of 1961 have become increasingly irrelevant to the income and well-being of most Japanese farm households. Income parity between urban and farm households was achieved in the 1970s, but not primarily because of the government's agricultural pricing policies. Growth in off-farm income was key to raising rural income as the agricultural component of farm household income dwindled from about 50 percent in 1960 to only 15 percent in 1987. Thus, it is rural industrialization and the availability of nonfarm jobs in rural communities that have sustained rural communities in Japan over the past 30 years and will be critical to their viability in the future. A phasing-out of agricultural price supports would *not* lead to massive social and economic dislocation in rural Japan. Many farm households could adjust to the loss of the farm component of their income; they could not adjust to the loss of the nonfarm component.

Both Egaitsu and Yoshioka recognize that some gradual reduction of agricultural price supports is in the long-term interests of Japan. The reduction of nominal rice price supports in 1987, 1988, and 1990 indicates an explicit understanding that these policies are no longer politically supportable. Egaitsu notes that other—presumably less trade-distorting—support policies need to be considered. Yet, apart from the realization that past policies have been ineffective and need to be phased out, no consensus has emerged on what policy alternatives would be appropriate for making agriculture an economically and socially viable sector.

One alternative that has considerable political appeal is to rely on demographic change to solve the farm problem. Eventually the aging of the farm population will lead to a consolidation of landholdings and an increase in efficiency. No politically divisive debate would be required to let events continue on their present course.

This option, however, fails to address the social objectives of the broader population vis-à-vis the rural sector. The maintenance of Japan's link with its rural heritage and the desire for a source of high-quality food will require an economically viable agricultural sector. This cannot be achieved by neglecting the long-term effects of rural demographic change. A more pro-active policy is needed. As Yoshioka has pointed out,

> [We] must do something to persuade people to stay in the villages and to make rural communities viable. Now is a good opportunity to shift the emphasis in spending on roads, water supplies, drainage and other public works away from urban areas and toward rural areas. We must create a better living environment and the cultural facilities necessary to keep young people in rural areas. It is time to put an end to the policies in effect from the Meiji era [1868-1912] that promote centralization and the abandonment of rural areas. (Yoshioka 1991)

The Japanese policy challenge is not very different from the challenge facing the United States and the European Community. Over the next decade, farmers in both the United States and the European Community will see a long-term decline in effective support levels for agricultural commodity production. Rural communities in the United States and, to a lesser extent, in Europe are suffering from a prolonged decline in the size of the working-age population in agriculture and, consequently, a fall in the level of rural services and schools. Off-farm income is a large and growing share of total farm income in these countries as well. And, like Japan, none of these developed countries has found a feasible set of policies that can sustain rural communities at or near their current levels.

Japan, with its limited size, large population, and well-developed infrastructure, probably stands as good a chance as any of the developed countries of generating adequate off-farm employment opportunities to sustain a village-like agricultural sector. The key to success of this endeavor may well be Japan's ability to develop for the rural sector the wages and amenities that have drawn most of the young people to the urban areas.

Notes

1. Authors acknowledge helpful comments from Ryuhei Matsumoto with the Japan Ministry of Agriculture Forestry and Fisheries and John Dyck with the Economic Research Service, U.S. Department of Agriculture.
2. See Baldwin (1984) for a review of the economics literature on trade policies.

References

ABARE. 1988. *Japanese Agricultural Policies: A Time of Change. Policy Monograph No. 3.* p. 118. Canberra.

Baldwin, Robert E. 1984. "Trade Policies in Developed Countries." *Handbook of International Economics. vol. I.* edited by R. W. Jones and P. B. Kenen. Elsevier Science Publishers B. V: Amsterdam.

Cassing, J. H. and A. L. Hillman. 1986. "Shifting Comparative Advantage and Senescent Industry Collapse." *American Economic Review* 76: 516-523.

Egaitsu, Fumio. 1982. "Japanese Agricultural Policy: Present Problems and Their Historical Background." in E. N. Castle, K. Hemmi and S. A. Skillings (eds), *U.S.-Japanese Agricultural Trade Relations.* Pp. 148-81. Washington, D.C.: Resources for the Future, Inc.

Hayami, Yujiro. 1988. *Japanese Agriculture Under Siege: The Political Economy of Agricultural Policies.* New York: St. Martin's Press.

Hemmi, Kenzo. 1987. "Agricultural Reform Efforts in Japan: Political Feasibility and Consequences for Trade with the United States and Third Countries." in *Agricultural Reform Efforts in the United States and Japan.* Pp. 24-46. D. Gale Johnson, editor. New York: New York University Press.

Konosu, K. 1982. *What Will Be the Agricultural Policies of Japan in the 1980s?* Tokyo: Japan FAO Association.

Management and Coordination Agency, Statistics Bureau. 1990. *Japan Statistical Yearbook: 1990.*

Webb, Alan J., Michael Lopes, and Renata Penn (eds). 1990. *Estimates of Producer and Consumer Subsidy Equivalents: Government Intervention in Agriculture. 1982-1987.* Economic Research Service. Statistical Bulletin No. 803.

World Bank. 1990. *World Development Report 1990.* Washington, D.C.

Yoshioka, Yutaka. 1991. "Thoughts on Japanese Agriculture." *Japan Agrinfo Newsletter,* Vol. 8, No. 8. Tokyo: Japan International Agricultural Council.

8

Policies and Profitability in Livestock Feed Sectors of the ASEAN Countries

Allan Rae, Liborio Cabanilla, Tan Siew Hoey,
Faisal Kasryno, and Suthad Setboonsarng

Introduction

It is well known that the Association of Southeast Asian Nations (ASEAN) has been one of the fastest growing regions of the world in recent times. GDP growth rates varied between 6 and 8 percent on average over the 1960-80 period in Indonesia, Malaysia, the Philippines, and Thailand, although 1980s' growth has been somewhat less spectacular, especially in the Philippines. With the likely continuation of above world average growth rates over the next decade, patterns of food consumption will continue to change in ways similar to those observed in Japan and the newly industrialized economies in Northeast Asia.

The demand for livestock products is usually elastic with respect to income levels in developing countries, which, coupled with rapid income growth, leads to the observed switch from consumption of foodgrains and staples to consumption of livestock products. Between 1965 and 1984, for example, per capita consumption of pork, chicken, and beef increased from 9 kg to 32 kg in Japan, while consumption of the same meats in South Korea rose from 6 kg to 10 kg between 1971 and 1981. Similar growth patterns can be expected in the ASEAN region, where per capita consumption of these three meats already averages around 10 kg. Assumptions of 5 percent future growth in income per capita, a unitary income elasticity, and 2 percent population growth suggests a 7 percent annual growth in demand for livestock products in this region.

Such trends in the ASEAN economies could result in increased imports of livestock products, depending on the rate at which domestic production can be increased. However, success by these developing countries in displacing such increasing imports by domestic production could lead to rapid increases in feed imports unless domestic production of feedstuffs can also be expanded.

A question that arises for policy-makers is this: What is likely to be the economic benefit to society from meeting such increased demands with imports of final product, compared with increased domestic livestock production based on either imported or local feedstuffs? In addition to any economic benefits, and not forgetting balance of payments implications, expansion of the livestock sectors in the ASEAN region may allow governments to more closely attain other rural development goals such as income growth and improved nutrition, especially given the smallholder nature of some livestock production systems.

Government planning agencies in the region have in the past been hindered by the lack of reliable data and analyses regarding the impact of policies on livestock production incentives and social benefits of livestock and feedstuff production. Therefore, at the First Workshop of the Livestock and Feedgrains Study Programme of the Pacific Economic Cooperation Conference (PECC), the ASEAN participants urged an economic examination of their livestock and feeds sub-sectors (Rae and Johnson 1987). The study was undertaken by study teams in Indonesia, Malaysia, the Philippines, and Thailand. Some preliminary studies were reported to the Second Workshop of the above PECC Task Force (Rae and Johnson 1988), while final results were summarized for the Third Workshop (Rae and Chadee 1990). Documentation prepared included four Country Reports (Kasryno et al. 1989, Tan et al. 1989, Cabanilla 1989, and Setboonsarng et al. 1989) and a Summary Report (Rae and Lough 1989).

In this study, policies that impacted directly or indirectly on the livestock and feeds sectors were described, and their influence on production and consumption incentives was measured. This involved surveys of farmers, processors, and traders in each country, the estimation of nominal and effective protection rates, and private and social profitability indicators for a number of livestock products and feeds. At the same time an assessment was made as to whether government assistance targeted commodities that were socially profitable.

The study emphasized regional patterns of production, consumption, and resource costs, since transportation can be a major component in countries like Indonesia and the Philippines. This highlighted issues such as the economics of transporting live animals or carcasses and the location of raw material production (e. g., liquid milk or grains) in relation to that of processing facilities.

The Livestock Production and Trade Situation

The major livestock enterprises in the ASEAN region are poultry (both meat and egg production) and pigs, which have developed into modern agribusinesses, especially in Malaysia and Thailand. The ruminant production sectors in most cases remain as "backyard" or smallholder operations integrated with the farm cropping system, while in the Philippines and Indonesia the household sector is also dominant in the production of poultry and pigs. In some countries, ruminants remain an important source of draft power and a form of savings.

Production growth rates in the region have been greatest for poultry products and pork; in Malaysia, for example, broiler output quadrupled, that of eggs tripled, and production of pork more than doubled over the 1970-1987 period. Generally, growth rates were lower in the Philippines than elsewhere.

Often encouraged by government programs, dairy production has also expanded rapidly, often based on cooperative principles, and milk powder is now manufactured from surplus milk production in Indonesia and Thailand. During the mid-1980s, the annual average growth of milk production in Thailand, Malaysia, and Indonesia averaged 22 percent, 20 percent, and 12 percent respectively.

Feeding systems on the commercial poultry and pig farms, which have been responsible for the rapid growth in output of these products, employ modern technology, while the smallholder production systems rely on indigenous feeds. Feedlot systems are not common in ruminant livestock farming, and where they exist concentrate feeding is low by Western standards. Otherwise, feed rations are based on roughage and agro-wastes. In Malaysia, efforts have been made to develop beef and sheep farming systems in conjunction with plantation cropping.

Each of the four countries is more or less self-sufficient in the production of poultry meat, pork, and eggs. Poultry meat is a major export of Thailand (one of its top 15 export commodities), while Malaysia and Indonesia are entering the export phase. Pork (or live pigs) and eggs are also actual or potential export items from these three countries. All four countries are net importers of beef and dairy products.

Each country has experienced a rapid expansion in the demand for feedstuffs due to growth in the poultry and pork sectors. Corn, soybean meal, and rice bran are major feed ingredients. Unlike some of its neighbours, Thailand is richly endowed in animal feeds, is a net exporter of corn and cassava (the world's largest in the case of the latter product), but a net importer of soybeans. Despite rapid growth in corn production almost to the point of self-sufficiency, Indonesia is a net importer of corn and soybeans. Like Thailand, Indonesia exports a major share of its cassava output. The Philippines imported more than one-half by value of its animal feed ingredients up to 1985, but since the imposition of a ban on corn imports, around 70 percent of feedstuffs are sourced domestically. Assisted by this policy, domestic corn production has expanded rapidly, but in the south of the country, far from the major feedmilling locations. Compared with the other ASEAN countries studied, Malaysia is an insignificant producer of conventional animal feeds, although like Thailand it has plentiful supplies of agro-industrial by-products and wastes. A major feedstuff produced is palm kernel cake, although returns available from exports to the EC (as with cassava exports from Thailand and Indonesia) discourage its use by local livestock farmers.

International Competitiveness of ASEAN Livestock Production

Some Initial Indications

While changes in consumption patterns in Southeast Asia may follow those already well established in the more developed countries of Northeast Asia, parallels need not be so evident on the supply side.

Tyers and Anderson (1985) draw from the Heckscher-Ohlin-Samuelson theory of comparative advantage in suggesting how changes in the structure of production in ASEAN economies might differ from those in Northeast Asia. They concluded that the greater per capita endowment of agricultural land in the four large ASEAN countries will result in their specializing in manufacturing at a later stage of economic development than the natural resource-poor Northeast Asian countries.

Supportive data taken from their study are presented in Table 8.1. In particular, note the small areas of pasture per capita in the ASEAN region but the somewhat higher availability of short-cycle cropland and land planted in tree crops. Thus one would expect these countries to have a comparative disadvantage in range-fed livestock systems but a stronger comparative advantage in either crop or plantation agriculture. The latter, of course, is relevant to the supply of feedstuffs in the region, which may be produced by these crops either directly or indirectly as by-products or wastes.

The revealed comparative advantage indicators calculated by Tyers and Anderson show clearly Northeast Asia's comparative disadvantage in agriculture relative to ASEAN, and the rapid decline in agricultural comparative advantage in Korea as that country industri-

TABLE 8.1 Some Indicators of Regional Comparative Advantage

	Land Availability[a] per capita			Revealed Comparative Advantage[b]			
				Food		Nonfood Agr.	
	Pasture	Short-cycle crops	Tree crops	1960	1980	1960	1980
Japan	5	37	5	0.4	0.1	0.3	0.2
Korea	1	55	4	2.3	0.7	1.8	0.5
Indonesia	81	97	36	2.5	0.7	6.7	3.6
Malaysia	2	74	243	1.0	1.8	3.4	7.8
Philippines	21	146	59	3.1	3.7	3.0	1.5
Thailand	7	350	37	3.1	4.6	6.4	2.8
Australia	31,166	3,051	12				

[a] Hectares per thousand people (1980).
[b] The ratio of the share of a commodity group in a country's exports to that commodity group's share of world exports.
Source: Tyers and Anderson (1985).

alized. In most cases, the ratios reveal a strong agricultural comparative advantage for the ASEAN countries, with indices well above the neutral value of unity.

The Measurement of Social Profitability

The study employed standard project evaluation methodology but applied to sector-wide data to measure average revenues and costs per unit of various livestock product outputs (Gittinger 1982). Costs included those incurred by farmers, processors, and traders. Social profitability per unit of commodity i was measured as:

$$SP_i = P_i^b - \sum_{j=1}^{k} a_{ij} P_j^b - \sum_{j=K+1}^{J} a_{ij} v_j^b \tag{1}$$

where P_i^b = border price of commodity i

a_{ij} = quantity of input j required per unit of output i

v_j^d = domestic valuation (net of taxes and subsidies) of the opportunity costs of non-traded inputs

$j = 1, \ldots, k$ = all traded inputs

$j = k+1, \ldots, J$ = non-traded inputs

OER = official exchange rate

SER = shadow exchange rate

$v_j^b = v_j^d \text{ OER/SER}$

Note that all components of this equation are valued in domestic currency. If $SP_i > 0$, production of that commodity produces a positive return to the nation.

Input-output coefficients and domestic prices were collected through sample surveys of farms, processing and marketing firms in each country, and from various secondary data sources. The financial data so collected often required adjustment to remove distortions such as those caused by policy interventions, so as to obtain the relevant border prices. Such adjustments first involved the deduction of all direct transfer payments, such as taxes and subsidies. Adjustments to the prices of traded items involved determination of the FOB price (for farm inputs such as feedstuffs that are also exported) or the CIF price (for imported inputs) converted to domestic currency at the official exchange rate. Such prices were further adjusted to incorporate domestic transport and marketing costs. Opportunity costs of non-traded items (e.g., land and rural labor) were determined using shadow prices, while other non-traded items (e.g., transport) with a significant imported component were decomposed into the imported and domestically produced components.

As regards the valuation of feed inputs, it should be noted that domestically produced feedstuffs that were defined as traded inputs were valued at border prices. Thus exported feeds (such as cassava from Indonesia or Thailand and palm kernel cake from Malaysia) that could be diverted into the domestic livestock sector were valued at their border prices adjusted for transport costs rather than decomposed into traded and domestic components. Later in the paper, the question of whether or not such feedstuff production is socially profitable will be addressed.

Border prices were averaged over the 1983-87 period, although sensitivity analyses were conducted in recognition of the rise in commodity prices towards the end of the 1980s.

The study was designed to draw attention to regional differences in resource endowments, productivity, and social profitability. This was particularly relevant in such island-based economies as Indonesia and the Philippines. Therefore, close attention was paid to the measurement of transport costs between production regions, processing locations, wholesale markets, and export/import points.

Government Policies Can Distort Profitability Measures

In each ASEAN country studied, government policies impact on the prices of livestock products and feedstuffs. These impacts may be direct or indirect. Policies such as a tariff on soybean meal imports or a tax levied on the export of live cattle will directly alter the domestic prices of these items. Other policies that do not directly target prices can have the same effect. Quotas on imports of dairy products or a ban on the import of corn will indirectly raise the prices of these products in domestic markets.

Such policies therefore can alter the apparent profitability of livestock production; the distortions may even be sufficiently severe to make production activities that provide a positive return to a country appear unprofitable, and vice versa.

The study derived estimates of nominal and effective protection rates to summarize the extent of such policy-induced distortions. The nominal measure simply compares domestic with border prices of the various livestock products, while the effective protection rate also includes the impact of policies on the prices of inputs such as feedstuffs. Results are given in Tables 8-2 and 8-3.

Protection of meat and egg production in the Philippines has declined over the last two decades, partly as a result of the government's trade liberalization program but also due to improvements in production technology and domestic competition. Of these commodities, protection is highest for poultry production, especially broilers. Beef production in the Philippines receives less protection. Although domestic beef prices exceed border prices of equivalent-quality beef by over 20 percent, hidden penalties in the beef marketing system reduce the effective level of protection to almost nil.

Domestic prices of chicken meat and eggs in Thailand are very similar to prices received for Thailand's exports of these commodities, reflecting the low level of government involvement with this sector. Nominal protection rates are above zero for pork and beef, especially

TABLE 8.2 Rates of Protection on Non-Ruminant Products

Rate of Protection (%)	Nominal Rates of Protection			Effective Rates of Protection		
	Broilers	Eggs	Pork	Broilers	Eggs	Pork
100 to 200				East Malaysia		
75 to 100						
50 to 75	Philippines East Malaysia				East Malaysia	
25 to 50		Philippines East Malaysia		Philippines	Philippines	
10 to 25		Lampung (Indo.)	Philippines Thailand East Malaysia		Lampung (Indo.)	Philippines Thailand East Malaysia
0 to 10	Thailand Pen. Malaysia	Thailand Pen. Malaysia	Pen. Malaysia	Pen. Malaysia	Pen. Malaysia	
-10 to 0			East Java	Thailand		Pen. Malaysia
-25 to -10			Central Java Bali, ENT		Thailand	Central Java
-50 to -25	Indonesia	West Java				
Below -50				Indonesia	West Java	Bali

Data for Peninsular Malaysia are averages of the North, Central, and South regions. East Malaysia data refer to Sarawak. The ENT region in Indonesia is East Nusa Tenggara.

TABLE 8.3 Rates of Protection for Ruminant Products

Rate of Protection	Nominal Rates of Protection					Effective Rates of Protection			
(%)	Beef	Sheepmeat	Milk	Skim Milk Powder	Anhydrous Milk Fat	Beef	Sheepmeat	Milk	Wholemilk Powder
Over 200						Pen. Malaysia		Philippines[1] Pen. Malaysia	Indonesia[2]
100 to 200			Pen. Malaysia	Indonesia	Indonesia	Thailand			
75 to 100	Thailand Pen. Malaysia							Thailand	Indonesia[3]
50 to 75			Thailand Philippines						
25 to 50		Pen. Malaysia					Pen. Malaysia	Philippines[4]	
10 to 25	Philippines								
0 to 10									
-10 to 0						Philippines			
-25 to -10									
-50 to -25	Indonesia					Central Java ENT			
Below 50						West Java			

[1] Mindoro
[2] Milk production from imported breeds
[3] Milk production from crossbred animals
[4] Mindanao
See also notes to Table 8.2.

the latter, with domestic prices about double the border price of beef of equivalent quality due to tariff protection. Trade barriers on the import of inputs used in production of meat and eggs in Thailand result in higher production costs for all livestock products, on the order of 10 percent to 15 percent for poultry and pork production and around 35 percent for beef production. When policy-induced increases in costs are taken into account, production of broilers and eggs is effectively taxed rather than protected. For pork and beef production, effective rates of protection are positive. In other words, the exported commodities are taxed, while import substitutes are assisted.

In Peninsular Malaysia, rates of protection for broilers and pork average close to zero. In Sarawak, however, domestic prices of poultry meat exceed border values by over 60 percent, reflecting higher levels of policy intervention in East Malaysia. Levels of protection are higher in beef production, and domestic beef prices exceed border prices of similar-quality product by up to 80 percent.

In contrast with the other three study countries, nominal and effective protection rates for all meat products as well as eggs are negative in Indonesia. Domestic prices of these commodities are less than world values by 10 percent to 50 percent, depending upon the product and region in question. This would appear to reflect the success of the government's export controls in providing assistance to domestic consumers. This, combined with other trade policies that impose further disincentives on livestock production by raising the cost of imported inputs, ensures that effective protection rates are also negative.

Dairy production in all four countries is heavily protected, with the highest rates estimated for Malaysia. Rates of protection were lowest in Thailand and one region of the Philippines, but even so, domestic milk prices exceeded milk prices based on the cost of imported ingredients by 50 percent to 65 percent. Protection of skim milk powder (SMP) and anhydrous milk fat (AMF) was studied in Indonesia because of the recent rapid expansion of the milk processing sector in that country. For both products, domestic prices exceeded import values by around 150 percent.

In summary, rates of protection on the non-ruminant livestock products tend to be highest in the Philippines and East Malaysia, and lowest in Indonesia and Thailand. All countries heavily protect their ruminant livestock sectors, with the notable exceptions of beef production in the Philippines and Indonesia.

The Results for Livestock Commodities

Social profits were calculated for a number of regions within each country and were also calculated separately by assuming the commodity in question was exported, was an import substitute, or was traded from surplus to deficit regions within the country. Results are summarized in Table 8.4.

With the exception of milk products, all commodities studied in *Indonesia* were socially profitable for the majority of regions. Poultry meat, egg, pork, and beef production were all found to be internationally competitive. Government trade policies have discouraged these enterprises by decreasing final product prices (through export restrictions) and increasing feed prices relative to international prices. Both beef and pork production were found to be more efficient on smallholder than on corporate farms, making future expansion consistent with social as well as economic objectives. Survival of the dairy industry has been dependent on a high level of government protection and was not internationally competitive at mid-1980s prices. The recent increase in world dairy prices made milk production on smallholder farms in Central Java socially profitable in supplying that local region, but could not compete with imports in supplying Jakarta.

Poultry meat, egg, and pork production was socially profitable as either import substitutes or exports in Peninsular *Malaysia*, but not East Malaysia. While beef, dairy, and sheep production is highly protected by the Malaysian government, these products were not socially profitable. For some commodities, the evidence indicated that market intermediaries were the main beneficiaries of government support rather than the targeted farmers. Protection of the ruminant sector has been given on the basis of its potential regarding rural income growth, employment, improved nutrition, and upgrading of smallholders' and landless workers' living standards. The income enhancement objective may not be realizable given that beef and sheep production did not generate positive private, let alone social, returns.

TABLE 8.4 Is Livestock Production Socially Profitable?

Product	Indonesia	Peninsular Malaysia	Philippines	Thailand
Broilers	Yes	Some regions	Some regions	Yes
Eggs	Some regions	Yes	Yes	Yes
Pork	Yes	Yes	Yes	Yes
Beef	Yes	No	Yes	Some regions
Milk	No	No	Some regions	Some regions
Sheep	N/S	No	N/S	N/S

N/S = Not studied.

The *Philippines* analyses indicated that production of all commodities was socially profitable in at least some regions although farm sample sizes were very small in many cases. The conclusion was marginal in the case of broiler production. Government policies resulted in positive incentives for the production of all commodities, so they were aimed at encouraging resources into uses that provided positive returns to society. However, protection of the marginally efficient broiler industry was greater than for several other commodities. Assisted by such incentives, private profits generally were positive, especially for cattle production. In several cases, traders appeared to benefit more than farmers from government assistance. The social profitability of pig and beef production was noteworthy given the role of these enterprises in smallholder farming systems and government objectives regarding rural income enhancement and agrarian reform.

All of the commodities studied in *Thailand*, with the exception of beef and dairy products, were socially profitable. Few government interventions directly affect the poultry sector, although product quality and market competition in the pork sector have been inhibited by public controls over the ownership of slaughterhouses. The government has made considerable efforts to promote beef and dairy production, as indicated by the relatively high rates of protection for these commodities in Thailand. Despite this intervention the production of beef, with the exception of that using pineapple waste as a feed, was non-competitive with imported supplies. Should recent levels of world dairy prices continue, milk production in Thailand would be socially profitable. Given its importance as a smallholder enterprise, such a possibility supports future public involvement in research to further improve productivity.

Is Regional Feed Production Efficient?

Those feedstuffs that were defined as traded inputs to livestock production were valued at border prices, irrespective of whether they were produced domestically or imported. As a result, conclusions about social profitability in livestock production do not answer questions about whether the ASEAN countries are economically efficient producers of feed inputs. To examine this issue, social profits were calculated for a few major feed crops produced in the region, along with measures of public assistance to their production.

Compared with the other countries, protection levels for maize and cassava production in the Philippines are relatively high. Up until 1984 (when the National Food Authority's monopoly on maize imports was ended), domestic maize prices had averaged 20 percent above world prices. This price distortion fell to only 7 percent the following year when imports were privatized, but since imposition of the maize import ban in 1986, domestic prices have exceeded world prices by over 60 percent. Dismantling of the government import monopoly on soybean meal in 1985 did not result in a significant reduction in domestic prices relative to world levels, since import licenses were granted to only a few firms.

In Indonesia, domestic maize prices have been kept below international price levels in the main producing regions of East Java and Sulawesi. The same two regions have the lowest (and negative) effective rates of protection of all Indonesia's maize-producing regions. For soybeans, domestic prices exceed world levels by 35 to 90 percent. Effective protection levels are also high due to government subsidization of inputs—the on-farm value of traded inputs has been up to 50 percent lower than their value at world prices. Domestic prices of dried cassava exceed border prices by up to 20 percent in the main exporting regions. In contrast to the subsidization of input costs to maize and soybean farmers, cassava producers pay up to 10 percent in excess of the border price valuation of inputs. As a result, the level of effective protection of dried cassava production is close to zero.

The impact of government policies on incentives for maize production in Thailand is relatively small. Domestic producer prices are close to, or a little below, international levels, while the costs to producers of traded inputs have been 15 percent to 20 percent above their border values. The production of soybean meal is more heavily protected, and the result of quotas on meal imports has been to drive domestic prices to levels 35 percent above border prices. The rate of effective protection of soybean meal production in Thailand is of similar magnitude.

The production of maize, cassava, and soybeans was socially profitable in Indonesia and Thailand, as were maize and cassava production in the Philippines (Table 8.5).

TABLE 8.5 Are Social Profits Positive in Feed Crops Production?

	Indonesia	Peninsular Malaysia	Philippines	Thailand
Maize	Yes	No	Most regions	Most regions
Cassava	Yes[1]	N/S	Yes	Yes[1]
Soybeans	Most regions	N/S	N/S	Yes[2]

[1] Production of dried cassava
[2] Soybean meal production
N/S = Not studied

From a policy viewpoint, it is noteworthy that policies in Indonesia give greatest encouragement to maize and soybean production in the less efficient regions of the country. Social profits were lowest from production elsewhere than in Java, while protection was greatest in Java. And in the case of maize, policy intervention actually resulted in disincentives (i.e., negative protection rates) to production in some regions with positive social profits.

The governments of both Indonesia and Thailand provide encouragement to their socially profitable soybean industries. However, the potential for a continuation of past rapid expansion in output in Thailand will likely be hindered by land constraints.

Feed maize production in Malaysia is still in an experimental phase, and data from trial results were used in the study. These results suggested that commercial maize production in Malaysia would not be profitable from either the private or the social point of view, and doubts also exist over the availability of land in sufficiently large units to support commercial production given the profitability of alternative crops.

Conclusions and Scope for Regional Cooperation

Each of the four countries is a socially profitable producer of broilers, eggs, and pork, but often not in the case of milk and dairy production. And additional calculations showed that all countries except Malaysia were economically efficient producers of corn, cassava, and soybeans for livestock feeds.

The Pacific Economic Cooperation Conference is particularly interested in promoting regional cooperation. Given the cooperative objectives of ASEAN, and their past efforts in agriculture, it is relevant to ask whether this particular study has indicated areas in which regional cooperation might be mutually beneficial.

The similarity of results across the four countries suggests that little scope may exist for mutual gains from a regional trade liberalization in non-ruminant livestock products. Intra-regional differences in beef social profits exist, but the smallholder nature of this enterprise means that some regional governments could find a trade liberalization program in conflict with their smallholder-targeted political objectives. On the feeds side, substantial volumes are already traded within the region, and future livestock sector expansion is likely to mean an increase in net imports into the region as land supplies and support for rice production constrain future feed production growth.

More scope for mutual gain could exist within a regional approach to livestock and feeds trade with the rest of the world. Some ASEAN nations already export broilers, eggs, and pork outside the region, and other nations could reach exporter status before long. These countries are also in a similar trade situation regarding their livestock sectors' import requirements of feed and live animals. Thus an ASEAN regional strategy for the future management of livestock product exports and the related importing and feed stockholding activities could be addressed.

Finally, past ASEAN cooperation in agriculture has emphasized technical projects and information exchange. Enhanced cooperation among national research centers and among national and international centers, or the creation of new regional institutions, may provide regional benefits since many of the remaining technical problems are shared across the region. Issues that might benefit from a heightened regional research approach include the eradication of foot and mouth disease, a lack of knowledge on technical and economic aspects of nontraditional feed use, feed crop production and post-harvest technology improvement, the need for continued improvement in cattle breeds and the development of processing and marketing facilities appropriate to the region's agricultural structure.

References

Cabanilla, L. S. 1989. *Government Incentives and Comparative Advantage in the Livestock and Feedstuffs Sectors in the Philippines*. Mimeographed report. University of the Philippines, Los Banos.

Gittinger, J. P. 1982. *Economic Analysis of Agricultural Projects*. 2nd ed., Johns Hopkins, Baltimore.

Kasryno, F., P. Simatupang, I. W. Rusastra, A. Djatihati, and B. Irawan. 1989. *Government Incentives and Comparative Advantage in the Livestock and Feedstuff Subsectors in Indonesia*. Mimeographed report. Center for Agro Economic Research, Bobor.

Rae, A. N., and R. W. M. Johnson, eds. 1987. "The Livestock and Feedgrains Study Programme of the PECC: Proceedings of the First Workshop," Agricultural Policy Proceedings No. 9, Centre for Agricultural Policy Studies, Massey University, Palmerston North, New Zealand.

———. 1988. "The Livestock and Grains Study Programme of the PECC: Proceedings of the Second Workshop," Agricultural Policy Proceedings No. 11, Centre for Agricultural Policy Studies, Massey University, Palmerston North, New Zealand.

Rae, A. N., and D. D. Chadee, eds. 1990. *Policies for Agricultural Trade Liberalisation and Adjustment in the Pacific Rim*. Centre for Agricultural Policy Studies. Massey University, Palmerston North, New Zealand.

Rae, Allan N., and Roger D. Lough. 1989. *Government Incentives and Comparative Advantage in the Livestock and Feedstuff Sectors in the ASEAN Region.* Mimeographed report.

Setboonsarng, S., B. Titapiwatanakun, and S. Tubpun 1989. *Research Report on Competitiveness of Animal Feed and Livestock Production in Thailand.* Mimeographed report. Thailand Development Research Institute.

Tan, S. H., Z. Mohamed, E. F. C. Chiew, and M. N. Shamsudin. 1989. *Government Incentives and Comparative Advantage in Livestock and Feedstuffs Sectors in Malaysia.* Mimeographed report. Institute for Strategic and International Studies, Kuala Lumpur.

Tyers, Rodney, and Kym Anderson. 1985. *Economic Growth and Agricultural Protection in East and Southeast Asia.* ASEAN-Australia Economic Papers No. 21, ASEAN-Australia Joint Research Project, Kuala Lumpur and Canberra.

9

The Response of Thai Agriculture to the World Economy

Ammar Siamwalla, Suthad Setboonsarng, and Direk Patamasiriwat

Introduction

No other sector in the Thai economy is as oriented to international markets as agriculture. Although it has been contributing less than a fifth of the Gross National Product throughout the 1980s, its share in Thailand's export trade remains close to a half. Most of the goods produced by the sector (accounting for about three-quarters of the value-added in the agricultural sector) are considered as traded goods; that is, they are traded in international markets. Movements in these markets thus have considerable impact on their prices, and consequently on producers' incomes.

Until quite recently, the dominance of the agricultural sector in Thailand's export trade was overwhelming—it contributed close to 60 percent of the gross value of exports in 1980, but there is a clear downward trend in the contribution of agriculture—its share in 1987 was only 45 percent. This relative decline (the absolute value and volume of agricultural exports has continued to increase) has prompted speculation that Thailand is becoming an industrialized country. More precisely, it is alleged that Thailand is acquiring comparative advantage in industrial goods and services, which presumably implies comparative advantage lost in agriculture. Agriculture is thus a natural candidate for a "sunset" industry.

The present paper examines the nature of comparative advantage in agriculture. Analysis of comparative advantage normally juxtaposes domestic production conditions against international opportunities. We therefore start the paper by examining the international environment, stressing in particular how the rules of the game in the international marketplace affect Thailand. Normally, these rules of the game are considered beyond Thailand's ability to manipulate. We feel, however, that they have a bearing on our approach to agriculture. We then look at Thailand's comparative advantage in three subsectors of agriculture, given world prices for the various commodities and their projected future movements. From the results of this examination, we draw inferences on the proper pricing and technology policies.

The Rules of the Game
Gains and Losses for Thailand Under the Present Regime

Two sections below will provide an account of the gains and losses to Thailand of the present regime. Before we proceed to discuss these, it is important to ask what Thai measures toward agriculture the government would have to dismantle, should GATT rules be universally applied.

Many things can be said about Thailand's agricultural policies, but one thing that cannot be said is that they have been heavily protectionist. Indeed, in the past, its policies have been quite the opposite, with rather hefty export taxes levied on major commodities such as rice and rubber. This is not to say that protectionist policies are entirely absent. Historically, and even now, sugar has been the favored sector—it is alone among the export sectors to be significantly subsidized, albeit implicitly. Among the import-competing sectors, two sets of commodities stand out as being among the more heavily protected, namely dairy products and oilseeds generally, with soybeans and palm oil being particularly favored.

Cassava stands in a class by itself. While it is true that the voluntary export restraint agreement with the EEC affects local farmers adversely, government policies, particularly the bonus quota system, have succeeded in limiting the adverse impact on the farmers somewhat. Essentially, a bonus quota system is a quota allocation scheme whereby exporters who succeed in exporting one ton of cassava chips or pellets to markets outside the EEC may export one ton to the EEC. The workings of this quota system may be construed as dumping, but since anti-dumping measures can only be taken by importing countries that apparently are quite happy with the consequences, Thailand is relatively safe from any GATT action.

We now turn to the impact of other countries' policies on Thailand, examining first the impact of EEC's Common Agricultural Policy.

The EEC's Common Agricultural Policy and Thailand

The impact of the EEC's Common Agricultural Policy (CAP) is many-layered. At the most basic level, the CAP has a favorable impact on Thailand, which is able to export large quantities of cassava because the CAP has raised cereal prices and thus encouraged the use of many kinds of cereal substitutes, among which cassava is one. It so happened that, back in 1967, during the Kennedy round of the GATT, the Europeans thought they could provide some largesse to the developing world and agreed to a bound tariff for cassava at 6 percent ad valorem. Combining cassava imported at 6 percent tariff with soybeans at zero tariff essentially allowed European feed compounders to create artificial maize at a much lower cost than that sold in the EEC. The boom in the cassava trade that followed surprised the Europeans and by 1980 affected their sensitivities sufficiently for them to request Thailand's "cooperation" in limiting its exports. For reasons best known to themselves, Thai government officials responded with alacrity to the request, and the result is the voluntary export restraint agreement (VERA), whereby Thailand has limited its exports to approximately five million tons per year since 1982.

Even thus constrained, the trade in cassava remains beneficial to the Thai economy. However, a balanced view of the CAP would require us to look at a wider range of commodities which Thailand exports and which are no less affected by CAP, namely sugar, rice and cereals. The CAP on these commodities have adversely affected the world prices of these commodities and thus indirectly lowered Thai export earnings.

In an unpublished paper by Setboonsarng and Tyers, this broader view was taken. Using a multimarket multicommodity model developed by Rodney Tyers and Kym Anderson of Australia, an attempt was made to get the full measure of the impact of CAP on Thailand. While it is true that the price for cassava for Thai producers would fall by 15 percent and its level of exports by 25 percent, the effect of the removal of CAP on other commodities would be quite favorable. Table 9.1 shows the impact on international prices and on the export earnings of three of Thailand's major export items other than cassava.

Unfortunately, the particular model employed does not have enough "room" for both sugar and cassava, so the large adverse impact of CAP on sugar is not represented in Table 9.1. There is another, almost identical, model which includes sugar but excludes cassava. This model was employed to estimate the impact of the EEC sugar policies on Thailand. While the figures obtained from this second model are not strictly comparable to those in Table 9.1, the results do indicate tenta-

TABLE 9.1 Effect of the Removal of CAP on Prices, Export Volumes and Export Earning of Thailand in Rice, Coarse Grains, Sugar and Cassava

	International Price (% Change)	Export Volumes (Change in thou. tons)	Export Earnings (Change in mill. $)	Producers' Gain (Change in mill. $)
Rice	8.40	426.00	204.50	396.10
Coarse Grains	5.60	143.00	62.10	76.80
Others	-	-	0.20	95.10
Cassava	-15.10	-2,380.00	-147.20	-151.30
Total	-	-	119.60	389.70

Source: Setboonsarng and Tyers (unpublished work).

tively that the impact of EEC policies on Thai sugar trade and producers' income is roughly of the same order of magnitude as that on rice.

The Rice Title of the U.S. Farm Act and Its Impact on Thailand

In contrast to the CAP, however, there is no ambiguity about the effect of the U.S. policies. In major items of Thai trade, namely rice, maize and sugar, U.S. policies have clearly affected Thai farmers adversely. True, there are a few items which Thailand imports which have been helped by U.S. subsidies, namely cotton, tobacco and soybeans, but total imports of these items do not add up to even a third of our rice exports. The United States has also been insisting that Thailand accept more U.S. subsidies by buying their cigarettes, and the matter is now being decided by a GATT panel.

It is fair to say that the major point of controversy between Thailand and the United States in the area of agriculture has been the Rice Title of the U.S. Farm Act. There is little doubt that Congress aimed that title squarely at Thailand, which succeeded in expanding its market share substantially during the life of the previous Farm Act, in 1981-1985, when U.S. prices were perched on a very high level because of the unrealistically high loan rate. A specially included section (Section 1165) of the Food Security Act implies that Thailand has unfairly encroached on U.S. market shares during 1981-1985 [Subsections (a)(7) and (a)(8)]. A reference was then made to a countervailing duty (CVD) petition then pending with the Commerce Department. The purpose of these insinuations was to show that the Thais were using the subsidies to encroach on the U.S. share in the world rice market. The Commerce Department's finding on the CVD petition did show that the Thais were indeed giving 0.75 percent subsidies to its rice exports. At the time the findings came out, Congress had already legislated a more than 100 percent subsidy on the United States' own rice exports. Another possible purpose behind this is to square the proposed subsidy with the GATT's requirement that it would not lead to the United States capturing a "more than equitable share of the world export trade" in rice.

The main impact of the 1985 Act has been to permit the Commodity Credit Corporation to unload onto the world market some 2 million metric tons of rice that it had accumulated between 1981 and 1985 during the lifetime of the previous Farm Act.

That the disgorgement of the rice stocks with the CCC in 1986 did reduce the world market rice price now admits of little doubt. A recent U.S. study of the U.S. rice program shows quite clearly that in that year, the United States itself transferred a substantial benefit (about $90 million worth) to foreign buyers of U.S. rice by dumping the rice abroad (Cramer, Wailes, Gardner and Lin 1989:16). The impact of that dumping on Thai prices is a bit more complex.

The expected release of the CCC stocks has an immediate impact in reducing the Thai price of 100 percent B rice by $30 to $40 per metric ton in early 1986, from the $210-$220 per ton range to about the $180-190 range. (Figures concerning export prices of rice during this period are somewhat murky, as the Thai authorities were then doctoring them more than usual.) How much of this $30-$40 fall can be attributed to the U.S. legislation remains debatable, as there were other shifts in the world market, shifts that could have cushioned the drop as much as they would have exacerbated it. An example of a cushioning shift is the rise in Brazilian demand that took place in that year. An example of an exacerbating shift is the lifting of the rice export tax in Thailand in January 1986.

That $30 fall in rice prices which we shall attribute to the rice title translates into about 400 baht a ton fall in paddy prices, which is about 15 percent of the then current farm-gate prices. A 15 percent fall in the price of rice is not a large drop, given the diversified structure of the Thai economy (Rice now constitutes only 4-5 percent of the GDP). What people tend to forget, however, is that even today one-third of the Thai households make a living from rice. In all the trade disputes between Thailand and the United States (with the United States being in all cases the demanders), no Thai action under dispute (even assuming that Thailand is the "guilty" party) has affected such a large swath of the U.S. population to such a degree.

Since 1987, the rice prices have climbed again, thanks to that year's drought in Thailand and the depletion of CCC stocks. Thai complaints about U.S. rice policies have also disappeared. The U.S. administration has also contributed by maintaining its acreage restriction program at a stringent level. Indeed, at times in 1988 and again this year, the world price of rice, worked back to rough rice (paddy) equivalents, came close to the U.S. target prices, so that the United States could claim that its subsidies are now close to zero and that the problem has disappeared.

The Food Security Act expires at the end of 1990. In designing new legislation it would be nice if the Congress could bear in mind the fact that the American rice lobby did say in 1985, with a straight face, that the purpose of the Food Security Act was to "orient" the American rice industry towards the market, and that the measures deployed between 1986 and 1990 were to bridge over the difficulties. Furthermore, the U.S. rice industry commissioned a study that showed that the burden of the rice program would taper off by 1990. Indeed, the general mood in the Congress appears to be that the marketing loan has been a great success, and that its application should be extended from rice and cotton to other crops.

Does "success" mean therefore that the American rice industry has attained full manhood of "market orientation" and can sustain itself without any government subsidies? Can the American rice industry go out and fight foreign competition on a level playing field? If the rice industry were to be held to the statements it has made, it should be ready to face the international market without any help from the long-suffering (and long-bamboozled) American taxpayer.

Realistically, it is likely that the American rice lobby will still press for and obtain a continuation of the existing program. Given the rather severe budget constraint, it is hard to imagine it acquiring an even greater subsidy. At the present level of subsidization (with its attendant price in the form of acreage restriction), it is unlikely that American exports would expand much beyond the 2.5-3 million ton range.

The Thai Government and the International Rules of the Game

The tasks facing the Thai government in the international arena can be divided into two parts: those dealing with multilateral issues, which mean primarily the Uruguay round negotiations, and those dealing with bilateral issues.

On multilateral trade negotiations, the Thai government's stand thus far has been logical. It has seen its interest clearly to lie in the direction of promoting world liberalization of agricultural trade. It has, as a result, been an active member of the Cairns group, and it has put a large proportion of its very limited staff on the tedious work of participating actively in the negotiations with a major focus on agriculture.

Among the three major issues discussed in the current round, the position of the Thais is very clear on export subsidies—it wants them removed. Its position on internal support is to ensure that what gets put in the so-called red box does not include items that it considers to be developmental, in particular, irrigation. In Thailand, water is provided free to farmers.

Its position on market access is quite unexpected. It would like some sort of safeguards, measures to prevent surges of imports during favorable weather periods. It argues (there is no clear evidence for it) that weather conditions in Thailand and other Southeast Asian rice exporters are correlated, and Thailand would like to reserve the right to impose temporary ban on rice imports. It is very difficult to understand the motivation behind this particular stand. An optimist would suggest that Thailand is serious about free trade and looks forward to the day when it will actually be importing rice (something unthinkable to most Thais) and is already planning for it. In any case, this situation has landed the Thai government in some difficulties with its Cairns group allies.

Two major bilateral issues face the Thai government. The first is the necessity to renegotiate the cassava agreement, which expires at the end of this year. The renegotiation is now complete, with things more or less to continue as usual.

On the U.S. front, the government needs to formulate a clear strategy of how it wishes to present its case to the Congress. Unfortunately, the lobbying effort is somewhat stymied by a lack of clear strategy which, in my view, should concentrate on American interests (other than the rice lobby). Instead, the Thais have tended to concentrate on how the Farm Act is hurting its economy, which while true, cannot win any vote on Capitol Hill.

The World Market and Thailand's Response: Some Preliminaries

Thailand's Comparative Advantage in Agriculture

That Thailand at the moment possesses considerable comparative advantage in agriculture is obvious. It is able to maintain a high level of net exports of agricultural commodities without subsidies (except for sugar) in competition with other suppliers, some of whom subsidize heavily.

Among its exports, the share of agriculture has been steadily declining, particularly since 1980, suggesting that its comparative advantage in manufactures has also been increasing. As Thailand demonstrates more comparative advantage in certain manufacturing items, its clear advantage in agriculture can no longer be taken for granted. The following pages explore what the future holds in store, in respect of Thai agriculture in the world economy.

Before we proceed to measure Thai comparative advantage, we must recognize that "agriculture" is many things. For some, agriculture appears synonymous with crop production: not altogether an unreasonable view, considering that it comprises about 68 percent of total value added in Thai agriculture. Usually ignored are three other sectors that should be included as part of agriculture, namely livestock, fisheries and forestry. In the following, forestry will continue to be ignored. Even though silviculture is growing in importance, the sector is generally small and declining.

The Measurement of Comparative Advantage

The very term "comparative advantage" requires us to look at the Thai situation relative to the rest of the world. One summary measure of the "comparative advantage" of agriculture in the rest of the world would be the prices in the world market of agricultural commodities relative to manufactured goods.

Among crop production, livestock and fisheries, the measurement of comparative advantage below follows different procedures, largely because the activities involved are quite different in nature. Crop production in general is constrained by the availability of basic resources, notably land in relation to the agricultural labor force. Traditionally, until about the late 1970s, land under cultivation had been expanding faster than labor. This is the fundamental source of comparative advantage of Thai agriculture. As land has become scarcer from 1980 onwards, Thailand's comparative advantage in crop production may be expected to decline, if world prices do not change. World price changes would, of course, have to be taken into account, but only in the context of shifting resource availability in Thailand.

Livestock production is in many respects similar to industrial processes, particularly for poultry and swine, the two larger activities within this category. Unlike crop production, there are no domestic natural resource constraints (such as land) to its expansion. One has to examine whether the present technology allows socially profitable use of domestic resources to produce livestock in competition with products available in the world market. Competition in the world market implies some comparison of the cost of domestic resources vis-à-vis world prices. Such a comparison assumes that the livestock sector can easily acquire, at a price, additional domestic resources (meaning mostly labor and other nontradable goods and services, e. g., transport) that it uses, simply by pulling them in from other activities in the economy. Contrast this easy augmentability with the difficulty of expanding land in the case of the crop subsector. For this reason we shall employ the domestic resource cost (DRC) analysis to measure comparative advantage in livestock. The details of the technique will be given below.

The fishery subsector is something of a hybrid. A part of it—that part depending on capture rather than culture—depends on the bounty of nature and is thus similar to crop production. The part depending on culture, the more rapidly growing one in recent years, is similar to livestock. Different approaches should be adopted for these two components of the fishery subsector. Lack of adequate data on the available natural resources prevents us from doing full justice to the capture part of the subsector. We have perforce adopted the DRC technique to examine the comparative advantage of both parts of the Thai fishery industry.

The World Market and Thailand's Response in Crop Production

Shifting Comparative Advantage in Thai Crop Sector

In the past, agriculture has grown slowly relative to the industrial and service sectors. There are many and complex reasons for the different expansion rates. Among them:

- The world terms of trade of agriculture relative to industrial and service sectors have been moving steadily against agriculture, even though within Thailand this tendency has been moderated by the gradual removal of the barriers against exports.
- Agricultural expansion is more natural-resource constrained, while the industrial and service sectors rely heavily on capital and labor, which are more easily augmented.
- The technologies in use in both the agricultural and nonagricultural sectors are backward relative to the best practices in the rest of the world. While the nonagricultural sector can easily acquire and adapt foreign technology and therefore grow rapidly on this basis, the acquisition and adaptation of foreign technology into Thai agriculture is by no means simple or in some cases even possible. Considerable effort has to be put into both adaptive and new technology before they can be put into practice. Crop output growth cannot therefore be as rapid.

Ultimately, shifts in the comparative advantage occur as a result of the shifts in the domestic resource costs (which, in the case of crops, depend primarily on changes in domestic resource endowments) interacting with changes in the relative world prices (which measure the opportunities faced by Thai agriculture). TDRI's agricultural supply model allows us to explore the impact of the above shifts. The speed of the transformation in the agricultural sector depends primarily on changes in land and labor, although we have included factors that enhance the productivities of these two inputs, namely public and private capital, schooling, and agricultural research. To take into account the changes in the economic environment facing Thai agriculture, price movements are also included in the analysis. The data which form the bases of this essentially long-term analysis came from Thailand's experience in the period 1960-1985. The analysis is reported extensively in Siamwalla, Patamasiriwat, Mundlak and Setboonsarng (1989).

The assumptions needed to employ the above model to forecast future changes are:

- Crop price forecasts
- Changes in the amount of land and labor as well as the productivity-enhancing factors mentioned above

Agricultural Price Forecasts to the Years 1995 and 2000

Table 9.2 reproduces the World Bank's crop price forecasts. It can be immediately seen that prices in 1987 were particularly low, which is why many of the forecasted prices show a rise in the future, sometimes by a substantial percentage.

The forecasts for crop prices not covered by the World Bank are based on our judgement or their historical trends.

In aggregate, these forecasts show that the price index for the 20 crops of importance to Thailand (deflated by the nonagricultural price) will increase at a moderate pace of 0.14 percent per annum on the average between 1987 and 1995. But this aggregative change hides a number of differing movements.

Rice. Rice price is forecast to fall slightly in real terms from the base level in 1987 at the rate of 0.3 percent per year to the year 1995.

Maize and Soybeans. Both maize and soybeans are expected to rise at around 2 percent per year from 1987 to 1995. The soybean price forecast should be treated with caution for at least two reasons: some economists anticipate that soybean prices will tend to decline as a result of the continued rapid expansion in Brazil and Argentina, and

TABLE 9.2 Price Forecasts for Agricultural Commodities

Commodity	Actual[1]			Forecast[1]		Increase or Decrease[2]	
	1970	1980	1987	1995	2000	1987-1995	1987-2000
Rice	396	416	177	173	166	-0.3	-0.5
Maize	161	120	58	68	73	2.0	1.8
Sugar	223	606	115	224	254	8.7	6.3
Sorghum	143	124	56	62	68	1.3	1.5
Soybean	322	284	166	198	148	2.2	-0.9
Soybean Oil	845	572	257	470	371	7.8	2.9
Rubber	1,270	1,560	860	1,150	1,060	3.7	1.6
Palm Oil	716	559	264	327	296	2.7	0.9
Copra	619	434	238	305	266	3.1	0.9
Cotton	1,740	1,960	1,270	1,230	1,160	-0.4	-0.7
Jute	754	295	248	243	236	-0.3	-0.4
Tobacco	2,717	2,205	1,471	1,492	1,439	0.2	-0.2

Source: World Bank 1989, Price Prospects for Major Primary Commodities (1988-2000).
[1]1985 U.S. $/metric ton
[2]percent per year

the World Bank itself expects soybean prices to decline in the period beyond 1995, the rate of decline being 0.9 percent per year, from 1987 to 2000.

Rubber. Rubber price is anticipated to increase in real terms at 2.7 percent per year during 1987-1995. An important development that may be of interest to Thai policy-makers is the shift taking place in Malaysia away from rubber towards oil palm. Malaysian economists argue that rubber is more labor-intensive, and as Malaysian wages have grown, Malaysia's comparative advantage has declined. Thai wages are still very much below Malaysian wages, and therefore it can be expected that the Thai share of world natural rubber production will increase at the expense of Malaysia.

Sugarcane. Strikingly, sugarcane prices are assumed to increase very strongly at the rate of 8.7 percent per year between 1987 and 1995. This growth is, however, from the very low base of the 1987 price level—this was the year after the United States released its stocks following the Farm Act. Furthermore, the World Bank includes as part of its projection the assumption that the United States will lower its target price (the receipt that the U.S. government guaranteed sugar growers) down from 18 cents to 12 cents per pound.

Expected Future Changes in Resources Devoted to Agriculture

The following are the assumptions (based largely on an extrapolation of past trends) that we have made to project future trends of resource use in agriculture:

- The amount of land per agricultural worker will be declining at the rate of 1 percent per annum over the next 10 years. This is essentially a continuation of a trend which began in the second half of the 1970s.
- Capital stock per worker will be increasing at the rate of 1 percent per annum.
- Irrigation will expand at different rates in the different regions, but nationally, the average rate of expansion will be 8 percent per annum.
- Schooling (an important factor explaining agricultural growth) will grow at 3 percent per annum.
- Agricultural research expenditures will be expanding at the rate of 5 percent per annum.

Results of the Projection

The projection exercise indicates that agricultural output in the next 10 years will continue to grow at 2.3 percent per year, a moderate rate of growth, no longer as strong as it was in the 1960s and the 1970s, when it was in excess of 3.5 percent. The breakdown by commodity groups is as follows:

Rice	1.4 percent
Upland crops	6.1 percent
Tree crops	5.5 percent

The rice sector will be lagging somewhat, because the world price is expected to fall, and even though irrigation is projected to expand substantially and thus favor rice production, it is not sufficient to pull up rice production. But even if the rate of its production growth is barely equal to the rate of population growth, rice exports will probably continue to grow, because rice consumption per capita is presently trending downwards strongly.

We may insert an observation here concerning the future of maize trade, even though at the moment the model is not detailed enough to allow us to forecast its output and exports. Recent developments both on the demand and supply side would tend to indicate that the surplus that Thailand has been enjoying on this commodity is fast dwindling and turning into a deficit. In anticipation of future shortfalls, the government has put in place a variable levy system to stabilize domestic prices and to protect domestic producers. Thus far, Thailand remains a net exporter.

The upshot of this exercise is that Thailand will continue to export agricultural products under the scenario assumed above. This continuing net export surplus, as we shall see below, is going to pose a problem for policy.

Thailand's Comparative Advantage in the Livestock Subsector

The dynamics of expansion in the livestock subsector is driven much more by the strength of domestic demand than by international developments. As incomes have grown, the people's diet has diversified from vegetable products, primarily cereals, towards livestock products, the income elasticities of consumption for these products being much higher for directly consumed crop products. Thus, the urban income elasticities for poultry and for pork, to take two examples, are 0.99 and 1.10 (Setboonsarng and Amaranand, unpublished), as against a probably negative income elasticity for rice. The growth rates of the various components of the livestock subsector are shown in Table 9.3. The figures in Table 9.3 mask the profound changes that have taken place in livestock production in Thailand. Take the case of poultry. Production in this sector in 1970 was still mostly in the backyards. This type of poultry raising still exists, but it is a very small component of the total now. The growth rate reported in Table 9.4 is a composite of the slow growth (or even possibly absolute decline) in this sector together with the far more rapid growth in commercial poultry operations, with each farm raising more than 10,000, sometimes more than 100,000, birds. This kind of operation requires much more intensive use of feed, which has implications for the amount of feed used in Thailand.

Although the livestock industry is driven primarily by domestic demand, international markets do exert considerable influence over the livestock subsector. Some of its products are traded in the world markets. Poultry exports from Thailand are now of some importance, and swine producers are hopeful of one day matching the performance of the poultry-raisers. On the import side, dairy products make up the largest category among Thailand's agricultural goods imports. Above all, livestock production requires for its raw materials many items in which

TABLE 9.3 Growth Rates of Value Added in Various Livestock Products at Constant Prices (1970-1988)

	Growth Rates (%)
Cattle and Buffaloes	3.1
Swine	5.5
Poultry and Eggs	7.5
Others	5.9
Total Value Added	6.1

Source: National Accounts (New Series), National Accounts Division, National Economic and Social Development Board.

TABLE 9.4 Comparative Advantage in Agricultural Production, 1986

Product	Domestic Resource Cost
Livestock[1]	
Chicken	16.15 - 17.01
Eggs	13.26 - 15.57
Pork	24.22
Beef	19.03 - 45.85
Dairy	32.87 - 36.91
Fishery[2]	
Shrimp	7.86 - 9.95
Shrimp farming[a]	6.55 - 10.48
Squid	11.79 - 24.10
Fish	11.26 - 16.24

[a]Shrimp farming consists of extensive farming, semi-intensive, and intensive farming.

Notes: Domestic Resource Cost (DRC)=$Cd/(Pb\$-Cb\$) \times SER$ where Cd is the primary and nontraded input cost for producing one unit of an output in baht. $Pb\$$ is the border price of output, in dollars, $Cb\$$ is the traded input cost per unit of output, in dollars, and SER is the shadow exchange rate.

Sources:

[1]Setboonsarng, S., "Competitiveness of Livestock and Feedgrain Subsectors in Thailand," paper presented at the Pacific Economic Cooperation Conference, Seoul 1989.

[2]Tokrisna, R., "Comparative Advantage of Thai Agriculture." Mimeo, Thailand Development Research Institute, 1989.

Thailand is an active trader, either on the importing or exporting side, for example, maize, soybean meal and fishmeal.

We estimate Thailand's comparative advantage in livestock production using the domestic resource cost approach. The top part of Table 9.4 presents the results of the domestic resource cost calculations that TDRI did for the Asian Development Bank (Setboonsarng, Titapiwatanakun and Tubpun 1989) for the year 1986. The numbers are given as a range, because the calculations were done for different regions of the country. The figures indicate clearly that Thailand has a comparative advantage in the poultry sector (both chicken meat and eggs) and equally clearly that it has a comparative disadvantage in the dairy sector, which at the moment can only be sustained by heavy protection. Thailand's comparative advantage in the swine sector is less glaring, but we would maintain that it is there nonetheless. These calculations are made for the year when Thailand still enjoyed a considerable maize surplus. It is not expected that the expected shift towards a deficit situation with respect to this key feed grain will affect the comparative advantage in poultry and swine substantially. The advantage in poultry that Thailand has is so large that the extra cost of imports (excluding tariffs) will not affect it, while the swine population in Thailand still depends largely on rice-bran rather than maize.

The beef sector is complicated, partly because of the enormous quality range, at least the quality as measured by the varying prices that people are willing to pay for a kilogram of beef. In Table 9.4, the results that are reported are merely for the high-quality beef that would compete with imports, which is a very small section of the beef market. The reason we confine ourselves to this small section is because there is no international trade in the kind of beef that is mostly consumed in Thailand—and therefore no question of comparative advantage could arise.

For the high-quality beef, the availability of the right kind of feed explains the wide range of results reported in Table 9.4. We obtain our data from three areas in the country: in Sakon Nakhon, in Tak, and in Ratchaburi. The last area is the only one which shows a domestic resource cost significantly below the exchange rate, whereas the other two show the cost to be much higher. The main reason for the profitability of the Ratchaburi operation is the availability of the pineapple waste from nearby canneries as roughage for the cattle, which also reduces the need for concentrated feed. The nearness to the large Bangkok market also helps.

The beef study shows the limitations of the domestic resource cost approach. Although it clearly shows that the Ratchaburi farms have a clear comparative advantage, it does not follow that Thailand as a whole would have comparative advantage in beef production. To draw that conclusion, the conditions in Ratchaburi must allow replication, which clearly is not the case here. On the other hand, our earlier results that chicken production generally has a low domestic resource cost, are more robust, because poultry technology can be easily replicated over wide areas in Thailand.

Thailand's Comparative Advantage in the Fisheries Subsector

The fisheries subsector is in the midst of a crisis stemming from an overintensive mode of fishing. As the marine fishery resources have been mined to the point of exhaustion, the Thai fishing fleet had to face rapidly rising costs, compounded in the 1970s by high fuel costs. As far as the inland fisheries are concerned, rural people are finding it more and more difficult to obtain fish from natural sources. These difficulties have a profound but unmeasured impact on the standard of living of most people, since traditionally, fish is second only to rice as an essential food item.

Surprisingly, despite all this, Thai fisheries exports (in the analysis below we exclude canned tuna fish) continue to grow. Of the major export items, only fishmeal exports have declined, so that in real terms its export value in 1986 is less than in 1977. Part of the growth in general fisheries exports came from the increase in aquacultural output. However, contrary to popular impressions, the overwhelming proportion (99 percent by weight and 90 percent by value) of Thailand's marine fisheries product still comes from capture rather than culture. Even for shrimp, only a fifth of the tonnage produced in 1986 comes from farms.

One way to get at the riddle of why Thai exports of fisheries products have been doing so well is to examine the comparative advantage of the Thai fisheries industry. In a specially commissioned paper prepared for TDRI, Ruangrai Tokrisna (1989) calculated the domestic resource cost of the various kinds of fishery products, taking into account different technologies of capture and culture. The results, displayed in the lower panel of Table 9.5, show unequivocally that Thailand has a clear comparative advantage in most sectors of fisheries production. The main exception is shrimp caught by otterboard trawl and fishmeal, which appear by 1986 to be a socially unprofitable way to obtaining foreign exchange.

TABLE 9.5 Research Expenditure per 100 Baht of Crop Value

Crops	1987	1988
Exportable Crops		
Rice	0.49	0.37
Rubber	0.46	0.54
Maize	0.52	0.20
Tapioca	0.20	0.18
Sugarcane	0.43	0.23
Mungbean	0.88	0.74
Sorghum	1.01	0.77
Importable Crops		
Soybean	0.79	0.66
Oil Palm	0.72	0.46
Cotton	4.35	2.30
Groundnut	1.20	2.30

Sources: Setboonsarng and Khaoborisuth (forthcoming), *Research Budget Allocation of the Department of Agriculture,* Discussion Paper for the Research Priorities in Thai Agriculture Project, Department of Agriculture, Thailand Development Research Institute (TDRI), Australian Center of International Agricultural Research (ACIAR) and International Service for National Agricultural Research (ISNAR).

Government Policies Towards the Agricultural Sector

We discuss government policies in two parts. The first section below analyzes government policies given the natural evolution of Thailand's comparative advantage in agriculture vis-à-vis other sectors. We confine ourselves to pricing policies (including trade intervention) because these, more than anything else, permit us to examine the interaction between comparative advantage and the incomes of farmers. The second section examines policies that modify that comparative advantage.

Pricing Policies and Trade Interventions

Efficiency requires that a country should follow the comparative advantage that it possesses in its resource allocation. The simplest way that a country can follow its comparative advantage is to pursue a free trade policy. Most governments wish, however, to pursue policies that aim for objectives other than efficiency. In particular, agricultural output prices are supposed to have powerful effects on income distribution, and the most effective way to manipulate these prices is through border interventions. Consequently, free trade is seldom practiced by most governments. In this respect, Thailand is no exception.

Traditionally, the Thai government has adopted two conflicting instruments to manipulate domestic prices for agricultural products. On the one hand, it has restricted trade, either by export or import duties. Such trade restrictions would lower the prices of exportable items and raise the price of import competing items. On the other hand, the government claims to be conscious of the fact that Thai farmers are poor, and therefore product prices have to be "supported" or "guaranteed" as a means of enhancing their incomes. Measures were then adopted to "support" and "guarantee" these prices. For exportable products, these two sets of measures stand in direct conflict with each other, but such contradiction has not prevented many governments from adopting both. Unfortunately the price "support" and "guarantee" measures have been generally ineffective in reaching their objective and have succeeded only in frittering away considerable amounts of taxpayers' money. The export taxation, on the other hand, has been all too effective in depressing domestic prices. Past pricing policies have therefore not only been inefficient, in that they have distorted incentives away from those dictated by comparative advantage, but also inequitable, in that they have imposed a burden on the farmers, who generally tend to be poorer than the nonfarming population.

From the beginning of the 1980s onwards, the government policies of export taxation on agricultural goods have been gradually dismantled.

The analysis above shows that Thailand's agricultural sector will remain competitive, in the sense that Thailand will retain at least the present level of exports in most of the items, with a few exceptions, even though the proportion of labor force engaged in agriculture will continue to decline.

In general, Thai farmers have been singularly unfortunate for being so efficient. As long as Thai farmers continue to churn out surpluses for export, then for the government to enhance their incomes through price measures, it has to expend fiscal resources to subsidize exports. This the Thai government has been most reluctant to do. The only successful example where domestic interests have pushed the government to subsidize exports has been the sugar industry. The peculiar industrial structure for sugar allows the government to implement a scheme to have the domestic sugar consumers cross-subsidize directly the exports, without any direct fiscal outlay (Siamwalla and Setboonsarng 1989). Otherwise, only producers of import-competing products, such as soybean meal and palm oil, enjoy domestic prices higher than world prices.

An interesting price and trade policy issue is now arising as Thailand is switching from a maize-surplus to a maize-deficit situation. Should Thailand enhance the income of its maize farmers by limiting imports? One by-product of such protection is that the demand for cassava as domestic feed might go up and therefore the income of cassava growers could also rise, the more so if soybean meal imports are less restricted than they are now. But equally clearly such protection, if substantial, will affect the viability of the livestock sector, particularly poultry, which is now being exported in some quantities. As pointed out above, the viability of the poultry sector from the country's point of view does not depend on whether we import or export maize, but its private viability (i.e., from the individual producer's point of view) depends very much on the kind of tariffs and trade restrictions that the government imposes on maize imports.

Most developed countries and Asian newly industrialized countries (NICs) do protect their agriculture heavily by providing hefty export subsidies, among other measures. As Thailand progresses toward that aspired NIC status, it could use its new-found industrial wealth to help out agriculture. To make such claims is to misread the recent history of many of these Asian NICs. Both Korea and Taiwan turned towards protecting their agricultural sector (particularly that benchmark commodity, rice) only after they became net importers. Both Korea and Taiwan were traditional rice exporters (before the war, as part of the Japanese Empire, they were assigned the task of supplying Japan with cheap rice), and Taiwan continued to export rice until the late 1960s. It was only after their farmers were unable to produce the rice needed domestically that they supported their farmers by giving them prices well above the world prices and by a concomitant policy of import restrictions. Japan, indeed, began a serious program of support for its rice farmers only after 1961, four decades after it began to import rice on a regular basis. (True, all these countries later turned out surpluses for exports which are subsidized—such exports, however, count as surplus disposals). Closer at home, Malaysia, well ahead of Thailand in per capita GNP, is supporting its rice farmers, but only because it is also an importer of rice. Most of its export commodities are subject to border taxation, and therefore to negative protection. The association between importer status and protection on the one hand, and exporter status and disprotection on the other, is too strong to be ignored, at least for countries near Thailand's level of income. It is therefore unlikely that the existing political economy will allow an increase in effective support for farmers, unless they grow import-competing crops.

Changing the Comparative Advantage Through Investment

Thailand need not take its comparative advantage as immutably given. It can attempt to modify it for many reasons, in particular, if a sector which appears to be losing its comparative advantage employs a large proportion of the labor force. If Thailand can continue to retain its comparative advantage in that sector, it will lead to a happy solution in that the painful costs of adjustment can be avoided without imposing any distortions on the economy.

Paradoxically, the Thai government, while penalizing the agricultural sector heavily with the price policy measures in the past, did invest rather large sums of money to enhance agricultural comparative advantage. Two avenues were followed. The first was the building of roads which lowers the marketing cost of agricultural produce. The second was the building of the irrigation systems, which had of course a direct impact on productivity, particularly of rice.

We shall not discuss the role of roads and road-building, because much of the gains from this public investment are behind us, now that much of the primary network has been built up. True, there is now congestion on many of these roads, but investments to relieve this congestion will affect agriculture relatively little.

For irrigation, on the other hand, the issue is at an altogether different level of complexity. Thailand has invested considerable sums into irrigation, probably the largest single form of investment in agriculture. Almost the entire system was designed for rice. As rice prices declined, and as the more favorable sites became irrigated, the return on investment in new sites, never very high, also declined. The issues facing the government now are whether to expand the irrigation and what to do with those areas already irrigated. On the first question, it appears unlikely that any major new irrigation scheme will be worthwhile. If one factors in the cost of irrigation, Thailand probably has no comparative advantage in growing irrigated rice. That lack of comparative advantage was becoming obvious in 1985-1986, when large amounts of land were taken out of rice in the central plains and put to other use, mostly horticulture and aquaculture, while at the same time more rice was being grown in the unirrigated Lower North and the Northeast, where more and more of wet season rice is coming from. Expensive irrigated land is best put to uses other than for rice, particularly if rice prices continue to drop, as the World Bank is projecting.

Indeed the question that has been subdued during the past two years of extraordinarily high domestic prices of rice is how to use the irrigated lands. Before this boom in rice prices, farmers in these areas have expressed their preferences by shifting to other, higher-valued crops.

Normally, over much of Thai agriculture, it is futile to ask what the government's land use policy should be. Farmers normally make these decisions themselves, and the government has little effective control over what the farmers can and cannot do with their lands—indeed it has little effective control over what people can do over the officially "public" lands. In the irrigated areas, things are a little more complicated. An individual farmer's choice of crops has a great deal of spillover effect, in both the literal and the technical senses of the term. Furthermore, farmers' decisions are significantly constrained by the timing of the water flow, which is a government decision. Unavoidably, therefore, the government plays a decisive role in how individual farmers in irrigated areas use their land.

Two levels of policy decisions have to be made. Given the present irrigation hardware, how should the water be allocated? And how much more investment should be made to modify that hardware? The present hardware has been designed specifically for rice, as is the water allocation system. Yet, over large areas of the central plains, during the years when rice prices were low, farmers have gone ahead and reshaped their lands for activities other than rice. This has implications for the water allocation system. If the government is to reform the water allocation system away from the present rice-only stance, it would necessarily become involved in decisions concerning cropping patterns, which in turn entail forecasting what individual crop prices would be during the forthcoming season. Is the government ready to do so? How much responsibility is it willing to take for its forecasts and decisions? When it makes a wrong forecast—as inevitably it will, no matter how sophisticated the methods employed are—will it share in the farmers' losses? These are issues that will be on the political agenda, as the irrigated areas move to a more complex cropping pattern.

The present rice-only design for the irrigation hardware is obviously less efficient than an alternative which would be less specific. To modify the existing system to become more flexible will require new investments. A study conducted by the World Bank (1985) concluded that such a modification would not be socially profitable. Unfortunately, the study assumed a shift away from rice toward the relatively low-valued upland crops, thus biasing the result downwards. It is not clear what the kind of returns would be for higher-valued products that would come from a shift towards aquaculture or horticulture.

Changing the Comparative Advantage Through Technology

The present comparative advantage between agriculture and industry can and will be modified by technological change. Technological change can in turn be accelerated or retarded, or its direction changed by government policies. Because we are discussing comparative advantage, strictly speaking, we should be addressing technology policies in both the agricultural and nonagricultural sectors. However, neither time nor competence allows us to tackle technology policies at that broad level. We shall confine ourselves to government policies to induce technological change in agriculture.

Each individual crop grown in Thailand has undergone relatively little technological change. By and large, there is little application of what is conventionally regarded in the rest of Asia as modern technology. There is little use of modern high-yielding varieties of rice, for example, and the rate of fertilizer application is well below that in most of the rest of Asia. Only in the use of machineries are Thai farmers somewhat ahead of their brethren in the rest of Asia. The outcome of this low application of modern technology is that agricultural yields in Thailand in general lag behind those of other countries.

To look at technological developments at the level of each individual crop, however, is to underestimate the technological dynamism displayed by the Thai farmer during the last three decades. While he has used age-old techniques to grow any particular crop, he has also been adopting new crops with speed, aided by the availability of abundant land resources. And it is due to this same abundance of land resources that he has been slower to intensify his practices and adopt the new high-yielding varieties and the associated use of fertilizers, generally known as the Green Revolution. As long as a farmer can extend his land, or his children can clear new areas, there is no reason for them to adopt a more intensive technique. But it must be remembered that acceptance of a new crop is no less an innovation than acceptance of a new technique or a new variety.

Government has expended resources to promote technological change, at least for the crop subsector. The amount of resources put in has, however, not been as large as it could be. In this respect, Thai agriculture has again suffered the misfortune of success. Because Thailand exports most agricultural commodities, there is not a sufficiently strong impulse for the government to invest heavily in research. In rice, for example, Thailand offers a sharp contrast to neighboring countries, such as Indonesia or India, where the drive for self-sufficiency has impelled their governments to put a great deal of resources into research. The same drive for self-sufficiency has also been at work with respect to import-competing crops in Thailand. For a long time, for example, research on cotton and soybeans has received a larger share of the research budget than would be justified by their importance in terms of the income that they generate for Thai farmers (Table 9.5). In these instances it can be said that the research policy has tended to lead to changes in comparative advantage.

For export crops, on the other hand, while the government has not been instrumental in introducing new crops to the farmers, once a crop becomes successful, the research budget has tended to expand *pari passu* with its importance in the economy. The reason for this strategy is to increase the income of the farmers growing these crops by making their farms more productive, not to protect the competitiveness of the particular crop. In these instances research policy follows the comparative advantage.

The key role played by private firms has been in introducing new crops to the farmers, but until recently they have played a minor role in researching new technology. Even in the poultry sector, where the private firms have played the dominant role, they have imported the technology from foreign multinationals. Domestic firms have confined themselves to adapting foreign technology to conditions here. Only recently have private firms in the hybrid maize industry begun to conduct research of their own (Setboonsarng, Wattanutchariya and Puthigom 1988), and much of that work has capitalized on the success of the Suwan varieties—a success of public sector research.

Not to be omitted are the unending experiments conducted by farmers themselves ever since humans started practicing agriculture 10,000 years ago. Thai farmers' trial-and-error methods have played an essential role in the progress of the horticultural sector and are playing some role in the swine and cattle industry. Such activities will no doubt continue. The potential of the farmers' own technologies is beginning to be realized in widening circles, not least by the Department of Agricultural Extension, which is now keen to diffuse such technologies.

Regardless of the source of new technologies, one undesirable consequence has been that they have with few exceptions tended to increase income inequalities among rural areas, for one simple reason. It is much easier to come up with new technologies or better varieties for areas that are agriculturally favorable; for example, while most of the new rice varieties are adapted to irrigated areas, the hybrid maize is best grown in areas with the more regular rainfall. Researchers inside and outside Thailand recognize the inherent bias in their work. Many organizations, for example the International Rice Research Institute (IRRI), have shifted the focus of their work toward such problems as drought tolerance and thus are more helpful to farmers in the less favorable growing environment, but so far with no results remotely matching their performance with the Green Revolution of the 1970s.

Such has been the experience in the past with government and private research activities to introduce new technologies to the Thai agricultural sector. What should be the strategy in a now-changed world agricultural environment?

First of all, it must be recognized that private firms will play an increasing role in research and diffusion of new technologies. Thai private firms still play a small role in generating new technology for agriculture. Nevertheless the success of poultry and feed firms, and mushrooming of the hybrid maize seed companies (Setboonsarng, Wattanutchariya and Puthigom 1988) suggest that their role will expand. From a social point of view, however, private firms have certain biases in the choices that they make. By and large, they prefer to confine their research activities to crops that are propagated by cross-pollination (for which they can offer a hybrid alternative more easily) and on animals. Crops that are self-pollinating or that are vegetatively propagated do not appeal to them, because farmers can easily reproduce the outcome and the investing firms cannot recapture the benefits from research to finance it.

This modest and biased entry of private firms into agricultural research suggests that public agricultural research will still continue to play a major, indeed the predominant, role. The rate of return to public sector research for all countries for which it has been measured—and there is no reason to suppose that Thailand is the exception—has always been very high, usually much higher than the return on irrigation.

But aside from conducting its own research, the government has also to police private sector technology. In particular, with the growth of private seed industry, the present laissez-faire stance of the government towards it will no longer suffice. Seed certification procedures and regulations will have to be devised to protect farmers against substandard seeds. True, the present method relies heavily on the incentive of private firms to protect their brand names by maintaining the quality of their seeds, but such methods tend to lead to an oligopolistic structure of the industry—not necessarily a desirable outcome either for the farmers or for the country as a whole.

A question that has been raised is whether Thailand should, for its own benefit (and not because of U.S. pressure), offer intellectual-property-right protection to people who invent new technology for agriculture. The present patent law specifically excludes agricultural machinery from products that can be so protected. Nor does Thailand have plant or animal variety protection. Little research has been conducted to measure the costs and benefits of such protection to the country as a whole. In our opinion, for the present level of agricultural technology, the benefits or costs of such protection are relatively small. Domestic production of technology that is patentable (patents require an invention which is a discrete step over and above what is known) is relatively small, and plant variety protection laws can be easily circumvented (even in developed countries). Import of foreign technology is also not much hampered. Under present technology, foreign firms build in their own protection to the genetic material which cannot be replicated (as genetic material), as can be seen in the case of poultry, oil palm, cattle and maize. They do not require any intellectual property protection.

Conclusion

World agricultural prices over the next decade will continue to be depressed by oversupply, and it is unlikely that the present GATT round of trade negotiations will be successful in making a sizable dent in the oversupply. Although prices are not expected to be as low as they were in 1987, they are expected to be only slightly above that on average.

These developments will not affect the trade orientation of Thai agriculture. The crop subsector is expected to continue to produce a net exportable surplus in the aggregate over and above domestic demand. A study of comparative advantage in the fisheries subsector indicates that Thailand enjoys favorable production conditions for much of that sector (except fishmeal), so it will probably continue to generate surpluses in this area as well. Our own studies show also that, within the livestock sector, the Thai poultry industry enjoys substantial comparative advantage. The swine industry also does, although the margin of advantage is not as decisive. Thailand, however, has no comparative advantage in the dairy industry, which can only be sustained by protection.

Despite some exceptions, Thai agriculture is therefore expected to be producing an exportable surplus, despite the expected fall in prices (relative to levels ruling in 1989). Therein lie some of the problems, for this expectation implies that without an increase in productivity, the producers' incomes cannot be expected to rise. Policies designed to shore up their incomes would imply a net outlay from the government, which, given past behavior patterns, is unlikely.

Increases in productivity can be generated only by putting more effort into research on new technology. Unfortunately, such research tends only to help farmers in areas that are already productive, and therefore would enhance inequalities among different regions in the country.

References

Cramer, Gail L., Eric J. Wailes, Bruce Gardner, William W. Lin. 1989. *Regulation in the U.S. Rice Industry, 1965-1989*. Staff Paper of the Department of Agricultural Economics and Rural Sociology, University of Arkansas, Fayetteville, Arkansas.

Johnson, D. Gale. 1989. *Soviet and Chinese Agriculture and Trade*. Testimony presented to the Joint Economic Committee of the U.S. Congress. September 7.

Perkins, Dwight H. 1988. "Reforming China's Economic System." *Journal of Economic Literature* XXVI: 2 (June), pp. 601-645.

Setboonsarng, Suthad and Piyaswasdi Amaranand. Unpublished. *The Vegetable Oil and Animal Feeds Model for Thailand*. To be published as a research report by Thailand Development Research Institute.

Setboonsarng, Suthad, Boonjit Titapiwatanakun, Somnuk Tubpun. 1989. *Competitiveness of Animal Feed and Livestock Production in Thailand*. Unpublished Research Report. Thailand Development Research Institute, Bangkok.

Setboonsarng, Suthad and Rodney Tyers. Unpublished. *The Impact of the European Common Agricultural Policies on Thailand*. To be published by the National Center for Development Studies, Australian National University.

Setboonsarng, Suthad, Sarun Wattanutchariya and Banlu Puthigom. 1988. *Seed Industry in Thailand: Structure, Conduct and Performance*. Research Report No. 32. Tilburg, the Netherlands, Development Research Institute, Tilburg University.

Siamwalla, Ammar, Direk Patamasiriwat, Yair Mundlak and Suthad Setboonsarng. 1989. *A Dynamic Analysis of Thai Agricultural Growth: Some Lessons from the Past*. Paper presented at the Workshop on TDRI Research Activities Supported by EPD II Project, Chiang Mai.

Siamwalla, Ammar and Suthad Setboonsarng. 1989. *Trade, Exchange Rate and Agricultural Pricing Policies in Thailand*. World Bank Comparative Studies on the Political Economy of Agricultural Pricing Policy. Washington, the World Bank.

Winham, Gilbert R. 1986. *International Trade and the Tokyo Round Negotiations*. Princeton, New Jersey: Princeton University Press.

World Bank. 1985. *Irrigation Subsector Review*. Washington: The World Bank.

10

China Agricultural Trade Developments and Prospects: With Emphasis on Pacific Rim Countries

Francis C. Tuan and Shi Ru

Brief Historical Perspective

With the opening of its door to global trade in the early 1970s, China's foreign trade began to develop rapidly. By the 1980s, following the basic reform of economic policies and institutions, the trade volume including many agricultural commodities expanded markedly. This paper begins with a brief historical perspective of China's foreign trade followed by an empirical review of the growth in trade of the 1980s particularly with reference to the Pacific Rim countries and also with respect to the agricultural trade policies of that period. The impact of the recent political unrest on agricultural production and trade is discussed before concluding with an outlook for agricultural trade with the Pacific Rim countries in the 1990.

In the 1950s, China actively pursued foreign trade with the Soviet Union and Eastern European countries. China's trade policy at that time focused on accelerating industrial growth and building up military capacities through large-scale capital goods and military-related matériel and equipment imports. About 60 to 80 percent of imports were from those countries (Eckstein, 1976).

China's relationship with the Soviet Union, however, deteriorated in the early 1960s. This coincided with an agricultural and economic crisis in China, particularly during the Great Leap Forward (1958-61) and resulted in a sharp drop in foreign trade. China greatly reduced machinery and defense matériel imports from the Soviet Union. It also began to allow more wheat, sugar, wool, cotton, and chemical fertilizer imports from countries other than the USSR and Eastern Europe. However, according to statistics published by China's Ministry of Foreign Economic Relations and Trade (MOFERT), China's total trade values did not regain the 1959 level until 1973 (Ministry of Agriculture, 1949-86).

During the 1970s, China increased domestic investment levels and, as a result, the Chinese economy began to grow. The country boosted exports in order to fund the foreign machinery, equipment, and technology imports for its accelerated economic growth. China made a historic change in the early 1970s to open up trade with more countries, and in 1971 barriers to Sino-American trade were removed as the two countries began to normalize political and economic relations. In 1978, in addition to a long-term trade agreement with Japan, China also signed a five-year trade agreement with the European Economic Community (EC).

China's foreign trade expanded rapidly in the 1980s, partly as a result of the country's decade of economic reforms. To accelerate economic development and improve people's living standard, China's leaders now realize the importance of international trade; therefore, the open door policy has been kept intact after the country experienced increased trade deficits and after the June 4th Beijing incident in 1989. In general, China has exported raw and processed products, including many agricultural commodities, in exchange for needed machinery, equipment, and advanced technology, in order to modernize the country (Tuan, 1990). In the last 10 years, the value of China's foreign trade increased 193 percent, reaching $111.63 billion in 1989, for an annual increase of 12.7 percent (Fig. 10.1).

Agricultural Trade Growth in the 1980s

China's overall trade expanded rapidly between 1981 and 1989, averaging 12.3 percent annually, according to China's customs statistics (see appendix for differences between MOFERT and customs statistics). Agricultural trade, which contributed between 12 and 20 percent of total trade during the last seven years, also grew at a comparable rate of 11.7 percent per year since 1983, the earliest year customs data were available.

The share of agricultural trade relative to overall trade declined in the first half of the 1980s, particularly in the mid-1980s, as agricultural commodity imports, mainly grains and cotton, were sharply cut. The share rebounded to about 15 percent in the second half of the decade.

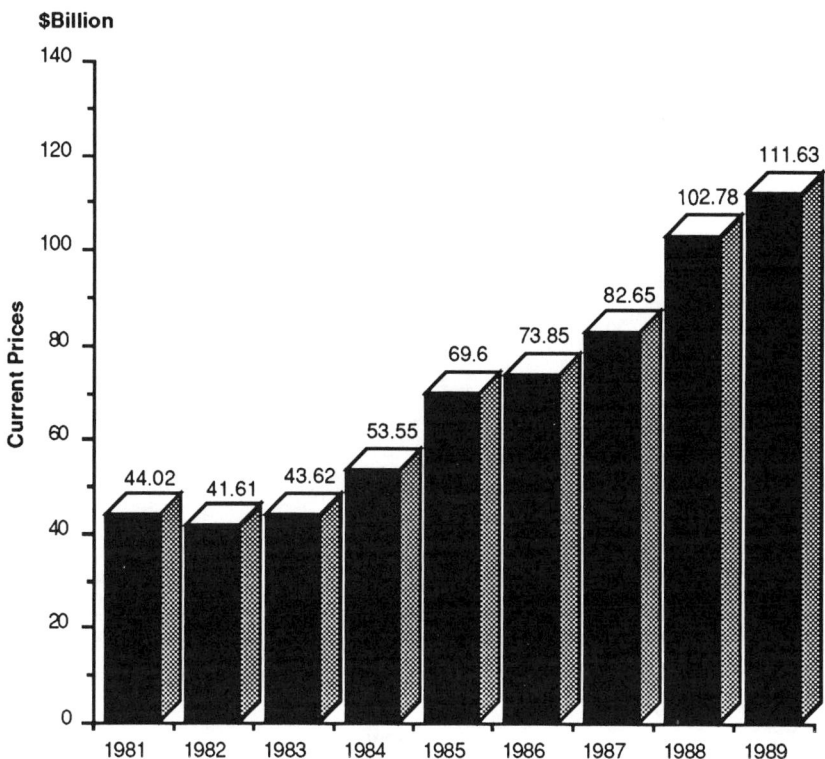

FIGURE 10.1 China's Total Trade

China's agricultural trade surpluses increased rapidly in the mid-1980s, as the country sharply cut imports and expanded exports when crop production peaked in 1984 (Fig. 10.2 & Fig. 10.3). China started shipping more corn, oilseeds and meals (such as soybeans and soymeal), and cotton to Japan, South Korea, the Philippines, Malaysia, Hong Kong, Singapore, Indonesia, and other Asian countries. The decision to increase exports was made mainly because of the lack of transportation and storage capacity between crop surplus and deficit areas. Rather than stockpile crop surpluses, some areas, especially those in the Northeast, found it more feasible and profitable to export.

Corn and cotton imports were largely eliminated for a number of years after crop production peaked in 1984, and wheat purchases were reduced to about 6 million tons in 1985 and 1986, compared with the pre-

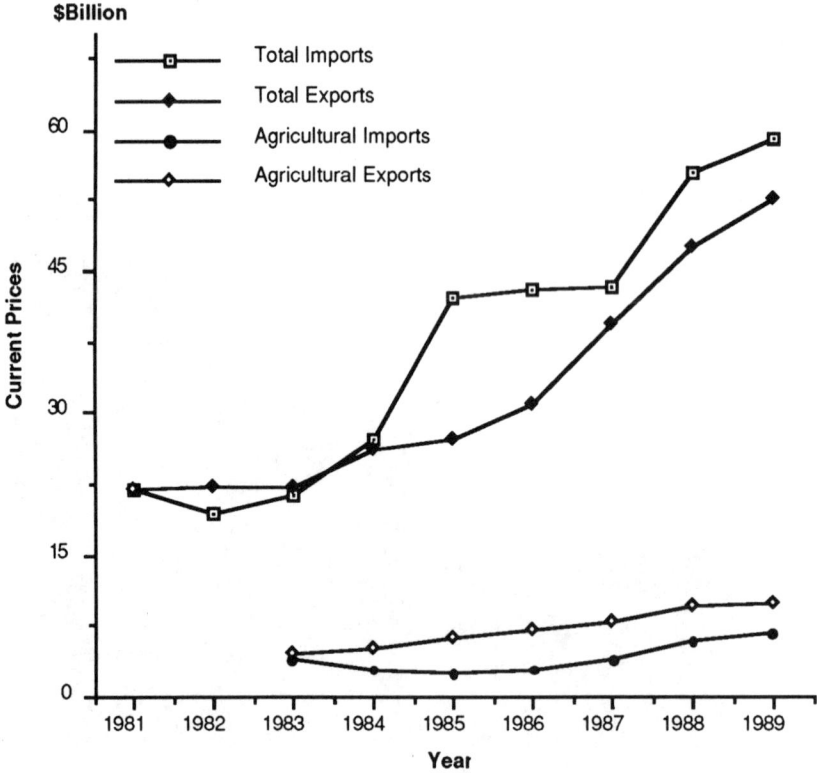

FIGURE 10.2 China's Total and Agricultural Trade

vious annual levels of 14 million tons in the early 1980s (Fig. 10.4). However, the agricultural trade surplus was gradually reduced in the latter half of the decade because commodity production, particularly grain and cotton, stagnated and domestic demand expanded. Wheat imports surged at the end of the 1980s because stocks began running low after three or four years of reduced state procurement and increased demand. The Export Enhancement Programs (EEP) of the United States, offering competitive wheat prices, also contributed to China's resumption of a higher level of wheat imports.

In all, agricultural trade surpluses, as high as $4.4 billion in 1986 and $4.1 billion in 1987, helped support imports of machinery, equipment, and advanced technology. Agricultural surpluses also helped reduce the country's overall trade deficits incurred during most of the 1980s.

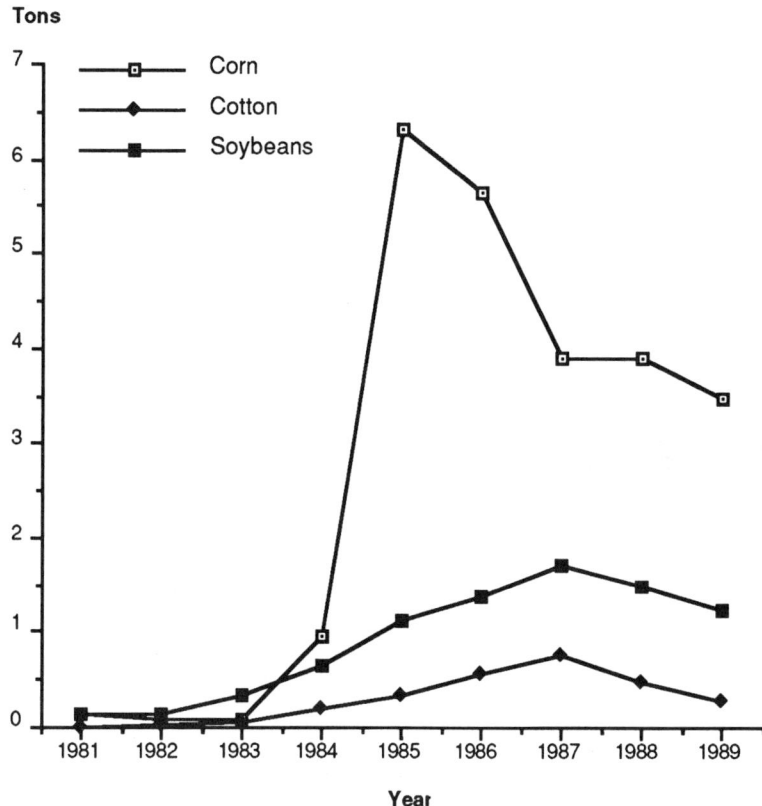

FIGURE 10.3 Major Agricultural Commodity Exports

Exports of agricultural products, however, have become much more diversified. Despite continual exports of grain and cotton in the late 1980s, China managed to expand exports of other agricultural products except animal fats and vegetable oils (Table 10.1). Besides fresh vegetables, fruits, and oilseeds, many of the exported goods were processed products, for instance, feed and canned foods.

Agricultural Trade with Pacific Rim Countries

Because of proximity and cultural ties, Pacific Rim countries have been China's major agricultural trade partners since it opened up its trade in the 1970s (Fig. 10.5 & Fig. 10.6). The major ones are Japan,

TABLE 10.1 Composition of China's Agricultural Trade, 1983-89 (thousands of U.S. dollars)

	1983	1984	1985	1986	1987	1988	1989
Imports							
Food, livestock	3,116,060	2,215,444	1,556,502	1,614,049	2,444,032	3,475,900	4,192,680
Grains	2,457,362	1,720,845	971,594	982,330	1,689,294	1,854,790	2,983,160
Sugar	440,401	248,172	283,223	217,435	299,436	866,060	441,490
Feed	76,054	88,054	84,711	98,019	135,550	324,390	324,400
Beverages and tobacco	46,490	118,491	208,363	175,211	263,427	345,900	201,470
Inedible material	673,447	341,241	557,738	739,003	829,161	1,636,780	1,435,710
Hides	56,011	39,345	103,814	76,839	68,109	70,480	43,830
Oilseeds	1,053	1,030	923	63,407	61,559	37,000	13,960
Textile fibers	540,522	225,694	354,619	518,171	569,936	1,384,310	1,264,760
Animal fats and veg oils	69,889	77,513	123,758	208,384	351,380	368,920	875,280
Veg oils	52,154	54,069	89,757	184,479	316,010	323,190	839,430
Total ag imports	3,905,887	2,752,690	2,446,362	2,736,649	3,887,999	5,827,500	6,705,140

Exports

Food, livestock	2,848,104	3,106,487	3,868,986	4,522,098	4,794,342	5,890,540	6,144,690
Grains	213,949	442,289	1,083,223	899,427	580,151	681,700	719,130
Sugar	803,806	794,000	840,314	1,112,280	1,292,031	1,617,390	1,623,190
Feed	197,009	216,496	241,455	422,981	489,920	862,670	743,570
Beverages and tobacco	103,746	105,504	107,995	120,357	175,371	235,510	313,720
Inedible material	1,495,217	1,883,621	2,167,065	2,355,871	2,975,788	3,256,350	3,157,690
Hides	87,837	111,224	121,150	123,772	136,990	176,410	122,170
Oilseeds	320,119	471,720	483,049	573,216	678,826	683,530	645,260
Textile fibers	671,327	878,806	1,157,534	1,164,397	1,513,194	1,672,010	1,545,820
Animal fats and veg oils	104,565	137,668	135,993	117,496	81,551	74,330	86,060
Veg oils	103,487	136,754	134,927	116,676	79,635	72,410	82,660
Total ag exports	4,551,632	5,233,280	6,280,039	7,115,882	8,027,052	9,456,730	9,702,160

Sources: China's Customs General Admin., various issues; Ministry of Agriculture, 1949-86.

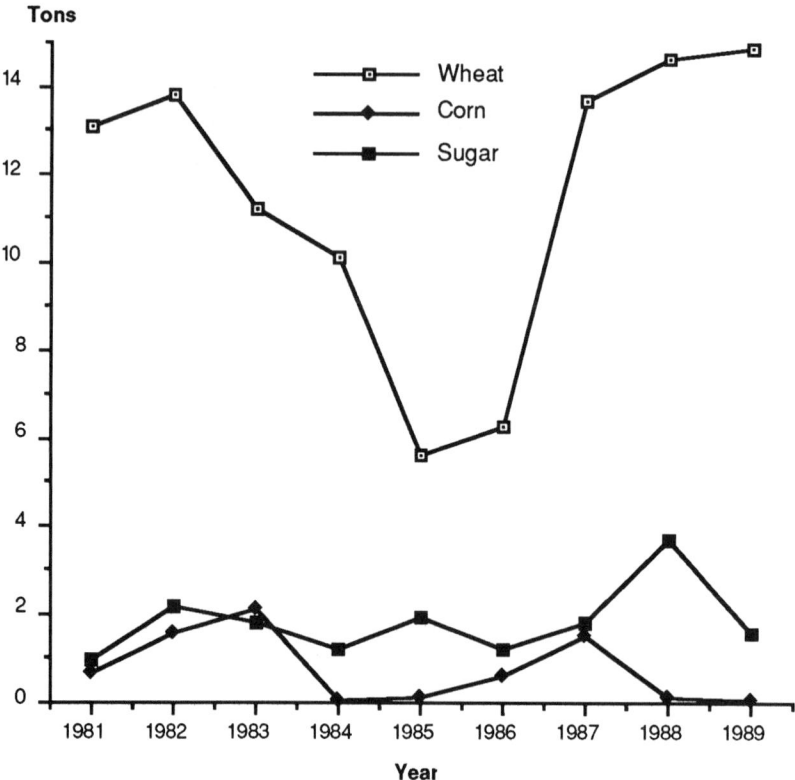

FIGURE 10.4 Major Agricultural Commodity Imports

Hong Kong, the Philippines, Malaysia, Singapore, Indonesia, Thailand, Macao, the United States, Canada, Australia, New Zealand, and the USSR, mainly the eastern part of the Soviet Union. Despite the relatively rapidly decreasing shares of China's agricultural imports from these countries in the 1980s, the share of their agricultural trade relative to China's total agricultural trade decreased only marginally and remained as high as 70 percent at the end of the 1980s (Table 10.2).

In value terms, China's agricultural trade with Pacific Rim countries has steadily increased since 1984. Among those countries, Hong Kong, Japan, the United States, the USSR, and Singapore have been China's most important export markets (Table 10.3). According to China's statistics, Hong Kong appears as China's largest agricultural as well as

TABLE 10.2 China's Agricultural Trade with Major Pacific Rim (PR) Countries, 1984-89[1]

	1984	1985	1986	1987	1988	1989
			Million $			
Ag imports[a]	2,752.7	2,446.4	2,736.6	3,888.0	5,827.5	6,705.1
From PR countries	2,313.3	2,018.0	1,944.9	2,870.8	3,722.3	4,319.9
Ag exports	5,233.3	6,280.0	7,115.8	8,027.1	9,456.7	9,702.2
To PR countries	3,476.2	4,474.2	5,013.4	5,769.0	6,919.9	7,093.0
Total ag trade	7,986.0	8,726.4	9,852.5	11,915.1	15,284.2	16,407.3
With PR countries	5,789.5	6,492.2	6,958.3	8,639.8	10,642.2	11,412.8
			Percent			
Ag imports[b]	100	100	100	100	100	100
From PR countries	84	82	71	74	64	64
Ag exports	100	100	100	100	100	100
To PR countries	66	71	70	72	73	73
Total ag trade	100	100	100	100	100	100
With PR countries	73	74	71	73	70	70

Notes:
[1]Pacific Rim countries include Hong Kong, Japan, the Philippines, Malaysia, Singapore, Indonesia, Thailand, Macau, the United States, Canada, Australia, New Zealand, and the USSR.
[a]Million $
[b]Percent

Sources: China's Customs General Admin., various issues.

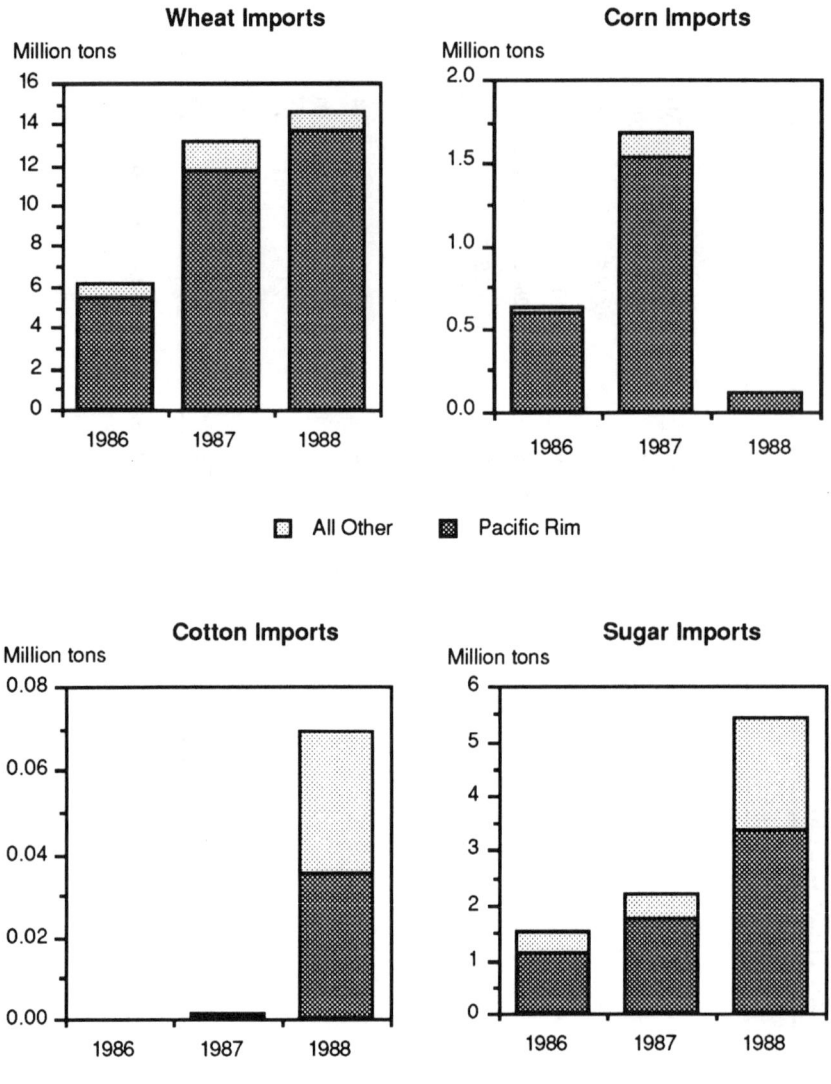

FIGURE 10.5 Major Commodity Imports from Pacific Rim Countries

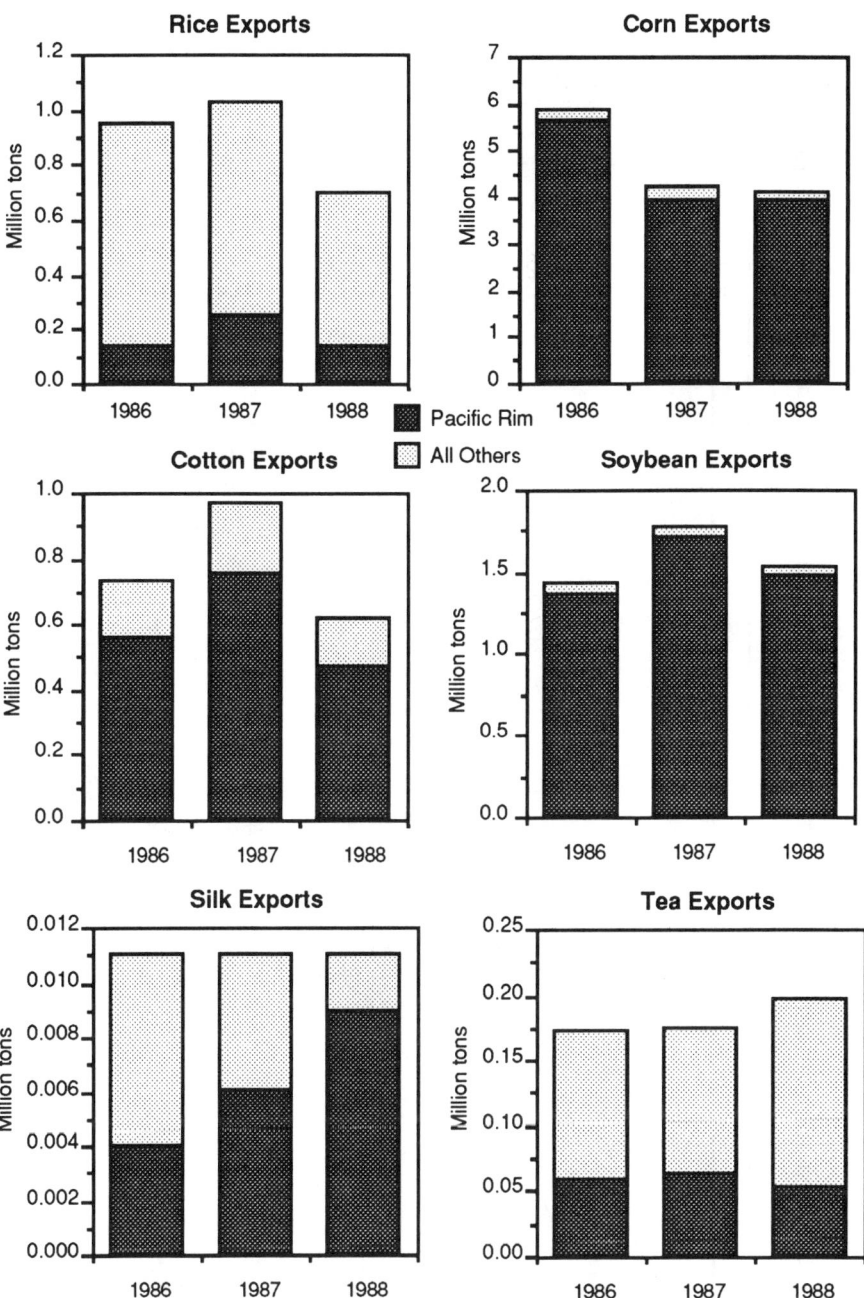

FIGURE 10.6 Major Commodity Exports to Pacific Rim Countries

TABLE 10.3 China's Agricultural Trade with Major Pacific Rim Countries or Regions 1984-89 (thousands of U.S. dollars)

	1984	1985	1986	1987	1988	1989
Imports						
Hong Kong	62.95	105.32	85.65	118.76	150.25	150.79
Japan	32.65	43.98	42.19	58.59	51.54	52.89
Philippines	39.63	35.20	18.41	26.19	38.54	21.15
Malaysia	21.65	43.52	23.94	34.63	89.84	184.12
Singapore	3.02	59.33	77.76	125.33	156.65	272.99
Indonesia	32.49	38.29	39.81	71.55	65.10	52.92
Thailand	111.22	151.58	166.58	219.01	325.17	432.94
Macau	.44	1.13	.57	2.46	1.46	7.71
United States	871.43	473.19	202.07	514.87	969.52	1,805.10
Canada	515.02	434.50	403.87	673.68	894.88	337.11
Australia	540.16	508.17	723.41	845.31	608.73	699.21
New Zealand	80.63	117.60	160.36	175.89	346.47	242.08
USSR	2.01	6.18	.29	4.53	24.19	59.97
Pac Ag Imports	2,313.30	2,017.99	1,944.93	2,870.80	3,722.34	4,319.88
World Ag Imports	2,752.69	2,446.36	2,736.65	3,887.10	5,827.50	6,705.14
Pacif Imports	18,938.49	29,888.28	28,489.21	29,818.59	37,997.29	39,699.79
World Imports	26,744.31	42,831.57	43,403.41	43,393.11	55,250.73	59,141.63
Exports						
Hong Kong	1,471.12	1,689.85	1,943.44	2,190.41	2,591.29	2,569.76
Japan	1,035.43	1,375.47	1,543.94	1,773.54	2,205.64	2,339.39
Philippines	54.75	54.30	54.55	42.06	71.10	62.18

Malaysia	81.09	88.35	89.31	95.86	107.53	118.90
Singapore	148.09	160.50	170.18	209.49	293.36	368.29
Indonesia	56.33	109.46	106.72	152.19	169.93	123.67
Thailand	44.69	36.93	54.28	103.52	132.68	119.83
Macau	67.00	65.92	62.34	75.02	77.76	73.95
United States	140.32	154.29	176.56	245.39	382.53	386.56
Canada	37.02	41.30	71.60	71.40	54.78	57.28
Australia	21.21	20.39	15.81	18.95	20.41	28.56
New Zealand	8.54	6.59	4.32	5.00	4.54	5.05
USSR	310.63	670.86	720.33	786.17	808.32	839.53
Pac Ag Exports	3,476.21	4,474.22	5,013.35	5,769.00	6,919.87	7,092.95
World Ag Exports	5,223.28	6,280.04	7,115.82	8,027.05	9,456.73	9,702.95
Pac Exports	17,167.63	20,271.45	2,343.98	27,990.04	35,318.15	40,887.03
World Exports	25,024.01	27,558.66	31,337.02	39,541.49	47,540.34	52,485.92
Pac Ag Trade	5,789.51	6,492.21	6,958.28	8,639.80	10,642.21	11,412.83
World Ag Trade	7,985.97	8,726.40	9,852.47	11,915.05	15,284.23	16,407.30
Pac Trade	36,106.12	50,159.73	49,833.19	57,808.63	73,315.44	80,586.82
World Trade	51,768.32	70,390.22	74,740.43	82,934.60	102,791.07	111,627.55

Sources: China's Customs General Admin., various issues.

overall trade partner, mainly because it transships to the United States, Taiwan, South Korea, and other countries. Statistics compiled by the United States tell a different story, however. According to the data published by the Bureau of Census, Department of Commerce, United States total imports from China amounted to $11.9 billion in 1989, compared with the $4.4 billion published by China's Customs Administration. With the U.S. data, the United States not only became China's largest export market, surpassing Japan for the first time, but also became by far its most rapidly growing market. Among U.S. trading partners, China became the ninth largest source of imports in 1989, rising from 12th place in 1988 (U.S. International Trade Commission, 1990).

The huge discrepancy between the U.S. figures on imports from China and China's figures on exports to the United States can be traced to Chinese products that initially enter Hong Kong and are then reexported. The United States counts these transshipments in compiling data on trade with China, but China treats Hong Kong as the destination for these goods and compiles no separate data on products that are reexported. For this reason, China's statistics for 1989 show Hong Kong, rather than the United States, as China's largest export market.

Another major discrepancy in China's export figures is caused by Hong Kong's reexports to Taiwan and South Korea. For example, MOFERT announced in March that total trade in 1989 between Taiwan and Mainland China totaled $3.83 billion, of which China's exports were valued at $587 million (Yingpu, 1990).

However, China's exports of agricultural commodities to Taiwan seemed insignificant. Only herbal medicines and preserved or processed products can be classified as agricultural (Yingpu, 1990). Reexports of China's agricultural commodities from Hong Kong to South Korea may be more significant because of corn and soybean meal shipments. China's total trade values with South Korea are not available due to the exclusion of trade data in Chinese official statistical publications, but they are estimated as being similar to those with Taiwan.

China's barter trade with the USSR has developed rapidly, especially in the last several years (Table 10.3). The USSR has imported large quantities of agricultural commodities, particularly soybeans and corn, from the most northeastern province, Heilongjiang. In return, China bought machinery and forest products.

China's most important sources of agricultural imports, mainly grain, wool, vegetable oil, and cotton, are the United States, Canada, Australia, Thailand, Malaysia, Singapore, and New Zealand (Table 10.2). According to United States statistics, U.S. exports of wheat constitute about 80 percent of the total agricultural export value to China in recent years. Cotton exports to China have picked up in the last couple of years, contributing a growing percentage of the value of U.S. agricultural exports.

China's wheat imports in the 1980s have been mainly from the United States, Canada, and Australia. Certain non-Pacific Rim countries, such as Argentina and France, have been minor suppliers. Vegetable oil imports have principally come from Malaysia and Singapore (palm oil) and the United States (soybean oil). Wool imports have been mainly from Australia and New Zealand (China's Customs General Administration, various issues).

Agricultural Trade Policies in the 1980s

Although China is a socialist country with a planned economy, some market forces have been incorporated into the economy during the last decade. The government set up a state trading system to manage international trade and has the ability to use trade to achieve not only economic but sometimes political objectives. The MOFERT makes annual and medium-term (two to five years) foreign trade plans under the guidance of the State Planning Commission. The plans are implemented by state-owned Foreign Trade Corporations (FTCs) and subordinate Foreign Trade Bureaus at the local level.

In agricultural trade, the state-owned China National Cereals, Oil and Foodstuffs Import and Export Corporation (CEROILFOOD), China National Native Produce and Animal By-products Import and Export Corporation (CHINATUSHU), and China National Textiles Import and Export Corporation (CHINATEX) handle most of the basic commodity imports and exports.

The main objective of China's foreign trade, as in many developing countries, is to import advanced technology and equipment that the country does not produce or has in only limited quantities. The volume of such imports is heavily dependent upon exports. China makes great efforts to export agricultural commodities, raw materials, and light industrial products to earn as much hard currency as possible. Meanwhile, the country limits unnecessary imports by imposing quotas or planned targets to save foreign currency. China's agricultural trade in the past 10 years has been closely guided by these policies and programs.

A secondary objective of China's agricultural trade is to balance domestic demand and supply for certain basic commodities. Rice exports and wheat imports are often used by the government officials to explain this objective.

China has specific programs to guide agricultural trade. During the late 1970s and the early 1980s, the government allowed more grains, particularly wheat, to be imported for urban use. The imports allowed farmers to retain more grain for their own consumption and, in some cases, helped government guarantee low fixed-price grain supplies to farm households specializing in non-grain production activities. When China managed to sharply increase grain output in 1981-84, the government ordered a drastic cut in grain imports and vigorously promoted and expanded grain exports, particularly corn, to Asian markets. In the late 1980s, however, grain imports increased because of stagnating domestic production and increased domestic demand.

Since 1987, the government has promoted exports by using contracts signed between central foreign trade corporations (FTCs) and provincial or local trade corporations. The contracts include targets for foreign exchange earnings from exports, the amount of foreign exchange to be transferred to the central government, and the responsibility for financial profit or loss (Tuan, 1989).

Agricultural commodity exports are classified in three groups according to the contract system adopted in 1987. Commodities in the first group, including rice, soybeans, cotton, and corn, may be exported only by designated central FTCs because they are closely related to people's daily livelihood. The second group of commodities, such as rabbit hair and silk, can be exported only by national and designated provincial or local FTC's because of limited world supplies in international markets. For instance, China exports about 90 percent of its raw silk to world markets and, without state coordination, could end up with severe price competition among its exporting provinces. The last group, including all remaining commodities, can be exported by any local FTCs.

Agricultural imports are also divided into three groups. The first group, including wheat and corn, may be exported only by central FTCs. Wool and paper pulp, included in the second group, can be handled jointly by national and provincial or local FTCs. The third group of items may be imported by all local trade corporations. However, a complete list of the above-mentioned import and export groups has never been released to foreign countries. Only partial lists have been published in the newspapers.

Impact of Recent Political Unrest on Agricultural Production and Trade

In general, China's agricultural production was not affected by the June 4th Beijing incident in 1989. Agricultural production grew a respectable 3.3 percent in 1989, and grain output, which had stagnated for four years before 1989, was a record 407.5 million metric tons, marginally surpassing the previous 1984 record crop of 407.3 million metric tons.

After four years of fluctuating grain harvests, China's government leaders reemphasized the importance of grain production and decided at the end of 1988 to raise 1989 grain procurement prices and increase both central and local government investment in crop cultivation. Despite some poor crop yields last year, particularly in the northeast, grain production as a whole reached a record, though still 2.5 million metric tons short of the 410 million target. This year, the government has continued its increased investment in crop production and raised procurement prices for cotton, oilseed and oil, and livestock products. Agricultural production is expected to grow between 3.5 and 4 percent and, with a record summer grain harvest in hand, largely wheat, grain output is likely to reach or even surpass its 1990 target of 412.5 million metric tons.

Foreign investment in China's agriculture was reduced because of the unrest in 1989, however, and has only gradually resumed. Foreign capital and loans have been granted more slowly to China in recent months than previously thought, partly because of the political and economic reforms taking place in Eastern Europe and the USSR. Although the World Bank resumed normal lending to China in early 1990, it appears that foreign investors are waiting to see if it is more profitable and more secure to invest in Eastern European countries than in China. This may affect the availability of foreign loans for improving China's rural infrastructure development such as transportation and storage, particularly in the long run. Capital shortages in China could result if the delays are prolonged. Most recent G-7 summit meetings, however, agreed to let Japan resume its six-year $5.4 billion loans to China. World Bank loans to China will be further relaxed but still will be based on the improvement of human livelihoods.

In the 1990s, China will continue to face the need to reform its rural economy. Austerity programs imposed by the government at the end of 1988 to adjust China's economy may work in the short run, but will not solve long-run farming problems. Using administrative measures to direct farming—for example, forcing farmers to plant grain crops or engage in certain production activities, recentralizing fertilizer distribution, monopolizing cotton procurement, and severely cutting loans and credits granted to rural industrial development—may be effective temporarily. However, reestablishment of the command economy system will not help to sustain long-run agricultural development.

Actually, China's grain production faces two pressing issues: improving an irrational price system and legalizing a land contract system.

Without a rational price system, China's crop production, particularly grains, will remain less profitable than cash crops. And without a legalized land contract system, farm investment by individual farmers will remain inadequate.

China's planners must also increase investment in the agricultural infrastructure, including irrigation and drainage, transportation, and storage. Since the implementation of the rural household production responsibility system in the early 1980s, government investment, including national and local investment in the farming sector, has fallen dramatically. The central government's investment in agricultural capital construction as a share of its total capital investment fell from 11.1 percent in 1979 to only 3 percent in 1988. During the same period, individual household capital investment shifted towards housing construction instead of farm improvement. Continued low household investment for land improvement and reduced government investment in capital construction will constrain long-term agricultural growth.

Other problems in the agricultural sector are inefficient marketing and information systems. The old government procurement system cannot deal efficiently with the rapid growth in farm products and the rising importance of consumer demand. The grain rationing system, which provides low and fixed-price grain to urban residents, not only encourages waste but also distorts the entire grain marketing system. Unless the system changes, producer incentives will be diminished, consumer dissatisfaction will grow, and increased subsidies will strain the government's budget.

Agricultural Trade Policies and Outlook for Trade with Pacific Rim Countries in the 1990s

Agricultural Trade Policies in the 1990s

In the next 10 years, China will have to maintain steady economic growth and continue to expand foreign trade, particularly exports, to be able to modernize the country and to pay increasing international debt payments in the 1990s. Some MOFERT specialists have estimated that an export growth rate of at least 8 or 9 percent per year will have to be maintained to reach the foreign trade target of about $200 billion, with exports and imports each around $100 billion (Shi, unpublished).

To achieve the target, China will also need to continue reforming the structure of its foreign trade system. These reforms include improving management, increasing efficiency and profits of trade enterprises, and delegating greater decision-making authority to local trade organizations.

There are two general guidelines set by the government for promoting exports in the next decade. The first is to increase the share of manufactured goods instead of exporting primary products. The second is to further increase the value-added component of export goods, including agricultural commodities, by upgrading processing techniques and output quality. Based on these two principles, together with the rich human resources in China, the fastest growing export areas are expected to be led by textile products, followed by machinery and electronic goods. The agricultural commodity export share is expected to decline, but the value of agricultural trade will continue to increase.

Outlook for Agricultural Trade in the 1990s

Agricultural trade will remain an important part of China's overall trade in the 1990s. Preliminary estimates by MOFERT specialists show that the export value of agricultural commodities and processed products may reach $19 to $20 billion by the year 2000, roughly double their value of $9.7 billion in 1989. Parallel to the general export guidelines, China hopes to increase the export value of its agricultural products by upgrading quality and processing, converting raw cotton to more and better-quality textile output, and expanding the exports of processed food, canned food, beer, leather shoes and clothes, and silk products.

Agricultural imports will also expand because continued population increases and economic development will require higher levels of grain consumption, especially wheat, and more raw materials, such as wool, cattle hides, and sugar, for processing or manufacturing industries. Preliminary estimates by some MOFERT specialists also predict an increase of about 100 percent in agricultural import value to $12 to $13 billion (excluding rubber and timber products) by the end of the century, compared with $6.7 billion in 1989.

China's agricultural trade in the 1990s will continue to be under the guidance of government policies. Trade values will grow steadily, but at a slower rate compared with the 1980s. On the one hand, growth will be based upon the increased demand for imported grains, particularly wheat; sugar; wool; and cattle hides. On the other hand, exports of agricultural products will be vigorously expanded at an annual average rate even higher than that of imports because foreign exchange earnings will be an important source for modernization of the country and fulfillment of the growing annual debt payments. The total agricultural trade value, based on the MOFERT specialists' forecast, may reach $32 to $33 billion by the end of the 1990s.

Pacific Rim countries will continue to be China's major trading partners. Recent establishment of political and economic relations between China and Indonesia should further enhance their trade development. Singapore will follow in Indonesia's footsteps to establish official diplomatic relations with China, likely by the end of this year. China's leaders also have visited the USSR and expect to further develop their already rapidly expanded trade in the 1990s. The United States, Canada, and Australia should remain leading suppliers of grains to meet China's growing demand. Japan, one of China's largest trading partners, will also continue to import large quantities of agricultural commodities as in the past because of its location and trade relations. The following is a summary of likely major agricultural trade developments for the 1990s.

Grains. China's demand for various kinds of grains, particularly wheat, will continue to grow as income and population increase and government procurement remains low. Despite more grains required by livestock development in the 1990s, China's imports of grains other than wheat may not increase significantly because of the country's continued food self-sufficiency policy and because of the changing structure of its livestock production. Levels of wheat imports are expected to stay close to those over the last couple of years, though with some differences because of output and stock variations. Wheat imports could approach 20 million metric tons towards the end of this decade, provided the foreign exchange situation does not deteriorate. Otherwise, the government will regulate wheat consumption by raising domestic procurement and/or lowering wheat rationing to slow import expansion. China's major sources of wheat imports will continue to be the United States, Canada, and Australia.

China's rice exports will continue and may increase slightly, especially if rice prices are favorable and wheat imports increase. Hong Kong is likely to remain one of China's major rice export destinations, although China's rice exports face competition from Thailand. Rice exports are not likely to grow dramatically, since rice consumption for the country is still increasing and only in big cities is it actually declining. Another factor that hinders China's rice export is its poor quality. China therefore will continue to feed large quantities of rice to livestock, particularly in the south, where the development of feed grain production has been slow and is not economical. Lack of transportation capacity will continue to prevent large amounts of feed grains from being transferred from the north.

Demand for coarse grains, mainly corn, expanded rapidly as livestock development accelerated in the 1980s. The government managed to meet the increased feed demand by reducing human consumption. In the latter half of the 1980s, when corn production was off, the government decided to turn down several requests by southern provinces to allow large quantities of corn to be imported. This policy of restricting coarse grain imports, basically because of the lack of hard currency, will continue in the 1990s as long as foreign exchange earnings are targeted for machinery, equipment, and technology imports.

China has also exported significant amounts of corn since 1985. Although the government currently encourages farmers to raise more animals with better feed convertibility, domestic demand for corn keeps growing. Corn exports may well continue, though they are expected to diminish gradually during the 1990s.

Soybean and soybean meal exports expanded in the 1980s but started to decline in 1989. Exports are expected to decline gradually over the next 10 years. In the 1980s, soybean crush increased rapidly and, from the mid-1980s, virtually no soybean meal was put back into the fields as fertilizer. Soymeal has gradually been integrated into the feed manufacturing system in the last few years. Future meal exports are expected to decline but not disappear entirely because certain joint ventures need to export soybean meal in order to earn hard currency to repay loans for processing-plant construction. The primary export destinations of China's soybean meal will continue to be Pacific Rim nations such as Indonesia, Singapore, the Philippines, and Japan.

Cotton. China's cotton trade experienced drastic changes in the 1980s. In the early 1980s, China was a major importer of U.S. cotton. But in 1983, China's domestic cotton supplies grew rapidly and were so far in excess of demand that the country not only started exporting cotton in 1984 but also began to restrict output by lowering cotton procurement prices in 1985. However, an unexpected surge in domestic demand and great successes in promoting exports since the mid-1980s led the country to urgently boost output again in the last couple of years. Unfortunately, increasing cotton production in 1988 and 1989 was not successful. Although China still continues to export cotton, it also purchases more cotton on international markets. In the 1990s, China's cotton exports will gradually diminish and the country will try to become self-sufficient in cotton.

Other Commodities. China's import demand for other commodities, such as sugar, wool, hides, and skins, will rise. Consumer tastes have diversified significantly, and demand for items such as soft drinks and beer has grown very rapidly. The food processing industry will expand to meet varied tastes as well as to export to help earn foreign exchange. Traditional export items such as silk, tea, pig bristles and casing, and Chinese herbs will continue to be exported to all Pacific Rim markets.

The government will seek advanced technology and modernized equipment to improve food processing and packaging.

Overall, the rapid growth of China's agricultural trade has slowed, but a country as big as China will continue to play an important role in Pacific Rim agricultural markets. China's potential as an agricultural exporter, particularly of major commodities, is gradually diminishing, mainly because of slowing growth of agricultural production and increasing domestic demand. However, the country will continue to remain a significant player in Pacific Rim agricultural trade as it develops better-processed and higher-valued products to export in the future.

References

China's Customs General Administration. Various issues. *China's Customs Statistics*. Hong Kong: Economic Information & Agency.

———. *Summary Surveys of China's Customs Statistics*. 1986, 1987, and 1988 issues. Beijing: Knowledge Publishing House.

Clarke, Christopher M. July-August 1987. "Two Views of China's Foreign Trade," *The China Business Review*. Washington, D.C.: U.S.-China Business Council, Washington DC.

Eckstein, Alexander. 1976. *China's Economic Revolution*. New York: Cambridge University Press.

Foreign Broadcast Information Service (FBIS). Dec. 19, 1989. "Economists Ponder Reduced Exports, Effects." *China Daily Report*. FBIS-CHI—89-242: 31.

Ministry of Agriculture. May 1989. *The Encyclopedia of China's Rural Economic Statistics, 1949-86*. Agricultural Publishing House: Beijing (Chinese).

Qu, Yingpu. March 22, 1990. "Taiwan-Mainland Trade May Top $4b." *China Daily*, p. 2. Beijing.

Shi, Ru. "China's Agricultural Trade in the 1980s and Outlook for the 1990s." Unpublished manuscript.

Tuan, Francis C. July 1990. "China's Agricultural Trade in the 1980s: Policy Changes and Performance." China Agriculture and Trade Report: Situation and Outlook Series, RS-90-5, ERS, U.S. Department of Agriculture.

———. Nov. 1989. "Major Agricultural Policy Changes in the Last Decades." China Agriculture and Trade Report: Situation and Outlook Series, RS-89-5, ERS. U.S. Department of Agriculture.

United States International Trade Commission. June 1990. Trade Between the United States and the Nonmarket Economy Countries During 1989, USITC Publication 2286.

Appendix: China's Trade Statistics

China's foreign trade statistics are compiled by the General Customs Administration and the Ministry of Foreign Economic Relations and Trade (MOFERT) using different procedures. MOFERT uses data on the trade activity of factories, mines, and other enterprises officially authorized to engage in foreign trade, for example, all retail sales made in China's domestic foreign currency stores (including Friendship Stores, Overseas Chinese Stores, and the Guangzhou Trade Fair). An expert in China's Foreign Trade Research Office commented in a recent press release that MOFERT's import figures are not accurate because they include incomplete reports of imports by local organizations.

China's Customs Administration views trade as the physical movement of goods. It compiles statistics from customs declaration forms that include virtually all goods that move across China's borders. It also includes import values such as non-trade items as foreign materials for processing in China. Customs statistics are grouped according to international trade classifications used by the United Nations Statistical Office and therefore are comparable to trade statistics compiled by other countries.

As for counter trade, customs statistics include the entire trade value, but MOFERT statistics do not, except for commissions.

The customs statistics are used in this analysis because they can be grouped to estimate the values of China's annual agricultural trade. The following categories of customs statistics, prefixed by SITC (Standard International Trade Classification), have been used to calculate China's agricultural imports and exports:

0 Food and live animals chiefly for food
1 Beverages and tobacco
2 Inedible materials, except fuels, including
   21 Hides, skins, and furskins
   22 Oilseeds
   26 Textile fibers, excluding synthetic and regenerated
   29 Other animal and vegetable materials
4 Animal fats and vegetable oils

Exports are valued on a FOB (free on board) basis, while imports are valued on a CIF (cost, insurance, and freight) basis.

11

Soviet Economic Reforms, Republic Sovereignty, and Pacific Rim Agriculture and Trade

Sergei B. Iliukhin and Kenneth Gray

Introduction

The USSR is presently going through a difficult, but necessary, period of economic and political change. Only through such an adjustment can the USSR become a genuine member of the world community. The period is necessarily difficult because it makes a sharp break with the previous 70 years of history.

This new experience involves devolution of authority once vested in the central government to the fifteen union republics, each of which in 1990 declared its sovereignty, or non-subservience to the central government's authority. The experience involves grueling deliberation on economic reform, giving way in a rush of events to economic disruption, including a severe and widely misunderstood food crisis. Also, foreign relations of the USSR, including foreign economic relations, are being fundamentally reassessed.

This report examines the food crisis of the 1990s and the emerging reforms which will likely affect Soviet agricultural trade. It makes specific comments on prospects for developments in the Soviet Far East, a region that directly touches the Pacific Rim and whose importance in world politics and economics is increasing rapidly.

The Difficult Course of Perestroika's Economic Reforms

The economic reforms as conceived in 1989 and 1990 were meant to rebuild the Soviet economic system on market principles—a process, however, which by 1989 and 1990 proved very difficult. By 1990 a large portion (if not yet perhaps the majority) of the Soviet people came to support the idea of a market economy, even if they often did not understand its full meaning. In addition, a large part of the Soviet people understood and accepted that the first steps of the transition toward a market economy would lower living standards.

But in 1990 the central government was increasingly bound by ideological dogma and in clinging to obsolete and ineffective institutions undertook inconsistent and contradictory steps toward reform. Many of its decisions were taken without much idea of where they would lead. Inconsistency of policy bred discontent among the populace, which in turn made the central government timid. In public opinion polls, which had become quite common, the approval rating of the government declined. It reached the point that the central government was hampered in devising and implementing sound radical reforms. At the same time there was such a loss of public confidence that there was little support for any program developed by the central government.

In 1990 a number of radical thinkers were at work on a wide range of specific areas to devise practical means for the central government to move the economy to a market basis. These thinkers found themselves more welcome by several of the governments of the 15 Soviet republics, including the important Russian Republic, than by the central government. An important "500 Days" program was adopted in principle by the Russian government, but after attempts it failed to be adopted by the Union parliament and government. The program would have sought (1) macroeconomic stabilization, (2) rapid privatization, and (3) price liberalization.

A "war of laws" between the union government and the republics broke out in 1990, leaving many wondering who was in charge. However, although the inability to resolve the division of powers between the republics and the union government presented a constitutional crisis in 1990, the republics were gaining power and began to undertake independent policies.

Centrifugal Economic Forces

With the occurrence of glasnost and political liberalization, long-standing ethnic and national resentments have surfaced in most of the Soviet republics. These tendencies have been reinforced by chaos in consumer markets and a food crisis caused by macroeconomic imbalance. A type of "reverse" protectionism became prominent in 1990, practiced by republics and lower jurisdictions which sought to retain food (and other) resources for themselves. Economic factors were important as the central government and peoples in the fifteen republics considered a new union treaty. These factors included fears about adequacy of food provision and different approaches to farm restructuring and agricultural policy in general.

Macroeconomic Imbalance

The overriding fact in the Soviet economic experience of the late 1980s and 1990 was the macroeconomic imbalance resulting from the growing state budgetary deficit and the undisciplined growth of the money supply. The budget deficit was first acknowledged officially in 1988 and was estimated by 1989 to be approximately 12 percent of Soviet GNP, compared to 3 percent for the United States. In early 1991 the chairman of the State Price Committee reported that from 1988 to 1990 money incomes increased by over 200 billion rubles, compared to 77 billion for the entire previous five-year plan.[1] Thus, money incomes grew at a faster rate than labor productivity, which gave rise to inflationary pressures.

The state budget deficit resulted from a number of factors relating to both expenditures and revenues. The reduction of enterprise profit taxes lowered state revenue. A growing expenditure from the budget was the subsidy required to maintain constant state retail prices for basic foodstuffs, in the face of increased farm prices. In 1990 this subsidy amounted to nearly 90 billion rubles, about 20 percent of the state budget.[2]

The 1990 Food Crisis

In 1990, fears of hunger were voiced as more and more local jurisdictions introduced various schemes for the rationing of common foodstuffs. By fall the USSR had become the recipient of food aid from private donors and Western governments including the states of the European Community.

Shortcomings in the Soviet food system have always existed. Growing food shortages shifted attention to long-standing problems of the collective and state farm system. However, the food crisis was intensifying not as the result of a collapse in food production but from increasing macroeconomic imbalances. In 1990 gross agricultural production declined, though only by 2.3 percent. Grain output of 235 mmt was, in fact, at a near record.

The immediate cause of the food crisis was the excess demand resulting from the budgetary imbalance and fixed retail prices, along with the partial collapse of the traditional system for state redistribution of foodstuffs among republics and the hesitant introduction of a new market mechanism for distributing food within the USSR.[3]

Americans who experienced gasoline shortages in the 1970s can understand the frustration experienced by Soviet consumers in 1990. A similarity is that in the United States, shortages were also artificial, engendered by price controls, hoarding and panic buying. For example, in the U.S. case, when there appeared to be "no gas" available in the summer of 1979, only slightly less was sold than in the same months a year earlier. However, the frustration in the Soviet case must have been much greater. By one report in early 1990, only 10 of 275 basic food and nonfood goods were readily available in state stores.

Until increases occurred on April 2, 1991, state retail prices for livestock products had not officially changed since 1962. For bread, pasta and other staples, they had not changed since the 1950s. While shortages grew in the state sector, products were available through other channels, including the black market, cooperative trade, and the collective farm markets, where in Moscow, for example, meat was readily available at a free market price 15 times the state price of 2 rubles per kilo. State stores in Moscow typically sold meat "out the back door" for a few rubles per kilo premium.

The food situation may have been greater in large cities such as Moscow and Leningrad which had been favored previously by privileged supplies of subsidized food. Residents in rural areas and small cities had benefited much less from the food subsidy and many did not view the situation now facing the largest cities as a complete tragedy, although the inconveniences of excess demand for most goods were present everywhere.

In general, widespread anticipation of long overdue farm and retail price increases contributed to hoarding and spoilage throughout the distribution system. Announcement by USSR Prime Minister Ryzhkov in May 1990 of the intention to raise retail prices led to a run on stores, which frightened the government into delaying the price increases. Anticipation of a previously announced one-third increase in the farm price of livestock products, to be effective January 1, 1990, led to a withholding of livestock from market and forced the RSFSR to advance the increase.

Reverse Protectionism and the Collapse of Distribution

It is interesting that whereas Western states commonly erect barriers to keep competitors' food *out*, jurisdictions in many socialist countries have erected barriers intended to keep food *in*.[4] This is due to general inflationary tendencies (sellers' market conditions) existing and the practice of stable state retail , which creates excess demand. Early in 1990 the Soviet republic Kazakhstan outlawed exports of food above those quantities specified in state orders. Kirgizia did likewise, in an effort to reduce excess demand engendered not by harvest failure but by excess money incomes. In general, the practice of embargoing or limiting food exports became general as the year progressed, and as the political power of the central government diminished.

This "reverse protectionism" was one manifestation of the collapse of the economic system of food distribution (as opposed to the collapse of the physical infrastructure).

State and collective farms had been formally relieved of obligatory quotas for deliveries to the state by regulations derived from the 1987 Law on State Enterprise and the June 1988 Law on Cooperatives. State procurement organs in the republics and oblasts were still obliged to meet planned contributions to the central mechanism for planned redistribution (the "all union fund"). Having intended to abandon coercion, the new State Commission on Food and Procurement attempted to guide food marketing but with increasingly ineffective administered prices. Having experienced a declining ratio of grain marketings compared to production since 1987, the central government increased grain purchase prices by an average of 50 percent in May 1990 without substantial effect.[5] Due to shortages of goods to buy with rubles, farms preferred to feed grain or give it to farm workers for that purpose. The search by farms for equipment to make their own sausages became widespread. By some reports "monetized sausage" superseded the ruble as the means of payment in transactions.

Besides the decline in the center's desire or ability to coerce and the ruble's declining ability to stimulate, the interruption the previous year of the growth of trade involving middlemen caused food distribution to be worse than it might have been. Operating under the auspices of the 1988 Law on Cooperatives, "trade-purchase" cooperatives had begun to buy from farms, often at prices higher than state prices, and resell, either with substantial processing or not. Labeled "speculators," hundreds of these cooperatives were shut down illegally by zealous party officials in early 1989. The new cooperative legislation was amended in a reactionary or perhaps populist action of the USSR parliament in October 1989—to control prices and otherwise restrict this activity.[6]

Emerging cooperative middlemen were particularly vulnerable to charges of merely reselling or "skimming" without adding substantial value-added because of the pervasive practice of farm price differentiation—paying different prices for exactly the same good. The prices the state pays farms have been highly differentiated by cost of production across a wide number of price zones, and in recent years, prices had come to be differentiated, even for neighboring farms.

Differing Approaches to Farm Privatization

Although their proximate cause is macroeconomic imbalance, shortages attending the current food crisis have focused useful attention on long-standing inefficiencies in state and collective farm management. Many of the proposals to establish individual "private" farms offered by the republics, particularly the Russian Republic, have been more radical than those of the central government. Only 50,000 state and collective farms, each averaging 10,000 hectares of farmland, control over 97 percent of the nation's arable land. The remaining three percent, allocated to their workers for part-time use as household plots, produce over one-quarter of the value of all Soviet agricultural production. As well, local authorities in various parts of the USSR have promoted the autonomy of individual farms from the 50,000 large state and collective farms.

In February 1990 the USSR Parliament approved a Land Code laying out guidelines for the long-term inheritable use rights to land for individual "family-type" farms. Details were to be worked out on land, small farm, and tax legislation of each republic. The non-Slavic republics generally took up more radical legislation. The Russian Republic in particular legalized a broader land tenure concept of ownership, including the right to sale after a proving period of ten years. The Baltic nations followed similar paths but added the principle of compensation or return of land to those who had owned land prior to their forced annexation by the Soviet Union in 1940. In the "war of laws" the central government pronounced these excesses of the republics illegal and sought a national referendum on the issue of private ownership of land.

While interest in individual farming was growing (over 40,000 such units were in existence by the beginning of 1991), several factors hindered development. One obstacle was fear that land tenure rights were not secure or could be reversed by communists whose intrinsic ideology is linked with farm collectivization. Another factor, cited even more frequently by farm people considering becoming independent farmers, was the lack of equipment for small-scale farming and the uncertain supply situation for critical inputs, like fuel, seeds, and agrochemicals.

On the other hand, as property throughout the economy began to be reserved by individuals, many even hard-line apparatchiks began to "hedge their bets" by starting to reserve the best of the farm assets for themselves and their children. The dynamic of this was just beginning to snowball by the spring of 1991.[7]

Progress in Rationalization of Farm and Retail Food Prices

In 1990 the Soviet state decreased the number of farm price zones and the degree of price differentiation. For example, for beef and milk there are now 4 to 5 price zones, versus 49 and 98 in the past. Thus, farms in low-cost regions (such as in the North Caucusus) which had previously received the lowest prices are now receiving considerably more.

The reduction of price differentiation reflects the state's diminished ability to dictate prices to republics and farms, which no longer want rents extracted from what they increasingly consider their own property. Although without well-developed marketing services, large farms had taken to marketing their own products, often through barter, throughout the country. Farm prices promise to become even freer as the state recognizes its inability to administer them and bows to developing market forces.

April 1991 also saw momentous retail price changes that were part of the revision upward for the first time in 28 years or more and partial freeing of prices. Faced with maintaining the price subsidy themselves, republic and oblast governments chose to raise them, often by several hundred percent. In part this was to recoup some of the rents being collected by the parallel market. In part it was also because local jurisdictions saw that their subsidizing prices led to leakages of the subsidy outside their jurisdiction. Estonia found that raising prices about the neighboring region caused goods to flow in and eliminated lines.[8]

External Economic Relations

Foreign Trade

Central government policy in the sphere of external economic relations has been inconsistent and unstable. About 17 thousand enterprises, cooperatives, and so on were allowed to export and import foreign goods and services (by the USSR Council of Ministers' resolution passed in December 1988). Foreign trade had previously been the exclusive right of foreign trade organizations housed in the Ministry of Foreign Trade. However, almost simultaneously a system of licenses was introduced. So, to import and export a broad range of goods one still has to obtain licenses issued by a corresponding ministry or other governmental body. These retain their monopoly position by preventing competition by enterprises independent of them. The introduction of this system of licensing hampered the fulfillment of many contracts which had already been written. It threatens the future development of foreign trade. So, in effect foreign trade transactions remain highly centralized and cause serious resource waste.

The USSR imports considerable quantities of machinery and equipment, though a significant part of it is later unused or underused. The importation of consumer goods whose domestic price is considerably higher than their world price is neglected, an omission which is criticized by Soviet analysts because these imports could help lower the state budget deficit.

Foreign Capital

Nor does the central government have a well thought out policy towards foreign investment. The numerous laws and regulations in this sphere are full of contradictions.

The laws regarding joint ventures are constantly changing. An example is the "re-registration" campaign launched in mid-1990. These changes have made it extremely difficult for potential foreign investors to know what Soviet partners, governmental bodies, and joint ventures are qualified to do. The law on free economic zones was prepared by the central government over two years ago, but so far there are no practical results. Lastly, among many of the shortcomings which could be mentioned, no practical steps have been taken as yet to make the ruble convertible. This remains the main factor hindering the inflow of foreign capital.

The Russian Republic's Foreign Economic Program

In mid-July 1990 the newly elected Russian Supreme Soviet adopted a resolution, called "On the Main Principles of External Economic Activity on the Territory of the Russian Republic." This represents one of, if not the most, radical government documents of the present time. The document contains a number of concrete measures which would radically change foreign economic relations, bringing them into line with normal market relationships. It would liberalize foreign investment policy and achieve ruble convertibility as soon as possible.

Another resolution adopted on the same day ("On Free Economic Zones") supports several regional soviets in their desire to create free economic zones on their territory. These include the Nakhodka city soviet and the Primorskii and Sakhalin regional soviets that are located in the Soviet Far East. The resolution called for the submission of practical measures for discussion within two months. The Russian Council of Ministers began work in 1990 on documents dealing with free economic zones. These involved their legal status, tax and investment regimes, and labor law. One member of the international relations committee has said that by doing this the Russian Supreme Soviet deliberately hoped to prevent passage of the central government's legislation, which he characterized as hopelessly insufficient.

The USSR in Pacific Rim Agricultural Trade

The Soviet Far East

The USSR has close economic ties with many Pacific Rim countries. The Soviet Far East is (and will continue to be) the part of the USSR most deeply involved in the Pacific Rim economic relationship.

The Soviet Far East (SFE) is a vast region, very rich in natural resources, but sparsely populated. Its share in the total Soviet land area is 27 percent, but it has only 2.6 percent of the total population. The region is rich in coal and waterpower as well as wood, chemical raw materials, and biological resources. Presently the region accounts for 2.9 percent of Soviet industrial production, about 1.4 percent of agriculture, and 2.8 percent of Soviet national income. The region's share in Soviet exports is higher—about 4.4 percent. The main constraints to economic development in the SFE are the lack of labor and capital resources.

Economic cooperation with the countries of the Pacific Rim can play an important role in the region's future economic development. This relationship is already close. For example, about 80 percent of SFE exports go to the Pacific region. But the potential is presently vastly underutilized.

The Food Sector

The food sector in the Soviet Far East is one of the likely spheres for cooperation with other Pacific Rim countries. The SFE is not self-sufficient with regard to the principal food commodities (see Table 11.1). About half the food consumed by the population of the SFE comes from outside the region. The share is lower for commodities like milk, sugar, grain and fruit.

Inferior climatic conditions lead to low levels of production and high costs of production. For example, in 1987 the cost of locally produced grain was three times higher than that of the southern European part

TABLE 11.1 Balance of Selected Food Products in the Soviet Far East (1985-1988 average, thousands metric tons)

	Production	Net Imports	Available Supply	Human Consumption[a]	Per Capita Consumption[b]	Self-sufficiency Ratio
	1000 mt				Kg/year	percent
Grain	1085	4495	5580	1380	175	20
Meat	317	269	586	564	71	54
Milk	1450	2063	3513	2879	363	41
Egg[c]	2171	379	2550	2347	296	85
Potatoes	1413	732	2145	794	100	66
Vegetables	484	463	946	842	106	51
Sugar	160	410	570	360	45	28

[a]Includes commodities supplied by other regions of the USSR as well as from abroad.
[b]Meat is in slaughter weight; milk is in whole cow's milk including milk processed for cheese and butter; potatoes and vegetables are in raw product weight; grain is in grain equivalents; and sugar is refined.
[c]Total consumption is in millions pieces. Per capita consumption is in pieces per year.
Source: Narodnoe Khoziaistvo RSFSR v 1988 godu.- Moscow, Finansy i Statistika, 1989, personal estimates.

of Russia (255 vs. 71 rubles per ton). Many other locally produced commodities cost 1.3 to 1.7 times more than the average costs for the Russian republic as a whole (see Table 11.2).

Most of the difference between local production and consumption is imported from western regions of the USSR. However, the low quality of these commodities, and the poor transportation and storage system, cause considerable waste (up to 50 percent) and result in high costs and prices.

From this point of view, a reorientation of the Pacific Rim as a source of food for the Soviet Far East seems economically sound. Countries like the United States, Canada, Australia, New Zealand, the Philippines, Thailand, and China are all important agricultural producers. The opening of trade with the Soviet Far East should interest them as a market for their agricultural (and other) exports.

ERS research shows that economic rationality (based on the relationship between domestic and world prices) supports an increase in Soviet meat imports.[9] The high relative cost of meat production in the Soviet Far East makes the region particularly suitable for expanded imports. Export of its vast natural wealth would finance the meat imports, particularly if the region were able to keep more of the economic rent from the extraction of its natural resources.

TABLE 11.2 Costs of Production of Selected Agricultural Commodities (in roubles per metric ton, 1981-1985 average)

	Soviet Average for		
	(1) Far East	(2) Russia	$\frac{(1)}{(2)} \times 100$
Potato	233	135	150
Vegetables	179	116	154
Milk	591	362	163
Eggs[a]	82	61	134
Beef	425	266	160
Pork	361	214	169
Poultry	219	166	132

[a] in roubles per 1,000 pieces.
Source: Kontseptia razvitia aropromyshlennogo kompleksa dal'nevostochnoi zony. Khabarovsk, 1989.

The Prospects for Foreign Investment

The conditions now being offered for foreign investment in the Soviet Far East are beginning to become more attractive than those of the "mainland." But they can still be improved. Some development goals should be prioritized and implemented by preferential treatment for foreign firms. Such goals should be established in the area of social development—to help sustain settlement in this sparsely populated area. Foreign involvement in food and agriculture, housing, transportation and communications should be actively encouraged.

There are several areas of possible cooperation in agriculturally related industries. The traditional export industries of the Soviet Far East are fishing and forestry. But the Soviet Far East could develop significant tourist and recreation industries. Any of these offer good prospects for joint ventures with the other countries of the Pacific Rim.

From the Soviet side there are a number of specific interests in the food and agricultural sphere. These include joint ventures in the livestock and meat industry (including stock breeding and meat processing), the dairy industry (baby food and low-fat milk products), the feed industry (especially soybean production and processing), transportation and packaging (refrigeration, polymer packaging materials), and a wide range of agricultural machinery adapted to the climatic conditions of the area.

A number of areas have known export potential. These include timber, reindeer breeding, and seafood production.

Nakhodka's Free Economic Zone

The State Foreign Economic Commission of the USSR Council of Ministers has established a program in principle for the creation of a free economic zone in the port city of Nakhodka. It is envisioned that this zone would assimilate foreign management experience and supply a number of goods to the Soviet market. Fishing and tourism would be the focal industries in the new zone. However, the implementation of steps to create this free economic zone is continually put off by the central government. In addition, the former regional authorities including the regional party organization have simply marked time. Advocates of the project are now turning to the new Russian Republic government for support. The Russian government's own stance, as early as the first announcement in July 1990 of the "500 days" program, provides for the active development of free economic zones.

Conclusion: The Future National Market and External Trade

In April and May 1991, first in an agreement with nine other republics and then in an agreement with thirteen, the central government progressively ceded to the republics powers it had once held for itself. The effect is to accelerate economic decentralization; the important Russian Republic of which the Pacific Far East is a part, for example, continues to press rapidly for privatization of property which the center now acknowledges the republic controls.

The center also conceded to the republics the right to control significant foreign exchange earnings and to license external trade. As of this writing (June 1991), the center seeks to maintain common tariff policy except for special enterprise zones and prohibit tariffs and barriers among republics.

There are reasons for the republics whose economies are highly interrelated to want to cooperate in this. The economy has already suffered significantly due to the interruption of normal commerce among its republics and is forecast to shrink by 10 to 15 percent in 1991.[10]

Eventual restraint of monetary growth, significant continued price liberalization, and continued development of interregional markets could establish for the USSR a basis for economic integration and national reconciliation.

If it emerges more or less intact, the Soviet Union will be changed in several ways that will alter its agricultural trade. The recent reform of retail prices will tend to restore order to retail markets and improve internal distribution as well as simply reduce consumption, all leading to fewer imports. The emerging rationalization of internal farm prices (reduction of artificial price differentiation) will have several effects. It will tend to improve specialization and at the same time allow the Soviets to better identify the opportunity cost of their own production versus imports. Changes in rents throughout the economy, and by region, will change demand patterns.

The Soviet Far East is likely to one of the gainers and through decentralized trade autarky, will be able to articulate new demands for traded food products in the Pacific Rim market.

Notes

1. V. S. Sechagov, interview in *Rabochaya Tribuna*, 19 March 1991 [trans. JPRS-UEA-91-017, 8 April 1991].

2. See Edward C. Cook, "Potential Soviet Budget Crunch Looming in 1991 as a Result of Agricultural Price and Subsidy Changes," *CPE Agriculture Report*, Vol. III, 6 (Nov.-Dec.), 1990, and "How Fiscal Policy Fueled Inflation in the USSR," *CPE Agriculture Report*, Vol. IV, 1 (Jan.-Feb.), 1991.

3. The phenomenon of excess demand has always colored perceptions of consumption achieved by Soviet citizens. For example, since the mid-1970s meat has not been readily visible in meat counters because it is rapidly snatched up or distributed through other channels available only to special workers, party members, etc. On the whole, average Soviet meat consumption (carcass weight as adjusted by the UN Economic Commission for Europe) was about 58 kilograms in 1988. This was less than one-half the American level of per capita consumption, but it compared not unfavorably to Britain at 67.5 and was less than Sweden at 54.3.

4. This tendency is also true of China and Yugoslavia. See the special section on regional agricultural production and trade in *CPE Agriculture Report*, Vol. IV, 2 (March/April), 1991.

5. The ratio of marketed to produced grain continued to fall in the Ukraine and Russia and went up slightly for the USSR in 1990 (from 30 to 31%) only because of bumper crops in sparsely populated Kazakhstan, which has little alternative to marketing grain.

6. Kenneth R. Gray, "On the USSR Law on the Cooperative System: Free at Last?" *CPE Agriculture Report*, Vol. I, 4 July/August 1988, and Kenneth Gray and Yuri Markish, "Recent Restrictions on Soviet Cooperatives to Halt 'Speculation,'" *CPE Agriculture Report*, Vol. II, 6, November/December 1989.

7. See K. R. Gray, "Individual Farms and Emerging Land Legislation in the Russian Federation," *CPE Agriculture Report*, Vol. III, 6 (Nov/Dec) 1990.

8. Yuri Markish and Kenneth Gray, "Soviet Retail Price Revision and Compensation: A Start," *CPE Agriculture Report*, Vol. IV, 2, March/April 1991.

9. William M. Liefert, Robert B. Koopman, and Edward C. Cook, "The Effect of Western and Soviet Agricultural Trade Liberalization on the USSR," USDA/ERS Staff Report, in process.

10. Report of CIA analyst George Kolt, *Washington Post*, May 17, p. 1.

12

Economic Reforms and New Zealand Agriculture

Ron A. Sandrey

The Setting

It is important to appreciate how regulated the New Zealand economy had become by mid-1984. Interest rates were controlled and lending policies directed; the exchange rate was fixed; and wages and prices were subject to a comprehensive "freeze." At the same time, several economic indicators were poor. The current account and budget deficits were very high and increasing, and inflation, artificially low due to a price freeze, was expected to accelerate sharply the following year. Agricultural assistance had doubled over a very short 3-4 year period to 30-34 percent of the final value of output (PSE), with much of the support being directed to sheep meats, although farm incomes were falling in spite of this assistance. Many of these indicators are shown in Table 12.1.

The fiscal deficit and overseas debt had climbed steeply, and New Zealand's relative standard of living continued to fall from its 1950s pinnacle. As the country's economic performance worsened, the impetus for change grew. A snap election in 1984 brought to power the Labor Party, with a Finance Minister committed to a less interventionist approach. This apparent contradiction of a traditionally left-wing democratic party espousing free market economic policies indicates the degree to which previous governments had drifted into intervention and the high level of disenchantment with such policies. Although some progress had been made in selected areas of reform prior to 1984, the breadth, depth and speed of the post-1984 changes was dramatic. Attention focused on lowering the fiscal deficit by reducing the role of government in many areas and increasing efficiency in others; liberaliz-

TABLE 12.1 Selected Economic Indicators, New Zealand, 1980-90

	1980	1981	1982	1983	1984	1985	1986	1987	1988	1989	1990
Total Ag Output ($ billion)	4.4	4.5	5.0	5.0	5.9	7.6	6.9	6.9	7.4	8.3	9.4
Agriculture as % of GDP	10.1	8.8	7.7	6.7	7.0	9.2	6.7	5.9	6.3	6.4	6.5
Total Assistance to Pastoral Output ($ million)	393	345	750	1179	1092	1060	874	525	539	291	240
% of Pastoral Output	15	13	24	33	30	23	23	13	12	5	2.3
Consumer Price Index (1982=1000)	746	861	1000	1074	1139	1316	1490	1724	1834	1924	2048
Real Trade Weighted Exchange Rate (1976=1000)	1039	1023	1012	1016	1004	867	1024	1022	1237	1171	1183
Real Net Farm Incomes											
Sheep and Beef Farms (1976=1000)	1066	807	686	663	503	832	329	475	474	440	429
Dairy Farms (1976=1000)	839	797	905	837	838	969	723	592	610	829	1018
Real Farmland Values (1982=1000)	812	914	1000	908	818	702	556	462	424	445	505
Agricultural Debt ($ billion)	3.5	4.2	5.2	5.8	6.8	7.4	8.0	8.0	8.0	7.8	—
Terms of Exchange in Agriculture	960	880	940	900	980	1050	770	760	710	790	—
Unemployment %	2.2	3.6	3.5	5.6	5.7	4.1	4.0	4.0	4.3	6.2	7.2
Terms of Trade	82	76	77	74	75	73	71	76	83	87	91
Current Account Balance (as a % of GDP)	-4.2	-3.6	-5.9	-6.3	-5.8	-9.4	-8.5	-4.7	-3.7	-1.6	-5.5

Note: There is some variability with the years in the above table, as different items have different reporting dates.
Sources: Ministry of Agriculture and Fisheries; New Zealand Meat and Wool Boards' Economic Service; Department of Statistics. 1988-1990 figures range from provisional to forecasts.

ing both currency and product markets; and achieving a sustainable low inflation rate.

While it was known that removal of direct assistance measures would disadvantage agriculture in the short run, it was expected that the simultaneous reform of macroeconomic, commercial and exchange rate policies, which had previously been more than offsetting direct agricultural assistance, would eventually result in better incentives for and consequential gain to the sector. It was also recognized that the costs of adjustment would precede the benefits. However, apart from a brief period after the 1984 devaluation, the benefits of reform for the agricultural sector have been very slow in coming.

This raises a number of questions. Was the sequence of reforms, in which some markets were fully liberalized while others were still subject to extensive regulation, the main factor explaining the poor performance of the agricultural sector? Although this was the case, it begs the question of whether any alternative was feasible given the circumstances facing the new government. Is it that the anticipated responses of the sector will be forthcoming, but far more slowly than expected, perhaps involving a 5-10 year transition period, or is it that lack of reforms in some other sectors, particularly the continuing protection to parts of the manufacturing sector, have negated the positive effects of liberalization?

These questions are addressed in the paper, albeit in summary form. For a more detailed analysis, the reader is referred to Sandrey and Reynolds (1990). The objectives of this paper are to document the reforms, outline the consequences for agriculture, draw some tentative conclusions and present the prospects for New Zealand agriculture. From a trade perspective, the emphasis has been on the supply side, but from now on, with agricultural support almost totally withdrawn, the emphasis will be on the demand side. This highlights the crucial importance of international trade reform to the sector and the country.

The Reforms

Macroeconomic

The New Zealand dollar was immediately devalued by the Labor Government and, in March 1985, floated. Central policy objectives have been the control of the deficit and a reduction in inflation. However, government expenditure actually increased in the first two years, and monetary policy was not tightened until 1987. Other policy initiatives were directed towards general market liberalization, removal of export assistance, lowering of import protection, changes in the taxation system to more indirect taxation and a widening of the tax base, privatization of government trading activities and a greater emphasis on public sector efficiency. Key indicators are shown in Table 12.1 and reflect an appreciating real (inflation-adjusted) exchange rate between 1985 and 1988, high short-term real interest rates, declining growth, rising unemployment, and an eventual fall in the inflation rate and improvements in the external account deficit.

Commercial Policies, Taxation and Regulatory Reform

The new Labor Government accelerated the withdrawal of agricultural supports: concessionary farm loans were progressively brought into line with market rates, cost-recovery plans were announced for agricultural product inspection and farm advisory services and farm input subsidies were terminated. By 1990 direct assistance to agriculture had been reduced to very low levels (a PSE of 3 percent, Table 12.1). However, government did absorb the considerable overdrafts in the producer board stabilization accounts, and a Rural Bank discounting scheme was introduced to restructure some concessionary farm loans. These represented substantial transfers to farmers, although the nature of the original supports was such that it is difficult to assess when the resource effect took place. The current industry support situation is uneven. Almost all assistance to agriculture has been removed, and, although there have been tariff reductions, the remaining assistance to import-substitution manufacturing constitutes an implicit tax on agriculture. The estimated 1990 ERA for the pastoral sector of -6 percent limits the sector's growth.

Much reform of the New Zealand Income Tax Act 1976 was undertaken during the 1984-89 period, with many of the changes having a significant effect on business decision-making in the primary sector. The objective of these changes was to achieve a simpler, broader-based, more investment-neutral and efficient system. Major sector-specific reforms concentrated on the valuation of livestock for taxation, deductibility of farm development expenditure and the tax-free status of producer boards and cooperatives. Many of these changes incorporated (generous) transition provisions and took place in a generally lower income and lower tax-potential environment. The broad conclusion reached is that the total tax burden (including GST on disposable income) has increased with the 1989 regime, although tax liability on the final sale of livestock has been reduced.

To understand how radical the shift in New Zealand's economic philosophy has been, it is instructive to look at the regulatory changes resulting from the fundamental reevaluations of the role of government.

Some of these changes, such as full charging of product inspection, user funding of research and changes in adverse events assistance, were part of the general reduction in assistance to agriculture. Other changes, such as local and regional government reform, resource management law reform and community irrigation scheme ownership changes, although less direct, still have significant ramifications for the agricultural sector. Adverse events assistance further demonstrates the evolution in policy. Beginning as a series of ad hoc policies administered on a relatively regular basis, it is now recognized that adverse events assistance must be consistent with overall economic policy objectives. The remaining assistance to the sector is concentrated in research and extension, animal health and quarantine and adverse events assistance.

The reform of domestic marketing regulations resulted in complete deregulation of the wheat and egg industries and a partial deregulation of the town (market) milk sector.

The Consequences

Farm (Input and Output) Prices and Farm Performance

During 1984 and 1985 the devaluation of the New Zealand dollar benefited producers, world prices for beef, wool and dairy were favorable, and assistance still supplemented output prices for pastoral commodities. However, from late 1985 until 1988 the prevailing prices for meats in world markets failed to improve, the exchange rate appreciated, inflation remained high (as did interest rates), and output assistance was removed. The only gains to farmers were through reduced margins (processing costs) and farm costs, which increased at a slower rate than inflation, although input prices were still increasing faster than those of overseas competitors and damaging international competitiveness.

From late 1988 prices turned to favour farmers. Farmers' terms of exchange strengthened as a result of the long-awaited gains from the reforms and the stronger world prices for pastoral commodities. World prices for dairy products and wool improved, followed by prices of meats during 1989. Some depreciation of the exchange rate occurred, together with significant reductions in inflation and farm costs. Farmers were more competitive against producers of nontradeable commodities and in the international marketplace. By 1990, however, the recovery in dairy prices was looking very fragile, and world wool prices had declined again.

During the assistance period, sheep numbers rose from their late 1960s and early 1970s level of around 60 million head to 70 million, with much of this expansion occurring at the expense of beef cattle numbers. Since 1984 sheep numbers have dropped back to below the earlier levels. Dairy cow numbers, meanwhile, showed a slow but variable increase. Output levels largely mirrored these changes, with the usual short-term negative supply responses and biological lags associated with pastoral farming.

Study of farming supply responses through the use of a computer-based model clearly indicates that producers' behavior before and since liberalization has not differed—all output and inventory changes can be explained as consistent, rational responses to prices, costs and seasonal conditions.

Farm incomes generally declined throughout the period to 1989, except for the upward surge in 1985 due to favorable exchange and climatic conditions (Table 12.1) and improved dairy farm incomes in 1989. Farmers were caught in a classic cost-price squeeze as incomes declined and expenses increased. These expenses were dominated by debt servicing costs and the resultant crowding out of discretionary expenditure. Overall, the capital base of farming declined.

Land Markets and Rural Debt

The period 1971-82 was one of accelerated growth in nominal (and real) farmland values. The period 1982-88 was one of divergence between farmland values and inflation—the farmland value index fell while the CPI rose. By 1987 nominal farmland values had reduced to near 1981 levels, while in real terms they had decreased to only about 40 percent of their 1982 peak values (Table 12.1).

These declines, coupled with higher interest rates and lower incomes, reduced farmers' security margins and led to concerns about debt levels. By 1988 rural debt had peaked and appeared to be moving downwards, a trend helped by a Rural Bank discounting scheme which saw a $229 million write-off of concessionary loans in exchange for market interest rates in 1987. Although relationships among farm incomes, expected future incomes and inflation are complex, the large increase in land values early in the 1980s demonstrates the way in which agricultural supports became capitalized into land values. This accentuated the debt problem later in the decade. An analysis of sheep and beef farms reveals that financial leverage is excessive for current conditions.

Labor Market Adjustments

Relative employment changes were apparent from 1984 to 1988. Employment in agriculture, agricultural services and processing fell both in numbers and in share of total employment during that period. At a disaggregated level the meat processing industry (over half of agricultural processing sector employment) has seen reductions only in the last two years, despite being under pressure for a decade. The two main agricultural input industries—fertilizer and machinery—both halved employment in the four years to 1988.

Although is it obvious that farming and related industries have experienced declining employment and falling real and relative wages, it is less clear whether the speed and nature of adjustment differs from that of other sectors. General labor market reform may have provided the mechanism for change, but most of the shocks have been related to product markets.

Responses in Agribusiness Firms and Marketing Boards

A survey of agribusiness firms indicated that only changes in the tax laws were judged to have had a significantly favorable effect on profits. On the other hand, increases in the cost of borrowed working capital, reduction in the profitability of exports (caused by changes in the New Zealand dollar), and reduced purchasing power of customers in the domestic market had important negative effects on profits. However, firms believed that the strategic adjustments they made in response to the changed environment contributed positively to profits, and about one-third of the agribusinesses believed that they had become more competitive in both New Zealand and foreign markets.

Compared with other sectors of the agricultural economy, the marketing channels for exporting have been relatively untouched by the liberalization process. The legislative changes which have taken place with respect to the existing commodity marketing boards have increased the boards' financial and decision-making autonomy and, it is to be hoped, their efficiency. In the case of kiwifruit marketing, producer autonomy has been further extended through the creation of a new single seller board.

While there is still considerable debate over the marketing advantages and economic efficiency of such institutions, little evidence was found to support the notion that the boards have provided increased returns to New Zealand products. On the other hand, meat processing highlights the manner in which government policy and producer board intervention can both delay and increase the cost of the rationalization process which would normally occur as a part of a liberalization program.

The Future

The important lesson emerging from New Zealand's experience has been the extent to which these broad policy changes interacted to adversely affect the agricultural sector. This arises because the agricultural sector consists largely of tradeable goods, and the macroeconomic policies greatly influence the structure of incentives facing the tradeable goods sector. Public sector deficits and the associated capital flows over the period prior to and immediately after liberalization, the floating of the exchange rate, the liberalization of capital markets, and the tight monetary policy adopted to control inflation all led to an appreciation of the currency. This discouraged investment and output in the tradeable goods sector in general and accentuated the effect of removing assistance to agriculture.

Whether or not the overall impact of these reforms could have been reduced by a different sequencing of policies is unclear. A more drawn-out program may well have lacked the credibility necessary to sustain the impetus of reform which was a feature of the New Zealand experience. Even if a different sequencing might have been more desirable, this begs the question of planning that optimal sequence. However, given the importance of the real exchange rate (expressed as the ratio of tradeable to nontradeable goods, both expressed in New Zealand dollars), it is clear that the attainment of a low rate of domestic inflation and the subsequent adoption of a neutral monetary stance and the elimination of the public sector deficit are necessary for growth in the tradeables sector.

Rural Debt

What was largely unanticipated was that it would take so long for adjustments in land ownership and the capital structure of farm businesses to take place. Lower land values and incomes have placed many farmers in financial jeopardy, and a heavy debt burden is borne by the agricultural sector. Efforts will be required from the financial sector to deal with this problem, as their approach to date has largely been one of "wait and see." This can be rationalized by possible earlier expectations of government assistance, the overshadowing of rural debt awareness by post sharemarket crash trauma facing banks during 1988 and the sunk cost nature of much of the unrecoverable rural debt. Certainly, farms in a negative equity position have little economic incentive to resolve their debt, and lenders have no incentive to write off debt provided the debtor has stabilized. That means lenders may be able to recover some capital in the future.

Further adjustment is necessary for the financial health of the sector. This would involve debt repayments, private sector debt write-offs, a transfer of ownership to new entrants at lower debt levels or better returns and lower interest rates. It is likely that a combination of all these will be necessary. Improvement in market prices for outputs would speed the adjustment process, as this may create more interest in farmland. Land markets were very "thin" during the rural downturn, but recent improvements in land prices are most encouraging for aiding adjustment. This is, however, a mixed blessing: while enabling existing farmers to exit with some capital and dignity, it creates an increased debt servicing problem for new entrants.

The New Zealand experience has some parallels with the United States during its farm crisis of 1982 to 1985. Nonperforming loans increased during this period as land values declined, but the adjustment process is more advanced in the United States. Rural debt fell from $US 206.5 billion in 1983 to under $US 140 billion at 31 December 1988, with much of the cost of the write-down borne by the U.S. taxpayer. Many New Zealand farmers have yet to go through such an assets adjustment process, and it is uncertain how much of the actual losses will be borne by each of the private sector groups concerned. Much of the cost already borne has not yet been fully recognized.

The government has effectively withdrawn from its previously dominant position as a rural lender with the sale of the Rural Bank, an increased private sector involvement in the Bank of New Zealand, the restructuring of Landcorp, and the sale and subsequent failure of the Development Finance Corporation (DFC). The solution of the rural debt problem is clearly one for the private sector, and government must be careful to ensure that any intervention does not distort private sector decisions about debt resolution.

Production and Trade Forecasts

The lags associated with pastoral farming have long been recognized. They are a function of the biological nature of pastoral livestock farming and the short-run supply responses from changes to new livestock levels and mixes. Reductions in the size of flocks and herds is associated in the early stages with increased slaughter and therefore increased meat production. Conversely, rebuilding of livestock numbers is initially associated with an output decline. These lags mean that the full impact of the reforms undertaken has yet to be observed.

Forecasts were made for the New Zealand livestock and horticultural industries to 1995, based on a real exchange rate set at the second half of 1989 average level, and international market conditions as at January 1990. As the bulk of New Zealand's agricultural production is exported, agricultural exports are largely determined by domestic production conditions, which are now driven by these market conditions. Increasingly, the Pacific is becoming a major focus of our hopes and aspirations. Trade is shifting to North America, Australia and the Asian countries; the Pacific is providing an increasing portion of our immigrants; and the awakening of our indigenous people's rights and culture is reminding us of the importance of these Pacific links.

The major factor influencing our agricultural trade will, however, be progress on the GATT Round. New Zealand is shown to be a big winner in most of the proliferation of trade models that have been developed to study the effects of unilateral trade liberalization. The high support prices of the United States and the European Community represent a double-edged sword to New Zealand. Market access is restricted and consumer prices are increased by the original programs, reducing consumption. Marginal producers remain in business, and the surplus is dumped into the decreasing number of "free" markets, adding insult to the original injury.

Multilateral liberalization benefits New Zealand in two ways. The first is the increased returns for our export produce. Dairy returns are directly impacted by protectionism. Red meat returns are more indirectly affected via a change in (subsidized) grain prices, which would change the relative prices between grain-fed pigs and poultry and beef and lamb as well as the relative prices of grain-fed beef and our grass-fed beef. The second point is that as our agricultural sector *is* facing an unsupported free market environment domestically, our producers do not have an adjustment process to go through. Others, including the paper by Professor Allan Rae looking at the Pacific, will no doubt discuss the GATT Round and trade prospects in greater detail at this conference.

New Zealand prospects are for sheep numbers to decline slightly, beef cattle numbers to increase and then stabilize, and a slight but steady rise in dairy cow numbers. As a result, total sheep and cattle stock units should initially increase and then remain virtually static. The forecast of a substantial increase in deer and goat numbers should counteract part of this lack of growth in traditional livestock, but total stock units (including deer and goats) are expected to remain below the peak levels of 1982. These livestock numbers and the following output forecasts, however, do need a qualifier, and they highlight the crucial importance of assumptions used in forecasting. Recent dairy market downturns and the uncertainty surrounding the Australasian wool market will have an effect.

Beef and veal production and exports are likely to fall in the near future but then return to around the 1988/89 levels. Output of lamb and mutton is projected to drop from current levels and, while domestic utilization should fall slightly, a greater decline in export availability is likely. With the projected substantial growth in deer and goat numbers, an increase in their associated outputs is expected, but production volumes will still be small relative to the traditional pastoral products.

It is important to note that the removal of agricultural assistance programs, which had bolstered returns to sheep, has allowed the market to determine the appropriate levels of production in competing enterprises. The efficiency gains thus realized should more than offset the effect of lower total production on producer returns. In addition, the diversified pastoral base should reduce the exposure of New Zealand agriculture to adverse international commodity price shocks, although the tendency for agricultural prices to be correlated both between commodities and with the levels of international economic performance makes this more difficult.

Unfinished Business

After six years into the liberalization program, some outstanding issues remain to be fully addressed. It is also important to recognize that continuing high levels of unemployment may diminish enthusiasm for reform and leave some changes unfinished. This makes it all the more important to identify where reforms are incomplete and the implications of this for the future viability of the agricultural sector.

Clearly, the "cost excess" facing agriculture due to protection elsewhere in the economy remains an issue. The reduction of protection to the manufacturing sector has not only been more leisurely but also rather uneven. This has resulted in a short- to medium-term implicit tax upon both certain manufactured goods and the agricultural sector. A continuing policy of removing industry assistance is vital to avoid this being translated into a long-term tax. There is symmetry between remaining manufacturing protection and the implicit tax on agriculture and other tradeable industries. There are only two ways in which this tax can be alleviated: by direct support measures for presently unassisted tradeables or by way of reduced protection elsewhere in the economy.

To move in the direction of providing compensating assistance to agriculture would clearly be a second best approach which would constitute a questioning of the rationale behind past policy changes. It would give rise to questions of credibility about the government's reform program, not only in the sense that the speed of reform was changing, but that even the direction of policy changes was in doubt. The negative effects of such a policy choice would be likely to far outweigh any short-term benefits.

Farming leaders, recognizing these dangers, are stressing the need for a more rapid reduction of protection for import-competing manufactured goods. It is important also that more attention be given to the reduction of disparities in protection levels with the manufactured goods category, bringing rates for goods under "industry plans" more rapidly into line with others and harmonizing rates of protection on both manufacturing inputs and outputs.

The same arguments apply to labor market flexibility. Although many changes have taken place in the agriculture and primary processing subsectors, and the Labor Relations Act (1987) has facilitated these changes, caveats must be introduced concerning labor market reform in general. A fundamental question remains about the need for an overall consistent framework to address the whole issue of labor market flexibility.

It is essential that flexibility in the labor market increase and that some of the resulting efficiency gains be reflected back in farmgate returns. At the same time, it must be recognized that political reasons exist for the delay of these reforms, one of which is the interaction between the government social welfare system and the lower pay rates.

Statutory Producer Boards and Other Issues

The debate over appropriate structures for the marketing of New Zealand's primary products continues. Amendments made to the legislation governing the major export-oriented producer boards during the liberalization period have been relatively minor and have had little effect on their operations. As government has withdrawn from involvement in the financial affairs of the boards, and as the boards have extended their involvement in commercial activities, it has become increasingly difficult to obtain sufficient information to assess their performance.

All the statutory boards have significant powers, conferred upon them by Parliament, over both producers and other participants in the industry. Strengthening the mechanisms by which the boards can be held accountable to Parliament and to producers for the exercise of these powers will be necessary to counterbalance the increased freedom of action the boards now have. The conduct of regular wide-ranging performance and efficiency audits, as is required for the new Kiwifruit Marketing Board, would help to assess board performance and evaluate the need for, and appropriateness of, their statutory powers.

The Meat Producers Board and the Wool Board are expanding their commercial activities in the industries they regulate. This has led to increased concern by other participants about potential conflict of interest. These concerns are unlikely to disappear unless greater efforts are made to distinguish between the boards' commercial and regulatory functions. In the case of the Apple and Pear Marketing Board and the Dairy Board, where the commercial and regulatory roles have in effect merged, pressures for them to justify the extent of their activities, particularly on the domestic market, may intensify as the deregulation of other sectors continues.

The debate over the future role and functions of the Ministry of Agriculture and Fisheries continues. The major policy issues involved are the role of government in inspection service, and future directions and levels of agricultural research and development (R & D) funding. These remain unresolved, particularly the desirability of, and mechanisms for, introducing further contestability into inspection services. Changes to the role of government in R & D conduct and funding have been an ongoing part of the economic reforms. MAF Technology has been required to increase its revenue targets annually, but attainment of these targets may be impeded by an inability to take capital positions in joint ventures of companies. This is likely to become an increasingly crucial question for MAF Technology as the percentage of contestable government funding increases to 50 percent by 1995. Over recent months some attention has been focused within MAF on the issue of conflict of interest between policy advice and delivery functions. This seems likely to lead to a greater degree of separation between the two activities by way of a restructuring.

While not strictly unfinished business, conflict and uncertainty over the ownership and use of resources have emerged as significant issues requiring policy responses. The mandate of the Waitangi Tribunal was broadened in 1985 to hear Maori land claims dating back to 1840 and led to the lodgement of claims affecting a significant part of the country. These claims, along with recent court decisions on other resource ownership rights of the indigenous population, have created a great deal of uncertainty and are likely to have an impact on the agricultural sector.

Increasing concern over the effects of resource use on the environment, and on the need to manage natural resources in a manner which provides for future generations, has resulted in a wide-ranging review of New Zealand's resource management legislation. New legislation on the government's agenda is expected to place greater emphasis on the conservation of resources and to provide for closer monitoring of the environmental effects of land-use practices. In the future, farmers are likely to bear a greater portion of the environmental costs of farming.

Conclusions and Lessons for Others

Three major, albeit interrelated, issues emerge from the analysis. Firstly, the macroeconomic factors of exchange and interest rates moved against the sector following liberalization. In addition, the sequencing of the overall liberalization program may have imposed further adjustment costs on the agricultural sector by way of an appreciation of the real exchange rate. Secondly, the necessary adjustment in the ownership and capital structure of farm businesses has been much slower than anticipated. Finally, the economic "playing field" is still not level, with several important areas of unfinished business remaining. Until protection elsewhere in the economy is reduced, the tradeable goods sector (including agriculture) will continue to be penalized.

The major concerns remaining for agriculture in New Zealand focus on the general area of "unfinished business"—those reforms yet to be completed—which will enable the agricultural sector to realize its full potential.

Specifically, further commercial policy reform is needed to reduce the protection afforded import-competing manufacturers. In addition, government efforts must be directed at continuing to improve flexibility in the labor market. There is considerable concern that continuing high levels of unemployment will temper the political enthusiasm for completing the reform program necessary to achieve a more competitive environment for tradeable goods in general, and agriculture in particular.

The completion of economic reforms is given added importance and urgency by the Uruguay round of GATT negotiations currently under way. A competitive agricultural sector is crucial if New Zealand is to take full advantage of any opportunities offered by a liberalization of global agricultural trade. Similarly, a genuine commitment is required from both the United States and the European Community to achieve the mutual gains which can be made from changes to the support regimes of those two blocs. GATT objectives might be met by creative "nontrade distorting" supports of agriculture, and the budgetary concerns could be met by taking intervention "off-budget." While *perhaps* within the letter of GATT, these actions would not be in the spirit of the agreement. Mutually reinforcing disciplines in the four major areas of domestic support, access, export subsidies, and sanitary and phytosanitary practices will be needed if the round is to result in any meaningful success. Cosmetic changes may be attempted but will be firmly resisted. Meanwhile, New Zealand's agricultural market is badly exposed, awaiting further reforms at home and abroad.

The New Zealand experience reinforces the growing evidence showing the importance for agriculture of macroeconomic and general economywide trade policies. These policies alter the incentives (the real exchange rate) facing the sector and have a powerful effect in either reinforcing or negating sector-specific policies. During the liberalization period in New Zealand more of the adjustment burden fell on agriculture than was warranted solely by the removal of the sectors' direct assistance, and in this respect our experience mirrors that of the Southern Cone experience in the 1970s and early 1980s.

References

Sandry, R. A., and R. G. Reynolds. 1990. *Farming Without Subsidies: New Zealand's Recent Experience.* Wellington, New Zealand: Ministry of Agriculture & Fisheries.

PART THREE

A Sampling of Applied Modeling Research

To better understand how agricultural trade will likely develop in the twenty-first century, we must understand the fundamental forces driving agricultural trade today. The following chapters provide a sampling of the ongoing applied academic research on agricultural trade patterns in the Pacific Rim countries. They represent a small fraction of the work of this type available at research and academic institutions.

As a principal exporter of agricultural commodities in the Pacific Rim, Australia has much to gain from trade development. It is, perhaps, not surprising that two of the three papers in this chapter have lead authors from that country. In the first paper (Chapter 13), the authors explain the livestock model developed at the Australian Bureau of Agricultural and Resource Economics (ABARE). The ABARE model is the only existing model capable of analyzing the worldwide impacts of the beef market liberalization programs in Japan and South Korea. Most Pacific Rim countries are free of foot-and-mouth disease and will not import beef or pork from countries where the disease exists. Additional Australian exports to South Korea in the short to medium term must therefore result in reduced Australian exports to either Japan or the United States. The ABARE model has estimated demand systems and supply response curves for all these countries and is thus capable of measuring global impacts and intercountry trade-offs.

The second paper (Chapter 14) examines how changes in real exchange rates influence agricultural prices and, by extension, agricultural exports in Pacific Rim countries. Among its other strengths, this paper provides an excellent review of the literature on the effects of macroeconomic shocks on agricultural exports. The paper also provides a simple and plausible model of the variables influencing the pass-through effects, which may not be entirely due to conditions of imperfect competition, and supports the model with econometric estimates of pass-through elasticities for Canada, Japan, and Hong Kong.

The third paper (Chapter 15) goes one step further in the policy analysis process by examining the factors on which governments base agricultural policy decisions; specifically, the paper examines Japan's recent decision to liberalize beef imports. The analysis indicates that the Japanese government has chosen an import level that will maximize tariff revenues. The authors argue that previous beef import laws were so restrictive that they have limited quota rents in a Laffer-curve-type manner. This analysis is important in that it may imply that the Japanese government has partially opened its beef market to generate tariff revenues and not because of any fundamental change in the political preference function. The test of this analysis will occur in 1993 when Japan will be under pressure to reduce the tariff from 50 percent. The analysis indicates that any reduction beyond 50 percent may reduce tariff revenues, which will make it less politically acceptable and could create additional tensions between Japan and the United States.

Dermot Hayes

13

EMABA: An Econometric Model of Pacific Rim Livestock Markets

David Harris and Ian Shaw

Introduction

Australia's three main broadacre agricultural industries, wool, wheat and beef, account for around half of the gross value of Australia's total agricultural output. In addition, the broadacre industries make a substantial contribution toward Australia's total export earnings. It is hardly surprising, then, that analysis of the issues affecting Australia's broadacre industries has figured prominently in the research programs of the Australian Bureau of Agriculture and Resource Economics (ABARE) and its predecessor, the Bureau of Agricultural Economics (BAE). Part of this research effort resulted in the development of EMABA, an acronym for a structural Econometric Model of Australian Broadacre Agriculture.

One of the important features of Australian broadacre agriculture is the extensive nature of the production process, which provides opportunities for production substitution between enterprises. Initially the development of EMABA focused on modelling these relationships. Subsequently, the model has been enhanced with the addition of more detailed representations of export demand for wool, beef, pigs and poultry. More specifically, the model has been expanded to include endogenous representations of the demand for and supply of livestock products in each of the main countries involved in the Pacific Rim meat trade, as well as the bilateral trade flows which link Pacific livestock markets. Perhaps now a more suitable acronym for the model would be EMPRA, an Econometric Model of Pacific Rim Agriculture. While the current model is focused on livestock, our intentions are to extend EMABA with representations of grain markets.

As beef, in particular, is extensively modelled in EMABA, the model is well suited to an analysis of the impact of policy changes in the Pacific Basin beef trade. Indeed, one of the objectives of this paper is to present some results of an analysis of the impact of an unrestricted beef trade in North Asian markets. More detailed results will be provided in a forthcoming ABARE discussion paper on North Asian beef trade.

However, first we will summarize the underlying structure of EMABA and provide updated estimates of the most important elasticities contained in the model. As all behavioral equations in EMABA are estimated, the internally generated elasticities are a convenient means of summarizing the current version of the model.

An Overview of EMABA

Model Features and Development Philosophy

EMABA is a non-linear, annual dynamic model that currently contains estimated representations of demand, supply, trade and price determination for up to seven commodities in 21 countries. A summary of the current version of the model is presented in Table 13.1. While the model is notable for its extensive coverage of the livestock commodity markets in the Pacific Basin, more importantly EMABA has structural features which distinguish it and in some cases make it unique from other commodity trade models. These features include the representation—through systems of behavioral equations and identities—of both the dynamic behavior inherent in livestock supply response and the modelling of meat demands as a two-stage budgeting process.

TABLE 13.1 Summary of Commodity Country Coverage in EMABA

Domestic Demands

Meat demands for beef, lamb, mutton, pig meats and poultry in Australia and New Zealand

Meat demands for beef, pig meats, poultry and seafood in Japan, South Korea and Taiwan

Meat demands for table beef, processing beef, pig meat and poultry in the United States

Meat demands for beef, pig meat and poultry in Canada

Beef demands in Southeast Asia[a]

Apparel wool demands in France, Italy, West Germany, the Netherlands, the United Kingdom, Belgium, Japan and the United States

(continues)

TABLE 13.1 (continued)

Domestic Supplies

Livestock supplies of beef, lamb, mutton, wool and pig meat in Australia and New Zealand

Livestock supplies of fed beef, non-fed beef and pig meat in the United States and Canada

Livestock supplies of wagyu beef, dairy beef and pig meat in Japan

Livestock supplies of beef and pig meat in South Korea

Pig meat supplies in Taiwan

Wool supplies in Argentina and Uruguay

Crop supplies of wheat, sorghum, barley, oats, winter oilseeds and summer oilseeds in Australia

Trade Demands

Total beef, lamb, mutton and wool export demands for Australia and New Zealand

Beef export demands for Australian and New Zealand sales to the United States, Canada, Japan, South Korea, Taiwan, Singapore, Malaysia, Hong Kong and the Philippines

Total wool export demands for Argentina, Uruguay and the rest of the world

Total beef import demand for the United States, Canada and South Korea

Total beef, diaphragm beef and pig meat import demands for Japan

United States imported beef trade with Australia and New Zealand

Canadian imported beef trade with Australia and New Zealand

Korean imported beef trade with Australia, New Zealand and the United States

Japanese imported beef and diaphragm beef trade with Australia, New Zealand, the United States and Canada

Japanese imported pig meat trade with the United States, Canada and Taiwan

Japanese imported poultry trade with United States; and Southeast Asian[A] imported beef trade with Australia, New Zealand, the United States and Canada

Price Determination

Market prices for beef, lamb, mutton, wool, pig meat and poultry in Australia and New Zealand

Market prices for fed beef, non-fed beef, pig meat and poultry in the United States and Canada

Market prices for wagyu beef, dairy beef, pig meat and poultry in Japan

Market prices for beef, pig meat and poultry in South Korea and Taiwan

Market prices for beef in South East Asia[A]

Market prices for wool in Argentina and Uruguay

---

[a]Southeast Asia includes separate representations for Singapore, Malaysia and Hong Kong.

The most significant distinguishing feature of EMABA, however, is that beef, pork and poultry are differentiated (non-homogeneous) in both production and trade. The livestock production systems of each Pacific Basin country have particular features which distinguish their products from those of other countries. In addition, different livestock production systems may exist within a country to yield a non-homogeneous domestic product. For example, the United States produces both grain-fed and grass-fed beef.

Livestock products may be differentiated on the basis of a number of factors, including the length of time on feed, the content of feeding rations, animal breed, climatic and associated feeding conditions, slaughtering ages, processing techniques and packaging. These factors affect the final form of the output and enable end users to distinguish between the range of products available. In some cases the differences may be small and products such as Australian and New Zealand grass-fed beef will be very close substitutes. In other cases the differences are substantial and the products such as Japanese wagyu beef and U.S. choice grade grain-fed beef may be relatively poor substitutes. With a differentiated product approach the model contains individual domestic price determinations for beef, pig meat and poultry in each and every represented country. Market prices are strictly determined by the market clearing structural identities which equate total demands with supply. For example, Australian and New Zealand beef prices are determined by the interaction of supply and total demands (domestic plus export).

Pacific Basin trade in beef, pork and poultry meat have likewise been modelled as differentiated products. End users and importers are assumed to adjust their purchases from each country according to movements in landed prices and the degree to which the different products are substitutable for one another. For example, the relative prices of U.S. grain-fed beef and Australian grass-fed beef determine each country's share of Japanese beef imports. EMABA contains explicit representations of the major Pacific Rim bilateral trade flows in these commodities and these trade equations form the linkage between industry developments in each country.

Restrictions on meat trade between Pacific Rim countries have also been incorporated where necessary. This includes a group of equations endogenizing the formula contained in the U.S. Meat Import Law. When import restraints are triggered by conditional on/off statements, another set of statements allocates the resulting Voluntary Export Restraints between supplying countries.

EMABA was initially described in Dewbre, Shaw, Corra and Harris (1985), with regression and validation statistics for each equation presented in a companion report by Harris, Corra, Shaw and Dewbre (1985). At the time, EMABA consisted largely of detailed representations for the three main broadacre sectors of Australian agriculture: cattle, sheep and crops. It also contained a model of the U.S. beef market as well as representations of export demands for Australian beef in other countries and total export demands for wool and mutton. The enhancements to EMABA have been documented in a number of subsequent studies and include:

- Domestic demands, export demands and domestic supplies for New Zealand's beef, wool and sheep meat industries, in Shaw (1986) and McLeish and Spill (1987);
- Apparel wool demands for the eight major OECD wool-consuming countries, in Dewbre, Vlastuin and Ridley (1986) and BAE (1987);
- Pig meat supplies for Australia and the United States, in McLeish and Spill (1987);
- Japanese beef supplies, in Corra, Dickson and Teal (1989), and Japanese meat demands, in Teal, Dickson, Porter and Whiteford (1987);
- Domestic meat demands and beef supplies for Canada, in Harris and Corra (1990);
- Korean meat demands, in Harris, Corra and Shaw (1989), and Korean beef supplies, in Dickson, Harris and Corra (1990); and
- Pig meat supplies for Japan, Korea, Taiwan, Canada and New Zealand, in Corra, Harris and Dickson (1990).

Both in developing EMABA and in subsequent model enhancements, emphasis was placed on estimating the economic parameters underlying the assumed behavioral relationships rather than necessarily explaining a high degree of historical variation. Accordingly, estimation of price and income elasticities was given higher priority than identifying and explaining variation in endogenous variables due to non-economic phenomena.

In total there are more than 500 equations in EMABA. They include groups of stochastic equations representing the assumed underlying behavioral relationships, a number of stochastic and non-stochastic accounting identities, and several market-clearing identities. In general, functional forms have been approximated by log linear or log linear first-difference equations which yield constant elasticity relationships. For individual equations the logarithmic difference form was chosen in favour of the simple log form in order to ameliorate problems with autocorrelation in residual error terms.

While almost all behavioral equations in EMABA have been estimated directly by ordinary least squares (OLS) regression, for some countries, we adopted Deaton and Muellbauer's (1980) Almost Ideal Demand System approach to estimate retail meat demands with the SUR technique. The annual time-series data used for estimation varies in length according to the period when a particular part of the model was developed. Since the original documentation, some components of EMABA have been re-estimated with the addition of more recent observations to the data set. In most cases, however, the regression estimation periods begin in the early 1960s and end in the middle to late 1980s.

More detailed discussion of the approach adopted in modelling the supply, domestic demand and trade components of EMABA, together with model estimates of the more important elasticities, are presented below.

Beef Supply Response

EMABA has an extensive coverage of beef supply response in Pacific Rim countries. Individual beef supply models have been developed for Australia, New Zealand, the United States, Canada, Japan and the Republic of Korea. In general, these models contain detailed structural representations of the cattle inventory dynamics in each country. As far as possible these models also acknowledge that beef produced in the Pacific Basin is a non-homogeneous product.

The model structure for each country's cattle (beef and dairy) sector was based on the theoretical framework of livestock supply response developed by Jarvis (1974). This approach involves the estimation of a number of behavioral equations in conjunction with several livestock and output accounting identities. The identities describe the inventory dynamics and ensure that the system of equations is closed. Behavioral equations represent the important decisions of beef producers, particularly those relating to female cattle slaughter and retention decisions, which are the most important source of long- and short-run changes in beef production.

Modelling cow slaughter and retention decisions is complicated by the role of these animals as both a source of current production and as capital stock for breeding. It is further complicated by the joint role of price as a measure of the current return from sale and as an important source of information for producers on which to base expectations of future returns. In general, the theory of decision-making in livestock production suggests producers are rational if they invest in breeding stock when the expected capital value of these animals exceeds their current value. This investment occurs in the form of retaining cows and heifers by reducing the level of slaughterings. Consequently, in the short run, there exists the possibility of a backward-bending supply curve for some types of livestock and perhaps total production.

The formation of producers' expectations is an important aspect of the dynamics of supply response. In EMABA, producer expectations of future values for a variable are postulated to be an estimated function of current and past realizations of that variable. However, during model development, numerous expectations processes were tested, including polynomial distributed lags and adaptive expectations models. These options were evaluated on the basis of the same expectations process applying across all industries and on the basis of regression diagnostics and theoretical credence. Subsequently, a three-year moving average of current and past values of a per output unit gross margin variable was found to give the best overall results.

An important characteristic of broadacre agriculture in Australia and New Zealand is the substitution possibilities that exist between alternative agricultural enterprises such as sheep, beef, crops and dairying. An attempt was made to capture this feature by including variables reflecting expected returns to alternative enterprises in the behavioral equations representing retention or slaughter decisions. However, in modelling beef supply response for other Pacific Rim countries, returns to other agricultural pursuits were omitted, reflecting the implicit assumption of no substitution possibilities.

This general approach to modelling beef supply response was adopted for most of the Pacific Rim countries represented in EMABA. The U.S. beef supply model incorporates the three interdependent production systems of calf rearing, non-fed cattle raising and feedlot fattening. This approach yields the two distinct beef outputs of grain-fed beef and grass-fed beef. Similarly, the Canadian beef supply model distinguishes between the grain-fed and grass-fed outputs.

EMABA's Japanese beef supply representation differentiates between wagyu beef and dairy beef. Wagyu beef production is modelled in a simple partial adjustment process involving an expected gross margin variable. Dairy beef production was modelled in the more detailed structural framework, with the expected gross margins based on both beef and milk prices. For Australia and New Zealand, beef is treated as a homogeneous product in the detailed structural representations of the beef and dairy cattle sectors of these two countries. This reflects the almost exclusive grass-fed nature of beef production in both countries. Although different types of beef are produced in Korea, deficiencies in the livestock time-series data required beef supply to be modelled as a homogeneous product.

A convenient means of summarizing (and to some extent validating) these beef supply components of EMABA is to estimate the associated supply elasticities. However, estimating beef supply elasticities by arithmetic means is a non-trivial exercise because of the highly non-linear and dynamic nature of the EMABA supply models. Nevertheless, elasticity estimates can be obtained by simulation experiment.

First, a dynamically stable solution from a fully endogenous model is generated by fixing all exogenous variables to constant values and solving the model a sufficient number of periods into the future to obtain a set of constant solutions for all endogenous variables. Typically, the set of constant values chosen is for a recent year for which final data are available. The next step is to remove model simultaneity by deleting all market-clearing identities and assigning the previously endogenous prices their stable solution values. This non-simultaneous model is then used to simulate separate, fixed percentage perturbations of each livestock supply price and compared with the stable solution values to yield estimates of the supply response.

Producing elasticity estimates in this manner has two advantages. First, it permits a complete time dimensioning of the supply response, as the dynamics inherent in both the expectations process and the natural biological constraints of livestock production have an impact on supply adjustment. Second, a valuable by-product of this procedure is that it tests the stability and convergence properties of the supply models. In fact, the reported long-run elasticity estimates are the difference between the stable solution values and solution values from the perturbed simulation after a new stable equilibrium has been reached.

The elasticity estimates presented in Table 13.2 were derived by simulation and are based on 1987 data. They suggest that short-run beef supply response is small but negative for range-fed beef in the United States, Japanese dairy beef and total beef output in Australia and Canada. This reflects the relatively high proportion of cows and heifers in the cattle herds of these countries. In New Zealand the cattle herd is predominantly based on the dairy industry and immediate response to a beef price change is positive as producers react to higher salvage values for dairy cows as they substitute into beef breeds.

Over the medium to longer term, supply elasticity estimates for all countries are unambiguously positive. As breeding herds expand, the larger calf supply results in higher slaughterings of male cattle and eventually higher slaughterings of females. Australia has the largest

TABLE 13.2 Estimates of Short-, Medium- and Long-Run Beef Supply Elasticities[a]

	Year 1	Year 5	Year 10	Long-run
Australia	-0.04	0.10	0.88	2.99
New Zealand	0.03	0.20	0.41	0.59
United States	-0.01	0.07	0.12	0.66
Canada	-0.05	0.12	0.42	0.69
Japan				
Dairy	-0.01	0.16	0.31	0.42
Wagyu	0.03	0.27	0.39	0.41
South Korea	0.09	0.57	0.82	0.86

[a]Percentage change in quantity supplied from an immediate and permanent 1 percent change in farm level prices. Elasticities derived from simulation experiments with all market clearing prices made exogenous to eliminate any second-round effects. Elasticity estimates were evaluated with 1987 data.

long-run supply elasticity, reflecting the possibilities for substitution into beef cattle and away from cropping and sheep. Long-term cross-price elasticities for the Australian cattle sector indicate that a change in the saleyard price of beef has a small substitution effect of approximately 0.25 on the quantity of wool produced and 0.20 on cropping areas.

Elasticity estimates reported in this chapter are not directly comparable with similar estimates from other studies. In general, other studies of beef supply response do not incorporate dynamic expectations processes in their models. Rather, it is more common to assume that any change in price is equivalent to an immediate and equivalent change in expected price. When the same assumption is imposed on EMABA's beef supply models the resultant own-price elasticity estimates are comparable with the range of results reported in other studies.

Pig and Poultry Meat Supply Response

Individual pig meat supply representations for Australia, New Zealand, the United States, Canada, Japan, Korea and Taiwan have been added to EMABA since the original documentation. For Australia and the United States, pig meat supply response was estimated in a detailed structural framework similar to the approach used for modelling Pacific Basin beef supplies. Behavioral equations for slaughterings, promotions, and births were estimated and combined with inventory identities. As for the beef supply models, a three-year moving average of expected gross margins was used to represent producer decision-making on output levels.

For the remaining countries, pig meat supply response has been estimated as a single-equation partial adjustment process. An element of dynamic supply response is introduced with the lagged dependent variable and the three-year moving average of expected net returns. More precise estimates of pig meat supply response in these countries could be obtained with the estimation of structural models similar to those for Australia and the United States. However, this simplified approach was adopted in order to obtain a complete set of Pacific Rim pig meat supply representations at minimal cost. Estimates of pig meat supply response for each country are reported in Table 13.3. They were obtained from the experimental simulation process described earlier. In general they indicate relatively small, positive pig meat supply elasticities in the short run which become progressively larger in the longer run. As EMABA is an annual model, poultry meat production in Pacific Basin countries was modelled as a constant cost industry. With a relatively short four-month production cycle, poultry producers are able to adjust output levels relatively quickly in response to within-year changes in demand. Consequently, Australian and U.S. retail chicken prices were modelled as a function of compound feed and other costs. For the remaining countries, retail prices were explained by compound feed costs only. This approach implies an infinite poultry meat supply response to a change in price and does not incorporate any dynamic behavior in the form of a price expectations process.

Supply Response For Sheep Products

The EMABA model contains endogenous representations of wool, lamb and mutton supplies in both Australia and New Zealand as well as wool production in Argentina and Uruguay. For Australia and New Zealand, detailed structural models of the sheep industry were estimated using an approach similar to that already described for beef. All three outputs are determined by inventory identities and a number of behavioral equations which represent the critical producer's decisions on slaughterings, retentions and promotions.

The dual role of female stock as a source of both capital stock and current meat production does not complicate Australian sheep meat and wool supply response to the same extent as it does for beef. Unlike beef, the slaughter value of adult sheep is relatively low when compared with their capitalized value in wool production. This result also appears to hold in the case of New Zealand even though their sheep

TABLE 13.3 Estimates of Short-, Medium- and Long-Run Pork Supply Elasticities[a]

	Year 1	Year 5	Year 10	Long-run
Australia	0.05	0.27	0.47	0.90
New Zealand	0.09	0.70	0.96	1.05
United States	0.07	1.21	1.95	2.34
Canada	0.01	0.92	1.52	2.00
Japan	0.11	1.08	1.87	2.63
South Korea	0.10	1.05	1.99	3.54
Taiwan	0.23	2.33	3.99	5.38

[a]Percentage change in quantity supplied from an immediate and permanent 1 percent change in farm level prices. Elasticities derived from simulation experiments with all market clearing prices made exogenous to eliminate any second-round effects. Elasticity estimates were evaluated with 1987 data.

industry is structured to produce prime lamb and around 70 percent of the wool clip is for non-apparel use.

Wool production in both Argentina and Uruguay is modelled by a single equation, due to the lack of detailed statistical series of sheep inventories for both countries. A partial adjustment specification was used to represent grower response. The perceived advantages of this approach are that it endogenizes wool production and ensures a dynamic supply response in two of Australia's major competitors in world trade in wool. An attempt to model South African wool supply in a similar manner proved unsatisfactory. Except in years of adverse seasonal conditions, historically there appears to have been relatively little variation in wool production in South Africa, and therefore the world's fourth largest wool exporter remains an exogenous component in the model.

The wool, lamb and mutton supply elasticity estimates in Table 13.4 were again derived from EMABA simulation experiments. For Australia, the estimates of supply response for all three outputs are positive and relatively small in comparison to those obtained for beef supply response. Most other studies have also reported estimates of an inelastic supply response for Australian sheep products. The long-term cross-price effects for the sheep sector indicate that a 1 percent change in the price of wool has a small substitution effect of around 0.29 percent for lamb supplies but a large impact of 2.11 percent for beef production. Similarly, the estimated wool cross-price effect on crop outputs is a small substitution effect of approximately 0.09 percent.

TABLE 13.4 Estimates of Short-, Medium- and Long-Run Sheepmeat and Wool Supply Elasticities[a]

	Year 1	Year 5	Year 10	Long-run
Australia				
Lamb supply	0.00	0.58	0.65	0.65
Wool supply	0.00	0.22	0.46	0.79
New Zealand				
Lamb supply	0.12	0.06	0.05	0.05
Wool supply	0.00	0.13	0.40	1.28
Argentina				
Wool supply	0.03	0.29	0.45	0.56
Uruguay				
Wool supply	0.04	0.36	0.56	0.70

[a]Percentage change in quantity supplied from an immediate and permanent 1 percent change in farm level prices. Elasticities derived from simulation experiments with all market clearing prices made exogenous to eliminate any second-round effects. Elasticity estimates were evaluated with 1987 data.

Australian Crops Supply Response

Given the potential importance of enterprise substitution in Australian broadacre agriculture, EMABA also contains a representation of domestic crops supply. The approach adopted was to assume that crop and livestock supply in Australia is characterized by a joint production technology where land used in crop production and for grazing of livestock is weakly separable from other inputs. It was also assumed that producers are profit maximizers and that the marginal rate of substitution between land sown to each crop (wheat, barley, oats, sorghum, winter oilseeds and summer oilseeds) is independent of the quantities of grazing land and other inputs demanded. These assumptions enable crop area allocation decisions to be modelled as derived demands in a two-stage process.

In the first stage, the (exogenous) total cultivated land base is allocated between aggregate margins for aggregate cropping and aggregate livestock activities. In the next stage, total crop areas are allocated between aggregate winter crops and aggregate summer crops area and then to the individual crops within these groups. The second-stage decisions are specified as functions of the ratio of expected per hectare, gross revenues for each crop. Unavailability of statistics on the costs of growing different crops prevented the use of gross margin variables in the second-stage allocations. Where appropriate, the dynamics of crop area response were captured as a simple partial adjustment process.

The elasticity estimates of Australian crop production in Table 13.5 are based on exogenous crop yields and were obtained by simulation experiments. These estimates are appropriately signed for the own-price effects, and the cross-price effects indicate significant substitution relationships amongst the different crops. However, it should be noted that in the current version of EMABA, crop supply elasticities may be underestimated because the (exogenous) total area of cultivated land does not respond to the overall profitability of broadacre agriculture. Estimates of the cross-price effects between crops and livestock suggest small substitution relationships. For example, the long-term effect of a concurrent 1 percent change in the price of every crop is a 0.33 percent change in wool output and a 0.04 percent change in beef production.

Domestic Demand Representations

Another feature of EMABA is the inclusion of domestic meat demand systems for Australia, New Zealand, the United States, Canada, Japan, Korea, and Taiwan as well as single-equation representations of beef demands in Singapore, Malaysia, Hong Kong and the Philippines. For the countries represented, domestic meat demands were estimated as a two-stage budgeting process. In the first stage, total consumer demand for a group of meats was determined as a function of real personal consumption expenditures and the weighted average price of the group of meats deflated by the consumer price index. In the second-stage, a system of equations determined the allocation of the total meat demand among the group of meats.

For the United States, Canada and Japan the expenditure share equations were estimated using Deaton and Muellbauer's (1980) Almost Ideal Demand System. In some cases (for example, Korea) this approach was estimated and rejected due to the implausibility of some elasticity estimates. For the remaining countries, a more simplified market share approach was used to allocate individual meat demands. Specified as a share of total meat demand, individual meat demand equations were estimated as functions of the ratio of the price of the individual meat relative to the weighted average price of all other competing meats. A total meat consumption variable is also included in some market share equations to allow for differences in the income elasticities of demand for each meat. More detailed information on the market share approach can be found in Dewbre, Shaw, Corra and Harris (1985).

TABLE 13.5 Estimates of Short-, Medium- and Long-Run Australian Crop Supply Elasticities[a]

	Year 1	Year 5	Year 10	Long-run
Wheat	0.00	0.39	0.45	0.46
Barley	0.00	0.47	0.50	0.51
Oats	0.00	0.76	0.77	0.77
Sorghum	0.00	0.93	1.36	1.45
Winter oilseeds	0.00	1.87	1.87	1.87
Summer oilseeds	0.00	0.52	0.76	0.81

[a]Percentage change in quantity supplied from an immediate and permanent 1 percent change in farm level prices. Elasticities derived from simulation experiments with all market clearing prices made exogenous to eliminate any second-round effects. Elasticity estimated were evaluated with 1987 data.

In estimating these meat demand systems the number of commodities explicitly represented varies across EMABA's country representations. For Japan, Korea and Taiwan the demand systems included beef, pig meat, poultry and seafood. The U.S. system was based on table beef (mainly grain-fed product), processing beef (mainly grass-fed product), pig meat and poultry while the Canadian demand system covered total beef, pig meat and poultry. For Australia and New Zealand, separate lamb and mutton categories were included with beef, pig meat and poultry demands.

The underlying own-price and income elasticity estimates for beef and sheep meats are reported in Table 13.6 and for pig meat and poultry in Table 13.7. In most cases EMABA uses simple price transmission margin equations to link the saleyard, wholesale and retail price levels. A 1 percent change in the farm level price has a relatively smaller consumer demand impact as it translates into a less than 1 percent price change at the retail level. Therefore, elasticity estimates are reported with respect to an own-price change at both the retail level and the saleyard level. The own-price effects are all appropriately signed and are generally within the bounds of previously reported estimates. While the cross-price elasticities of demand have not been reported due to space limitations, in almost all cases the uncompensated effects are positively signed. For those negatively signed cross-price effects, the compensated estimates generally indicate zero or very small, positively signed results.

TABLE 13.6 Estimates of Uncompensated Own-Price and Income Elasticities of Demand for Beef and Sheep Meats[a]

	Retail Price	Farm Price	Income
Beef			
Australia	-0.92	-0.37	0.26
New Zealand	-1.08	-0.37	1.36
United States			
Processing	-0.43	-0.16	0.40
Table	-0.49	-0.30	0.66
Canada			
Processing	-0.77	-0.67	0.31
Table	-0.52	-0.43	0.31
Japan	-0.67	-0.24	1.15
South Korea	-0.69	-0.38	1.09
Taiwan	-0.55	N/A	1.22
Lamb			
Australia	-1.20	-0.62	0.14
New Zealand	-1.10	-0.31	1.26
Mutton			
Australia	-2.31	-0.61	-0.32
New Zealand	-2.33	-0.34	2.89

[a]Percentage change in quantity demanded for a 1 percent change in retail price, farm price, and (real, per person) private consumption expenditures, respectively. Elasticity estimates were evaluated with 1987 data.

N/A = Not modelled.

EMABA Trade Representations

EMABA's country representations are linked together by equations endogenizing world trade in apparel wool and the Pacific Basin trade in beef, pig meat and poultry products. In general, trade representations are based on a differentiated product approach with total imports by a particular country and the (export) supplying country shares of that total determined by relative price movements. These endogenous bilateral trade flows into the importing country are linked up with corresponding bilateral export trade flows out of the supplying countries. Each of these individual export demands becomes part of the market clearing identity in the supplying country, which determines

TABLE 13.7 Estimates of Uncompensated Own-Price and Income Elasticities of Demand for Pig and Poultry Meats[a]

	Retail Price	Farm Price	Income
Pig Meat			
Australia			
Pork	-1.39	-0.55	0.22
Bacon and Ham	-0.73	-0.13	0.21
New Zealand	-0.39	-0.16	0.41
United States	-0.98	-0.58	0.18
Canada	-0.35	-0.19	0.19
Japan	-0.31	-0.16	1.10
South Korea	-1.14	-0.75	1.10
Taiwan	-0.68	-0.26	0.51
Poultry Meat			
Australia	-0.79	–	0.21
New Zealand	-0.63	–	0.01
United States	-1.09	–	0.25
Canada	-0.37	–	0.68
Japan	-0.54	–	1.10
South Korea	-0.54	–	0.41
Taiwan	-1.30	–	0.66

[a] Percentage change in quantity demanded for a 1 percent change in retail price, farm price, and (real, per person) private consumption expenditures, respectively. Elasticity estimates were based on expenditure shares. Elasticity estimates were evaluated with 1987 data.

market prices. Consequently, a change in import demand simultaneously affects the landed prices and the import market shares of each supplying country.

Time-series data limitations on market prices have so far prevented the explicit representation of the differentiated products approach at the retail level of importing countries. In some cases these limitations have also restricted the application of this approach at the wholesale or landed product stage of import demands. As a result the landed (border) prices that determine import demands have had to be proxied by the respective supplying (export) country's saleyard or wholesale level market prices. This applies to all of EMABA's trade representations for wool, beef, pig meat, sheep meat and poultry. In addition, for estimation purposes the differences in transport and handling charges have been ignored and assumed to be constant.

EMABA's wool trade representations involve total apparel wool demands by Japan, the United States, the EC-Six and a rest of the world category to account for Soviet and Chinese wool purchases. These total wool demands are allocated between the supplying countries of Australia, New Zealand, Uruguay, Argentina and South Africa on the basis of relative market prices for raw wool denominated in a common currency.

The model's meat trade representations are focused on trade flows within the Pacific Basin. They include:

- U.S. poultry trade with Japan;
- U.S., Canadian and Taiwan pig meat trade with Japan;
- Australian and New Zealand sheep meat trade with all countries;
- Australian, New Zealand, U.S. and Canadian beef trade with Japan, Korea, Taiwan and other Southeast Asian countries; and
- Australian and New Zealand beef trade with the United States, Canada and the rest of the world.

For the Japanese poultry trade, imports are modelled as a share of total demand and determined by the relative retail prices of Japanese and U.S. chicken meat. Supplying country shares of the Japanese pig meat trade are determined by relative market prices, with total imports dependent on the ratio of Japanese market prices and a policy-determined stated price of pig meat imports.

Australian and New Zealand sheep meats are treated as differentiated products with relative prices determining their respective shares of total world trade. Beef trade with the Southeast Asian countries is determined by prices but total beef imports by Japan and Korea are restricted by exogenous import quotas. Although the exporting country shares of the Japanese beef trade are determined by endogenous market prices, there were insufficient observations to estimate similar market share equations for the Korean beef trade. Consequently, EMABA imposes fixed shares on the exporting country allocations of the Korean import quota.

For the North American beef trade, EMABA includes a group of equations to represent the formula used in the U.S. Meat Import Law. A set of conditional if-then statements determine if import controls are triggered and if voluntary export restraints are to be imposed. At present, EMABA's Canadian import controls are also triggered by these U.S. conditional statements, which reflects the close relationship between the North American beef industries. In the absence of import restrictions the total level of trade is determined by the ratio of the U.S. or Canadian domestic cow beef price and the (import share) weighted average price of Australian and New Zealand beef.

TABLE 13.8 Estimates of Short-, Medium-, and Long-Run Aggregate Export Demand Elasticities[a]

	Year 1	Year 5	Year 10	Long-run
Australia				
Beef	-0.64	-0.88	-1.37	-1.25
Lamb	-1.62	-3.11	-3.20	-3.22
Mutton	-0.51	-0.66	-0.66	-0.66
Wool	-0.45	-1.93	-1.98	-1.95
New Zealand				
Beef	-0.64	-0.88	-1.37	-1.25
Lamb	-0.47	-1.30	-1.35	-1.35
Mutton	-0.26	-0.30	-0.31	-0.31
Wool	-0.14	-0.26	-0.29	-0.30
United States				
Beef	-0.41	-0.71	-0.78	-0.85
Pig meat	-0.70	-1.06	-1.42	-1.34
Canada				
Beef	-0.41	-0.71	-0.78	-0.85
Pig meat	-0.70	-1.06	-1.42	-1.34
Taiwan				
Pig meat	-1.64	-1.90	-1.87	-1.87

[a]Percentage change in quantity exported from an immediate and permanent 1 percent change in farm level prices. U.S. poultry export demand elasticity evaluated at retail price level. Elasticities derived from simulation experiments with market clearing prices for all other commodities made exogenous to eliminate any second-round effects. Elasticity estimates were evaluated with 1987 data.

A summary of the estimated export demand elasticities underlying EMABA's trade representations are provided in Table 13.8. These elasticities are evaluated with respect to auction level price changes and indicate the percentage change in the total quantity of product demanded (exported) for a 1 percent change in market price in the supplying country. The estimated beef export demand elasticities are the same for both Australia and New Zealand because, in the current version of EMABA, Oceania beef is regarded as a homogeneous product in trade. Similarly the pig meat export demand elasticities for the United States and Canada reflect the same assumption imposed on North American pig meat supplies.

The estimate for Australia's beef export demand response reflects the removal of Japanese import quotas and their replacement by a 70 percent tariff. Therefore, the resulting aggregate elasticity estimate partially reflects an assumption imposed on the Japanese component of EMABA that dairy steer prices will decline to a level equivalent to the landed price of U.S. choice grade steers (that is, adjusted for exchange rates, tariffs, transport and handling charges). Additive marketing margins and conversion to a product weight basis would yield a corresponding elasticity for a border price change which is substantially higher. However, it should be noted that the imposition of U.S. beef import controls would result in a substantial reduction in the estimated aggregate export demand elasticity for Australian beef.

An Application of EMABA: Liberalization of the North Asian Beef Trade

While EMABA is used as an analytical framework to support ABARE's short- and medium-term commodity outlook work, it is policy analysis for which the model is mainly used. Recent moves toward liberalization of the North Asian beef trade have important implications for the future prosperity of Australia's beef industry. In addition, the current Uruguay Round of GATT negotiations may result in further moves toward a lowering of trade barriers affecting Japanese and Korean beef imports.

The Pacific Basin beef trade is essentially a collection of regional trade flows separated from beef trade in the rest of the world by trade policy restrictions. In general it is defined to include the regions of Oceania (Australia and New Zealand), North America (the United States and Canada), North Asia (Japan and Korea), Southeast Asia (Taiwan and other countries), and the Central American countries. The separation in trade is largely the result of countries in this region imposing bans on trade with supplying countries where foot-and-mouth disease is endemic.

Australia, New Zealand and the United States account for more than 90 percent of beef trade among Pacific Rim countries. Beef from the European Community which is free of foot and mouth disease has restricted access to Pacific markets due to the Andriessen Kerin Agreement and some GATT-sanctioned minimum access restrictions.

In a paper by Harris, Corra and Shaw (1989), EMABA was used to provide some preliminary estimates of the Pacific Basin impacts from changes to the beef import policies of Japan and Korea. A forthcoming ABARE report on the North Asian beef markets will provide more recent estimates of these impacts, based on EMABA forecast simulation experiments.

A baseline simulation was generated for the 1991-95 period and used for comparisons with alternative simulations involving changes to North Asian beef import policies. In generating the baseline simulation a number of important assumptions were imposed on the model. A summary of some of the key exogenous assumptions is reported in Table 13.9. Of equal importance are the assumptions concerning North Asian beef trade policies.

For Japan, import quotas were replaced by a 70 percent tariff in 1991, 60 percent tariff in 1992 and 50 percent tariffs for the 1993-95 period. Tariffs on diaphragm beef remained unchanged at 15 percent and beef stocks are assumed to decline by 30 kt in 1991. For Korea it was assumed import quotas expand by 10 kt (shipped weight) a year from a base level of 80 kt in 1990 through to 130 kt by 1995.

With the removal of Japanese import quotas, an assumption was required for the endogenous determination of Japanese beef prices in the new trading environment. For the purposes of the analysis it was assumed the saleyard price of Japanese dairy steers would reach a level equivalent to the landed price of U.S. grain-fed steers (that is, a saleyard price adjusted for exchange rates, tariffs, transport and handling charges). This assumption implies these two products are perfect substitutes. As market price differentials suggest these two products are differentiated (Mori, Lin and Gorman 1989), this assumption will overestimate the price changes in Japan to the extent they are less than perfect substitutes. For simulation purposes it was also assumed the aggregate retail beef price in Japan was determined by a weighted average of wagyu and dairy beef prices and the border prices of U.S. and Australian beef.

A selection of results for the baseline simulations are provided in Table 13.10. For the assumptions imposed, Japanese retail beef prices in 1991 are expected to be around 19 percent lower than in 1990, causing beef consumption to rise by around 7 percent in 1991. Total quota beef imports rise by around 13 percent to 467 kt shipped weight. Over the medium term, the projected lower prices for beef encourage even higher consumption levels and higher imports. By 1995, 42.4 percent of total Japanese quota beef imports of 733 kt are supplied by Australia, while 53.8 percent are supplied by the United States. As a result, Japanese beef consumption reaches an estimated 9.1 kg per person (retail weight) in 1995 compared with 6.7 kg per person in 1989.

The quota restrictions in Korea result in higher beef prices and a limited expansion in domestic output. With the assumed fixed trade shares

TABLE 13.9 Major Exogenous Assumptions For EMABA Simulation Results

	Unit	1990^s	1991	1992	1993	1994	1995
Personal Consumption Expenditures[a]							
Japan	%	4.0	3.5	3.5	3.5	3.5	3.5
Korea	%	6.0	6.0	6.0	6.0	6.0	6.0
Taiwan	%	6.0	5.0	5.0	5.0	5.0	5.0
United States	%	2.0	3.0	3.0	3.0	3.0	3.0
Canada	%	2.0	3.0	3.0	3.0	3.0	3.0
Australia	%	1.2	3.7	3.0	3.0	3.0	3.0
New Zealand	%	2.4	2.0	2.0	2.0	2.0	2.0
Exchange Rates[b]							
Japan	Yen	115	106	101	97	93	90
Korea	Won	522	526	531	536	542	548
Taiwan	NT$	19.81	19.32	18.72	18.16	17.62	17.14
United States	US$	0.76	0.76	0.74	0.73	0.71	0.75
Canada	CN$	0.89	0.88	0.87	0.86	0.85	0.84
New Zealand	NZ$	1.29	1.26	1.24	1.21	1.19	1.17
Grain Prices[c]							
Wheat	US$/bu	3.91	3.61	3.65	3.67	4.02	4.37
Corn	US$/bu	2.69	2.88	3.06	3.27	3.48	3.73
Sorghum	US$/bu	2.52	2.84	3.01	3.23	3.43	3.67
Soybean meal	USc/lb	14.09	14.70	15.16	15.62	16.18	16.41
Australian Wool Marketing[d]							
Floor price	Ac/kg	870	700	700	700	700	700
Producer levies	%	8.5	18.0	18.0	18.0	15.0	15.0

[a]Real percentage growth rates in constant 1989 values. The 1989 base levels were Japan Yen224.3 billion; Korea 64.1 billion won; Taiwan NT1769.2 billion; United States US$3485.7 billion; Canada CN$376.4 billion; Australia $A175.1 billion; New Zealand NZ$38.2 billion. Calendar year growth for countries except for Australia (year ended 30 June) and New Zealand (year ended 30 September).
[b]Calendar year exchange rates per Australian dollar.
[c]Crop year prices received by farmers except for calendar year price of (44 percent) soybean meal.
[d]Assumes no revolvement of producer levies. Floor price in clean terms.
^{s}ABARE estimate.

of 75 percent for Australia, 15 percent for the United States and 10 percent for New Zealand the gradual expansion in Korean beef imports primarily raises the demand for Australian product. Overall Australian beef prices increase steadily during the simulation period in response

TABLE 13.10 EMABA Baseline Simulation for Pacific Basin Beef Trade[a]

	Unit	1989[p]	1990[s]	1991	1992	1993	1994	1995
Japan[b]								
Production	kt	548	535	559	588	603	614	614
Consumption	kt	1,199	1,267	1,355	1,381	1,472	1,612	1,683
Imports	kt	349	414	467	514	579	678	733
from Austr.	kt	177	209	215	230	243	275	311
from US	kt	152	180	227	258	311	375	394
Diaphragm imports	kt	103	95	58	41	29	22	17
Retail price	¥/kg	3,646	3,882	3,145	3,233	3,168	3,199	3,282
Wholesale price[c]	¥/kg	1,254	1,372	888	907	855	872	911
Korea[b]								
Production	kt	120	110	107	109	115	120	124
Consumption	kt	218	222	233	249	269	288	306
Imports	kt	70	80	90	100	110	120	130
Retail price	Won/kg	10,166	11,534	12,542	13,241	13,886	14,677	15,702
Farm price[d]	Won/kg	4,186	5,867	7,672	7,992	8,197	8,528	9,091
Australia								
Production	kt	1,491	1,660	1,601	1,498	1,536	1,628	1,788
Consumption	kt	683	673	646	619	615	612	602
Exports	kt	578	703	680	623	655	726	851
Farm price[e]	Ac/kg	210	218	217	229	241	251	261
United States[b]								
Production	kt	10,633	10,671	10,897	11,033	11,142	11,090	11,938
Consumption	kt	11,137	11,160	11,201	11,386	11,461	11,431	11,364
Imports[f]	kt	600	624	531	587	608	656	712
Exports	kt	326	385	405	427	476	540	559
Farm price[g]	USc/kg	160	168	170	174	179	190	206

[a]Prices expressed in nominal terms; production and consumption in carcass weight equivalent; imports and exports in shipped weight.
[b]Calendar year ended December.
[c]Dressed weight wholesale price of dairy steers.
[d]Price recieved by farmers for 400 kg male native cattle.
[e]Weighted average saleyard price of beef in estimated dressed weight terms.
[f]Excludes trade with Canada.
[g]Liveweight saleyard price of choice grade steers (900-1100 lb), Omaha.
[p]Provisional.
[s]ABARE estimate.

to increased export demand and lower beef supplies as producers expand their breeding herds.

By 1995 Australian beef production reaches 1,788 kt (carcass weight) and during the ensuing period the greater beef sales to North Asian markets are at the expense of domestic consumption and lower export volumes to other markets such as the United States. Fed-beef prices in the United States increase gradually as do beef exports in response to the higher Japanese demand for grain-fed beef. The higher prices strengthen the desire for a limited expansion of the U.S. cattle herd and by 1995 total beef production reaches 11,938 kt.

In the context of the current Uruguay Round of GATT negotiations there is some interest in the impact of removing all restrictions affecting the North Asian beef trade. To examine the impact of complete trade liberalization an alternative simulation was generated assuming the immediate removal of all quotas and tariffs on restrictions of Japanese and South Korean beef imports. Again the Japanese dairy steer price was assumed to adjust to a level equivalent to the landed price of U.S. grain-fed beef. For South Korea, the market price of beef was assumed to fall to a level equivalent with the (import share) weighted average landed prices of U.S. and Australian beef. A 30 percent price premium was added to allow for the reported differences in quality between Australian grass-fed beef and South Korean native quality beef (see Harris and Dickson 1989).

The percentage impacts from a comparison of this alternative simulation with the baseline results are reported in Table 13.11. Overall retail beef prices in Japan are substantially lower, resulting in higher levels of beef consumption and higher beef imports. By 1995 quota beef imports are 25 percent higher than the baseline simulation level of 733 kt. The U.S. market share increases dramatically at the expense of Australia and beef consumption in Japan reaches an estimated 10.2 kg per person, 12.2 percent above baseline results.

Removal of South Korea's trade restrictions causes retail beef prices to approximately halve. This results in lower domestic beef production and a 84 percent higher level of beef consumption by 1995. Korean beef imports expand continuously to an estimated 330 kt by the end of the simulation period. Much of this growth in beef imports is supplied by Australian product due to the fixed market shares imposed on the model. Consequently, the Australian price impacts are larger than the U.S. price impacts, which improves the competitiveness of U.S. beef in the Japanese market. These impacts are likely to be overstated as a move to free trade in South Korea would more than likely encourage a larger demand for U.S. grain-fed primal cuts and hence increase the U.S. share of South Korea's imported beef trade.

TABLE 13.11 EMABA Alternative Simulation Results for Unrestricted North Asian Beef Trade[a]

	1991	1992	1993	1994	1995
	%	%	%	%	%
Japan					
Production	0.0	-1.6	-2.8	-4.5	-6.2
Consumption	15.3	15.9	13.1	12.3	12.2
"Quota" imports[b]	34.9	35.1	28.2	25.4	24.8
from Australia	6.6	-3.4	-.5	-14.1	-7.4
from US	64.5	72.5	65.7	56.3	51.8
Diaphragm imports[c]	-28.3	-45.9	-53.4	-57.7	-60.7
Retail price	-17.6	-18.2	-15.4	-14.6	-14.4
Wholesale price[d]	-32.5	-32.6	-27.8	-25.9	-25.4
Korea					
Production	-20.1	-27.6	-38.2	-49.8	-55.6
Consumption	83.6	84.0	82.3	83.4	84.2
Imports[e]	171.3	171.3	172.0	178.5	179.1
Retail price	-55.4	55.5	-54.8	-55.1	-55.3
Farm price[f]	-78.5	-78.5	-77.8	-78.0	-78.2
Australia					
Production	-0.6	-4.2	-5.5	-3.0	-0.4
Consumption	-9.7	-9.8	-10.2	-8.3	-8.0
Exports	5.7	0.4	2.5	0.2	4.8
Farm price	29.8	26.3	27.0	22.3	22.4
United States[b]					
Production	0.5	0.0	-0.4	-0.9	-1.4
Consumption	-2.5	-3.3	-3.7	-3.9	-4.1
Imports	-11.2	-9.4	-7.6	-3.0	-0.9
Exports	47.5	55.7	55.3	51.8	50.2
Farm price	2.7	5.2	6.7	8.2	9.1

[a]Percentage impacts from comparison of alternative simulation with baseline simulation results presented in Table 13.10.
[b]Assumes no import quotas and a tariff rate of zero percent.
[c]Assumes a tariff rate of zero percent.
[d]Japanese saleyard price of dairy steers assumed to adjust to a level equivalent with the landed price of U.S. choice grade steers (adjusted for exchange rates, transport and handling charges).
[e]Assumes no import quotas and a tariff rate of zero percent.
[f]Korean native steer price assumed to adjust to a level equivalent with a weighted (by import shares) average landed price of U.S. choice grade steers and the weighted average Australian beef price (that is, adjusted for exchange rates, transport and handling charges) plus fixed 30 percent price premium.

The higher demand for beef by North Asian markets results in higher beef prices, lower domestic consumption and a larger herd expansion in both Australia and the United States. Initially Australian beef prices are 30 percent higher than base levels, which encourages a stronger rate of herd buildup and lower domestic beef production. The higher prices for grass-fed beef also result in lower shipments of Australian beef to the traditional markets of the United States and Canada. In net present value terms the estimated total gains for Australian beef producers are estimated at $A2676m. Combined with the estimated losses for Australian beef consumers of $A1006m, the net gain to the Australian economy would total $A1670m.

Future Directions for EMABA

Efforts are under way to update and revise EMABA. Currently the model is being transferred from TROLL onto the SAS (ETS Version 6) software. As part of this transfer, regression bounds for the older components of EMABA will be updated and equations reestimated and/or respecified where necessary to provide a consistent set of parameter estimates across countries and commodities. These revisions are bound to result in changes to the underlying elasticities contained in the model.

Future EMABA development work could proceed in a number of different directions. One of the more interesting areas of model development is to expand the commodity coverage by including greater detail on Pacific Basin grain markets. EMABA has extensive representations of grain-fed beef, pig meat and poultry production in Pacific Rim countries and a natural progression is to model the linkages with feed grain markets. Currently work is proceeding on the development of feedgrain demand systems in the United States, Japan and Australia with appropriate linkages to intensive livestock production.

Subsequently feed grain demand systems for other Pacific Rim countries could be added to the model. The development of grain supply models for the United States and Canada and the addition of domestic wheat demand representations for Pacific Rim countries would then provide EMABA with the opportunity to endogenize grain prices. At the same time, these developments would provide the basis for testing the appropriateness of a differentiated products approach to modelling Pacific Basin grain trade. The successful addition of these developments into EMABA would greatly enhance the model's forecasting capabilities and its capacity to examine policy issues such as the U.S. farm bill.

For meats, the extension of the application of the differentiated product approach to the retail level is constrained by difficulties in obtaining prices for the different types of available product. However, the opportunities for obtaining the necessary price data are more promising at the wholesale level. With improved price information, a systems estimation approach could be used to estimate the wholesale level demands and substitution relationships for the various types of domestically produced and imported products. Part of an existing ABARE research project is currently examining the possibilities for this type of approach in the context of Japanese beef trade liberalization. If successful, the estimated relationships may be used to enhance EMABA's representation of Japanese beef demands.

Finally, further research is warranted to examine the approach used to model the production substitution possibilities that exist between alternative agricultural enterprises. The same issue arises when considering the question of alternative outputs within an aggregate enterprise such as cropping. At present, EMABA acknowledges these resource allocation possibilities only for Australia and New Zealand, albeit in a restricted manner. In Australian broadacre agriculture this is an important issue in both forecasting and policy analysis work and requires further attention. The impact of North Asian beef trade liberalization and future developments in Australian wool pricing arrangements will highlight the significance of these Australian broadacre substitution possibilities. It is anticipated that some alternative approaches to modelling these Australian production substitution relationships will be considered as part of the current EMABA revision exercise.

References

BAE (Bureau of Agricultural Economics). 1987. *Returns from Wool Promotion in the United States: An AWC-BAE Analysis.* Occasional Paper No. 100, AGPS.

Corra, G., A. Dickson, and F. Teal. 1989. *Why Has the Supply of Beef in Japan Grown So Rapidly?* ABARE paper presented at the 33rd Annual Conference of the Australian Agricultural Economics Society, Lincoln College, Christchurch, New Zealand, 7-9 February.

Corra, G., D. Harris, and A. Dickson. 1990. *Pacific Basin Meat Trade: The Impact of a Change in Feed Grain Prices.* ABARE paper presented at the 34th Annual Conference of the Australian Agricultural Economics Society, University of Queensland, Brisbane, 13-15 February.

Deaton, A. and J. Muellbauer. 1980. "An Almost Ideal Demand System." *American Economic Review* 70: 312-26.

Dewbre, J., I. Shaw, G. Corra, and D. Harris. 1985. *EMABA: Econometric Model of Australian Broadacre Agriculture.* Bureau of Agricultural Economics, AGPS, Canberra.

Dewbre, J., C. Vlastuin, and H. Ridley. 1986. *An Analysis of Demand for Apparel and Apparel Fibre Including Wool*. BAE paper presented at the 30th Annual Conference of the Australian Agricultural Economics Society, Australian National University, Canberra, 3-5 February.

Dickson, A., D. Harris, and G. Corra. 1990. *South Korean Beef Industry: Potential Impact from Liberalization*. ABARE paper presented at the 34th Annual Conference of the Australian Agricultural Economics Society, University of Queensland, Brisbane, 13-15 February.

Harris, D. and G. Corra. 1990. *The U.S.-Canadian Free Trade Agreement and EC Beef Sales to Canada: Implications for Australia*. ABARE paper presented at the 34th Annual Conference of the Australian Agricultural Economics Society, University of Queensland, Brisbane, 13-15 February.

Harris, D., G. Corra, and I. Shaw. 1989. *Policy Changes Affecting Pacific Basin Beef Trade: A Preliminary Analysis*. ABARE paper presented at the workshop on Agricultural Policy, Trade and Development, Pacific Economic Cooperation Conference, Seoul, Republic of Korea, 15-18 May.

Harris, D., G. Corra, I. Shaw, and J. Dewbre. 1985. *EMABA: Econometric Model of Australian Broadacre Agriculture: Technical Documentation*. Bureau of Agricultural Economics, Canberra.

Harris, D. and A. Dickson. 1989. "Korea's Beef Market and Demand for Imported Beef." *Agriculture and Resource Quarterly* 3(1): 294-304.

Jarvis, L. S. 1974. "Cattle as Capital Goods and Ranchers as Portfolio Managers: An Application to the Argentine Cattle Sector." *Journal of Political Economy* 82(3): 489-520.

McLeish, R. and M. Spill. 1987. *Livestock Feed Grains Linkages in the Pacific Basin: The Impact of a Fall in Grain Prices*. BAE paper presented at the Livestock and Feedgrains Study Programme, Pacific Economic Cooperation Conference, Napier, New Zealand, 19-21 October.

Mori, H., B. Lin, and W. D. Gorman. 1989. *The New U.S.-Japanese Beef Agreement: Some Implications for the U.S. Beef Industry*. University of Idaho, College of Agriculture, Bulletin No. 696, Idaho.

Shaw, I. 1986. *Modelling New Zealand Wool and Sheep Meat Supply: An Alternative Approach*. BAE paper presented at the 30th Annual Conference of the Australian Agricultural Economics Society, ANU, Canberra, 3-5 February.

Teal, F., A. Dickson, D. Porter, and D. Whiteford. 1987. *Japanese Beef Policies: Implications for Trade, Prices and Market Shares*. ABARE Occasional Paper 102, AGPS, Canberra.

14

Exchange Rate Pass-Through Effects in Agriculture

Julian M. Alston, Colin A. Carter and Marilyn D. Whitney

Introduction

During the 1970s the United States experienced dramatic increases in the value of its agricultural exports. In an influential 1974 paper, Schuh argued that devaluations in the U.S. dollar were largely responsible for the rapid growth of exports and high U.S. domestic prices of the early 1970s. His hypothesis attracted further attention among agricultural economists after a sharp appreciation in the dollar from 1979 through 1985 was accompanied by slumping U.S. exports of farm products. The strong dollar of the early 1980s came to be perceived by many economists and government officials as a "problem" for U.S. farmers.[1]

Many agricultural economists now attach great importance to relative currency values in explaining prices and trade flows in agricultural goods markets. For example, Shane (1990) states that "exchange rates are now the single most important variable in determining the economic environment for agricultural trade." However, the empirical evidence to date has been less conclusive regarding the significance of exchange rate changes for agriculture. The "Schuh hypothesis" has been tested empirically by several authors, with mixed results (e.g., Konandreas, Bushnell and Green, 1978; Chambers and Just, 1981; Batten and Belongia, 1986; Johnson, Grennes and Thursby, 1977; Greenshields, 1974; Vellianitis-Fidas, 1975; Orden and Fackler, 1989; and Henneberry, Drabenstott, and Henneberry, 1987).[2]

One view of the existing econometric evidence was recently summed up by Penson (1988) and Gardner (1988, p. 1016): "Empirical studies tend to suggest that U.S. commodity prices are exchange rate elastic and that exchange rates are important determinants of agricultural trade flows." However, of the econometric studies whose findings support that view, several have weak statistical results. For example, Konandreas et al. estimated U.S. wheat export demand for five importing regions and concluded that export demand is responsive to nominal exchange rate changes, but virtually all of their regression coefficients were statistically insignificant. Chambers and Just (1981) estimated the impact of nominal exchange rates on the wheat, corn and soybean trade and arrived at a similar conclusion, even though the exchange rate variable turned out to be statistically significant only in the case of corn. Much of the other evidence has been obtained by simulation approaches rather than by direct estimation (e.g., Johnson, Grennes and Thursby, 1977; Longmire and Morey, 1983).

Other empirical studies have found that the exchange rate effect on export prices and volumes is relatively small (e.g., Greenshields, 1974; Vellianitis-Fidas, 1975; Orden and Fackler, 1989; and Henneberry, Drabenstott, and Henneberry, 1987). Greenshields found only a minor impact of *real* exchange rate changes on U.S. wheat, corn, and soybean exports to Japan. Vellianitis-Fidas found that the *real* exchange rate was not significant in explaining U.S. exports of corn, wheat and soybeans. Orden and Fackler (1989) examined monetary impacts on agricultural prices using a vector autoregressive (VAR) model. The estimated coefficients fail to show a strong statistical relationship between the exchange rate and agricultural prices. Henneberry et al. (1987) tested the relationship between real exchange rates and U.S. wheat exports and concluded that the exchange rate was not very important as an explanatory variable.

Against this background of mixed empirical results, it is difficult to have strong views either way on the importance of exchange rates for agriculture. This lack of consensus among empirical studies may be due in part to differences in methodology, such as the use of nominal versus real variables and bilateral versus effective exchange rates in estimating exchange rate effects. Additionally, a number of authors ignore "secondary" or "feedback" effects of exchange rate movements acting through prices of other tradeable goods such as competing products and farm inputs. Given the dependence that U.S. farmers now have on export markets, the questions of how both export prices and export volume adjust to exchange rates remain important.

The purpose of this chapter is to explore further the relationship between the exchange rate and U.S. agricultural prices, as measured by the so-called elasticity of exchange rate pass-through. Our main extension over previous analytic work on exchange rate pass-through is to emphasize the role of trade in factors of production and in substitute goods. Using a competitive model, we estimate pass-through coefficients for a number of U.S. farm commodities. We also show that the choice of bilateral versus multilateral exchange rates is important for empirical work.

The chapter proceeds as follows. In the next section we present a selective review of the literature on exchange rate pass-through, both in agriculture and in general. Following that we develop a model of exchange rate pass-through in a competitive industry (such as agriculture) and use that model to illustrate the differential effects of real exchange rate changes among agricultural industries that differ in terms of their market parameters, their use of traded inputs, and the extent of government intervention. In the third main section we develop some quantitative evidence with examples from Pacific Rim agriculture during the 1970s and 1980s.

Previous Literature

Exchange Rate Pass-Through in Manufactured Goods Markets

A significant body of recent literature uses models of exchange rate pass-through to analyze the effects, within particular sectors or industries, resulting from changes in exchange rates. Exchange rate pass-through refers to the extent to which a particular country's prices of internationally tradeable goods are affected by changes in exchange rates; however, the precise definition varies by author. For example, Ohno (1989, p. 550) provides the following definition:

> Roughly speaking, pass-through is said to be complete when the exporter does not adjust prices in his home currency, so that exchange rate fluctuations are reflected entirely in local import prices abroad. By contrast, if import prices in local currencies remain stable, it is prices received by exporters that must adjust to exchange rate shocks. In this case pass-through is said to be zero.

An alternative view is that exchange rate pass-through is the degree to which a single country's price of a good is affected by a change in its currency's value relative to another currency or to a bundle of other currencies, whether that country is a net importer or a net exporter of that good. This is the definition used here. In our empirical work we are concerned with pass-through of changes in the relative value of the U.S. dollar into U.S. commodity prices. Under our definition, "complete pass-through" occurs when all of the adjustment to changes in the exchange rate occurs in the U.S. prices and other (foreign) prices are unaffected.

The literature on this topic has focused mainly on exchange rate effects in markets for industrial and manufactured goods and includes papers by Dornbusch, 1987; Feenstra, 1989; Giovannini, 1988; Knetter, 1989; Ohno, 1989 and 1990; Schembri, 1989; and Woo, 1984 inter alia. The prime motivation for the work of Dornbusch and others was the empirical observation that exchange rate pass-through did not appear to be complete for many goods (e.g., U.S. prices of imported Japanese cars did not rise by as much as the 1985-87 U.S. dollar depreciation against the yen would imply).

Two theoretical explanations for incomplete pass-through have predominated in the literature: (1) "pricing to market" and (2) path-dependent firm behavior, or "hysteresis." Each of these assumes some form of imperfect competition. Models of pricing to market (which assume that firms are short-run profit maximizers who are able to price-discriminate by destination market) were used by Knetter (1989), Ohno (1989), Mann (1986), Hooper and Mann (1989), Krugman (1987), Feenstra (1989), Marston (1989), Woo (1984), Schembri (1989), Dornbusch (1987), Giovannini (1988), and Feinberg (1986). In these models, unless importers' elasticities of excess demand are constant, exporters will vary their markup of price over marginal cost in response to exchange rate movements, thus tempering the transmission of exchange rate shocks to importers' prices.

In models of path-dependence, current supply of and/or demand for a firm's output depends on its prior market share. For example, the "beachhead effect" (Baldwin, 1988) results when a favorable exchange rate shock induces foreign suppliers to incur sunk costs in establishing distribution and service networks in the importing country. Some of these entrants will remain to compete with domestic producers even if the exchange rate returns to its initial level, due to the asymmetry of entry and exit costs. In a similar fashion, Froot and Klemperer (1988) suggest that an exchange rate movement that enhances a firm's market share can cause a permanent outward shift in the demand for that firm's product as a result of habit formation among consumers, again resulting in asymmetric price responses to large exchange rate shocks.

For the analysis of exchange rate pass-through in markets for most traded agricultural goods, models of imperfect competition are likely to be inappropriate.[3] This view is supported by Dornbusch (1987), Hooper and Mann (1989), Ohno (1989) and Woo (1984). We therefore will assume perfect competition throughout our analysis. Additionally, we are concerned that the use of unit-value data can lead to the appearance of price discrimination where none may exist, even for manufactures, since destination-specific differences in product quality or variety, port of export, type or size of packaging and timing of purchases are difficult to control for. Thus we take issue with Giovannini's proposition that any observed deviations from the "law of one price" indicate *ex ante* price discrimination, unless one's data is disaggregated to a level far beyond the ordinary and specifies the exact timing of transactions.

Exchange Rate Pass-Through in Agriculture

Compared to the industrial sector, there has been less work done on the question of how exchange rates are "passed-through" to border prices in agricultural markets. Much of the literature on exchange rates and agriculture relates to this question but has been concerned more with effects on trade volumes than with border prices. Longmire and Morey (1983) identify three notable studies (Chambers and Just, 1981; Johnson, Grennes and Thursby, 1977; and Collins, Myers and Bredahl, 1980).

Chambers and Just (1979) developed a theoretical model of pass-through in competitive agricultural markets that allows for indirect exchange rate effects acting through prices of substitute goods, but they did not apply it empirically. A key point was their contention that exchange rate pass-through elasticities could be greater than 1. As described by Chambers, this claim provoked some discussion (e.g., Grennes, Johnson and Thursby, 1980; Reed, 1980; Orden, 1986). Subsequently Chambers and Just (1981) provided some empirical support for their claim (for wheat, corn, and soybeans they found elasticities greater than 1) but the issue remains unresolved. Johnson, Grennes and Thursby (1977) found a *real* exchange rate pass-through elasticity of 0.69 for U.S. wheat (where the U.S. dollar rate changes relative to all other currencies). The contribution of Collins, Myers and Bredahl was to introduce the importance of domestic and foreign trade barriers in modifying pass-through effects.

Chambers (1988, p. 6) suggested that the paper by Longmire and Morey (1983) "represents the most ambitious attempt to ascertain the effects of exchange rates on agricultural trade and prices. This paper combines the arguments of Chambers and Just (1979) and Collins, Myers and Bredahl into a single model. Although they did not estimate the relevant elasticities, this paper (in my opinion) represents the most thorough empirical examination of this issue." The study by Longmire and Morey is indeed a comprehensive analysis of exchange rate pass-through into U.S. commodity markets. It is a simulation rather than a statistical analysis. The authors report effects of real devaluations of the U.S. dollar on the real prices of wheat, corn, and soybeans and their results imply long-run exchange rate pass-through elasticities in the range of 0.5 to 0.8 for most of the cases that they analyzed.

Some more recent papers have focused on exchange rate pass-through more directly. Carter and Pick (1989) examined the U.S. agricultural trade balance and found some evidence to support the J-curve theory: following a depreciation, the trade balance may initially deteriorate before it improves. They reasoned that the J-curve exists for U.S. agriculture because (a) most trade takes places in U.S. dollar denominated contracts and (b) there are lags between the time when a contract is signed and when trade actually takes place. Jabara and Schwartz (1987) studied the pass-through of U.S. exchange rate changes to Japanese domestic prices. They found an asymmetric response. Pass-through was high when the dollar was appreciating, but low during periods when the dollar depreciated. Carter, Gray and Furtan (1990) estimated pass-through elasticities for a range of agricultural product and factor markets in Canada. Their results indicate that differences in institutional factors and the use of tradeable factors may be important determinants of different exchange rate pass-through effects among commodities. Pick and Park (1991) applied Knetter's model of "pricing to market" to estimate exchange rate pass-through to U.S. export prices of wheat, corn, cotton, soybeans, soybean meal and soybean oil. Assuming imperfect competition, they found the strongest evidence of pricing to market for the case of wheat. For the other commodities there was little indication of price discrimination.

Issues in Pass-Through Models

There is considerable confusion and disagreement in the literature regarding the proper definition of exchange rate pass-through and the relevant variables to include in empirical analysis. Some of this is purely semantic; some of it is substantive. Four major issues concern (a) nominal versus real pass-through, (b) the meaning of "incomplete" and "complete" pass-through, (c) the distinction between partial and total elasticities, and (d) the choice of bilateral versus multilateral exchange rates. These are discussed below.

Nominal Versus Real Pass-Through. In general, the literature on exchange rate pass-through takes a partial equilibrium approach to analyzing the effects of exogenous exchange rate changes within a particular industry. Even though it is clearly appropriate to take exchange rates as being exogenous to agriculture, it is still pertinent (especially when undertaking econometric work) to have in mind some notion about the causes of the changes in exchange rates—especially to discriminate between real changes and purely inflationary ones.[4] Much of the literature does not draw a clear distinction between *nominal* and *real* terms either in relation to exchange rates or the effects of exchange rate changes. Even those that do define their terms differ in their definitions. For instance, pass-through is treated by many in nominal terms (Mann, 1986; Hooper and Mann, 1989; Chambers and Just, 1981; Feenstra, 1989). However, Ohno (1989) and Feinberg argue that if inflation leads foreign prices to rise and simultaneously causes the foreign currency to weaken, pass-through to domestic prices should be negligible or zero. This implies that the nominal pass-through is not unique but varies according to the degree that shocks are real. We tend to agree with this viewpoint, and our analysis will focus on the effects of *real* exchange rate changes on *real* prices (regrettably, this choice introduces another difficult set of measurement issues related to the choice of a deflator).

"Complete" and "Incomplete" Pass-Through. There seems to be some confusion in the literature in the usage and interpretation of the terms "complete" and "incomplete" pass-through. Some seem to interpret them in relation to incidence of price changes; others in relation to measures of market distortions arising from imperfect competition. Under *perfect competition*, the law of one price is assumed to hold. Any exchange rate movement will be transmitted completely to prices by assumption; the question of pass-through refers to which country's prices are affected and by how much. An exchange rate shift between a "small" importer or exporter and the currencies of other nations' trading in that commodity should be reflected completely in the small nation's prices (provided the country is not large in some other relevant market, such as that for a key input).[5] For a larger country, the incidence of an exchange rate effect will fall in part on the country's trading partners. Under this paradigm, "imperfect pass-through" can result when a country is large, uses traded inputs, has elastic domestic demand or supply, and so on; imperfect pass-through does not imply any market failure or barriers to arbitrage. An alternative notion of pass-through that prevails in much of the *imperfect competition* literature appears to equate incomplete pass-through with violations of the law of one price: price transmission between markets is incomplete due to absorption of exchange rate shocks into firms' profit margins. Here we employ the former definition.

Partial or Total Elasticity of Price with Respect to the Exchange Rate?

One issue that isn't always clear is whether the interest is in the total elasticity of a product price with respect to the exchange rate (allowing for all of the effects of exchange rates on a particular commodity through effects on prices of tradeable factors and competing products, for example) or a partial elasticity (holding factor prices and other product prices constant). Hooper and Mann (1989) state that either definition can be correct and seem reasonable, depending on the purpose to which the estimates are to be put. We suspect that most authors have in mind total elasticities but most estimates are actually partial ones. As noted by Chambers and Just (1979), failure to account for the multiple avenues by which exchange rate movements can affect prices may lead to biased estimates of pass-through elasticities or incorrect interpretation thereof. The challenge to distinguish these partial and total effects is both conceptual and empirical and we will address this question later.

Bilateral and Multilateral Exchange Rates. Some studies model the effects of changes in bilateral rates whereas others use some weighted average of several bilateral rates or some other exchange rate index. Most of the studies of exchange rate pass-through outside agriculture have used bilateral rates; the majority of agricultural examples have used some multilateral rate. The appropriate choice of which to use depends on the purpose of the analysis. In empirical work, however, it will rarely be appropriate to use a single bilateral exchange rate without paying attention to other exchange rates. The reason is straightforward: unless all other bilateral rates are constant, there is likely to be a problem of "left-out variables." This may be particularly troublesome if, for example, a devaluation of the U.S. dollar against the yen is a reflection of an appreciation of the yen against all currencies; leaving out other currencies is tantamount to assuming that the dollar devalued against all other currencies, a very different phenomenon. Thus in a regression model, even where the interest is in the effect of a particular bilateral exchange rate, it may be necessary to include several exchange rates as explanatory variables. When a multilateral rate is more clearly appropriate—as would be so, for example, when exploring the effects of U.S. monetary policy in general on U.S. agriculture—the problem arises of choosing which exchange rate index is appropriate. Dutton and Grennes (1985) have suggested using different exchange rate indexes for imported and exported goods. Chambers (1988) discusses this issue at some length.

Comparative Statics of Exchange Rate Pass-Through

In this section we develop a model that extends previous exchange rate pass-through models (e.g., Dornbush, 1987; Feenstra, 1989; Ohno, 1989) by paying particular attention to the role of traded substitutes and inputs in the determination of elasticities of exchange rate pass-through ($\varepsilon_{P,E}$).[6] Using this model we illustrate that exchange rate pass-through may vary considerably among industries, depending upon market characteristics and parameters, the extent of trade in factors, intermediate goods, and competing products, and government intervention in trade.

The Basic Model

Consider the case of competitive trade in a product between two countries.[7] From the point of view of the exporter, the first direct implication of an exchange rate change is a shift of export (excess) demand (defined with prices denominated in the exporter's currency). Clearly the size of the exporter's domestic price change in response to that demand shift depends on the elasticities of supply and demand. At the same time, export (excess) supply may shift. The size of any export supply shift due to an exchange rate change will depend on whether (a) domestic supply has shifted as would occur if the industry uses traded inputs or there were other changes in factor markets due to exchange rate-induced changes in other product markets or (b) domestic demand has shifted due to exchange rate-induced changes in other product markets. Similarly, there may be second-round shifts in the excess demand due to exchange rate-induced changes in underlying supply and demand in the importing country. These ideas are illustrated in Figure 14.1.

Figure 14.1 depicts a representative market where Country A is an exporter and Country B an importer. The domestic market for Country A (e.g., the United States) is shown in panel (a) and that for Country B (e.g., Japan) is shown in panel (d). The excess supply curve for the United States (ES_{US}) and the excess demand curve for Japan (ED_J) are shown in panel (b), which represents the international market. For convenience, the initial exchange rate between the United States and Japan is par as shown by the 45° line OA in panel (c).[8] In the initial equilibrium the market price (in both Japanese yen and U.S. dollars) is P and the initial trade volume is equal to Q.

Consider the effect of the Japanese yen appreciating relative to the U.S. dollar. When the yen appreciates, OA rotates to OA' in panel (c) and as a result the excess demand in panel (b) rotates to the right from ED_J to ED'_J. The volume of trade expands to Q_1 and the exporter's price increases from P to P_1. At the same time the price in Japan falls from P to P_4. This is basically the model used by Schuh (1974) and Chambers and Just (1981), among others, to analyze the impact of exchange rate changes on U.S. agriculture. However, Chambers and Just (1981) also account for the exchange rate impact on substitute goods and the consequent feedback into ED'_J. When inputs used in the United States are

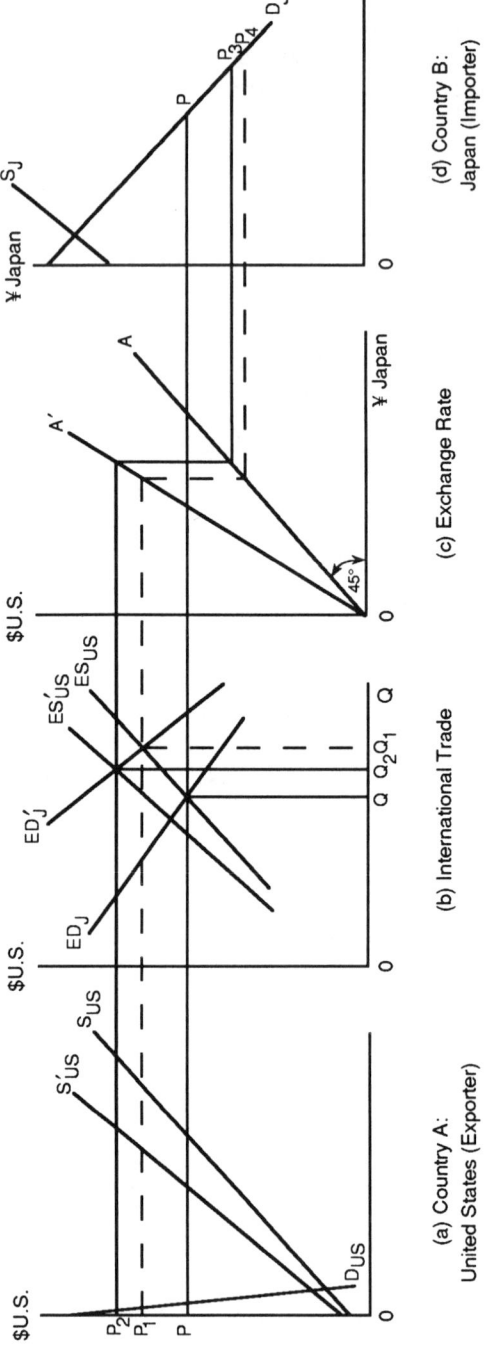

FIGURE 14.1 Exchange Rate Pass-Through in a Partial Equilibrium Model

tradeable the excess supply curve will also shift.[9] The rotation of OA to OA' in Figure 14.1 represents a depreciation of the U.S. dollar and with tradeable inputs the excess supply curve rotates from ES_{US} to ES'_{US} in panel (b) of Figure 14.1. The increased cost of production in the United States reduces the volume of trade from Q_1 to Q_2 and raises the price from P_1 to P_2. With a lower trade volume the price in Japan rises from P_4 to P_3.

This diagram illustrates two key points. First, if we were to ignore the tradeability of factors we would expect the U.S. price to rise from P to P_1 (and the Japanese price to fall from P to P_3). The extent of this rise (fall) is clearly a function of the slopes of excess supply and excess demand in panel (b). Any view that the exchange rate pass-through is too little (or too great) must be conditioned on explicit or implicit assumptions about these elasticities. Second, any such prior view is also conditioned on the implicit assumption that there are no traded inputs. Even when we use the correct elasticities of supply and demand, ignoring trade in inputs will yield the wrong pass-through elasticity. In the Dornbusch framework the failure of U.S. exporters to lower the yen price to P_4 (e.g., it "only" falls to P_3) would be taken as an indication of imperfect competition. Yet, as shown in Figure 14.1, there are two alternative explanations as to why the price may not fall as far as expected, maintaining an assumption of competition. The first is that the true elasticities of excess supply and demand may have been overestimated; the second is that input costs may have changed as a consequence of the depreciation. Similarly, in the Schuh framework, failure to account for the pass-through to inputs leads to an overestimation of the effects that exchange rates have on trade volumes.

The equations of a model that incorporates these ideas are:

Excess Supply: $P = S(Q, B)$ (1)

Excess Demand: $P = E P^* = E D(Q, A)$ (2)

In these equations, all of the monetary variables are defined in real terms. P is the *real* price of the good in domestic (exporter) currency, P^* is the *real* price of the good in foreign (importer) currency, and E is the *real* exchange rate, defined as the U.S. dollar equivalent (e.g., \$/yen). The real prices (P, P^*) are defined as the nominal prices (p, p^*) deflated by a general price index (e.g., the CPI). The market clearing condition is one of competitive arbitrage: $E = P/P^*$. For consistency this requires that the real exchange rate be defined as the nominal exchange rate (e) multiplied by the ratio of the price indexes ($E = eCPI^*/CPI$). Q is the quantity traded. B represents supply shift variables and A represents variables that shift demand, some of which may be functions of the exchange rate. Taking a logarithmic differential approximation to this model yields:

Excess Supply: $d\ln P = \varepsilon^{-1} d\ln Q + \beta\pi$ (1')

Excess Demand: $d\ln P = \pi + d\ln P^*$

$\qquad\qquad\qquad = \pi - \eta^{-1} d\ln Q - \alpha\pi$

$\qquad\qquad\qquad = (1 - \alpha)\pi - \eta^{-1} d\ln Q$ (2')

where ε is the elasticity of excess supply with respect to price, η is the absolute value of the elasticity of excess demand ($\eta > 0$), and $\pi = d\ln E$ is the percentage change in the exchange rate. The other terms (containing α and β) reflect the effects of exchange rate changes feeding into the underlying supply and demand equations. It is assumed that exogenous shift variables other than the exchange rate are constant in these comparative statics.

When both α and β are zero, we have the simple model as shown in Figure 14.1, where only the excess demand shifts, and it does so by the full extent of the change in exchange rates. Consider the example of an exporter's currency depreciating. In equation (1'), β is the vertical shift *up* in excess supply due to the exchange rate change, reflecting effects of the exchange rate on input prices and domestic demand in the exporting country. In equation (2'), α is the vertical shift *down* in the excess demand *in importer's currency* due to the exchange rate change, reflecting effects of the exchange rate change on the importer's domestic supply and demand. Thus the net effect of the exchange rate in shifting the excess demand *in exporter's currency* is $(1 - \alpha)$. Since the equations are in terms of relative changes, the shifters (α and β) are in the form of elasticities with respect to the exchange rate.[10]

The equations in this model correspond to the curves in panel (b) of Figure 14.1. To illustrate further the comparative statics described above, consider Figure 14.2, which duplicates panel (b) of Figure 14.1. Panel (a) of Figure 14.2 shows the impact effect of U.S. depreciation, assuming no effects of exchange rate changes on underlying supply and demand conditions in either country ($\alpha = \beta = 0$). Here, as a result of the depreciation, the excess demand facing the United States rises (vertically) by π percent, the equilibrium U.S. (export) price rises from P_0 to P_1 and the traded volume grows from Q_0 to Q_1.

Panel (b) shows this equilibrium with a second-round adjustment to

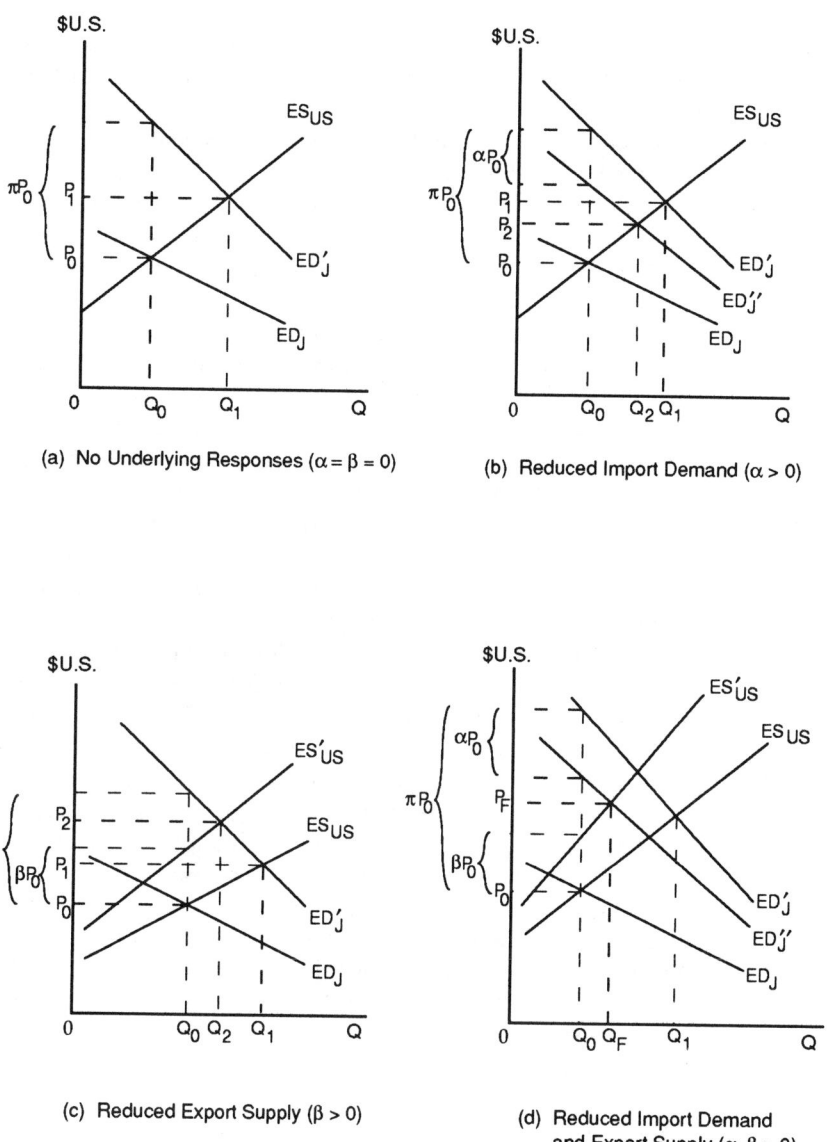

Figure 14.2 Components of Pass-Through Effects

incorporate a reduction in the Japanese demand for imports of the U.S. product due to the appreciation of the yen (this could be due to lower yen prices of traded inputs or lower yen prices of traded substitutes in consumption, for instance). The second-round adjustment is a shift of excess demand back from ED'$_J$ to ED"$_J$. As a consequence the final equilibrium U.S. price and quantity traded are P$_2$ and Q$_2$. In this case, the second-round adjustment reduces the effects of the depreciation on both quantity and price. In some alternative cases, considered below, the effect on price may be in the opposite direction to the effect on quantity traded.

Panel (c) shows adjustment of the equilibrium in panel (a) to incorporate a (second-round) reduction in the U.S. export supply *due to* the depreciation of the $U.S. (this could be due to higher $U.S. prices of traded inputs or higher $U.S. prices of traded substitutes in consumption, for instance). The second-round adjustment is shown as a shift of excess supply back from ES$_{US}$ to ES'$_{US}$. As a consequence, the final equilibrium U.S. price and quantity traded are P$_2$ and Q$_2$ in panel (c). In this case, when we allow for the second-round adjustment, the effects of the depreciation on quantity traded is smaller but the effect on price is greater compared to the initial effects shown in panel (a).

Finally, panel (d) shows the results when exchange rates feed through and shift both excess supply and excess demand. The final equilibrium is given by the intersection of ES'$_{US}$ and ED"$_J$ at Q$_F$ and P$_F$. Here, the second-round supply and demand shifts are both to the left (when α and β are positive) so that the quantity response to the $U.S. depreciation is unambiguously reduced (Q$_F$ < Q$_1$) — in fact we cannot rule out the possibility of a net reduction in volume of trade (which occurs when $\alpha + \beta > 1$) even when the exchange rate pass-through to price is positive. However, the effect of these second-round adjustments on price is ambiguous — allowing for second-round effects may increase or decrease the price change (i.e., the pass-through elasticity), depending upon the relative sizes of the supply and demand shifts (i.e., α and β). These issues are more clearly seen in the equations below for exchange rate pass-through elasticities.

Exchange Rate Pass-Through Elasticities

Solving (1') and (2') yields the following reduced form equations:

$$d\ln Q = \varepsilon\eta\pi(1 - \alpha - \beta)/(\varepsilon + \eta) \qquad (3)$$

$$d\ln P = \pi[\beta\varepsilon + (1 - \alpha)\eta]/(\varepsilon + \eta) \qquad (4)$$

Then, the elasticity of the exporter's real border price (P) with respect to the real exchange rate (E) is:

$$\varepsilon_{P,E} = d\ln P/\pi = [\beta\varepsilon + (1 - \alpha)\eta]/(\varepsilon + \eta) \tag{5}$$

Similarly, using equation (2'), the elasticity of the importer's real price (in importer's currency) with respect to the real exchange rate is:

$$\varepsilon_{P^*,E} = d\ln P^*/\pi = \varepsilon_{P,E} - 1 = -[\alpha\eta + (1 - \beta)\varepsilon]/(\varepsilon + \eta) \tag{5'}$$

Using this simple competitive model we can show how these exchange rate pass-through elasticities will vary, depending on the size of the supply shift (β) relative to the demand shift ($1 - \alpha$) and the sizes of the elasticities of supply and demand. A number of scenarios will lead to the result that $\varepsilon_{P,E} = 1 - \alpha$ and, in the case when $\alpha = 0$ (i.e., when there are no feedback effects in underlying supply and demand in the importing country) $\varepsilon_{P,E} = 1$. These scenarios are: (a) when the exporter is a small country in trade (taking the limit as $\eta \to \infty$); (b) when excess supply is fixed ($\varepsilon = 0$); and (c) when supply and demand shift by identical vertical amounts (i.e., $\beta = 1 - \alpha$).[11]

It is easy to see, also, how erroneous assumptions about underlying structure will lead to erroneous prior beliefs about the pass-through elasticity. For instance, suppose there are in fact no tradeable inputs and no other second-round effects ($\alpha = \beta = 0$) so that the pass-through elasticity is $\varepsilon_{P,E} = \eta/(\varepsilon + \eta)$. Clearly, using an overestimate of the demand elasticity or an underestimate of the supply elasticity will lead to overestimation of the pass-through elasticity. Alternatively, suppose these two elasticities are estimated accurately but there are second-round effects which are ignored. Then, we will overestimate (underestimate) the pass-through elasticity whenever $\beta\varepsilon$ is less (greater) than $\alpha\eta$.

One pertinent question is whether the elasticity is bounded between zero and one: i.e., is $0 < \varepsilon_{P,E} < 1$ implied by reasonable model assumptions (e.g., see Chambers and Just, 1979, and the comments by Grennes et al., 1980, and Reed, 1980)? We can say that this will be so, surely, when $0 < \alpha, \beta < 1$. This is a plausible scenario, but not the only one. The key question is whether we can bound the values of the elasticity of excess supply (marginal cost) with respect to the exchange rate (β) and the elasticity of excess demand (demand price expressed in terms of foreign currency) with respect to the exchange rate (α). These elasticities (α and β) reflect the effects of exchange rate changes in shifting the underlying supply and demand functions in both countries either through changes in factor prices or changes in prices of competing products or income. It seems to us that, for disaggregated goods, it is not possible to bound the elasticity of exchange rate pass-through to be less than 1 when there are second-round effects of adjustments in markets for factors and substitute products.

Trade in Productive Factors

In terms of the model developed so far, trade in factors of production (or intermediate products) could contribute to shifts in the exporter's excess supply function (reflected in β) or shifts in the importer's excess demand function (reflected in α) in response to changes in the exchange rate. This is conceptually straightforward, as is the related topic of trade in products that are substitutes or complements in production or consumption for the product of interest.

We can derive an equation for the elasticity of the export supply (in terms of percentage vertical shifts of excess supply) with respect to exchange rate changes (β) using a simple two-factor production model with one tradeable factor.[12] The elasticity (β) is a function of the cost share of the tradeable factor (k_1), elasticities of supply of traded and non-traded factors of production (e_1 and e_2, respectively), the elasticity of factor substitution (σ), the fraction of production consumed domestically (k_d), the elasticity of supply (ε_s), the elasticity of domestic demand (η_d), and the exchange rate pass-through elasticity for the traded factor (β_1):

$$\beta = \frac{\beta_1[k_1 e_1(\sigma + e_2)]}{[\sigma + k_1 e_2 + (1-k_1)e_1][\varepsilon_s + k_d \eta_d]} \quad (6)$$

Clearly, for a given pass-through of exchange rate changes into factor markets, there remains a multiplicity of possibilities for effects on export supply functions in different industries, depending upon the technology in the industry (factor shares and substitution possibilities in production) and depending on the market characteristics (the share of the product traded, the elasticity of total supply, and the elasticity of domestic demand). With typical parameters, however, a value of $0 < \beta < 1$ would be expected when $\beta_1 = 1$.

Similar equations could be developed to illustrate the determinants of effects of trade in productive factors on shifting importer's excess demand (i.e., α). Further, an exercise could be carried out to show the effect of substitution in consumption. Rather than do that here, we refer the reader to Chambers and Just (1979), who show equations for exchange rate pass-through derived from a model with a full set of general equilibrium type interactions among commodities in both production and consumption, treating all products as being tradeable. Their model does not explicitly incorporate factor markets but could, in principle, be extended to do so. The main conclusion from these manipulations is that the impact of trade in productive factors and other products on pass-through is an empirical matter that depends on a range of market characteristics that will differ among commodities.

Trade Distorting Policies

There can be no doubt that trade distorting policies can have direct and important effects on exchange rate pass-through.[13] For instance, prohibitive trade barriers (such as embargoes or import quotas) that completely insulate a domestic market from international markets will prevent any pass-through effects into the insulated product markets.[14] In the absence of indirect effects through trade in substitute products or factors of production, such goods would have exchange rate pass-through elasticities of zero—as would goods that would be "non-traded," even in the absence of trade distorting policies.

Even for products that are subject to prohibitive trade barriers, there may be some indirect exchange rate pass-through effects arising from trade in factors or trade in competing products. Indeed, given the likelihood that they will have relatively small demand elasticities (compared to traded goods), non-traded goods may have *greater* pass-through elasticities than traded goods in many instances. Thus prohibitive trade barriers have ambiguous effects on pass-through elasticities.

This example (of prohibitive trade barriers) shows that it is difficult to generalize much about the consequences of trade distorting policies for exchange rate pass-through. Moreover, attention should not be confined to border policies in this context. Any policies that modify the conditions under which production and trade take place are capable of changing pass-through effects; it may be best to assume that interventions in factor markets or product markets are unlikely to be neutral with regard to exchange rate pass-through. Some policies may increase pass-through from factor markets while reducing pass-though from product markets. Some policies may alter pass-through simply by altering elasticities (e.g., supply controls on U.S. tobacco make export supply relatively inelastic and *increase* exchange rate pass-through into U.S. tobacco prices). When policies distort product markets in ways that make effective export demand relatively elastic (inelastic), pass-through into the exporter's prices is increased (reduced); when policies make export supply relatively inelastic (elastic), pass-through into exporter prices is increased (reduced).

Contractual Arrangements

A related topic is the role of contractual arrangements. Like trade distorting policies, forward contracts will mean that contemporaneous data may not reflect continuous market clearing. They will also modify pass-through elasticities, in ways that depend on the currency used in the contract (e.g., see Carter and Pick, 1989). For example, suppose all Australian wheat sales are sold on forward contracts written before February each crop year by the Australian Wheat Board but deliveries are spread throughout the year. Further, suppose all contracts are written with the price specified in $U.S. Then, in terms of returns to Australian wheat growers, shipments after February (say in March and April) will be characterized by exchange rate pass-through elasticities of 1.0 (with respect to changes in the $U.S./$A rate) or 0 (with respect to other $A rates). More realistically, the short-run pass-through elasticities will be modified somewhat by contractual arrangements in the directions suggested by this argument, emphasizing pass-through in relation to the key currency (or currencies) and dampening it with respect to the others.

A similar (but opposite) phenomenon may arise in relation to products that involve leads in commitment of production to particular destinations—implying fixed short-run quantities, independent of demand conditions. This may arise when particular destinations require specific packaging, labelling, or other preparation of products and the product is perishable. When the quantity destined for a particular market is fixed independent of market conditions (i.e., the relevant excess supply is perfectly inelastic), the burden of adjustment will fall entirely upon the exporter's prices.

Both of these situations are ones where the impact effects of exchange rate changes may differ in important ways from the long-run effects due to short-run inflexibility of either supply or prices. Prices related to current shipments may bear little relation to current exchange rates for contracted goods where price is inflexible, even when exchange rates are very important in the longer term; on the other hand, prices may overreact in the short term for some goods when supply is inflexible. Both types of phenomenon are likely to be important for agricultural goods given the extent to which goods are traded under contract and the perishable nature of many agricultural products. The implication is that exchange rate pass-through is dynamic and therefore, especially when using relatively frequent data (say monthly), the econometric model should be designed to allow the dynamics of pass-through to be expressed.

Price Versus Volume Effects

As pointed out above, there have been few papers written that clearly separate the exchange rate effect on agricultural trade prices from the effect on trade volumes. This is a simple but important distinction which must be made when debating whether or not "exchange rates are important." For example, Schuh (1974), and Chambers and Just (1981) (and many others) concluded that both trade volume and price were highly dependent on the exchange rate. This is also true of most of the USDA studies, which argue exchange rates are important to both trade flows and trade prices.

An important contribution by Kost (1976) has been overlooked in much of this discussion. Kost showed that when the domestic supply and demand elasticities are both small (in absolute value), exchange rate changes will lead to large fluctuations in prices but will not appreciably affect export volume. In a theoretical context, Kost argued that a devaluation would generate a relatively larger change in price than in quantity traded for agricultural goods compared to manufactures. This can be shown with the model drawn in Figure 14.1 or using the result in equation (3). When the excess supply curve is highly inelastic, a shift in the excess demand curve will lead to a relatively large price effect but a relatively small quantity effect (in the same direction). In the empirical analysis which follows we focus on the *price* effect of exchange rate changes. However, our results have implications for the *trade volume* effect, given the inverse relationship between the sizes of the two effects.

Implications

The comparative statics have illustrated some key determinants of exchange rate pass-through elasticities in a competitive model. In particular, elasticities of excess supply and demand are important. For a small-country exporter or importer (i.e., a price taker), exchange rate pass-through is complete in the sense that the elasticity of domestic (border) price with respect to the exchange rate is unitary. This is so regardless of whether prices of factors or substitute products in the small country are affected by the exchange rate. However, the pass-through elasticity may be modified if other countries' prices of other goods or factors are affected in ways that affect their prices of the good in question.

In bilateral trade the incidence of exchange rate changes is smaller in the larger country (i.e., the one with the greater potential market power in trade).[15] By these arguments, exchange rate pass-through will differ among agricultural commodities, depending upon market structure. We would expect, for example, exchange rate pass-through to be less in Australian wool than in any other Australian agricultural commodity; due to its large share of the world supply of apparel wool, the elasticity of demand for Australian wool is fairly small (about -1 according to Mullen, Alston and Wohlgenant, 1989). Information on export demand elasticities may thus provide a partial basis for *ranking* exported commodities according to their likely pass-through elasticities. Thus, for certain goods where demand elasticities for U.S. exports may be relatively small, exchange rate pass-through elasticities may be expected to be significantly less than unitary. However, it is important not to neglect the supply side. For several commodities (e.g., chicken, pork) the long-run competitive supply elasticity is likely to be very large so that the direct exchange rate pass-through may be very small (elasticities near zero), regardless of demand elasticities. In these cases, second-round effects (e.g., through feedgrain prices) may be the main avenue of exchange rate pass-through.

In the small-country case, trade in factors of production and competing products may not be important (so long as there are not consequences of a change in the small country's exchange rate for world prices of the commodity in question). However, in the large-country case, trade in factors of production or competing products may lead to second-round adjustments in supply or demand, modifying the pass-through elasticity. This raises the issue of distinguishing between the direct effect (the partial elasticity) and the total effect including the second-round adjustments (a total elasticity).

The effects of government policies, contracting, and so on, on exchange rate pass-through may be thought of in terms of modifications of the relevant elasticities of supply or demand. This is clear-cut for supply controls and prohibitive trade barriers, for example. Contracting makes the relevant supply (or demand) perfectly elastic in the key currency. Government policies have implications for long-run pass-through; contracting has implications for short- versus long-run distinctions and brings the issue of dynamics to the forefront. In general we would expect elasticities of both excess supply and excess demand to increase with length of run. The key, for pass-through, is which elasticity increases most and fastest.

All of these factors, together, mean that it is difficult to have very strong prior views about the size of a particular pass-through elasticity. Any such priors must rely for their strength on priors about underlying elasticities and other information about market structure, government intervention, and so on. This is so under a maintained hypothesis of competition. It would certainly be difficult to draw any strong conclusions about departures from perfect competition based on evidence of exchange rate pass-through elasticities alone. While we cannot have strong prior views about the magnitudes of pass-through elasticities (unless we are convinced that a small-country assumption is applicable, in which case a unitary elasticity would be expected), we do have some information about their determinants, which we will explore in the empirical work below.

Economic Models and Hypotheses

General Form of Models

We propose to estimate pass-through elasticities for a range of U.S. primary product exports. We have in mind reduced-form pricing equations in which monthly prices of U.S. agricultural export goods are regressed against a range of exogenous variables including (a) various measures of currency exchange rates, (b) prices of tradeable factors, (c) prices of tradeable substitute goods, and (d) other variables representing shifters of underlying domestic and foreign supply and demand curves. All of the monetary variables are expressed in real terms. The results below are preliminary in that we have been able to consider only a subset of commodities (beef, pork, cotton, corn, oranges, soybeans, lumber) and a only subset of the models, with very limited treatment of shift variables.

Another dimension for model variations is in the specification of the functional form and the dynamics. To limit the specification search we arbitrarily chose to use a specification that is linear in logarithms so that the regression coefficients are elasticities. With monthly data, there are likely to be some significant lags in price response and we will wish to allow effects over time of the exogenous variables, especially exchange rates. Thus there are choices to be made about what restrictions to impose on the functional forms and lengths of the lag distributions applying to the various exogenous variables. In summary, our empirical model is of the following general form:

$$ln P_t = \alpha + \Sigma_k \beta_k ln E_{t-k} + \Sigma_m \Sigma_k \gamma_{mk} ln X_{m,t-k} + \varepsilon_t \qquad (7)$$

where, in time t, P_t is the *real* U.S. dollar price of U.S. exports of a particular good; E_t is a *real* U.S. dollar exchange rate (e.g., \$US/yen or a multilateral index); and $X_{m,t}$ (m = 1,...,M) are shift variables (expressed in *real* U.S. dollar terms) including prices of other goods and, possibly, other exchange rates.

The Greek letters represent the model parameters. The exchange rate pass-through coefficients are the β_k's. Each of these may be interpreted as a partial direct exchange rate pass-through elasticity. The sum of them may be interpreted as a total direct pass-through elasticity: it measures the total direct effect of changes in the exchange rate but it does not include the indirect effects through factor markets or through competing product markets.

Distributed Lag Specification

To simplify the econometric task, as a preliminary step we chose to restrict the lag distribution to be of the geometric (Koyck lag) form. To motivate this specification, suppose that the long-run relationship is:

$$lnP^*_t = \alpha + \beta lnE_t + \Sigma_m \gamma_m lnX_{m,t} + \varepsilon_t \tag{8a}$$

where P^*_t is the long-run equilibrium price. The assumption of geometric partial adjustment towards the long-run equilibrium can be represented as:

$$lnP_t - lnP_{t-1} = \theta[lnP^*_t - lnP_{t-1}], \text{ or}$$

$$lnP_t = \theta lnP^*_t + (1-\theta)lnP_{t-1} \tag{8b}$$

where θ is the coefficient of adjustment so that θ percent of the long-run adjustment of price to an exogenous shift is made in the first month. Substituting (8b) into (8a) and consolidating terms yields:

$$lnP_t = a + b lnE_t + \Sigma_m c_m lnX_{m,t} + d lnP_{t-1} + e_t \tag{9}$$

where the coefficients may be interpreted in terms of the long-run parameters as:

$$\alpha = a/(1-d); \beta = b/(1-d); \gamma = c/(1-d); \text{ and } \theta = 1-d.$$

This specification has the significant advantage of reducing the econometric problem to manageable proportions. The short-run direct (partial) exchange rate elasticity is b, the long-run direct (partial) elasticity is β, obtained by dividing the short-run elasticity by the adjustment coefficient (θ).[16] The approach has some advantages and disadvantages that are well known. Of course, it is very restrictive. The lag distribution is of the geometric form and infinitely long. The same lag distribution applies to all of the right-hand-side variables. To the extent that these strong restrictions are inappropriate, the results will be biased and perhaps those biases will be important. Further work will consider alternative lag specifications. For the moment, attention is confined to the class of models represented in equation (9) and even within that restricted model there are many choices to be made.

Data and Estimation

Models were estimated using SHAZAM (White et al., 1988) with monthly data for the period 1975:1 to 1988:12, a total of 168 monthly observations. In each regression, all of the variables were expressed as natural logarithms. The dependent variables were f.o.b. unit values of U.S. exports of pork, beef, fresh oranges, corn, soybeans, cotton and lumber. For every commodity we used unit values of U.S. exports to Japan. In addition, to show the effect of different destinations, in two cases we used values for exports to other destinations (U.S. beef to Canada and U.S. oranges to Hong Kong). The prices were expressed in real terms by dividing by the U.S. Consumer Price Index (for all goods) base 1967 = 100.

The explanatory variables included (in addition to the lagged value of the dependent variable) various measures of exchange rates and variables to represent supply and demand shifters. The exchange rates were all real exchange rates, all obtained from the USDA-ERS on a Lotus 1-2-3 spreadsheet. They included bilateral rates between the United States and the relevant importing country (either Japan, Canada, or Hong Kong) and two types of multilateral rates. The multilateral rates differed in their use of weights for individual real bilateral rates according to shares of imports of U.S. agricultural products ("Importers' Trade Weights") or according to competition with the United States for export markets ("Exporters' Trade Weights").[17] The shift variables included prices of tradeable substitutes in consumption or production and tradeable inputs (e.g., price of corn in the equations for prices of beef and soybeans) and general shift variables (e.g., GNP per capita) and, in the case of the models using bilateral rates, other bilateral rates for currencies of key competitors.

Base Model Results

In our base model we included only one exchange rate variable along with the lagged dependent variable, and no other (i.e., shift) variables. The results for these regressions are reported in Tables 14.1 and 14.2. These tables include the coefficients on the exchange rate and the lagged dependent variable (with t-values in parentheses), estimates of the pass-through elasticities in the short run (S.R.) and long run (L.R.),

TABLE 14.1 Summary of Base Model Results (bilateral exchange rates)

Dependent Variable (U.S. Price)	Exchange Rate	Lagged Dependent Variable	Pass-Through Elasticity S.R.	Pass-Through Elasticity L.R.	Mean Lag	R^2	h
Pork to Japan (using $US/Yen)	0.066 (1.787)	0.852 (21.431)	0.07	0.45	6.8	0.79	-1.08
Beef to Japan (using $US/Yen)	0.011 (0.245)	0.759 (15.123)	0.01	0.04	4.1	0.58	-2.04
Beef to Canada (using $US/$Can)	0.770 (2.641)	0.419 (5.915)	0.77	1.33	1.7	0.28	-4.07
Oranges to Japan (using $US/Yen)	0.005 (0.058)	0.619 (10.114)	0.00	0.01	2.6	0.38	3.49
Oranges to H.K. (using $US/$HK)	0.260 (2.106)	0.685 (11.997)	0.26	0.82	3.2	0.53	2.73
Corn to Japan (using $US/Yen)	0.002 (0.048)	0.956 (43.064)	0.00	0.05	22.7	0.94	1.39
Soybeans to Japan (using $US/Yen)	0.020 (0.255)	0.846 (20.548)	0.02	0.13	6.5	0.73	1.31
Cotton to Japan (using $US/Yen)	0.262 (1.155)	0.525 (7.894)	0.26	0.55	2.1	0.29	4.25
Lumber to Japan (using $US/Yen)	0.061 (0.259)	0.519 (7.776)	0.06	0.13	2.1	0.27	3.62

the mean lag, the R^2 and Durbin's h-*statistic*.[18] The estimated coefficients were of the expected signs and the magnitudes were plausible. The more interesting contrasts are between corresponding models using multilateral and bilateral rates, and between models of the price of the same good going to relatively open and relatively closed markets. On the whole, the models using multilateral exchange rates make much better sense to us than the ones using bilateral rates. Their statistical results are better and the exchange rate pass-through elasticities are generally more plausible.

Bilateral Versus Multilateral Exchange Rates. To facilitate comparisons, Table 14.1 is a summary of results for bilateral rates. With only three exceptions (beef to Canada, pork to Japan, and oranges to Hong Kong), the bilateral exchange rate is statistically insignificant.[19] In the case of beef to Canada, it is probably true that neither the short- nor long-run bilateral pass-through elasticities (0.77 and 1.33) are sig-

TABLE 14.2 Summary of Base Model Results (multilateral, exporter weights)

Dependent Variable (U.S. Price)	Exchange Rate	Lagged Dependent Variable	Pass-Through Elasticity S.R.	L.R.	Mean Lag	R^2	h
Pork to Japan (using $US/Yen)	0.147 (2.852)	0.805 (18.042)	0.15	0.75	5.1	0.80	-0.94
Beef to Japan (using $US/Yen)	0.237 (3.679)	0.627 (10.423)	0.24	0.63	2.7	0.61	-1.03
Beef to Canada (using $US/$Can)	0.992 (6.222)	0.196 (2.562)	0.99	1.23	1.2	0.37	-3.18
Oranges to Japan (using $US/Yen)	0.079 (0.717)	0.615 (10.010)	0.08	0.20	2.6	0.39	3.53
Oranges to H.K. (using $US/$HK)	0.217 (1.932)	0.686 (11.915)	0.22	0.70	3.2	0.53	2.83
Corn to Japan (using $US/Yen)	0.133 (2.245)	0.920 (36.968)	0.13	1.66	12.5	0.94	1.50
Soybeans to Japan (using $US/Yen)	0.443 (3.597)	0.724 (13.970)	0.44	1.61	3.4	0.75	2.18
Cotton to Japan (using $US/Yen)	0.436 (1.543)	0.517 (7.749)	0.44	0.91	2.0	0.30	4.29
Lumber to Japan (using $US/Yen)	0.538 (1.817)	0.490 (7.204)	0.54	1.06	2.0	0.28	3.96

nificantly different from 1.0. And, the response occurs relatively quickly with a mean lag of less than 2 quarters. This may imply that the United States is effectively a small country in beef trade with Canada (i.e., Canadian beef prices are unresponsive to the $U.S./$Can exchange rate). Alternatively, it may mean that the bilateral price is a good proxy for the world price and movement in the bilateral exchange rate is a good proxy for movement of more general rates.

For exports of fresh oranges to Hong Kong, the short-run elasticity with respect to the bilateral rate is significantly less than 1, but the long-run elasticity probably isn't. The mean lag is still fairly short at 3.2 quarters. The Durbin h-statistics indicate autocorrelation problems in most of the equations using bilateral rates.[20] We suspect that these equations are misspecified (in particular, in that we have left out other exchange rates) and that could account for the residual problems. We did some limited experimentation with other bilateral rates as additional explanatory variables. In the case of U.S. beef exports (to both Japan and Canada) the $U.S./$A exchange rate was statistically significant (with short-run elasticities of 0.24 and 0.62, respectively) and the other coefficients were affected, indicating that the left-out variable problem is not negligible. This type of result reinforces our prior belief that the models using single bilateral rates are very questionable.

Table 14.2 summarizes the results for the regressions using multilateral exchange rates (weighted by competing exporters).[21] In these regressions the exchange rate pass-through elasticity is significantly greater than zero (using the one-tailed test) in all of the regressions except two (those for the prices of exports of oranges and cotton to Japan). Once again, as with the bilateral rates, serial correlation seems to be present, possibly a reflection of left-out variables (e.g., other prices or other shifters) in the model.

Short-Run Versus Long-Run Elasticities. The estimated pass-through elasticities in Table 14.2 are all plausible, and in the range of previous estimates. All of the short-run elasticities are between 0 and 1; most of them are quite small (the elasticity for beef exports to Canada is a pronounced exception at 0.99). The long-run elasticities are mostly much larger and generally close to 1. Two notable exceptions are in the case of corn and soybeans (1.66 and 1.61, respectively), but these elasticities are probably not statistically significantly different from 1. In most cases the mean lag is less than 4 quarters, which nonetheless indicates a significant lag in price response to exchange rate changes. Corn is a notable exception with a mean lag of over 12 quarters. This seems to be an implausibly slow response and suggests that an unduly large coefficient on the lagged dependent variable may account for the large long-run elasticity. Based on this evidence, we cannot reject the hypothesis that the United States is a price taker in these markets—therefore exhibiting complete pass-through of exchange rate changes into U.S. prices—in the long run. However, in the short run (of up to several years) there may be significant real price effects elsewhere as a consequence of incomplete pass-through of changes in the value of the dollar into U.S. prices.

Effects of Policies. Our experimental design is not complete enough for us to separate out commodity and country (and therefore policy) effects completely, but we can draw some tentative implications. First, Canada and Hong Kong are relatively open in agricultural trade with the United States compared to Japan, and that could account for the relatively large and rapid response of U.S. prices of exports to those countries to changes in the value of the $U.S. In both citrus and beef,

Japan has imported under quotas for the period of the analysis. In a two-country model, an import quota will mean that pass-through into either country's internal prices is zero: all exchange rate effects are reflected entirely in changes in quota rents in response to changes in the importer's border price. This could account for the results for oranges and beef using the bilateral exchange rates. In the multicountry context of the data used here, Japanese import quotas could be expected to reduce—but not eliminate—exchange rate pass-through into U.S. prices; even though Japan is the main destination for U.S. exports of both commodities, the bilateral trade does not take place in a vacuum. Notice, also, that for the commodities not subject to quotas (e.g., corn, soybeans, cotton, lumber) pass-through is greater.

Second-Round Effects

To illustrate the second-round effects discussed in detail above, we tried including explanatory variables to represent tradeable factors or tradeable competing products. We had mixed success with this, but the results support the idea of including such variables and indicate that not doing so will mean that the estimated elasticities are partial ones and may be biased as well.[22]

For brevity we will discuss only the regressions using multilateral exchange rates with exporter weights. First, consider corn as an input into livestock production. The real price of corn exports to Japan was a statistically significant explanatory variable in the equations for the price of U.S. beef exports to Japan (with a short-run elasticity of about 0.06) and to Canada (with a short-run elasticity of 0.26). The estimated elasticity on the price of soybeans in the same regressions (instead of corn) was about the same size but was not statistically significant. Neither feed grain price was significant in the equations for pork prices. This was surprising to us. More work is needed, perhaps with some index of livestock rations. It will be interesting also to include chicken in further analysis.

Alternatively, consider feedback from goods that are substitutes or complements in production and consumption. In the regressions for prices of U.S. soybean exports to Japan, the price of corn was a highly significant explanatory variable with an elasticity of 0.52. Thus, feedback from corn into soybeans is likely to be a significant omission in the base model for soybeans. We also tried some general demand or supply shift variables (GNP per capita and interest rates) but they were uniformly insignificant explanatory variables. Better luck might result if more specific shift variables were used.

Conclusion

Previous studies of exchange rate pass-through outside agriculture have focussed on imperfect competition as a central reason for incomplete pass-through. In contrast, agricultural economists have for the most part used a maintained hypothesis of perfect competition so that incomplete pass-through is attributed to imperfectly elastic supply or demand. Our comparative statics indicate that—unless we are dealing with a small country in trade—exchange rate pass-through elasticities can be anywhere between 0 and 1 (and even beyond that) under an assumption of competition. Pass-through elasticities greater than 1 are unlikely, but possible as a consequence of second-round adjustments to price changes in markets for factors or related products. In this, we concur with Chambers and Just (1979). By way of qualification, we recognize that the possibility of exchange rate pass-through elasticities greater than 1 becomes smaller as we deal with increasingly aggregated goods.

We have argued for the use of variables defined in real terms because there is no unique pass-through from nominal exchange rates to product prices. In our empirical work, real f.o.b. unit values for a range of U.S. agricultural exports were regressed against real exchange rates. We suggest that the use of multilateral exchange rates is likely to lead to more robust estimates of exchange rate pass-through and, so far, our results reinforce that view.

Our preliminary results are encouraging. A relatively simple specification yields plausible estimates and illustrates some important points. Dynamics are important; second-round effects from factor markets or competing products exist and may be significant; policies seem to matter. These results have implications for specification of exchange rate pass-through models in general. Our estimates of long-run exchange rate pass-through elasticities tend to support the view that the United States is to a great extent a price-taker in agricultural trade although there may be significant lags before pass-though is complete.

Further work is warranted in a number of areas. In particular, it would be desirable to use a greater number of commodities and to use a more general measure of U.S. border prices in addition to the prices for products to particular destinations. The results indicated autocorrelation problems were present in most of the models. More sophisticated time-series approaches to model the dynamics should be tried, even though that may mean a loss of transparency in the results. More work should be done with shift variables. Finally, a systems approach (dealing with both simultaneity and contemporaneous error correlations) may be fruitful.

We began this study with a view to drawing on the exchange rate pass-through literature to inform discussions of exchange rates and agriculture. Since then we have learned more about both bodies of literature. It seems to us now that the literature on exchange rates and agriculture has lessons for work on exchange rate pass-though in general. In particular, the assumption of perfect competition is a more plausible approximation for most markets than the extreme forms of imperfect competition that are often assumed. Even under an assumption of perfect competition there are significant possibilities for incomplete exchange rate pass-through. It would seem to us to be better to make sure that other explanations are exhausted before resorting to arguments of monopoly power of firms in international markets.

Notes

1. See, for example, "Embargoes, Surplus Disposal and U.S. Agriculture," USDA-ERS Agricultural Economics Report No. 564 (December 1986). One of the key conclusions of this massive study was that the high value of the U.S. dollar was a major determinant of the farm "crisis" of the 1980s. Other U.S. government reports on the importance of the exchange rate include those by Shane (1990); Longmire and Morey (1983); and Krissoff and Morey (1986).

2. For a thorough and insightful review of the literature on exchange rates and U.S. agricultural trade, see Chambers (1988). Some related work on exchange rates and agriculture from an Australian perspective may also be pertinent; among these are papers by Gregory (1976) and Stoeckel (1979).

3. Exceptions might be found among commodities for which major importers and exporters control trade through marketing boards or other government agencies having substantial market power, or where governments provide destination-specific subsidies. This is consistent with Pick and Park (1991), who found some evidence of pricing to market in U.S. wheat exports, but not for cotton, corn, soybeans and soybean meal.

4. The source of an exchange rate change almost always will have implications for reasonable assumptions about which economic variables may be taken as constant and which are changing along with the exchange rate. For instance, are the prices of competing products and traded and non-traded factors taken as being (a) constant, independent of the exchange rate change, (b) affected by the exchange rate change directly, (c) affected by the factors that caused the exchange rate changes, or (d) themselves the cause of the change in exchange rates? In relation to causes of exchange rate changes, it may be difficult to say much anyway. For example, Meese and Rose (1990) present a very pessimistic viewpoint on this issue. They argue that there is little evidence that conclusively links the bilateral exchange rates of typical OECD

countries to "fundamental" macroeconomic determinants of exchange rates such as money, output, relative prices, or interest rate differentials.

5. Here, "large" refers to the nation's relative importance in the market for a particular commodity, and its concomitant ability to affect the price of that commodity rather than the overall size of its economy.

6. This model is similar to that of Chambers and Just (1979). Both models pay attention to secondary effects through related markets but we emphasize effects of traded factors (i.e., vertical market linkages) while they emphasize effects of traded substitutes in consumption (i.e., horizontal market linkages).

7. Strictly speaking, this analysis is correct only when either (a) there are only two countries involved in the trade in the product (and all related products and factors) or (b) we have aggregated across countries to a bilateral case of the home country and the rest of the world.

8. For example, assume the exchange rate was 100 yen per U.S. dollar initially. Rescaling this exchange rate by dividing by 100 gives the 45° line in Figure 14.1.

9. Tradeable does not necessarily mean the inputs are actually traded but rather it implies that their prices adjust to reflect changes in international prices (e.g., see Kyle, 1990).

10. The convention of defining the exchange rate elasticities (α and β) as entering the equations with negative and positive sign, respectively, is arbitrary but convenient. They do make some sense in relation to incorporating effects of traded inputs in which case they can both be assumed to be positive fractions (i.e., $0 < \alpha, \beta < 1$). For instance, suppose a traded input has a pass-through elasticity between 0 and 1 so that the exporter's input costs will be reflected as a reduction in supply and excess supply (positive β); a decrease in the importer's input costs (in importer's currency) will be reflected as an increase in supply and a decrease in excess demand (a negative effect with a positive value for α). Negative values for α and β, due to feedback from markets for related goods, are possible but unlikely.

11. This last case is a type of neutrality result. When supply and demand shift by equal vertical amounts, the quantity of trade is unaffected: $d\ln Q = 0$ when $\alpha + \beta = 1$. Another special case is that of zero pass-through (i.e., $\varepsilon_{P,E} = 0$), which will occur when either excess supply is perfectly elastic ($\varepsilon = \infty$) or excess demand is perfectly inelastic ($\eta = 0$) and there is no feedback ($\alpha = \beta = 0$).

12. The details of the derivation are available from the authors. The supply elasticity is a function of the factor cost shares and the elasticity of factor substitution.

13. See Collins et al. (1980) and Longmire and Morey (1983). They also have some effects that are similar to exchange rate effects. The "symmetry" hypothesis is discussed by Feenstra, 1989; some further analytic results related to this hypothesis, with allowance for trade in factors, are available from the authors.

14. Thus the presence of policies that act like import quotas (e.g., VERs in beef and automobiles may have contributed to "surprisingly" low pass-through in the markets for some goods). See Jabara and Schwartz (1987).

15. An important distinction is that between market power of nations and market power of firms. Our maintained hypothesis is that firms have no market power. Thus, the fact that a country can influence the international price for a product does not imply "pricing to market" or any other form of price discrimination other than that applied through government policies.

16. These are partial elasticities in the sense that exchange rate changes can affect product prices indirectly through the other explanatory variables as well as directly. The *total* elasticity will involve indirect effects through factor markets and other product markets as well as the direct effects (through β's).

17. For details of the two multilateral rates used here, see Shane (1990).

18. The long-run elasticity is computed by dividing the short-run elasticity by the estimated co-efficient of adjustment (θ) which is computed as $\theta = 1 - d$ where d is the co-efficient on the lagged dependent variable. The mean lag may be computed as the reciprocal of $\theta = 1 - d$.

19. For a two-tailed test with H_0: $|b| > 0$, the 95 percent critical value of the t distribution is 1.96. For the current analysis, a one-tailed test is more appropriate and for H_0: $b > 0$, the 95 percent critical value of the t distribution is 1.645.

20. The h-statistic is asymptotically distributed as a standard normal. The test for serially correlated residuals then becomes a standard z-test and when $|h| > 1.96$, we reject the hypothesis of no serial correlation at the 95 percent confidence level.

21. The results using the alternative multilateral rate (Importers' Trade Weights) are available from the authors. They were generally very similar to those in Table 14.2, although the models using the exchange rate with competing exporter weights tended to perform slightly better.

22. With good luck, the bias may be of the type that means the direct (partial) elasticity does provide an unbiased measure of the total elasticity. This will be so (we think) when the left-out explanatory variables (e.g., other exchange rates or tradeable factor prices) are uncorrelated with the included variables other than through the exchange rate so that they are uncorrelated with the residuals from the model that includes the exchange rate.

References

Baldwin, R. 1988. "Hysteresis in Import Prices: The Beachhead Effect." *American Economic Review* 78: 773-85.

Batten, D. S. and M. T. Belongia. 1986. "Monetary Policy, Real Exchange Rates, and U.S. Agricultural Exports." *American Journal of Agricultural Economics* 68: 422-27.

Carter, C. A. and D. H. Pick. 1989. "The J-Curve Effect and the U.S. Agricultural Trade Balance." *American Journal of Agricultural Economics* 71: 712-19.

Carter, C., R. Gray and H. Furtan. 1990. "Effects of Exchange Rate Changes on Inputs and Outputs in Canadian Agriculture." *American Journal of Agricultural Economics* 72: 738-43.

Chambers, R. G. 1988. "An Overview of Exchange Rates and Macroeconomic Effects on Agriculture." In R.L. Paarlberg and R.G. Chambers, eds., Ch. 1., *Macroeconomics, Agriculture and Exchange Rates*. Boulder: Westview Press.

Chambers, R. G. and R. E. Just. 1979. "A Critique of Exchange Rate Treatment in Agricultural Trade Models." *American Journal of Agricultural Economics* 61: 249-57.

Chambers, R. G. and R. E. Just. 1981. "Effects of Exchange Rate Changes on U.S. Agriculture: A Dynamic Analysis." *American Journal of Agricultural Economics* 63: 32-46.

Collins, K. J., W. H. Myers and M. E. Bredahl. 1980. "Multiple Exchange Rate Changes and U.S. Agricultural Commodity Prices." *American Journal of Agricultural Economics* 62: 656-65.

Dutton, J. and T. Grennes. 1985. "Measurement of Effective Exchange Rates Appropriate for Agricultural Trade." Department of Economics and Business, North Carolina State University, Raleigh, N.C. Economic Research Report No. 51, November.

Dornbusch, R. 1987. "Exchange Rates and Prices." *American Economic Review* 77: 93-106.

Feenstra, R. C. 1989. "Symmetric Pass-Through of Tariff and Exchange Rates Under Imperfect Competition: An Empirical Test." *Journal of International Economics* 27: 25-45.

Feinberg, R. M. 1986. "The Interaction of Foreign Exchange and Market Power Effects on German Domestic Prices." *The Journal of Industrial Economics* 35: 61-70.

Froot, K. A. and P. D. Klemperer. 1988. *Exchange Rate Pass-Through When Market Share Matters*. NBER Working Paper 2542. Cambridge, Massachusetts: National Bureau of Economic Research, March.

Giovannini, A. 1988. "Exchange Rates and Traded Good Prices." *Journal of International Economics* 24: 45-68.

Greenshields, B. L. 1974. *Changes in Exchange Rates, Impact on U.S. Grain and Soybean Exports to Japan*. USDA-ERS, Washington, D.C., Foreign Agriculture Report No. 364.

Gregory, R. G. 1976. "Some Implications of Growth of the Mineral Sector." *Australian Journal of Agricultural Economics* 20: 71-91.

Grennes, T., P. R. Johnson and M. C. Thursby. 1980. "A Critique of Exchange Rate Treatment in Agricultural Trade Models: Comment." *American Journal of Agricultural Economics* 62: 249-52.

Henneberry, D., M. Drabenstott and S. Henneberry. 1987. "A Weaker Dollar and U.S. Farm Exports." *Federal Reserve Bank of Kansas City: Economic*

Review 72: 22-36.

Hooper, P. and C. L. Mann. 1989. "Exchange Rate Pass-Through in the 1980s: The Case of U.S. Imports of Manufactures." *Brookings Papers on Economic Activity.* 1: 297-337.

Jabara, C. L. and N. E. Schwartz. 1987. "Flexible Exchange Rates and Commodity Price Changes: The Case of Japan." *American Journal of Agricultural Economics* 69: 580-90.

Johnson, P. R., T. Grennes and M. Thursby. 1977. "Devaluation, Foreign Trade Controls, and Domestic Wheat Prices." *American Journal of Agricultural Economics* 59: 619-27.

Knetter, M. M. 1989. "Price Discrimination by U.S. and German Exporters." *American Economic Review* 79: 198-210.

Konandreas, P., P. Bushnell and R. Green. 1978. "Estimation of Export Demand Functions for U.S. Wheat." *Western Journal of Agricultural Economics* 3: 39-49.

Kost, W. E. 1976. "Effects of an Exchange Rate Change on Agricultural Trade." *Agricultural Economics Research* 28(3): 99-106.

Krissoff, B. and A. Morey. 1986. "The Dollar Turnaround and U.S. Agricultural Exports." ERS Staff Report No. AGES861128. International Economics Division, USDA-ERS, Washington, D.C. December.

Krugman, P. R. 1987. "Pricing to Market When the Exchange Rate Changes." In S. W. Arndt and J. D. Richardson, eds., *Real-Financial Linkages Among Open Economies.* Cambridge: MIT Press.

Kyle, S. 1990. "Pitfalls in the Measurement of Real Exchange Rate Effects on Agriculture." Mimeo. Department of Agricultural Economics. Cornell University, April.

Longmire, J. and A. Morey. 1983. "Strong Dollar Dampens Demand for U.S. Farm Products." Foreign Agricultural Economic Report No. 193. International Economics Division, USDA-ERS, Washington, D.C., December.

Mann, C. L. 1986. "Prices, Profit Margins, and Exchange Rates." *Federal Reserve Bulletin.* June: 366-379.

Marston, R. C. 1989. "Pricing to Market in Japanese Manufacturing." Unpublished. Philadelphia: University of Pennsylvania, March.

Meese, R. A. and A. K. Rose. 1990. "Nonlinear, Nonparametric, Nonessential Exchange Rate Estimation." *American Economic Review* 80: 192-196.

Mullen, J. D., J. M. Alston and M. K. Wohlgenant. 1989. "The Impact of Farm and Processing Research on the Australian Wool Industry." *Australian Journal of Agricultural Economics* 33: 32-47.

Ohno, K. 1989. "Export Pricing Behavior of Manufacturing: A U.S.-Japan Comparison." *IMF Staff Papers* 36: 550-579.

Ohno, K. 1990. "Exchange Rate Fluctuations, Pass-Through and Market Share." *IMF Staff Papers* 37: 294-310.

Orden, D. 1986. "A Critique of Exchange Rate Treatment in Agricultural Trade Models: Comment." *American Journal of Agricultural Economics* 68: 990-993.

Orden, D., and P. L. Fackler. 1989. "Identifying Monetary Impacts on Agricultural Prices in VAR Models." *American Journal of Agricultural Economics* 71: 495-502.

Penson, J. B. and B. L. Gardner. 1988. "Implications of the Macroeconomic Outlook for Agriculture." *American Journal of Agricultural Economics* 70: 1011-22.

Pick, D. H. and T. A. Park. 1991. "The Competitive Structure of U.S. Agricultural Exports." *American Journal of Agricultural Economics* 73: 134-41.

Reed, M. 1980. "A Critique of Exchange Rate Treatment in Agricultural Trade Models: Comment." *American Journal of Agricultural Economics* 62: 253-5.

Schembri, L. 1989. "Export Prices and Exchange Rates: An Industry Approach." In R. Feenstra, ed., *Trade Policies for International Competitiveness*. Chicago: Univ. of Chicago Press.

Schuh, G. E. 1974. "The Exchange Rate and U.S. Agriculture." *American Journal of Agricultural Economics* 56: 1-13.

Stoeckel, A. 1979. "Some General Equilibrium Effects of Mining Growth on the Economy." *Australian Journal of Agricultural Economics* 23: 1-22.

Shane, M. 1990. "Exchange Rates and U.S. Agricultural Trade." Agricultural Information Bulletin No. 585. International Economics Division, USDA-ERS, Washington, D.C., January.

Vellianitis-Fidas, A. 1975. "The Exchange Rate and U.S. Agriculture: Comment." *American Journal of Agricultural Economics* 56: 692-5.

White, K. J., S. A. Haun, N. G. Horsman, and S. Donna Wong. 1988. *SHAZAM: Econometrics Computer Program Version 6.1 - Users Reference Manual*. New York: McGraw-Hill.

Woo, W. 1984. "Exchange Rates and the Prices of Nonfood, Nonfuel Products." *Brookings Papers on Economic Activity* 2: 511-530.

15

The Japanese Beef Policy: Political Preference Function

Thomas Wahl, Dermot Hayes, and Andrew Schmitz

Introduction

In an effort to maintain beef self-sufficiency and to protect the incomes of politically powerful domestic beef producers, Japan has restricted beef imports since the early 1960s. Prior to April 1, 1991, the primary mechanism used to protect the domestic beef industry was a quota on the quantity of beef that could be imported. On April 1, 1991, the quota was replaced by a 70 percent tariff, which is scheduled to be reduced by 10 percent per year for two years.

In a paper published in 1979, Hayami argued that the beef quota could be replaced with a deficiency payment funded by a tariff on beef imports. Hayami showed that consumers and taxpayers would gain and producer welfare would be maintained. In 1983, however, Anderson argued that the quota was rational. Anderson disputed the pareto optimality of the deficiency payment approach and argued that when the lobbying power of beef distributors and tariff visibility are included, quotas are optimal and will remain so for as long as the interests of "bureaucrats and politicians" diverge from those of society. Now that Japan has replaced the quota with a tariff, it seems that the government has found it optimal to accept Hayami's advice, which, in terms of Anderson's framework, means that the interests of bureaucrats, politicians, and society coincide.

One possible explanation for this shift in government preferences is that U.S. and Australian negotiators applied intense pressure during Japanese-U.S. and Japanese-Australian negotiations. A second possibility is that the government continues to optimize the political preference function (PPF) implicit in Anderson's model.

The purpose of this paper is to examine the validity of the second possibility. We begin by estimating the implicit weights in the PPF. Anderson's treatment of the beef import regulations as those that would emanate from an optimizing middleman is adopted. Because it is not clear how the government will distribute the tariff revenues, the interests of bureaucrats and politicians are combined and the government is modeled as a middleman. This approach differs from that used by Hayami, in which the PPF weights are implicitly set equal to one. The approach followed in this paper also involves a slight variation from the standard PPF approach of Rausser and Freebairn or Oehmke and Yao, for which the government is seen as a redistributor of wealth; i.e., the weights the government attaches to itself lie between those of producers and consumers. The variation we introduce allows the government weight to be greater than either the weights for producers or consumers; that is, we allow the government to act in its own interest.

In the first section of this paper, the optimal conditions for the government to act as a middleman are derived; in the second section, the parameters of a recently published model of the Japanese livestock sector are used to derive the weights implicit in the PPF. These estimated weights are consistent with Anderson's hypothesis of nonredistributing government behavior. One interesting result from this analysis is that, although the implicit weights in the PPF are greater for the government than for consumers and producers, the results indicate that the 1990 quota level was lower than that which would have existed had the government been optimizing. The model is then simulated to project the trade-offs that will occur in 1993; i.e., the effects of population and real income growth are projected so that the optimal level of imports in 1993 can be predicted. The results for 1993 show that the tariff agreed to in the negotiations is close to the predicted tariff when the optimizing government approach is used. These results indicate that the liberalization may have been rational in that it moved the government toward its optimal position. Finally, it is argued that, if the hypothesis just discussed is valid, it will be difficult to convince Japan to make significant reductions in the tariff after 1993.

Optimal Government Behavior

Japanese beef imports are controlled by a governmental agency, the Livestock Industry Promotion Corporation (LIPC), which was created in 1962 to promote livestock production. The power of the LIPC gradually increased to include beef price management by use of a beef import quota. In 1975, the LIPC was empowered to buy and sell beef to allow fine-tuning of the price stabilization scheme. The government, through the LIPC, acts as a middleman in the beef market by dictating the form (fresh or frozen), quality, quantity, and price of imported beef. The LIPC then resells the beef in the Japanese wholesale meat market at its discretion, supposedly to stabilize domestic beef prices. The difference between the purchase price and the resale price of the imported beef generates revenues that are then used to fund the LIPC.

Because the stabilization price has been set at a level that is significantly higher than world prices, large quota rents have been generated. It has never been clear how the Japanese government distributed these rents, and it is therefore difficult to model explicitly the behavior of each of the various middle agents. In what follows, Anderson's approach of lumping all the middle enterprises together and treating them as a single entity called *government* is adopted.

The optimal behavior for the government acting as a middleman is to maximize the revenues generated by the quota or tariffs. The increase in government revenues from the tariff (or quota rent) from additional imports is greater than the reduction in revenues caused by lower overall tariffs. The results that follow demonstrate that, at import levels at or near those that currently exist, the consumer welfare gains and losses from changes in imports dominate those of producers and the government combined. This concept is illustrated in Figure 15.1,[1] where setting the quota to the level at which the marginal revenue curve of the excess demand curve for beef in Japan intersects the excess supply curve for the rest of the world maximizes the revenue from the quota.[2] Quota rents are generated by the difference between the revenue from the domestic sale of imports $P_d * Q_1$ and the cost of the imports on the world market, $P_w Q_1$. Government rents are maximized when the marginal sales revenue equals the marginal cost of imports. The resulting domestic price is P_d, and the world price is P_w. Under free trade, the intersection of ES and ED would determine the free-trade price, P_F, and quantity, Q_F. The government welfare-maximizing import level is Q_1.

Government revenues generated by the quota are zero if the quota is zero (or the tariff is prohibitive), as reflected in the lower panel of Figure 15.1. As the quota increases (or the tariff decreases), government revenues increase; that is, the marginal benefit is still greater than MC. At Q_1 when MR=ES and the marginal benefit of another increment of imports equals the marginal cost, the government revenues reach a maximum and the government's welfare is maximized. As the quota increases or the tariff decreases, government revenues decline and eventually reach zero at the free-trade level of imports.

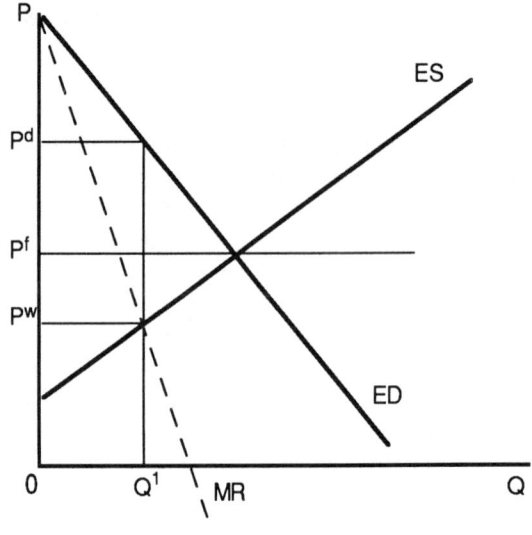

Optimal Government Behavior

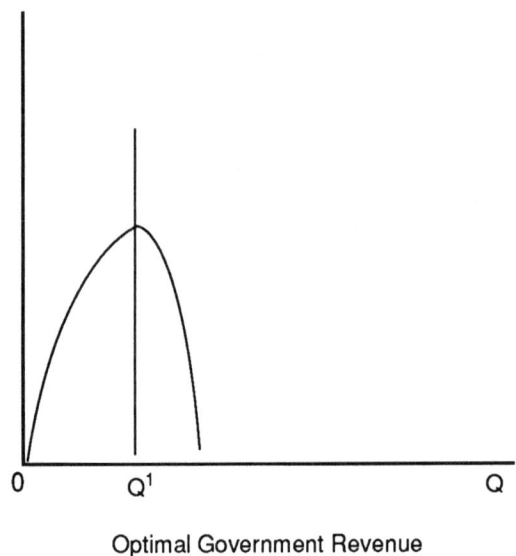

Optimal Government Revenue

FIGURE 15.1 Optimal Government Behavior and Revenue

Estimating the Implied Weights of the Political Preference Function

The implied weights of the PPF for various levels of the Japanese beef import quota were calculated by using the parameters of a Japanese livestock model obtained from Wahl, Hayes, and Williams. Following the approach used by Rausser and Freebairn or Oehmke and Yao, marginal changes in the quota were made and the changes in the welfare of the government, producers, and consumers were observed. The implied weights were then calculated. The essence of this approach is that if a one-unit change in the quota changed the welfare of consumers by $10, the welfare of producers by $5, and the welfare of the government by $1, then it could be concluded that the government values its own welfare relative to the welfare of consumers and producers with the weights 1:5:10, where 1 is the weight on consumers, 5 is the weight on producers, and 10 is the weight on government welfare.

The changes in government welfare can be measured by examining the revenue or rents generated by the quota or the tariff. The resulting quota revenue captures the government's intervention and interference at the wholesale level. The welfare of producers and consumers is estimated by using the areas over the supply curve and under the demand curve, respectively.

The changes in producer and consumer welfare and government revenues for various levels of the import quota for 1987 are presented in Figure 15.2. These results show that any increase in imports would simultaneously benefit consumers and the government. This result makes it difficult to determine whether the government changes the quota to increase its own revenues or to increase consumer welfare. In what follows, it will be shown that the government's behavior is consistent with revenue maximization by the government. However, it cannot be concluded that government behavior was not influenced by consumer welfare.

Figure 15.3 presents an expanded look at the quota rents captured by the government. The results indicate that in 1987 the government was not maximizing quota rents because the observed quota level, Q, is less than the maximum revenue level, given the underlying assumption of the model about world prices and own-price elasticities.[3]

Table 15.1 presents the estimated trade-off measures normalized on consumers. The results indicate that the society's trade-off in 1983 for producers was 1.5 and for the government was 4.6; i.e., society was willing to take 1.5 yen away from consumers to give one more yen to producers and to take 4.6 yen away from consumers to give one more yen to the government. The results are consistent with the hypothesis that

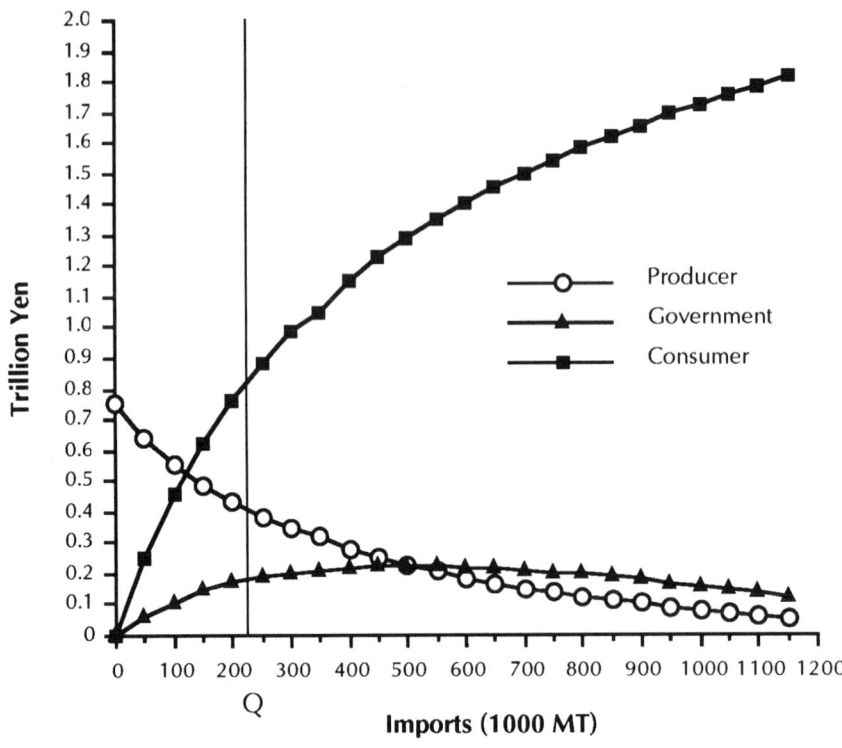

FIGURE 15.2 Changes in Producer and Consumer Welfare and Government Revenue at Various Levels of the Beef Import Quota in 1987

Japanese society values the government to a much greater degree than it values producers, and it values producers to a greater degree than it values consumers.

As the quota level increases from its 1983 level to its 1989 level, the implicit weights in the government's policy function change dramatically. For example, the government's implicit weight on its own welfare increases from 4.6 to 9.9. This increase demonstrates how the quota increase actually increased the welfare of the government acting as a middleman. The drop in the 1987 weights relative to 1985 weights may have occurred because the 1985 measure is closer to the optimal government revenue in 1985 than the 1987 measure is to the optimal government revenue in 1987 because of a relatively large increase in imports that occurred in 1987.

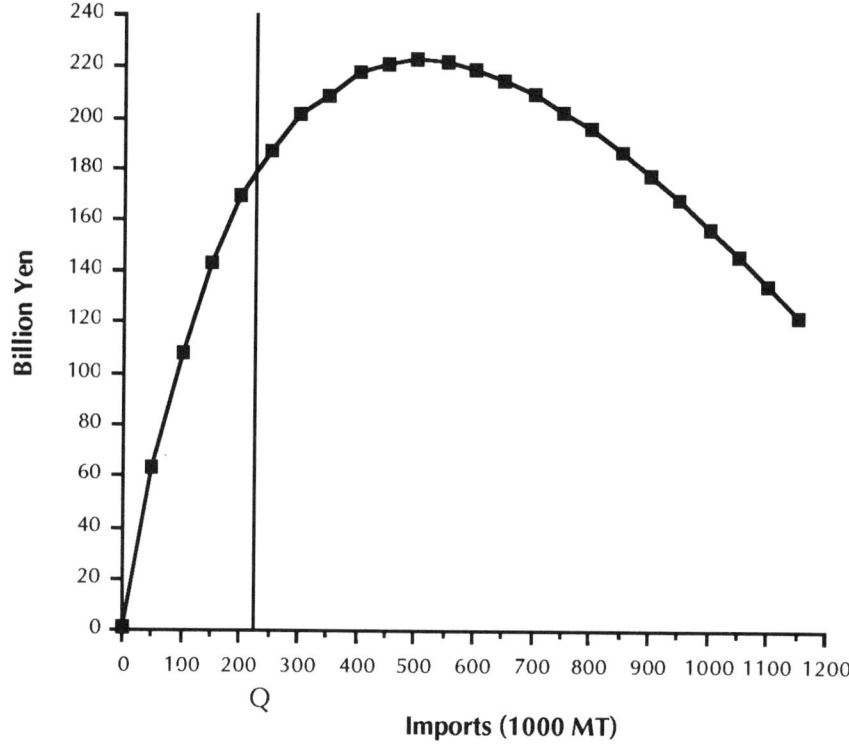

FIGURE 15.3 Government Revenues for 1987

The last line in Table 15.1 indicates how large the quota would need to be for the implicit weight on the government in the government's welfare function to be approximately one. This quota level is close to the free-trade beef import level reported by Wahl, Hayes, and Williams. This means simply that as we approach free trade, the implicit weights move toward the equality that is implicit in Hayami's paper. The fact that actual import levels are substantially lower than this level suggests that the government has not adopted Hayami's suggestion.

As real income and population grow in Japan, the optimal import level increases. This result raises the question of how close the liberalization agreement came to optimizing the government's welfare. To evaluate this, we simulated the dynamic model through 1993 and repeated the analysis with the projected data. Figure 15.4 presents the projected government revenue in 1993 for various levels of the import tariff. We use tariff equivalents in place of quotas for convenience. The

TABLE 15.1 Estimates of the Implied Weights for Consumers, Producers, and the Government

	Imports	Consumers	Producers	Government
1983	134	1	1.5	4.6
1985	150	1	1.5	6.2
1987	220	1	2.5	5.9
1989	334	1	3.1	9.9
1989	1,000*	1	1.2	0.9

*How large the import quota would have to be.

tariff levels presented are the tariff equivalents consistent with the beef import levels used in Figures 15.3 and 15.4, which range from 1 metric ton (mt) to 1.3 million mt. The maximum level of government revenue occurs at a 69 percent tariff equivalent, which corresponds to 650,000 mt of beef imports.

This result suggests that the liberalization agreement is consistent with optimizing government behavior. If the agreement is implemented without the emergency provisions, the tariff in that year will be 50 percent.[4] If the emergency provisions are implemented, the actual tariff is 70 percent. These prospective levels are surprisingly similar, especially given the degree of error that is typically associated with econometric models. These results indicate that the government may in fact have been acting in its own best interests when it agreed to liberalize, because government tariff revenues will increase as imports increase. The results also indicate that the government may have overshot the mark when agreeing to a 50 percent tariff when in fact 69 percent was optimal.

If the argument just presented is valid, there are two practical implications. First, there may be some Japanese interest in imposing the additional tariff. Second, it is unlikely that the Japanese government would agree to further reductions in the tariff because any reduction would unambiguously reduce government revenues. If the government has had the interests of consumers at heart, however, further liberalization can be expected.

Summary and Conclusions

Japan has recently agreed to open its beef market gradually. At first glance, this move would seem to indicate that the government has at least begun to act on behalf of consumers at the expense of producers. Hayami has argued that this behavior is rational by using a model

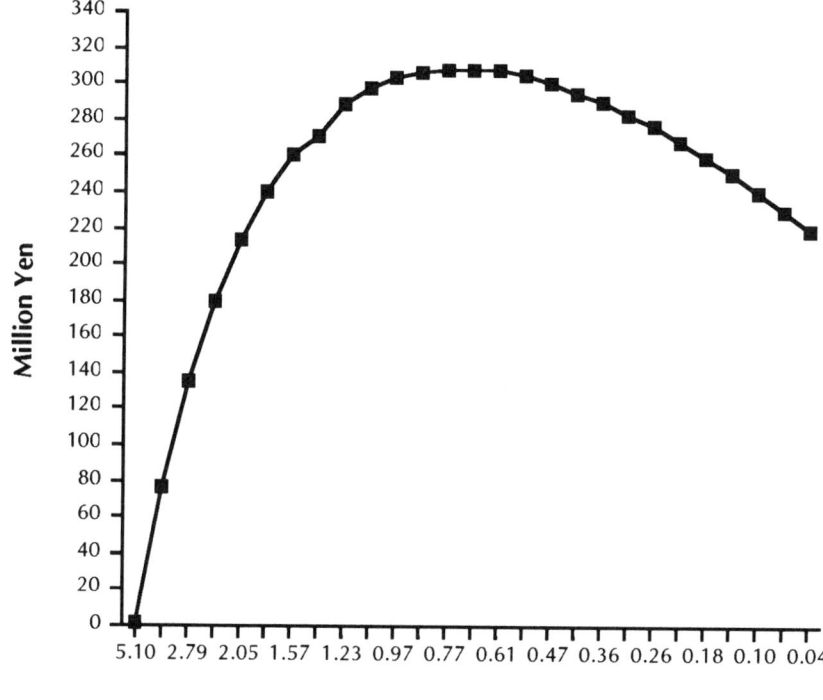

FIGURE 15.4 Government Revenues for 1993

that implicitly equates the welfare of producers and consumers. The liberalization agreement, however, allows the government to retain a significant tariff on imported beef. This tariff is quite close to that which would exist if the government had decided to maximize its revenues from the tariff. The government's behavior is therefore consistent with the hypothesis first proposed by Anderson that the Japanese government acts as a self-interested middleman.

It is difficult to determine if the government liberalized to benefit consumers or to increase its tariff revenues. Future government behavior should, however, provide some evidence in this regard. If the former case is valid, the government will eventually agree to further reduce the tariff. If the latter is true, then the tariff will remain at 50 percent and there may be some move to implement an emergency provision to increase the tariff to 70 percent.

Notes

1. Throughout the paper, we move between the tariff equivalent of the quota and tariffs by using the measured price wedge caused by the quota as the tariff equivalent.

2. The optimal behavior for the government acting as a middleman is to maximize the government's quota revenues (R) generated from the sale of imported beef in the domestic market ($P_d * Q_m$), minus the cost of the beef ($P_w * Q_m$) or

$$R = P_d * Q_m - P_w * Q_m.$$

These revenues are maximized when the marginal revenue (MR) of excess demand is equal to marginal cost or excess supply (ES) or

$$\frac{\partial R}{\partial Q_m} = P_d + Q_m \frac{\partial P_d}{\partial Q_m} - P_w - Q_m \frac{\partial P_w}{\partial Q_m} = 0.$$

Rearranging,

$$P_d + Q_m \frac{\partial P_d}{\partial Q_m} = P_w + Q_m \frac{\partial P_w}{\partial Q_m}.$$

Here, the left-hand side reflects marginal revenue and the right-hand side reflects marginal cost. This equation is a slightly adapted form of the standard monopolistic case (see Henderson and Quandt, p. 177), in which the excess supply from the rest of the world is substituted for the firm's marginal cost.

3. To examine the sensitivity of the results to world prices and own-price demand elasticities, the model was simulated for a 20 percent increase and decrease in world prices and a decrease in the own-price elasticity for wagyu beef. The 20 percent changes in world beef prices result in substantial changes in producer, government, and consumer welfare measures, suggesting that the welfare measures are sensitive to world price levels. The results, however, suggest that the welfare measures are much less sensitive to the own-price elasticity for wagyu beef. The results of the sensitivity analysis for 1987 are available from the authors.

4. The agreed-upon quota level for 1990 is 394,000 mt. Beginning in 1991, the quota is replaced by a 70 percent tariff, which will be reduced to 60 percent in 1992 and 50 percent in 1993. An emergency clause in the agreement allows a 20 percent increase in the tariff if beef imports increase by more than 25 percent over the level in the previous period. For example, if imports reach 472,000 mt in 1991, the tariff will increase to 90 percent. In 1993, the tariff will be 70 percent if imports reach 680,832 mt.

References

Anderson, K. 1983. "The Peculiar Rationality of Beef Import Quotas in Japan." *American Journal of Agricultural Economics* 65: 108-12.

Hayami, Y. 1979. "Trade Benefits to All: A Design of the Beef Import Liberalization in Japan." *American Journal of Agricultural Economics* 61: 342-7.

Oehmke, J. and X. Yao. 1990. "A Policy Preference Function for Government Intervention in the U.S. Wheat Market." *American Journal of Agricultural Economics* 72: 631-40.

Rausser, G. and J. Freebairn. 1974. "Estimation of Policy Preference Functions: An Application of U.S. Beef Import Quotas." *Review of Economics and Statistics* 56: 437-49.

Wahl, T., D. Hayes, and G. Williams. 1991. "Dynamic Adjustment in the Japanese Livestock Industry Under Beef Import Liberalization." *American Journal of Agricultural Economics* 73(1): 45-78.

PART FOUR

Problems and Issues for Future Research

16

Problems and Issues for Future Research on Pacific Rim Agriculture and Trade

Hiroshi Yamauchi

Since the early 1960s, various proposals have attempted to define the Pacific Basin region as a distinct economic community of interdependent trading countries. In all such attempts, the problem of exclusion implied by the selection of countries to include has been, and continues to be, a major obstacle to formalizing an international agreement on a Pacific free trade bloc. In keeping with the informal concept of the Pacific Rim (or Pacific Basin) as an open and dynamically growing region of interdependent trading countries, the chapters in this book present a perspective of the agricultural trade and adjustment problems of the region as we approach the twenty-first century. The region is too large and diverse for equal coverage to be given to all the countries within the time and resources allotted for the symposium. Thus, the strategy was first to address the major issues of the region from a global perspective, and then to take a closer in-depth look at the particular problems of selected countries within the region. The knowledge gained from this exercise serves as a useful baseline for revising hypotheses for further research work on the continuing problems and issues of agricultural trade and development of the Pacific.

This final chapter draws directly on the concluding statements of panel speakers who were asked to summarize their thoughts on the major problems and issues they saw as important for future research on Pacific Rim agriculture and trade. These were unprepared statements formulated with the creative ideas and impressions developed during the two days of discussions, and related only with the aid of notes over a final two-hour panel session with discussion from the floor. The comments from the floor and rejoiners are also included.

Concluding Statements of Panel Speakers

Lawrence Klein: Agribusiness, Technological Change, Land Reform

There are three issues that were shortchanged and would be worthwhile investigating at future sessions. First, agribusiness was not discussed very much until the last session. That was a very good session and we need to learn more about agribusinesses and their role in high-technology development and transfer.[1]

The second issue concerns technological change. Will there be a new phase in the green revolution that will significantly increase yields and supplies? I don't see a significant demand problem if we can get more efficient or cost-effective supplies. We need more intensive investigation into what technological change can produce—in particular, biotechnology.

Third, land reform was only lightly touched upon in historical terms for the Japanese and Taiwanese cases. But there is enormous potential here. Of course, there's the case of the Philippines that has been on the verge without happening. There's a legislative act but no significant action. Possibilities exist that could be significant steps forward on the supply side and also living standards in the countryside. The Taiwanese case of land reform, for example, helped pave the way for later industrialization. Having a very efficient agriculture was what made it possible for Taiwan to industrialize.

Kym Anderson: Political Economy, Transparency, General Equilibrium Modeling

We need to understand why we have the policies we have in place and what might happen to them over time. A better understanding is necessary for at least two reasons. First, until we understand why governments do what they do, we will not be in a position to suggest better ways in which they might do their thing. Second, we will be poorly equipped to project market opportunities if we don't somehow correctly include government policy developments in our modeling work. So we need a better understanding of the political economy of government policies.

One of the things that has struck me in recent years is the extent to which the modeling efforts at the OECD, USDA, and IIASA have had an effect on improving the transparency of existing policies, giving us an idea of the extent of distortions by measuring producer and consumer subsidy equivalents (PSEs and CSEs) and measuring the effects of policies. I think we still have a long way to go, and Andy Schmitz's point on the need to include the details of policies correctly in modeling is well taken. If we don't correctly include the details of such programs as land set-asides and quotas in our models, then we won't be capturing the full effects of the policies. It's not sufficient to have just price wedges in there.

That's only the beginning of the type of transparency that is needed. We certainly need more dynamics in our models to get an idea of the time paths of adjustments that would take place in response to policy reforms, such as the partial liberalizations that might be suggested in the Uruguay Round or actually be implemented in the 1990s. We need to know, for example, what would happen to absolute levels of production in different countries, to self-sufficiency rates, and to world prices.

Let me just give you an example of the need for each of those. With respect to production levels, what is often feared by farmers in protected countries such as Japan is that if there were some liberalization, there would be wholesale disappearances of farms—that the entire farm sector might even disappear. We had that discussion earlier with respect to rice in Japan. In fact, of course, most agricultural sectors are expanding over time due to investments in productivity growth, etc.; and the types of liberalization that are likely to be feasible, that is, partial and gradual liberalizations, are likely only to slow the rate of increase in production levels, not to cause major decreases in those production levels. In some recent work, we tried to look at the impact of partial liberalizations through tariffication of existing protection rates and gradually halving those tariffs over the 1990s. We could find almost no commodity or country for which there was a reduction in production. That is, the expected rate of increase in output, if policies were to continue, was sufficiently large to more than offset the decline in production that would come about through some price reductions, especially in the context of multilateral, as distinct from unilateral, liberalizations. That's very important in allaying the fears of farmers whenever there's talk of some reform.

Secondly, on self-sufficiency, for countries like Japan where food security is a major concern, saying something about the actual self-sufficiency ratios that might result is important. Again in the tariffication exercise we did, we found that, especially if one were to relax the land set-asides in Japan, the resulting numbers did not indicate substantial reductions in self-sufficiency in rice. They were rather modest, and we would be very interested in having the reactions of our Japanese colleagues as to the sensibilities of those results.

And thirdly, on world price effects, that is also crucially important because, if you consider the sort of issues John Mellor mentioned earlier—i.e., huge increases in grain imports as a possibility for

India—or the numbers in my paper on what might happen in China if they were to remain open with massive increases in grain imports, it's a legitimate concern on the part of Indian or Chinese governments to know what price they would have to pay for those imports. Would that sort of increase in world demand, say a 25 to 50 percent increase in the volume of world trade, have a huge impact on world prices so that the foreign exchange costs of those imports would be very high? There would not only be a quantity increase but also a price increase. Again, our modeling work suggests that those price increases will not be very high and that's because the rest of the world is very price responsive in aggregate. While one gets a large increase in volume, that doesn't necessarily imply a large increase in price. A better understanding of that set of dynamics is important for easing the process of reform.

Finally, the partial equilibrium models we have are not adequate, even with the multicommodity ones, because there are lots of ways in which one can influence the political process of reform by having a better general equilibrium understanding of the effects of policies and of policy changes. In particular, one can show more clearly with general equilibrium models who would be the gainers from liberalization in the domestic market, which is liberalizing rather than just focusing on the gains to agricultural exporters elswhere in the world. And, clearly, in EC countries and in Japan, it would be the other tradable sectors or the manufacturing exporters that would gain from liberalization of farm products. Steve Magiera's point was to emphasize who would gain and I think that's one way we could do that. It's not that I think computable general equilibrium (CGE) models necessarily will provide us with precise estimates that are close to the mark—far from it. What quantitative modeling work can do is to give politicians and other advocates of policy change some numbers that attract headlines. The work of the OECD and the USDA in recent agricultural trade modeling exercises have really shown how successful they can be in altering the political process. I'm sure we wouldn't have had agriculture so high on the agenda and discussed so much if it weren't for those results being available for top level ministers to go out and talk about the costs and benefits of reform in terms of hundreds of millions of tons and hundreds of millions of dollars.

John Mellor: Foreign Development Assistance and Commercial Interests, Intersectoral Growth Rates, Rural Part-time Farming

I want to make four rather brief comments. Two flow out of what I had to say earlier in my paper, and two are more broadly based.

There is a tremendous commercial interest for American agriculture to see development proceed rapidly in developing countries, particularly those in Asia. Therefore, there really should be an intelligent debate in the United States about what foreign assistance is all about and how it relates to those interests. I haven't seen any intelligence in that debate for at least the last 20 years.

I despair that once opportunities have gone by, they'll never come back, but there is a good deal that could still be done for developing markets. Obviously Africa could get development assistance on an intelligent track from the point of view of long-term U.S. commercial interests. There's also a good deal that still could be done in Asia that would be of some relevance, particularly in South Asia, and in at least a few Southeast Asian countries.

The two other remarks I wanted to make are more along substantive lines. As I look at the development process, which provides rapid growth in effective demand for food and leads—generally speaking in developing countries—to increasing food imports, I feel we have much better knowledge now than we did a quarter of century ago about how you get agriculture moving—how you accelerate the pace of technological change in agriculture, etc. I think we have that understood broadly. There's obviously a great deal of continuing research to be done in the same way that the land grant colleges continue to do useful research in the United States even though we don't fully understand the processes. Where we're very short of knowledge is in the kinds of policies and the processes into which they fit that increase the size of the multipliers between accelerated growth in agriculture and accelerated growth in the nonagricultural sector. Why is it that Taiwan and the Philippines both had very successful records in agriculture, one that was converted into extraordinary growth in the nonagricultural sector and eventually got a life of its own, and the other that wasn't? What's the difference between Taiwan and the Philippines in growth? They were pretty similar in agriculture; if anything, the edge would be with the Philippines. The difference is in the relationship between what happened in agriculture and what happened in the nonagricultural sectors. We know in Taiwan that nonagricultural growth grew very much out of agriculture in the early days long before export-led growth had come along. We know it was widely dispersed in rural areas, but we don't understand the processes very well. To some extent they're market driven, so you don't have to understand them. But there are some policy lessons in all of that in terms of public expenditures on infrastructure, education, health, social institutions, etc., that we don't understand. That was driven home to me very sharply last night when I read [a paper by Paul Collier on Kenya] that's being prepared for a conference we're running in Taiwan in September in which we're looking at nine different countries with different records in this relationship between agricultural and nonagricultural growth. You travel around in rural Kenya, the smallholder tea areas, and it's pretty obvious that there's a tremendous impact of prospering agriculture on the nonagricultural sector—the market towns and rural communities are vibrant places. Paul has done all sorts of statistical analyses and can't find any significant relationships. Well, that tells you something there. There's obviously a relationship, but we don't understand it well enough to do our statistical analyses in such a way as to bring it out. So that's an area in which we're clearly short of knowledge and probably ending up with inappropriate policies except in lucky countries like Taiwan, which seems to have stumbled onto the right set of policies.

The other comment I wanted to make about research needs is somewhat complex. And it was prompted very much by the reference to part-time farming in Japan and to some extent elsewhere. Mr. Egaitsu's paper is an extremely interesting paper and one that we should be paying a lot of attention to with respect to the implications for protectionism, growth, social processes, and so forth in all the densely populated parts of Asia. You have in Japan this tremendous dominance of part-time farming. It's partly because of the way "part-time" is defined that makes for more part-time in Japan than in the United States, but also it's very substantially real. There is tremendous part-time farming in Taiwan. Why? Because in both countries, you have very strong stimulation from agriculture for a very dispersed pattern of nonagricultural growth. You have very high population densities throughout most of the rural areas. As a result it is very easy for people to have one or some of the family members doing some farming and older family members working in the nearby increasingly modern and increasingly large-scale industries. I would think this is a pattern that could likely occur in Java, where you have very high population densities, through parts of South Asia that include 60, 70 to 80 percent of the population in rural areas, and possibly in quite a number of other Southeast Asian and South Asian countries. What are the implications of that for efficiency in agriculture, for agricultural policies, for social policies of all kinds? Certainly, Mr. Egaitsu's paper suggested that in Japan, it's considered that some desirable social and political effects come out of maintaining a much larger rural population through part-time farming than would be possible if you had only full-time farming ventures. And I have a suspicion that this system, which has some advantages, is also conducive to some degree of protectionism without necessarily lowering factor productivities very much for a wide range of factors. This is something we should think about if we're concerned about the development process in those countries and the commercial relationships we're going to have with them.

Allan Rae: PECC Task Force Agricultural Task Force Priorities[2]

Just a few words on the expansion on Pacific Basin research and the prevalence of issues for research in the region. We have major producers, major exporting and importing countries, major gainers from liberalization, including a range of the most protected to the least protected countries, a range of commodities from the temperate to the tropical. Pacific Basin markets are very important for a range of products like beef and grains and dairy products like milk powder with Southeast Asia and Latin America. Also what makes it exciting is that policies are on the move. We've heard about New Zealand policies earlier in the day, and also in Japan we know they're liberalizing, and in Korea agricultural policies are to be liberalized by 1997 in accordance with its new "graduate" status in the GATT. So there are all sorts of opportunities in a very exciting part of the world to work in.

Let me return to what we've been doing in the Pacific Economic Cooperation Conference (PECC) Task Force on Agricultural Policy, Trade and Development. The tripartite structure of the PECC is something unique to this organization, where we deliberately try to involve academics, government officials, and business people. We stress to government officials that they are there in an unofficial capacity. That's not always an easy line to push. It was my experience a few years ago, when we started our agricultural research task force, that it wasn't difficult to get government officials from certain countries involved. But, as the GATT round got under way and things got more and more politicized, we found that, for one reason or another, it was not possible for some countries or their officials to be present and to be able to attend workshops. So there's that sort of problem.

The other difficulty we have had is getting a full involvement from business people. This doesn't refer to just the agricultural task force, but it involves all of the PECC's activities. They see the PECC as being largely a collection of government officials and academics, and perhaps not as relevant as they'd like to what's going on in the real world of business. So we've got a bit of a task to make sure that what we do is relevant to business.

The first thing we had to do when the Task Force was set up in 1985 was to establish a research network. Those of you who have tried to do it know that it involves a lot of time, effort, travel, and also quite a lot of persuasive talk. But when you get around the Pacific, you find that there are a lot of excellent agricultural economists and a lot of very reputable research institutions, from Japan, Korea, Taiwan, all the way to Southeast Asia. (Incidentally, there is a new association of Southeast Asian agricultural economists that is having its first meeting right about this time. We need to know more about them and what they're doing.) All of that helps in the collaborative approach to research that is going to be necessary to push this Pacific Basin cooperation in agriculture along a bit further.

Currently, the PECC Agricultural Task Force has a network of about 20 institutions, and about 11 or 12 Pacific Rim countries. Some of us here are very familiar with these institutions, but others aren't, and there are all kinds of opportunities to make contacts with mutual gains to all parties. What we've being doing in the last few years in that Task Force is to set up a research agenda, which, first of all, started off with trying to understand what each country was trying to do in their agriculture, what their policies and objectives were, and whether or not their policies matched their objectives. That led to the study we talked about yesterday that focused on whether or not the policies for livestock were appropriate and, if not, what might be better policies.

Then the GATT round got under way and we focused more and more on getting additional work done and on publicizing the benefits of trade liberalization. Kym has spoken about the very real benefits that follow that. Academic researchers ought to be proud of the efforts and progress made in this area. The extent to which politicians accept that work is largely due to the efforts of researchers such as those in the IATRC.

We also tried to focus on agricultural adjustment issues. Perhaps here I can begin to focus on one or two ideas that we can try to introduce and put on the research agenda. Each time we've had our workshop we decided that adjustment issues ought to be researched. We've tried to get some people to do it and we've done a little, but not a whole lot. That suggests that we haven't thought deeply enough on what these adjustment issues are and how they can be confronted and solved.

We have spoken of such things as rural industrialization, which I gather has been quite successful in Japan but not in Korea, which is one reason Koreans give for maintaining high levels of agricultural protection. What's the role of part-time farming? Land reform has been covered because that's a very important constraint to agricultural development and reduction of production costs in some of the Northeast Asian areas.

A concern I have had for some time is whether or not the Southeast Asian countries would increase agricultural protection as happened in Japan, Korea, and Taiwan. I was thinking that they wouldn't although yesterday I was a bit concerned to hear Dr. Siamwalla say that protectionist forces were building up in Thailand. That's something that we might monitor and keep an eye on and try to influence in one way or another.

At our most recent meeting of our Task Force in Bangkok, Thailand, last month, we talked about our future research agenda. It was obvious that something was likely to happen at the end of the current GATT round, and whatever it was, there was going to be scope for further research next year. Hopefully the Uruguay Round will come up with a new set of rules, so that there will be a whole set of research to be done on just how those rules might be practically implemented in various countries—i.e., what sort of national policies can be used that would be consistent with whatever the new set of rules might be?

Finally, an area we identified to be very important currently has to do with environmental issues. A lot of environmental issues are due to agricultural policies, and as those environmental issues force change in agricultural practices, there are likely to be implications for agricultural trade. Food safety concerns will also have some impact on production technologies and trading patterns. So I suspect there are a whole set of green issues out there that will change things, and how those changes will have an impact on trade will need some sort of research.

Ammar Siamwalla: Thailand, Relative Sectoral Growth, Technological Change, Communities, Forgotten Sectors

Over the past five to six years, we have been going through fairly rapid changes in Thailand—what some people like to call "development." More recently a number of issues relating to trade and agriculture have come up that members of this group might want to look into. These issues concern not only Thailand but other countries as well.

We are interested in a sector. In retrospect, I think it is relative sectoral growth (in the sense of Kym's and my papers) that is the basic thrust. When one talks about relative sectoral growth, one must look at the resources that go into that growth and what kinds of technological changes are occurring relatively across the various sectors.

Let me start with technological change. I think there are certain issues that relate to trade policy questions. I would like some thinking from this group to go into the notion that we are encouraging, through policy, certain kinds of technological change that comes in and we cannot forget about once the policy is removed. Let me give an example of that. It seems to me that the development of high-fructose corn syrup was a result of high sugar prices in developed countries. The technology was invented and we have it around now. But what if, by some miracle next year, the United States and the European Community come to an agreement and all protection of sugar disappears? We will still have the capital invested in the technology for high-fructose corn syrup, but it may no longer be economical to produce. When you wipe out past policy, you don't go back to square one to a situation as if there were no policy in the first place. We cannot forget certain things about the way technological change has taken place or been encouraged in certain areas by policy distortions and then remain well after the policy has been removed. What are the social consequences of such dynamic changes over time? This is an issue that needs to be closely studied.

Let's turn to the issue of relative factor inputs in different sectors. I happen to be working on some labor market issues now after working on the credit market, which is not much of a problem. When we address questions about the labor market, we talk about the share of labor in agriculture and how it changes over time. But when we talk about labor shares, we get a bit schizophrenic about it. We know that there are lots of farmers who do other work. They are on the farm part-time and work in other sectors the other part of the time. Yet we talk about labor in agriculture, and we count heads as if people can be split off into the agricultural labor force; we succumb to various statistical conventions that divide people in some arbitrary fashion, and we just take it as that. We have a whole bunch of empirical literature and statistical tables that show the importance of nonagricultural sources of income for farm households. It is not hard to accept the claim that nonfarm income is important, but can one say a little bit more than that? That's an issue that one needs to look at in various trade and policy contexts; how is it (labor) related to other factor markets, particularly the land market? In the three East Asian markets that have a high incidence of part-time farming, how much of that is attributed to the land policies that are being followed? With all of these issues, I don't have a good sense of the analytical accounting of the various impacts that one can use in other contexts and other countries.

Concerning this labor movement between sectors, in the last year or so I have been having lunch with a colleague who is an anthropologist. He has brainwashed me with certain ideas that are probably anathema to most economists and certainly were anathema to me when I started talking to him. In most developing countries, people in the rural areas are much poorer income-wise than people in the urban areas. Most of us here have at one time or another come from the rural agricultural sector, and most of us revel in thinking that this is progress—a great thing. This anthropologist friend of mine works in small communities, and he thinks in terms of communities. He thinks of all those farmers sharing certain life-styles and so on. I'm sort of making fun of him, but to some extent at this stage in Thailand and in many developing countries, these are real things. The loss of community and all that goes with it is also very real. There is a sense in which people do put some utility in having a community, and we can even give some practical reasons for a community.

Earlier, there was mention of crime rates and divorce rates in cities. I think it's a little bit more than that in that communities are measures of social control. When we get detached from a community and get lost in some anonymous city, that social control becomes less. You need more policemen and a number of other things for control, and these are costly things. There is a social cost to the dissolution of rural community. I'm not necessarily saying that the social cost is so enormously large that we must physically prevent people from leaving the farm. But we ought to do some careful calculations and at least give some serious thought to a whole set of issues around that. We have, on the one hand, a very romantic notion of rural communities, and, on the other hand, economists who say the hell with all that stuff—they move to the cities, they get more income, and they're happier. We make some simple calculations and say it's good. I would like to put this on the research agenda, something we might want to look into. I haven't a clue about how that research is going to be done, but that's not my problem.

My final set of issues is one that I call the "forgotten sectors." Particularly in the development literature, people talk about agriculture and about industry, as if those are the only two sectors. The industry they talk about is the manufacturing and/or the tradable part of it. But there is another huge sector. In Thailand, it's more than a half of GNP; it is the nontradable service sector. What happens to this sector in the development process? Even in the short term, when one talks about exchange rate pass-through and other things, one has a sense that in agricultural markets the price formation is a matter of commodity markets, so it responds pretty quickly to demand-supply imbalances. The market clears almost every day. One has a sense about the manufacturing industry; that there is a stickiness to the prices and wages in that market. I don't have a clear sense of how price formation takes place in the service sector. As I said earlier, it's a very large sector, a very large part of GNP, a large part of the consumer price index (CPI). And before we have anything to say about exchange rate pass-through, we have to have a sense of how this particular sector responds to demand-supply imbalances. From the standpoint of those working in agriculture, the service sector is like the antechamber for most people leaving the farms. They go and mill around in the service sector before they get into the manufacturing sector.

The service sector is, in some sense, also very close to agriculture when we're talking about processing, marketing, transportation, etc. These are all service sector activities. It's a very large and important area we need to look into. Whether by economists or agricultural economists, it doesn't matter, the work needs to be done.

Fumio Egaitsu: Japan, Extra-Market Values and Uncertainties

I'd like to make only a short additional comment on my earlier presentation. I recognize that Japan faces a very different problem because, in our present situation, we are in a sense "suffering" from a very good economic performance. Suffering from a very good economic performance sounds a little strange, but the trade surplus, as you know, is one of the most serious problems for us. I don't think that this trade surplus can be recognized as a result of a very bad economic performance. So, in a sense, we are suffering from a very good economic performance.

What I'd like to say is that we can maintain very good economic performance even if we lose all our domestic agricultural production. We have about 6 to 7 percent of our total labor force in the agricultural sector, and 2 percent of national income is produced from agricultural sources. Our rate of economic growth is about 4 to 5 percent per year, and the general forecast for the coming several years is that we can maintain this rate for at least the foreseeable future. So under this 4 to 5 percent of economic growth, I think we can move all our resources from the agricultural sector to the industrial or other expanding sector within five or 10 adjustment periods. Of course it is necessary for us to have five or 10 years of adjustment time; but after that transition period, even if we lose all our domestic agricultural production, I think our overall economic performance will be almost the same. And also our trade surplus could be almost the same. So the Japanese stance to maintain the current level of domestic production doesn't come from the economic point of view. It comes from the noneconomic or extra-market point of view.

There is much uncertainty in what is meant by liberalization. If tariffication in the American proposal in the GATT negotiations means reduction of tariffs to zero percent within 10 years, then this tariffication means, at least to Japan, losing almost all of its domestic agricultural production. This liberalization is somewhat similar to liberalization of the labor market. In Japan, the liberalization of the labor market is currently one of the very hot issues, like the liberalization of the agricultural market. The liberalization of the labor market may surely bring better economic performance to Japan and to the Pacific Rim and the rest of the world, just like the liberalization of the agricultural market. But, it may cause Japan very serious damage in noneconomic or extra-market aspects of our living. So this, I think, is the very special concern that is very important in Japan. It may not be so important in countries like the United States, Canada, Australia, and New Zealand, but it is still very significant to Japan and in places like Korea and Taiwan today and may also be so in the near future in Thailand and other similarly growing countries.

Ken Gray: USSR, Price Variability and Food Security, Rural Development

The topic of price variability and food security comes to mind as an issue for research. I'm struck by Dermot Hayes' comments on a more secure world and by John Mellor's remarks that much more can be done in the way of mutual assurances. I recall the role of the Centrally Planned Economies (CPEs) in the increased apprehension of food security during the 1970s. It was particularly the USSR that played such a large role in increased food demand and prices of that era. We've done some calculations that show that, in regard to grain markets, the CPEs have played a very large role in the year-to-year variations in prices of import demands. What we might want to consider, when we talk about food security and price variability in a changing world, is what effects increased marketization would have on the variability of import demand from the USSR and from China. Our calculations show that these two countries can account for about 85 percent of the year-to-year variations of grain imports from 1970 to, say, 1988.

My hypothesis is that you can expect some good news. If, in fact, these countries are more market oriented, if they have price signals that can influence internal storage, and if they have more mobility from one region to another, then, when one region fails in huge countries like China and the USSR, other regions in these countries can pick it up. The law of large numbers should decrease the variability and increase price changes and cause demand responses that might spare the rest of the world some shocks from these countries. The mere elimination of certain administrative decisions in the purchase and use of grain could be a big factor.

There's one other aspect of this that loosely connects with a lot of things that I'd like to bring up. I'm struck that Japan has so much part-time farming, that rice makes so little difference in the average farm household income, because there's so much other nonfarm income. I'm struck by how that differs in development patterns of the nonmarket economies where statistics show there are sectors that have been discriminated against because they are smaller. Service sectors and trade have not even been accounted for in GNP accounting. Light manufacturing and food processing are the kinds of industries that central planning has not helped very much. In fact, they've suffered. They didn't have priority and, at any rate, were small scale and were the kind of industries that should be rural industries.

I'm struck by China's experience with their liberalization, with the great surge in rural development that has occurred in China, and thinking that's what we can look forward to in the USSR and Eastern Europe as well. The theme of rural development as it affects income security and creates a community where people can live in rural regions, partly engaged in international trade but also involved in all kinds of other activities—where the eggs are in different baskets, some in agriculture and others in nonagriculture: that's what comes to my mind for a research agenda.

Francis Tuan: China, Regional Distribution, Policy Modeling, Long-term Costs of Self-sufficiency

This past couple of years, China studies have attracted an increasing number of researchers who have been doing some very good work in spite of data limitations. There is a need to continue this research on the country's agriculture, especially in its grain sector.

The researchers have been doing interesting work on modeling China's economy, its agricultural economy and grain sectors. But it's the regional distribution system that we haven't been able to get a good handle on. A regional distribution study is very crucial to understanding China's future trade. We understand China's trade from aggregate stock levels, total production, and available hard currencies, but we need to understand the regional impacts better since it is the internal adjustments that govern the overall external trade decisions.

How policy variables can be adopted in modeling is critical. We have been doing some PSE and CSE estimates in which we have a certain degree of confidence, but we really don't know yet how good they'll turn out to be. So we will continue to refine our calculations and welcome more cooperation from researchers as well as from our counterparts in China.

Finally, a big issue for China is the long-term costs of its self-sufficiency policy over the last 30 to 40 years. This is a very important area of research, especially if it can be shown how the self-sufficiency policy has been affecting China's overall agricultural development. Better references for future policy are badly needed in this area.

Ron Sandrey: New Zealand, Time Path of Adjustment, Gainers and Losers

The time path of adjustment is an issue that has fascinated me and to some extent driven me in the work I have been doing over the last 18 months. This issue has been alluded to by Kym, but I think what is particularly important in this question of the time path of adjustment is also the gainers and the losers. It was particularly relevant in our New Zealand situation when we had almost no growth through a fairly long period after liberalization. When you're looking at some of the countries where there may be some adjustments, you've got very high growth; and it seems to me that it's much easier to accommodate changes and adjust your gains and losses in a situation where you're having high growth. I agree with Siamwalla that the social costs of some of these issues are important and need to be properly accounted for. It's a political economy question as much as just a pure economics question, and it's a rather fascinating research issue—the time path of adjustment, the gainers and the losers.

Dermot Hayes: Changing Patterns of Grain Versus Meat Trade

I'd like to share one thought, a germ of an idea that I've been developing throughout the course of this conference. I first got the idea as I listened to Allan Rae talk about comparative advantages in feedgrains and livestock in the Pacific Rim, and then at the luncheon address (by Mellor) I got some more intuition. And what finally clinched it for me was when K. K. Kodama (Mitsui & Co., Ltd.) indicated that it was cheaper to produce poultry in Thailand and ship the meat to Japan than to ship the 2 or 3 pounds of grain to Japan and produce the meat there. I can give you some facts that I've picked up during the conference and share the conclusions I'm starting to draw.

Labor costs in countries like Japan, as we've heard, are increasing faster than in the United States; that was the reason given for it to be more efficient to produce meat in Thailand than to ship it directly to Japan. I know from other work I've done that the technology for transporting meat itself is improving dramatically, much more so than that for transporting grains. We can now ship chilled meat to Japan for about $0.18/lb. with vacuum technology and shelf-life extension technology, whereas it was costlier before because we had to freeze it. The U.S. meat transportation system has become very efficient. We have the boneless boxed beef that saves us from shipping the bones around. And also, the workers in that industry are very competitive. I'm sure you've all read about that industry in the newspapers.

We heard that there's going to be a boom for meat in the Pacific Rim area, and that is, of course, where I'm leading. I know from other research I've done that our feed conversion ratios are perhaps better than those of some of the Asian countries. We see lots of barriers being removed, particularly those that were restricting beef or meat in general rather than the feedgrains. For instance, we have these new supermarket laws in Japan that will reduce the prices of meat, but there is not a lot of movement to reduce whatever it is that causes the feedgrain prices to be marked up so much in Japan. Also, we have a reduction in food security concerns. For instance, countries may have wanted to produce their own meats in the past despite economic considerations simply because of food security reasons. But now with some move toward increased security in the world, that's not as important as it used to be and we're looking more towards economic efficiency.

One last thing is that meat decisions are made at the margin. That is, if you want an extra ton of beef in Japan, and if you have two ways of doing it, you need to import all the grain because there's not a lot of extra forage there. It's a decision that's made at the margin. And so from that, I'm starting to think that, in the future, patterns of trade may change to where there's more of the final product that is exported rather than the inputs–i.e., the processed meat rather than the feedgrains. We may see the grain or grass surplus countries increasing their meat rather than feedgrain exports, so that some of the current emphasis on feedgrain exports may be misplaced.

From the Floor and Rejoinders

John Lee: Administrator, Economic Research Service, USDA: Liberalization, Rural Communities

I don't think that liberalization means that agriculture will go out of production altogether, whether it's Japan or any other country. Some of the land may go to housing but other lands, particularly in the rural areas, will certainly continue to produce something, whether vegetables, rice, or whatever. Resources will not go out of production entirely; they'll continue to produce something.

On some of those comments about political economy and of the desired social aspects of rural life and rural communities, I think it's important not to toss them out or to let them disappear, but there's always more than one way to get there. You can always provide assistance to rural areas without distorting prices and trade.

The point to remember is that most of the people in rural areas are not farming and have only a tangential relationship to farming. This is true in Japan and other industrializing countries in the Pacific Rim including the United States. Rural farming is not the same thing as agriculture.

From the Floor: Pacific Trading Bloc

Coming from the other side of the world and not being part of the Pacific Basin, I have some discomfort with the idea of a *Pacific trading bloc*. Any talk of such a trading bloc is questionable and should be an issue for research. Is that a good idea, and if so, should it perhaps include Latin America (Chile, Mexico, etc.)? I think it requires further explanation why there is this Asia, North America, Australasia concept to the Pacific Basin. Part of the research question should be what is it that is to be achieved out of this. I was interested to hear David Swanson's (Central Soya Co., Inc.) justification. He was hoping for codes of conduct, labelling legislation, lowering of tariffs, etc., all of which should be dealt with in a multilateral GATT context. I would suggest that the sensible strategy for North American, Japanese, and other agribusinesses is to look all over the world for trading opportunities, certainly not to believe that they're closed out of Eastern Europe; that there is plenty of opportunity in Africa and elsewhere. And that countries that do adopt the appropriate strategies and open up their economies should be rewarded wherever they are and not simply if they're in this region. Of course, there are joint interests in this region, transportation cost similarities, cultural and other identities, but I think it would be very dangerous indeed if they were allowed to eclipse some of the other wider multilateral issues.

Allan Rae: PECC, APEC, Cooperation Versus Pacific Trading Bloc

The PECC is a rather loose organization for regional economic cooperation, and it is happy to see itself evolve to wherever all sorts of forces push it. It has been very careful up to now not to take on the impression of being the beginnings of some sort of Pacific OECD or what have you. Sometimes leading politicians or journalists come away from PECC conferences and say those kinds of things because they misunderstand what is going on. But it is certainly not the PECC view that the time for a Pacific trading bloc is here as yet. And also, Australian Prime Minister Hawk has been very careful to point out that the Asian Pacific Economic Council (APEC), which just met the other day, is not about, at least at this stage, a Pacific trading bloc. As far as the country representation is concerned, the issue of who joins these organizations becomes very political. The PECC is quite proud of the fact that we managed to get both China and Chinese Taipei in as members. The next hurdle we thought we would have crossed a couple of months ago and didn't was to get Mexico and some of the other Latin Americans in as well, but that will happen before long, I think.

From the Floor: Technological Change, Tariffication

I just wanted to pick up on Professor Klein's comment on technology that we haven't discussed enough. We know or at least the experience has been that things don't move linearly or even geometrically anymore. We get these dramatic shifts in not only economies but also technologies. Take the example of hormones that affect livestock feeding. I don't know exactly where it stands since I'm not an expert on it, but in pigs, which are very important in the Pacific Basin, if you have a hormone that comes along that makes pigs use less feed, what impact will that have on all this discussion of the great grain trade? The same thing applies with changes in transportation, irradiation (if allowed), in the trade of meats.

Another comment is on tariffication. How are you going to tariffy with unstable exchange rates? In the Pacific Basin we have a situation of countries with large trade surpluses. I was interested in hearing about what would happen if Japan went to zero tariffs, but what's really interesting is, what happens if the yen goes to 90 with 90 percent or 50 percent tariffs. These could be quite dramatic moves. How would these be dealt with in a country that has been used to very stable prices?

William Meyers: Free Trade and Economic Performance

I have a feeling in this discussion that we are involved in a little bit of a contradiction sometimes because we, on the one hand, espouse or feel that free trade is good, and yet the countries we are pointing to as being such great performers have not necessarily pursued those policies. I think maybe the common denominator is not free trade but good policies or appropriate policies. John Mellor spoke about the comparison between the Philippines and Taiwan. I think if you go back far enough you can say something similar about the United States and Argentina. At one time they were at a similar stage of development and with similar potential for future growth, but what happened many years later was quite different. So I think the importance of good policy is a correct conclusion to come to, and it's appropriate intervention and not just no intervention at all.

Wrap-up

A general theme that emerges from these statements concerns the relationships among trade, economic development, and sustainable growth. There are important gaps between theory and practice in these areas that constrain our understanding of how the various economic systems in the Pacific are structured, how they function, and why they perform as they do. The challenge to understanding the basic relationships involved is not easy since the theories and principles that one can rely on to guide the research in these areas have not yet been perfected, much less integrated into a consistent paradigm. Thus, the contributions of our panelists in identifying the major problems and issues are valuable first steps in helping to formulate hypotheses for empirical testing.

References were made to intersectoral growth rates and relationships between agriculture and nonagriculture with emphasis on the importance of the "forgotten service sector," the uncertainty costs of instability, and the extra-market values in rural communities. This broadens the research scope far beyond agricultural trade to the broader concerns for rural development and economic growth. The issues were discussed in both the national and international contexts with all the implications for changes in technology, institutions, and preferences that accompany economic development and growth. Structural changes were initially described in terms of broad transitions from primary to secondary and tertiary sectors. However, identifying and analyzing the relationships between intersectoral growth rates over time will encounter definition problems as well as specification and measurement errors since the processes of growth are much more complex than the simple structural transitions from primary to secondary and tertiary sectors.

In an international context, trade and investments in the Pacific have even broader consequences and implications for regional growth and development. The sequences of structural transitions occur on an international level through trade and direct foreign investments that influence the international division of labor. Reallocation of resources are not only between sectors of a national economy but more importantly across international boundaries. The horizontal division of labor that has become so evident in the trade of manufactures is also becoming evident in the trade of agricultural commodities as increasing value is added to the primary products that leave the farm gates. The analyses of trade issues involving high vs. low value added agricultural products (e.g., the promotion of higher valued livestock products vs. lower valued feedgrains) clearly must take into account the differential effects on international division of labor.

An underlying motive for applied research is to influence economic policies that may fall within the two interrelated spheres—international policies such as the multilateral GATT and domestic policies that affect international trade and growth. The development of new political economy modeling approaches promises to help advance our understanding of the functional role of governments in setting policies, while the computable effects of these policies may eventually be mastered through advances in general equilibrium modeling.

Finally, research work can proceed at different levels. Logic distinguishes among three such levels: descriptive, functional, and theoretical. Some of the chapters in Part 2 of this book approached the more pressing regional and country issues from the descriptive to functional and theoretical levels; the authors in other chapters, particularly in Part 3, approached more narrowly defined technical issues from the opposite direction—i.e., from the theoretical to functional and descriptive levels. From whatever direction the economic issues are defined and addressed, the analytical approach will likely encounter methodological issues that will need to be subjected to theoretical and empirical testing before the final results can be verified and made to serve decision-making at all policy, institutional, and operating levels.

Notes

1. The views of agribusiness were discussed by Mr. David Swanson (CEO, Central Soya Co., Inc.) and Mr. Kazaya K. Kodama (CEO, Mitsui and Co., Ltd.) in a panel session moderated by Ed Rossmiller (Director, National Center for Food and Agricultural Policy, Resources for the Future). Agribusiness is one of the largest growth industries in the Pacific region.

2. These priorities have recently been refined and put forth as suggested future activities for discussion within a PECC Coordinating Group as follows: (i) agricultural policy reform—beyond the Uruguay Round, (ii) adjusting Pacific agriculture to the new trading environment, (iii) Pacific agriculture and the environment, (iv) a database for Pacific Rim agricultural policy analysis, ("Pacific Economic Cooperation Conference Task Force on Agricultural Policy, Trade and Development Report to Coordinating Group – January 18, 1991").

About the Book and Editors

This is a comprehensive, up-to-date, and forward-looking volume on the economic and political forces shaping agriculture and trade in the Pacific region. As rapid industrialization and agricultural policy reform take hold in many Pacific Rim nations, Japan and the newly industrialized countries of East Asia will provide important and growing import markets for agricultural products well into the next century. In this book, leading scholars provide new information about policy reform in Japan, the meaning of economic deregulation for New Zealand agriculture and trade, the potential role of the Soviet Union and China in the Pacific, and the prospects for agriculture in the Southeast Asian nations.

Underscoring the region's promise and importance for global agricultural markets at a time when the world's attention is fixed on Europe and the Soviet Union, this book promises to be valuable for scholars and policymakers interested in the political and economic forces shaping world agricultural trade.

William T. Coyle is chief of the Developed Market Economies Branch of the United States Department of Agriculture. **Dermot Hayes** is assistant professor of agricultural economics at Iowa State University. **Hiroshi Yamauchi** is professor of agricultural economics at the University of Hawaii.

Contributors

Julian M. Alston, Associate Professor, Department of Agricultural Economics, University of California, Davis, California 95616 U.S.A.

Kym Anderson, Currently on assignment with Economic Research and Analysis Unit, General Agreement on Tariffs and Trade, CH-1211 Geneva 21, Switzerland

Liborio Cabanilla, Associate Professor, University of the Philippines, Los Banos College, Laguna, Philippines

Colin A. Carter, Professor, Department of Agricultural Economics, University of California, Davis, California 95616 U.S.A.

William T. Coyle, Chief, Developed Market Economies Branch, Agriculture and Trade Analysis Division, Economic Research Service, U.S. Department of Agriculture, 1301 New York Ave., N.W., Washington, DC 20005 U.S.A.

Fumio Egaitsu, Professor, Department of Agricultural Economics, University of Tokyo, Yayoi 1-1-1, Bunkyo-ku, Tokyo 113, Japan

Kenneth Gray, Chief, Centrally Planned Economies Branch, Agriculture and Trade Analysis Division, Economic Research Service, U.S. Department of Agriculture, 1301 New York Ave., N.W., Washington, DC 20005 U.S.A.

David Harris, Senior Economist, Australian Bureau of Agricultural and Resource Economics, MacArthur House, Northbourne Ave., GPO Box 1563, Canberra, 2601 ACT, Australia

Dermot Hayes, Associate Professor, Center for Agricultural and Rural Development, Iowa State University, Ames, Iowa 50011 U.S.A.

Tan Siew Hoey, Senior Research Analyst, Institute of Strategic and International Studies, Kuala Lumpur, Malaysia

Sergei B. Iliukhin, USSR Academy of Sciences, Institute of World Economic and International Relations, 23 Profsoyazoaya Street, Moscow, USSR

Faisal Kasryno, Director, Bureau of Planning, Ministry of Agriculture, Jl. Harsono, Room 3, Jakarta Selaton, Indonesia

Lawrence R. Klein, Professor, Department of Economics, 3718 Locust Walk Cr., University of Pennsylvania, Philadelphia, Pennsylvania 19104 U.S.A.

John W. Mellor, President, John Mellor Associates, Inc. Formerly Director, International Food Policy Research Institute, 1776 Massachusetts Ave., N.W., Washington, DC 20036 U.S.A.

Direk Patamasiriwat, Thailand Development Research Institute, 163 Asoke Rd., Bangkok, Thailand

Allan Rae, Professor and Director, Centre for Agricultural Policy Studies, Department of Agricultural Economics and Business, Massey University, Palmerston North, New Zealand

Shi Ru, International Trade Research Institute, 28 Donghouxiang, An Dingnen Waiy St, Beijing, PRC

Ron A. Sandrey, Economist, Ministry of External Relations and Trade, Stafford House, 40 The Terrace, Private Bag, Wellington, New Zealand

Andrew Schmitz, Professor, Department of Agricultural and Resource Economics, University of California, Berkeley, California 94720 U.S.A.

Suthad Setboonsarng, Researcher, Thailand Development Research Institute, Raja Pack Bldg., 163 Asoke Road, Bangkok 10110, Thailand

Ian Shaw, Australian Bureau of Agricultural and Resource Economics, MacArthur House, Northbourne Ave., GPO Box 1563, Canberra, 2601 ACT, Australia

Ammar Siamwalla, Program Director, Agriculture and Rural Development, Thailand Development Research Institute, Raja Park Building, 163 Asoke Rd., Bangkok 10110, Thailand

Francis C. Tuan, Leader, China Section, Agriculture and Trade Analysis Division, Economic Research Service, U.S. Department of Agriculture, 1301 New York Ave., N.W., Washington, DC 20005 U.S.A.

Thomas Wahl, Assistant Professor, Department of Agricultural Economics, Washington State University, Pullman, Washington 99164 U.S.A.

Alan J. Webb, Senior Economist, Agriculture and Trade Analysis Division, Economic Research Service, U.S. Department of Agriculture, 1301 New York Ave., N.W., Washington, DC 20005 U.S.A.

Marilyn D. Whitney, Assistant Professor, Department of Agricultural Economics, University of California, Davis, California 95616 U.S.A.

Hiroshi Yamauchi , Professor, Department of Agricultural and Resource Economics, University of Hawaii, Honolulu, Hawaii 96882 U.S.A.

Yutaka Yoshioka, Chairman, Japan International Agricultural Council, Zenkoku Nogyo Kyosai Kaikan, 19, Ichiban-cho, Chiyoda-ku, Tokyo 102, Japan

Index

Afghanistan, 19
Africa, 313, 325
Agriculture, 4–6, 159 (table)
  agribusiness, 219–220, 310
  comparative advantage, 29, 45
  irrigation, 160, 168–169
  research, 160, 170–171, 309, 315–317
  trade, 165–166, 265–266, 286–288
  See also under individual countries
Agricultural Basic Law, 121–122
Agricultural Cooperative Law, 91–92
Agricultural Land Law, 121–122
Alston, J. M., 280
Anderson, Kym, 41–42, 51–53, 119, 121, 129, 295, 297, 310
APEC. *See* Asia Pacific Economic Cooperation Council
Argentina, 158, 189, 242, 243, 244(table), 326
ASEAN. *See* Association of Southeast Asian Nations
Asia, 15, 18, 325
Asia–Pacific, as a common market, 15–17, 20
Asia Pacific Economic Cooperation Council (APEC), 8, 54, 325
Association of Southeast Asian Nations (ASEAN), 3, 5, 15, 38, 41
  agriculture, 37–38(table)
  economic trends in, 10, 48, 133
  livestock, 50(table), 133–147, 248(table), 254(table), 256(table)
  protectionism, 43–44(table)
  regional cooperation, 146–147
  trade, 250(table)
Atlantic nations, 16, 18
Australasia, 33, 47–49, 51, 55, 325
Australia, 3, 5, 8, 15, 208, 295, 321
  agriculture, 39(table), 40(table), 182, 188–189, 194, 233, 241–245, 246(table)
  broadacre agricultural industries, 222, 233–237, 239
  economy, 2(table), 20, 29
  land, 38
  livestock, 50(table), 53, 137(table), 236, 238, 241(table), 243(table), 244(table), 247(table)
  minerals, 18, 27
  trade, 34–35(table), 53
Austria, 16

Baldwin, R., 58, 264
Bangladesh, agriculture, 83(figure)
Batten, D.S., 261
Beef, 234–236, 238–241
  See also under individual countries; Livestock
Beef and Citrus Agreement, 53, 127
Belongia, 261
Border prices, 265, 288
Bowen, H.P., 32
Brazil, 96, 153, 158
Bredahl, M.E., 265
Broadacre industries, 222, 233–237, 239
Brunei, 10
Burma, 20, 82
Bushnell, P., 261

Cairns group, 154
Cambodia, 4, 48
Canada, 1, 3, 29, 38
  agriculture, 40(table), 182, 188–189, 194, 208, 266, 321
  beef, 241(table), 247(table), 283–284, 286
  economy, 2(table), 16, 18, 20
  livestock, 50(table), 237–238, 241, 243(table), 248(table)
  trade, 34–35(table), 250(table)
Caribbean, 16, 53
Carter, C.A., 266, 278
Cattle. *See* Beef; Livestock
CCC. *See* Commodity Credit Corpora-

335

tion
Centrally planned economies (CPE), 321
 See also China; Eastern Europe; USSR
Cereal, 71, 80–82, 87
 See also Corn; Feedstuffs, Rice
Chambers, R.G., 261–262, 265, 267, 269, 276, 279, 288
Chile, 58
China, 4, 68–69, 71, 179, 208, 312, 325
 agriculture, 3(table), 8–10, 33, 36(table), 37–38(table), 40(table), 49, 76(table), 80(table), 83(figure), 175–196, 179(figure), 180–181(table), 182(figure), 183(table), 184(figure), 185(figure), 186–187(table), 322
 ASEAN and, 38, 48
 cotton, 49, 78, 79(table), 195
 economy, 2(table), 8–9, 15–17, 20, 26, 47, 55–56, 70(table), 176, 189
 foreign investment, 191
 government programs, 190, 193–196
 grain, 50(table), 73–74(table), 189, 194–195
 Great Leap Forward, 175
 infrastructure, 192
 international debt, 191–192
 June 4th Beijing, 190–191
 livestock, 50(table), 75(table), 194
 protectionism, 9, 43–44(table), 189
 self–sufficiency, 322
 subsides, 9–11
 technology, 176–178, 189, 196
 trade, 9, 16, 34–35(table), 52(table), 175–189, 177(figure), 178(figure), 192–193, 196, 320–321
 vegetable oils, 77(table)
Cold War, 48, 98
Collier, Paul, 313
Collins, 265
Commodity Credit Corporation (CCC), 153
Common market
 Asia–Pacific, 18

 See also European Economic Community
Competition, 264, 267, 271, 288
Consumption, 27(table)
Corn 48, 71
 See also under individual countries
Corra, 236–237
Cotton, 49, 77, 195
 See also under individual countries; Textiles
CPE. *See* Centrally Planned Economies
Currency, 261, 272
 See also Exchange rate

Dairy, 217
 production, 135, 139, 146, 161
 protectionism, 48–49, 142
Deaton, A., 238
Debt, 15, 26, 213, 192, 218, 220–221
Developing countries, 41, 87
 agriculture, 81–84, 96
 Eastern Europe and, 67
 trade, 67, 81
Development, 312–317, 321–322, 326
Dewbre, J., 236–237
Dickson, A., 237
Dornbusch, R., 264, 268, 271
Drabenstott, M., 261, 262
Drysdale, P., 54
Durbin, 284
Dutton, J., 267

East Asia, 3(table), 47
Eastern Europe, 1, 26, 54, 67, 79, 98, 322
East Germany
 China and, 175, 191
 development, 16, 18
 economy, 16–17, 47
Econometric Model of Pacific Rim Livestock Markets (EMABA), 234(table), 235(table), 239, 253(table)
 development, 234–238
 elasticities, 237, 240
 supply, 239, 241–242
Economic reform, 5, 9, 199–211, 213–220

Index 337

See also under individual countries
Economic growth, 5, 6, 67–68
  See also under individual countries
EEC. *See* European Economic Community
Egaitsu, Fumio, 119–120, 121, 125, 130, 314, 320
Elasticities, 271–273, 276, 278, 286
  exchange rate pass–through, 274, 275
  livestock, 237, 240
EMABA. *See* Econometric Model of Pacific Rim Livestock Markets
Engel's Law, 30, 84
Environment, 28, 56, 57, 225–226, 317
  See also under individual countries
Europe, 1, 17, 53, 55
  Common Market 15, 18, 27
European Economic Community (EEC), 5, 8, 9, 16, 122, 131, 136, 151–152, 176, 222, 226, 317
Exchange rate
  demand and, 269–275, 279, 288–289
  pass–through elasticities, 262, 265–266, 279–280, 288–289, 319
  pass–through statics, 268–269
  trade and, 267, 277, 279–280, 284–286
Exports, 167, 269, 280

Fackler, P.L., 261–262
Farming, 210, 221
  comparative advantage in, 29–33
  European Community, 122, 131
  farmers, 92, 216–219, 311
  part–time, 124–129, 312–315, 318, 324
  privatization, 203–204
  products, 30, 33, 45–46
  subsidies, 41–45
Farmland Law, 91–92
Feedstuffs, 79–80, 135–136, 138–139, 144–146, 323
  See also under individual countries; Livestock
Feenstra, R.C., 264, 267, 268
Feinberg, R.M., 267
Fertilizers, 39, 99, 171

First Workshop of Livestock and Feedgrains Study Programme of the Pacific Economic
Food, 30, 31, 33, 86
  crisis, 199, 201–202, 204
  security, 29, 51, 321–322
  See also under individual countries
Foot and mouth disease, 147
France, 102, 130(table), 189
Free economic zones, 207, 210
Free Trade, 10–11, 48, 165, 326
  See also under individual countries
Freebairn, J., 296, 299
Froot, K.A., 264
Furtan, H., 266

Gang of Four, 69, 74, 76, 78, 80
Gardner, B.L., 261
Garnaut, R., 47, 54
GATT. *See* General Agreement on Tariffs and Trade
GDP. *See* Gross Domestic Product
General Agreement on Tariffs and Trade (GATT), 5, 8, 53–56, 59, 87, 153–154, 173, 222, 226, 320, 325, 327
  Japan and, 93, 98, 120
  Uruguay Round of negotiations, 120, 242–243, 311, 315–317
Germany, 17, 130(table)
Giovannini, A., 264
GNP. *See* Gross National Product
Gorbachev, Mikhail, 48
Grain, 71, 92, 99, 189, 194–195
  wheat, 48–49, 74
  See also under individual countries
Gray, Ken, 266, 321
Green, R., 261
Green–house gases, 57
Greenshields, 261, 262
Grennes, T., 261, 262, 265, 267
Gross Domestic Products, (GDP), 25(table)
Gross National Products (GNP), 24(table)
Growth, 130, 312–315
  sustainable, 326–327

See also under individual countries
Gulf crisis, 48

Harris, D., 236
Hawk, Prime Minister, 325
Hayami, Y., 119–120, 295, 296, 301–302
Hayes, Dermot, 299, 301, 321, 323–324
Heckscher–Ohlin–Samuelson theory, 136
Henneberry, D., 261, 262
Henneberry, S., 261, 262
Hillman, A.L., 58
Hong Kong, 1, 3, 4, 15–17, 26, 33, 47, 75, 177, 182, 194
   agriculture, 37–38(table), 76(table), 80(table), 83(figure)
   cereal, 73–74(table)
   cotton, 79(table)
   economy, 2(table), 19, 20, 70(table)
   government policies, 283–284, 286
   livestock, 75(table)
   population, 68–69
   trade, 34–35(table)
   vegetable oils, 77(table)
Hooper, P., 264, 267
Horticulture, 75–76, 87
   See also Agriculture
Hungary, 27

IATRC. *See* International Agricultural Trade Research Consortium
IMF. *See* International Monetary Fund
Income, 33, 41, 45, 67
   per capita (YPC), 32, 133
India, 19, 26, 68–69, 71, 77, 78, 170–171, 312
   agriculture, 76(table), 80(table), 83(figure)
   cereal, 73–74(table)
   cotton, 79(table)
   economy, 70(table)
   livestock, 75(table)
   vegetable oils, 77(table)
Indochina, 9
Indonesia, 10, 15, 17, 49, 170–171, 177, 182, 194, 195
   agriculture, 31, 33, 38, 40(table), 76(table), 79, 80(table), 83(figure), 96
   cotton, 79(table)
   economy, 2(table), 70(table)
   grain, 73–74(table), 74, 82, 145(table), 145–146,
   growth rate, 68–69, 142
   livestock, , 75(table), 133–135, 137(table), 143(table), 146
   protectionism, 138–139, 140–141(table), 142
   trade, 34–35(table), 77
   vegetable oils, 77(table)
Industry, 29, 45, 57, 59
Inflation, 202, 213, 218, 220, 267
Infrastructure, 192
Interest rates, 213, 218, 226, 267
International Rice Institute (IRI), 171
International Monetary Fund (IMF), 16, 87
International Agricultural Trade Research Consortium,(IATRC), 1–3
Investment, foreign, 191, 206
IRI. *See* International Rice Institute
Irrigation, 160, 168–169
Israel, 53

Jabara, C.L., 239
Japan, 3, 5, 53, 58, 176–177, 179, 188, 191, 194, 195, 241, 266, 269, 283–284, 310–312, 315, 316, 324
   agriculture, 6–8, 33, 36(table), 37–38(table), 40(table), 41, 42(table), 56, 75, 80(table), 83(figure, 91–95, 99–100, 101–117, 119–123, 123(figure), 125–132, 320
   agricultural commodities, 127(figure)
   Agricultural Cooperative Law, 91–92
   agricultural produce, 126(figure)
   agricultural work force, 125(figure)
   beef 6, 53, 97, 127–128, 236–239, 241(table), 247(table), 254(table), 256(table), 295–304, 300(figure), 298(figure), 301(figure), 302(table), 303(figure)

cereal, 73–74(table)
cotton 49, 77, 79(table)
Democratic Socialist Party, 98
democratization, 91–92
economic growth, 6, 27, 69, 91–94, 97, 121
economy, 2(table), 70(table)
environment, 120, 129
exchange rates, 273(figure), 284(table)
extra–market values, 15–18, 320–321
farmers, 11(table), 111(table),
farming, 41, 92, 103–105, 121–134, 320–321
Farmland Law, 91–92
food, 67–68, 91–92, 95, 101–102, 311
fruits and vegetables, 76(table)
GATT, 93, 98, 120
grain, 92, 95–96, 71, 99
income, 124(figure)
Japan Communist Party, 98
Japan Socialist Party, 98
labor, 99, 323
land reforms, 6, 46, 120
Liberal Democratic Party, 97
liberalization agreement, 301–302
livestock, 50(table), 74, 75(table), 94, 102, 137(table), 248(table), 296–299
living conditions, 114(table)
pork, 243(table)
population 33, 47, 301
protectionism, 6, 43–44(table), 94, 98–100, 104(table), 103–107, 108(table), 120, 123–124, 126, 129–130
rice, 92–95, 98–101, 109(table), 111(table), 124–128, 167
rural sector, 99, 131
socioeconomic indicators, 130(table), 155(table)
trade, 34–35(table), 67, 93, 96–97, 120–121, 250(table), 301
vegetable oils, 77(table)
Java, 314
Johnson, P.R., 261, 262, 265
Joint ventures, 206

Just, R.E., 58, 261, 262, 265, 267, 269, 276, 279, 288

Kazakhstan, 203
Keesing, D.B., 32
Kenya, 313–314
Kirgizia, 200–203
Klein, Lawrence, 310
Klemperer, P.D., 264
Knetter, M.M., 264, 266
Kodama, K.K., 323
Konandreas, P., 261, 262
Korea, 15, 53, 237–239, 241, 316, 321
    agriculture, 36(table), 37–38(table), 40(table), 42(table), 82–85
    cotton, 78
    economy, 2(table)
    grain, 68, 71, 74, 80
    livestock, 241(table), 243(table), 247(table), 248(table), 254(table), 256(table)
    population, 69
    protectionism, 43–44(table), 76–78, 166–167
    trade, 34–35(table), 250(table)
    vegetable oils trade, 76
Kost, W.E., 279
Krueger, Anne, 31, 47, 54, 58, 264

Labour, 31, 41, 320, 323
Land, 120–121, 204, 220, 242, 244, 324
    reform, 46, 310
    See also under individual countries
Latin America, 1, 18, 53, 325
Leamer, 32
Lee, John, 324
Livestock, 4, 41, 49, 51, 67, 68, 71, 79, 94, 216–217, 221–223, 236, 322–324
    ASEAN nations, 133–147
    comparative advantage indicators, 136–144
    Cooperation Conference, 134
    growth rates, 135
    protectionism, 139–142
    social profitability, 134, 137–139, 142–144

trade, 74, 75
See also under individual countries
Longmire, 262, 265

Macao, 182
Maekawa Report 97
Magee, 58
Maize, 158, 160–161, 166
Malaysia, 8, 10, 17, 38, 68–69, 138, 159, 167, 177, 182, 189
  agriculture, 40(table), 76(table), 80(table), 83(figure)
  cotton, 78, 79(table)
  economy, 2(table), 70(table)
  grain, 71, 73–74(table), 74, 137(table), 145(table)
  livestock, 75(table), 143(table), 146, 133, 135
  protectionism, 140(table), 141(table), 142–144
  trade, 34–35(table), 77
  vegetable oils, 77(table)
Mann, C.L., 264, 267
Markets, 18, 47, 210, 222, 236, 313, 315–317, 321,
  development 86
  Pacific 18
  structure, 280
  See also ASEAN; European Economic Community
Marston, R.C., 264
McLeish, R., 237
Meat. *See* Livestock
Mellor, John, 311–312, 321, 323, 326
Mexico, 16, 18, 33, 34–35(table), 38, 41, 50(table), 53, 325
Meyers, William, 326
Most Favored Nation, 54
Models, 269–276
  agricultural trade, 312
  Commodity trade models, 233–259
  EBABA regressions, 283, 285–286, 287–288
  equilibrium, 310–312
  pass–through, 266–267
  policy, 322
Morey, A., 262, 265

Muelbauer, J., 238
Mullen, J.D., 280
Multi–fibre Arrangement, 53
Myers, W.H., 265

Nakasone, Prime Minister, 97
Nakhodka, free economic zone, 210
Nepal, 19, 83(figure)
New Zealand, 3, 5, 8, 15, 18, 27, 29, 237, 238, 239, 241, 182, 188–189, 208, 236, 315, 321–323
  agriculture, 10–11, 40(table), 56, 222–224, 215–217, 219–220, 225
  Australia and, 53
  debt, 213, 218
  dollar, 215, 217, 219
  economic reforms, 20, 27, 48, 213–227
  economy, 2(table), 214(table)
  Labor Party, 213
  land, 225–226, 242–244
  liberalization, 219–223
  livestock, 50(table), 218, 222, 239, 241(table), 243(table), 244(table), 247(table)
  privatization, 224–226
  taxation, 216–217, 219
  trade, 34–35(table), 53, 222–223
  pigs and poultry, 248(table 13.7)
  trade, 250(table 13.8)
Noh, President, 48
North America, 9, 15, 20, 33, 48, 51, 55, 222, 325
North Korea, 9, 20, 48, 53, 56
Northeast Asia, 33
Norway, 16

Oceania, 1, 3(table), 9
OECD. *See* Organization for Economic Cooperation and Development
Oehmke, J., 296, 299
Ohno, K., 263, 264, 267, 268
Oil, 15, 27, 31
Olson, M., 58
Orden, D., 261, 262, 265
Organization for Economic Cooperation and Development (OECD),

Index

25(table), 38, 39(table), 53, 59, 107, 310, 312, 325
Ozone, 57

Pacific Rim, 16, 175, 207, 209, 263
  agriculture, 3, 46
  cotton, 77–78
  economic community, 211, 309
  economic adjustments, 29, 39
  food, 67
  livestock, 323
  trade, 1–11, 45, 121, 234–236, 309, 325
Pacific Economic Cooperation Conference (PECC), 134, 146, 315–317, 325
Pakistan, 19, 26
Park, T.A., 266
PEEC. *See* Pacific Economic Cooperation Conference
Penson, 261
Pesticides, 39
Philippines 4, 10, 177, 182, 195, 208, 326
  agriculture, 40(table), 68–69, 76(table), 79, 80(table), 83(figure), 310–313
  cotton, 79(table)
  debt, 19, 26
  economy, 2(table), 70(table), 71, 133
  grain, 73–74(table), 82, 137(table), 145(table)
  green revolution, 82
  growth 71
  livestock, 75(table), 134–136, 143(table)
  protectionism, 139, 140–141(table), 142–144
  trade, 34–35(table), 77
  vegetable oils, 77(table)
Pick, D.H., 266, 278
Pineapple, 163
Poland, 27
Pollution, 57
  See also Environment
Poultry, 135
  elasticity, 240–241
  supply, 241–242
PRC. *See* China

Price, 205, 279
  controls, 202
  elasticity, 267–268
  liberalization, 200, 210
  Price support policies, 130
  variability, 321–322
Privatization, 204, 210
  See also under individual countries
Protectionism, 53, 59, 226, 314
  agriculture, 6–8, 167, 120–121, 129–130, 222–224
  livestock, 48, 139, 144–146
  reverse, 200–204
  See also under individual countries

Quota, 203, 277, 295, 297
  See also under individual countries

Rae, Allan, 315, 323, 325
Rausser, G., 296, 299
Reed, M., 265
Regional cooperation, 146–147
  agricultural policy, 10–11
  economic cooperation, 325
  Western Pacific, 8–9
  See also ASEAN; European Economic Community
Rents, 205
Rice, 158, 160, 168
  dumping, 153
  import, 49, 74, 101
  mechanization of production, 74, 94
  protection, 74
  See also under individual countries
Richardson, J.D., 58
Ridley, 237
Russia, 200, 204, 210
  See also USSR

Samoa, 20
Sandrey, Ron, 322
Schembri, L., 264
Schmitz, Andy, 310
Schuh, G.E., 269, 271, 279
Schuh hypothesis, 261
Schultz, T.W., 41
Schwartz, N.E., 266

SFE. *See* Soviet Far East
Shane, M., 261
Shaw, I., 236–237
SHAZAM, 283
Sheep. *See* Livestock; Meat
Shortages, 201–203
Sianwalla, Ammar, 317–320
Singapore, 10, 15, 17, 18, 182
   agriculture, 33, , 73–74(table), 76(table), 80(table), 82, 83(figure)
   China and, 194–195
   cotton, 79(table)
   economy, 2(table), 70(table)
   food, 68
   imports, 75
   livestock, 75(table)
   population, 69
   trade, 34–35(table)
   vegetable oils, 77(table)
South Africa, 243
Southeast Asia, 1, 3(table), 8, 313–317
Southern Europe 27
South Korea, 3, 5, 26, 56, 177, 188
   agriculture, 7–8, 33
   currency, 16–17
   livestock, 133
Soviet Far East (SFE), 207, 208(table), 209, 209(table)
Soviet Union. *See* Union of Soviet Socialist Republics
Soybeans, 48–49, 94–95, 158
Sri Lanka, 19, 88
Steel, 59
Subsidies, 205, 222, 310–312
   See also under individual countries
Sugar. *See under* Thailand
Supply elasticities, 240, 245
   See also EMABA
Swanson, David, 325
Sweden, 59
Switzerland, 16

Taiwan, 26, 58, 188, 237, 241, 310, 313, 314, 321, 326
   agriculture, 3, 7, 33, 36(table), 37–38(table), 40(table), 42(table), 76, 76(table), 80(table), 83(figure)

China and, 47
   cotton, 78, 79(table)
   currency appreciation, 15–18
   economy, 2(table), 70(table)
   farming, 41
   food, 68
   grain, 73–74(table), 82, 316
   livestock, 75(table), 243(table), 247(table), 248(table)
   protectionism, 43–44(table), 166–167
   trade, 34–35(table), 250(table)
   vegetable oils, 77(table)
Tariffs, 296, 301–303, 326
   See also under individual countries
Tax, 5, 57, 167, 201, 219, 223
   See also under individual countries
Teal, F., 237
Technology, 47, 317–320, 244, 326
   agriculture, 67, 76, 310
   fisheries, 164
   intellectual property rights, 172
   livestock, 135
   policy, 82, 85
   See also under individual countries
Textiles, 31, 32, 49, 59
Thailand, 29, 49, 135, 136, 138, 182, 194, 208, 323
   agriculture, 33, 40(table), 56, 76, 76(table), 80(table), 83(figure)149–151, 155–161, 162(table), 165–166, 168–173, 318
   climate, 155
   cotton, 78, 79(table)
   economy, 2(table), 70(table)
   farming, 41
   fisheries, 156–157, 164–165, 165(table), 173
   grain, 73–74(table), 74, 137(table), 143–146, 158, 166
   Green Revolution, 170
   livestock, 75(table), 84, 135, 139, 142–144, 143(table), 156–157, 161–164, 162(table)
   protectionism, 139, 140–141(table), 142, 150, 165–167
   Ratchaburi operation, 163
   rice, 87, 153, 158, 160, 168–169

Index 343

rubber, 159
service sector, 317–318
soybean, 158
subsidies, 166
sugar, 151–152, 159, 166
taxation, 165, 167
technology, 150, 156–157, 164, 170–173, 317–320
trade, 34–35(trade), 150–152, 152(table), 155, 165, 317
vegetable oils, 77(table)
water, 155, 169
Thursby, M.C., 261, 262, 265
Trade, 263
　agriculture, 266
　border prices, 277
　foreign, 175, 327
　grain, 323–324
　liberalization, 76, 222
　livestock, 323–324, 326–327
　policies, 226–227
　regional trade liberalization, 146–147
　world, 21–22(table)
　See also under individual countries
Treaty of Rome, 8
Tuan, Francis, 322
Turkey, 55
Tyers, 51, 53

UK. *See* United Kingdom
Union of Soviet Socialist Republics (USSR), 1, 9, 16, 67, 98, 175, 182, 188, 191, 194, 199–202
　currency, 202–203
　economic change, 199–202, 204, 206–207
　farming, 59, 203, 204–205
　food, 199–200, 204, 321–322
　foreign economic relations, 199, 205–207
　licenses, 205–206
　livestock, 202, 208
　lobby groups 45, 59
　political liberalization, 199–200
　protectionism, 200
　trade, 199–211
　war of laws, 200, 204

United States (U.S.), 1, 5, 6, 8, 16, 18, 178, 182, 188–189, 194, 202, 208, 221–222, 226, 269, 295, 313, 317, 321, 323, 326
　Agricultural Adjustment Act, 91
　agriculture, 39(table), 40(table), 68, 108(table)
　border prices, 288
　Department of Agriculture, 310, 312
　developing countries and, 67, 68, 81–88
　dollar, 261, 263, 266, 271–274
　exchange rates, 270(figure), 273(figure), 284(table)
　economy, 2(table), 20, 29, 53, 102
　farming, 131, 152–154, 159
　food, 67, 86
　grains, 50(table), 80
　Japan and, 128–130
　land, 38
　laws, 121–122
　livestock, 50(table), 236–237, 241(table), 241–242, 243(table), 247(table), 248(table), 254(table), 256(table)
　rice, 154–155
　socioeconomic indicators, 130(table)
　trade, 17, 34–35(table), 68, 93, 95–9, 250(table), 261, 284
United Kingdom, 9, 102, 130(table)
Uruguay, 244(table)
Uruguay Round (of negotiations). *See under* GATT
U.S.-Canadian Free Trade Agreement, 8
USSR. *See* Union of Soviet Socialist Republics

VAR. *See* Vector autoregressive model
Vector autoregressive model (VAR), 262
Vellianitis–Fidas, 261, 262
VERA. *See* Voluntary export restraint agreement
Vietnam, 4, 20, 34–35(table), 48, 56
Vlastuin, C., 237
Voluntary export restraint agreement

(VERA), 151

Wahl, T., 299, 301
Water, 57, 155, 169
Welfare, 299–303
West Germany, 16, 102
Western Europe, 30, 41–45, 55, 56, 67–68
Whalley, J., 57
Whiteford, D., 237
Williams, G., 299, 301
Wohlgenant, M.K., 280
Woo, W., 264
World Bank, 158, 159, 168, 169, 191

Yao, X., 296, 299
Yoshioka, Yutaka, 130–132